TRANSITIONAL JUSTICE IN THE MIDDLE EAST AND NORTH AFRICA

T0386702

CHANDRA LEKHA SRIRAM

(*Editor*)

Transitional Justice in the
Middle East and North Africa

جـامـعـة جـورجـتـاون قـطـر
GEORGETOWN UNIVERSITY QATAR

Center *for* International *and* Regional Studies

HURST & COMPANY, LONDON

Published in Collaboration with
Center for International and Regional Studies
Georgetown University-Qatar

First published in the United Kingdom in 2017 by
C. Hurst & Co. (Publishers) Ltd.,
41 Great Russell Street, London, WC1B 3PL
© Chandra Lekha Sriram and the contributors, 2017
All rights reserved.
Printed in India

The right of Chandra Lekha Sriram and the Contributors to be
identified as the author of this publication is asserted by them in
accordance with the Copyright, Designs and Patents Act, 1988.

A Cataloguing-in-Publication data record for this book
is available from the British Library.

978-1-84904-649-7 *paperback*

www.hurstpublishers.com

CONTENTS

CONTENTS

ACKNOWLEDGMENTS

I wish to express my gratitude to colleagues in the Center for International and Regional Studies of the School of Foreign Service, Georgetown University, based in Doha. I thank Zahra Babar and Mehran Kamrava for developing the concept for the project that generated this book, on transitional justice in a region which experienced a surge in practice after 2011 but remains under-examined in the transitional justice literature, and for their kind invitation to act as editor. I also thank their colleagues, Barb Gillis, Suzi Mirgani, Dwaa Osman, and Elizabeth Wanucha, who ably organized meetings in February and August 2014 bringing authors together, which helped us all to hone our own analysis and develop comparative analyses. I also want to thank all the contributors to this volume for their intellectual efforts and patience throughout the editing process. I wish to express particular thanks to Dionysus Markakis, without whose expert editorial assistance we might never have completed the volume.

Grateful acknowledgment goes also to the Qatar Foundation for its support of research and other scholarly endeavors.

Chandra Lekha Sriram   London, February 2016

1

INTRODUCTION

TRANSITIONAL JUSTICE IN THE MENA REGION

Chandra Lekha Sriram

The social and political uprisings in the Middle East and North Africa (MENA) region, designated the "Arab Spring" because the most visible ruptures appeared in the spring of 2011, drew global attention not only because they presented broad-based political protest against regimes which were long-entrenched, whether authoritarian or monarchical. They were landmark events because they led to the removal of several heads of state, and prompted discussions of institutional reform. Notably, they also entailed a broad range of human rights claims, both those related to abuses by prior regimes of civil and political rights and bodily integrity, but also of socio-economic rights. In short, they not only put transitional justice on the political agenda in a region of the world where it was seldom discussed (despite limited experiments in Morocco), but also put forward a broader view of transitional justice than that which has traditionally been implemented. However, many of these transitions have since stalled, leaving transitional justice similarly stalled, stunted, or manipulated for political ends. These phenomena are not unique to the

MENA region, but rather experiences from elsewhere with limited or frozen transition may be informative to the region. Similarly, experiences in the MENA region should help to inform academic and policy debates in transitional justice.

The chapters in this volume, written largely by experts in the region, draw upon pre- and post-Arab Spring use of transitional justice mechanisms in a range of countries, including Algeria, Egypt, Tunisia, Yemen, Libya, Morocco, and Bahrain. While these countries have diverse histories, political institutions, and experiences with accountability, most have experienced non-transition, stalled transition, or political manipulation of transitional justice measures, highlighting the limits of such mechanisms. Their experiences should impel analysts to rethink presumptions about the purpose, operation, and scope of transitional justice not just in the MENA region, but also more generally.

Transitional justice: Theory and practice

Transitional justice is an ever-expanding field of academic study and practice which, broadly speaking, involves a range of measures to address past serious human rights abuses in the wake of transition, usually from authoritarian rule and/or violent conflict. While mechanisms of post-atrocity justice can be identified throughout history and more commonly after the Second World War, they became a more frequent element of political transition to a limited degree in Southern Europe in the late 1970s, and more extensively through transitions in Central and South America in the 1980s and 1990s and the post-communist revolutions in Eastern Europe in the 1990s.[1] While transitional justice was initially implemented largely in post-authoritarian societies, it has become increasingly common in countries emerging from internal and cross-border conflicts, and in countries with ongoing conflicts and limited democracy or democratization in parts of Asia, sub-Saharan Africa, and in the MENA region.[2] While transitional justice mechanisms and scholarship have broadened significantly, particularly in relation to peace-building and development activities, and both the concept and execution of transitional justice have been challenged in academic literature and by grass-roots actors, several core elements of transitional justice can be identified.[3]

As articulated by the United Nations, transitional justice:

comprises the full range of processes and mechanisms associated with a society's attempts to come to terms with a legacy of large-scale past abuses, in order to ensure accountability, serve justice and achieve reconciliation. These may include both judicial and non-judicial mechanisms, with differing levels of international involvement (or none at all) and individual prosecutions, reparations, truth-seeking, institutional reform, vetting and dismissals, or a combination thereof.[4]

Transitional justice mechanisms

The most commonly used transitional justice measures are amnesties, prosecutions, commissions of inquiry, restorative measures such as reparations and memorials, and vetting and lustration.[5] Each of these five measures has been used in countries in the MENA region in limited ways before, and in more significant ways after the Arab Spring. Traditional justice measures are also frequently used elsewhere, primarily although not solely in sub-Saharan Africa.[6] Transitional justice measures are regularly linked to processes of security sector reform and (in post-conflict states) disarmament, demobilization, and reintegration of ex-combatants, and to rule of law reform and promotion globally, and similar linkages have been attempted in the MENA region.[7]

Amnesties are a controversial transitional justice measure, frequently operating as cynical measures of self-protection by leaders who wish to insulate themselves from accountability in the event that they choose to leave power, or passed precisely as they step down. They have fallen out of favor, particularly in peace mediation managed by the UN, but remain legal in certain contexts.[8] Further, they remain preferred not only by possible abusers, but by those who argue that they help to facilitate stability and reconciliation.

Prosecutions, in stark contrast, are seldom favored by those exiting power, and favored by those replacing old regimes only in some instances. Prosecutions may take a range of forms, whether domestic, international, or transnational, but all involve individual criminal responsibility for specific acts, usually international crimes such as genocide, war crimes, crimes against humanity or torture, but in some instances also corruption or terrorism. In some instances these are responses to demands of victims, attempts to engage in legal retributive justice, to deter future crimes, or to help develop future rule of law and democracy; in others these are also driven by calls for vengeance.[9] They tend to have relatively limited remits, trying a small number of accused, and their impact on domestic politics or institutions varies by context.

Commissions of inquiry are frequently treated as a compromise between amnesty and prosecution, or alternatively arguments are made for their own specific virtues.[10] The most familiar form is the truth commission, or truth and reconciliation commission, which receives testimony from a wide range of victims, usually in relation to crimes committed over a specific period of time. Variations include commissions of historical clarification, and commissions for the interrogation of specific incidents. In general, these commissions issue reports, often with recommendations regarding reforms to prevent future abuses; otherwise they can vary significantly in terms of mandate, legal capacities, and whether or not they identify individual or collective abusers by name. Their impact is shaped by their mandates, and by the political climate in which they operate.

Restorative processes encompass a range of activities, including apologies, memorials, and restitution and reparations. These are often presented as important to address the needs of victims and/or to promote wider societal reconciliation. In some instances they are developed alongside or in tandem with truth-telling processes or even prosecutions, but in other instances they are used in the context of no other transitional justice measures, or only with amnesties, and may be criticized as too limited to address the gravity and scale of past abuses. In some instances they may involve the return of individuals who were held as political prisoners, of people from exile, and their restoration to previous employment.

Vetting, or lustration as it was commonly termed in the Eastern European processes, involves the removal or exclusion of individuals implicated in previous abuses from positions of public trust, particularly in government. Its aims are several, including the loss of position as punishment, the prevention of specific individuals from holding posts from which they may commit further abuses, and offering a symbolic break with the past. However, vetting can also be used as a punitive measure against those associated with the former regime when applied too broadly, and can also destabilize transitional situations.[11]

Related activities

As discussed here and in Chapter 2, transitional justice is linked to an ever-expanding set of activities, including peace-building, development, and economic justice. It is most notably linked, however, to two key features of transitional institutional development and reform: rule of law promotion and security sector reform, which are themselves inextricably linked. The relationship between rule of law and transitional justice seems evident, and is even made explicit in the title of the landmark reports of the UN Secretary General on transitional justice and rule of law. Not surprisingly, expectations are that transitional justice and rule of law are mutually reinforcing, specifically that transitional justice mechanisms such as trials can help to promote future rule of law in a country, and that bolstering domestic rule of law capacity can help to address past abuses or contribute to preventing future ones.[12] Transitional justice processes may also identify flaws in the judicial system and recommend reforms. At the same time, the reform of the security sector is essential for rule of law promotion, as it is necessary to have a functioning system of police, prisons, and other security providers for a judicial system to function. It is also tied to transitional justice insofar as mechanisms such as truth commissions may recommend institutional reform of the security sector or trials and vetting may target specific perpetrators within that sector.

Challenges and themes

Countries in the MENA region have their own distinct histories and experiences with transitional justice, both before and after the Arab Spring. However, many of the challenges and lessons which arise from the chapters are not dissimilar to those in other countries around the world.

Transitional justice without transition

Increasingly transitional justice measures are being implemented in countries with ongoing conflict, incomplete democratization, or otherwise limited or non-existent transitions. While transitional justice literature and practice have tended to assume a "traditional" model, reality increasingly diverges from a model of mechanisms introduced in the wake of a clearly delineated transition from conflict or authoritarian rule.[13] While the uprisings of the Arab Spring were frequently touted as revolutionary, few generated fundamental changes in power, and even those which did remove top leaders did not necessarily promote more fundamental reform. Transitional justice measures implemented prior to the Arab Spring often came in the absence of significant political change. Thus the amnesty in Algeria and the first commission of inquiry in Morocco utilized the form of transitional justice, but in the context of regimes seeking to reinforce their own power or legitimacy. In Tunisia, Egypt, and Libya, where leaders were removed and some measures of transitional justice initiated, only Tunisia has seen significant implementation and potential impact of such measures. In part, a key obstacle to transitional justice and related reforms has been the endurance of key elites and institutions, regardless of the removal of a head of state and his inner circle. While it may seem obvious, a key lesson from many of the chapters in this volume is that transitional justice mechanisms cannot contribute to wider reform and transition in the absence of genuine political support for them.

Substantive and temporal scope

As discussed in Chapter 2, transitional justice has increasingly been expected to address numerous issues beyond direct redress for serious human rights abuses. It is expected to address development, peace-building, economic injustice, and gender inequality.[14] This has, not surprisingly, generated strong debates about the role of transitional justice generally, and in the region. In particular, several of the uprisings in the MENA region highlighted economic disparities and corruption, and demands of activists for accountability thus extended beyond addressing violence and repression. While trials in countries such as Egypt have addressed corruption, they have not managed to address wider socio-economic patterns. Similarly, while gender-based violence may be raised by activists, experiences in Tunisia suggest that transitional justice has been unable to address gender discrimination. At the same time, transitional justice has increasingly been deployed to address longer timeframes or historical injustices, and its temporal scope is frequently contested as choices about this shape who and what abuses are addressed. In Tunisia, debates over the temporal scope of justice have been politicized.

Knowledge and impact

Finally, transitional justice research is currently experiencing upheavals regarding methodology and ontology, and practitioners as well as academics are debating the impact of various mechanisms. In part, this is due to a lack of agreement regarding the purpose of specific measures, as well as the appropriate ways to measure impact. This upheaval is evident in discussions in the MENA region, because of the diversity of demands presented during the 2011 uprisings, ranging from human rights and democracy to socio-economic reforms, and because of the limited, and often politically malleable, use of specific measures.

Experiences in transitional justice

The chapters in this volume are organized into three sections. Part I presents core challenges, questions of scope in transitional justice, illuminated through comparative examination of experiences in the MENA region. Part II examines comparative experiences from the region, with chapters focusing upon specific dimensions, such as gender, martyrdom, and the monarchy. Part III treats the experiences of Egypt as an intensive case study, with discussions of collective memory, rule of law and the judiciary, and security sector reform.

Part I: Transitional justice: Challenges, themes, and scope in context

The chapters in Part I discuss several core challenges in transitional justice, including defining its scope, its relationship to human rights and other values, demonstrating the effects of transitional justice mechanisms and choices about peace and justice, in the context of experiences globally and in the MENA region.

Chapter 2, by Chandra Lekha Sriram, offers comparative lessons and challenges in understanding transitional justice from a global perspective, with some examples from and reflections for the MENA region. She identifies four types of challenges in discussing the topic, which have arisen from experiences in other regions but are equally relevant in the region. The first is how the impact of transitional justice can be assessed, if at all. The second is that of who is calling for transitional justice, and what the views of it are, particularly from the grass-roots level. The third is that of the effects of institutional design of specific transitional justice measures. And the final challenge is the appropriate scope of such measures, including whether they should include a range of social and economic concerns. She concludes that although there is no one-size-fits-all approach, and no prescriptions which may simply be applied based on experiences elsewhere, it is important for scholars and practitioners preparing for options or implementing them in the MENA region to recognize both the limitations of existing knowledge, and the likely challenges and risks so that they can ask the right questions in planning.

Chapter 3, by Susan Waltz, addresses several of these challenges as well as other themes in a distinct way, drawing upon experiences before and after the Arab Spring from several countries in the region including Egypt, Morocco, and Tunisia. She first draws attention to the apparent gaps between a set of universal human rights standards enshrined in international treaties, the practice of transitional justice with its focus on gross human rights abuses, and the expectations which have been raised of transitional justice, including of addressing questions of economic injustice. She then interrogates different facets of the problem of "impact" of transitional justice. These include the challenge of addressing what is termed a culture of impunity. This is linked to the challenge of institutional reform, particularly that of the security sector. And finally, she raises critical methodological problems, including measurement of indicators, challenging the assessments in some databases by drawing on experiences from Morocco and using similar sources.

Chapter 4, by Ibrahim Fraihat and Bill Hess, examines three of the major transitional justice measures used globally in the context of pre- and post-Arab Spring experiences in the region. Examining the use of prosecutions, amnesties, and commissions of inquiry in both periods, they argue that there is a propensity for governments to select mechanisms that pursue either justice, i.e. criminal accountability, or peace, i.e. amnesty, but achieve neither. Drawing upon experiences from Algeria, Iraq, and Morocco, they argue that each government chose its own approach to consolidate power, and that the tendency to use only one mechanism rather than several affected the possibility of achieving peace with justice. This, they argue, is substantiated as well by academic quantitative and qualitative studies suggesting that the use of more than one mechanism, and in particular the use of amnesties along with trials, is correlated with positive change in the key indicators of democracy and human rights. These patterns are also found to hold in early experiences of post-Arab Spring changes in Libya, Yemen, and Tunisia. They thus find that patterns found elsewhere hold in the MENA region, and identify lessons from the region for future transitions locally and elsewhere.

Chapter 5, by Christopher K. Lamont, further elaborates on critical debates regarding the scope of transitional justice processes. Drawing upon the Tunisian transition, he observes that one of the important debates has been over the appropriate temporal and substantive scope of any transitional justice mechanisms. He argues that transitional justice literature may not understand these debates well, not only because it has not until recently engaged with the MENA region, but because the former literature has been driven by legalism, while debates in Tunisia (and perhaps other countries in the region) over transitional justice issues have been driven by state-building contestation. He suggests that this is partly to do with the fact that in this region justice is understood as more than legal justice, also encompassing Islamic conceptions of social justice, and because decisions relate to political contestations about state identity. Thus, not surprisingly, there are significant discussions regarding the temporal period to be covered by mechanisms such as commissions of inquiry, as well as the coverage of topics not frequently addressed by any transitional justice mechanisms, such as economic justice and corruption.

However, while the chapter identifies divergences which may appear specific to Tunisia or the region, these are very much part of contemporary debates in the wider transitional justice literature.

Part II: Transitional justice experiences in the MENA Region: Comparative lessons

The chapters in Part II of this volume draw out comparative lessons from transitional justice experiences in several countries in the region, focusing upon a particular dimension of practice or a cross-cutting issue, such as gender, martyrdom, political exclusion, or implementing truth-telling processes in Arab monarchies. Most chapters examine these dimensions through the experience of several countries; all have implications for other countries in the region and beyond.

Chapter 6, by Doris H. Gray and Terry C. Coonan, discusses the role of transitional justice mechanisms in Tunisia in reframing gender narratives. They focus on one mechanism, the national truth commission, and the roles of women in it. Building on in-depth interviews, they identify a range of complex debates regarding the status of women visible in post-revolution Tunisia in the context of debates over Islamism and secularism. They argue that examining transitional justice through the lens of gender is important not only because transitional justice has tended to ignore this dimension, but also because in the case of many abuses which women experience, there is continuity before and after transitions. That is to say, gendered abuses by the state, as well as domestic violence and sexual harassment, are not necessarily altered by political change, or properly addressed by post-transition mechanisms. They document ongoing patterns of abuses of female opponents and sympathizers to the pre-transition regime, and emphasize the need for the commission to reflect multiple narratives, including those specifically relating to gendered violence. They also consider the impact that the experience of mechanisms in Tunisia has had in the Maghreb, including in Morocco, as well as in countries such as Sierra Leone in other regions.

In Chapter 7, Thomas DeGeorges argues that martyrdom has played an important role in the transitional justice processes both before and after the Arab Spring of Algeria, Tunisia, and Morocco. While martyrdom and transitional justice are not traditionally associated with one another, he makes the case that martyrs involve people who are victims of what may be framed as political violence, whether committed by state security forces or unknown perpetrators. In this context, martyrs may be understood in the frame of victims addressed by transitional justice, but also as icons for social or political transformation. Broadly speaking, claims regarding martyrdom were important in these countries insofar as martyrs were held up as symbols for whom reform must be pursued. In Algeria, he argues that this has not enabled stabilization. In contrast, he finds that in Tunisia and Morocco the broad claims relying on martyrs to justify social change were tempered by transitional justice bodies. Instead, he argues, mechanisms such as truth commissions and institutional reforms have helped to respond to the sacrifices made by martyrs and to address social demands for historical justice without the same disruptive effects as were seen in Algeria.

In Chapter 8, Marieke Wierda and Mieczysław P. Boduszyński discuss a mode of transitional justice which is less frequently discussed than the other commonly used mechanisms: vetting. They examine Libya's Political Isolation Law as an instance of retributive transitional justice, arguing that although the conditions may have been ripe for a wider range of transitional justice activities, these were not pursued. Specifically, they argue that although the collapse of the former regime and Libya's traditions of mediation and reconciliation between tribes might have encouraged the use of non-retributive mechanisms as well, this did not take place. Instead, political exclusion was used in a punitive fashion, frequently against members of the revolution rather than of the former regime. They suggest that this is a result of a wider struggle for legitimacy and power, in which this process was a tool. Further, in line with Fraihat and Hess, they see a dangerous impact from the use of only retributive mechanisms in the absence of reconciliation measures.

In Chapter 9, Elham Fakhro examines the use of truth and fact-finding commissions in two monarchies, pre- and post-Arab Spring. She argues that in Morocco and Bahrain the absence of regime change has not prevented the use of truth-telling. However, that same absence of reform has constrained the scope of these mechanisms, preventing the naming of alleged perpetrators or units. And, she argues, the wider political settlement between regimes and reformers has limited the potential for the creation of other transitional justice mechanisms, or for truth-telling to act as a catalyst to reform. Finally, in common with the chapters by Sriram and Waltz, she interrogates methodological issues. Specifically, she suggests that there remains a lack of clarity about what truth commissions ought to be able to do, what they could potentially do in the absence of democratization, and difficulties therefore in determining how to assess the efficacy of such bodies.

INTRODUCTION

Part III: Key dimensions of transitional justice: Lessons from Egypt

Egypt's tumultuous experiences during and following the Arab Spring present a range of issues common to the region, as well as to countries around the world experiencing transitions or attempted transitions, including trials, debates over the role of the security sector, attempts at rule of law reform, and contestations over collective memory. The three chapters in Part III each interrogate a dimension of transitional justice and related activities in Egypt.

In Chapter 10, Judy Barsalou discusses the trajectory of efforts at transitional justice in Egypt. She argues that while the protesters demanded reform, and united around the need to remove Mubarak, their further political demands, including those related to accountability, were less clear and sometimes divergent. They had, in particular, a range of demands regarding what transitional justice should do: whether it should promote democracy, focus on socio-economic justice, or address other goals. She observes, building on her own interviews, surveys, and a poll by Pew Charitable Trust, that there was strong support amongst ordinary Egyptians for institutional reform, particularly of the security sector and the judiciary, presumably because so many had been victims of the abuses of these. In the absence of consensus on transitional justice, international advisers entered the scene, pushing for implementation of transitional justice. In this context, she argues, there were ongoing efforts by citizens to develop collective memorialization, but these were somewhat sidelined by ongoing political developments and the push for implementation of technical "fixes."

In Chapter 11, Sahar Aziz discusses rule of law and judicial independence in the context of the Egyptian transition. She argues that while many external observers have viewed the Egyptian judiciary as relatively independent, political control by the Mubarak regime limited that independence successfully, and rendered the judiciary conservative. Further, she argues, while the concept of rule of law has been operational in the country, rather than a thick understanding of rule of law, there has been a hybrid version, of thin rule of law combined with rule by law. These phenomena operate in the context of patterns of patronage and the "deep state" to limit the prospect of reform. Indeed, she argues that there has not been a serious transition, despite the removal of former President Mubarak and his inner circle, because there has instead been a reshuffle of elites within the same basic authoritarian system. In such a context, wider reforms and transitional justice mechanisms are not viable.

In Chapter 12, Omar Ashour and Sherif Mohyelden examine the linked demands for transitional justice and security sector reform during and after

11

the uprisings in Egypt. They trace the targeting of security and intelligence forces during the uprising, as perpetrators of particular abuses, and the demands in the post-Mubarak period for transitional justice and specific measures of security sector reform. These were initiated in limited ways, such as through fact-finding committees, but further steps were not taken, and following the coup in 2013, the military authorities did not support reform of the sector or transitional justice. Although human rights and transitional justice bodies were established by the government, few substantive steps were taken and the prospects for reform are slim. The authors identify eight sources for the failure of security sector reform after the 2011 uprising. These include political divisions amongst pro-change actors and resistance from anti-reform groups, a range of institutional and capacity limitations, and regional actors hampering or failing to support change.

Conclusion

Transitional justice in the MENA region, like the transitions there, is far from complete and faces many of the challenges seen elsewhere in the world. Scholars and practitioners may glean some cautionary lessons from these experiences to date. Most notably, it is clear that pursuing transitional justice mechanisms is not very effective while transitions are frozen or incomplete, or countries have lapsed into new stages of violence and authoritarian rule. Even where transitions have proceeded somewhat more smoothly, transitional justice is still subject to political manipulation. And even where leaders have been replaced, transitions may stall because core elites, whether political, military, or institutional, remain embedded. Further, where transitional demands include socio-economic reforms and equity, transitional justice processes have not accommodated these well. As many authors note, these incomplete accountability measures, alongside failed or incomplete reform, create risks for future instability or have enabled repressive institutions to endure.

PART I

TRANSITIONAL JUSTICE

CHALLENGES, THEMES, AND SCOPE

2

TRANSITIONAL JUSTICE
IN COMPARATIVE PERSPECTIVE

LESSONS FOR THE MIDDLE EAST

Chandra Lekha Sriram

Introduction: Three decades of transitional justice

Transitional justice is a vast, amorphous, and seemingly ever-expanding field. The questions it addresses range from the specific, such as dealing with past atrocities, to broader questions of how to promote conflict prevention and resolution, peace-building, rule of law, democratization, traditional justice processes, and social and economic justice.[1] Internationalized criminal justice and domestic accountability for abuses of prior regimes date back to the Nuremberg and Tokyo tribunals and beyond. However, the contemporary practice of what is now termed transitional justice is generally understood to begin with transitions in the Southern Cone in Latin America, notably the prosecutions of former members of the military junta in Argentina following its return to democracy in 1983.[2] Rather than review the extensive literature and practice, this chapter will discuss lessons and gaps from some three dec-

15

ades of practice in comparative perspective. Drawing upon the author's previous research in Latin America, South Asia, and sub-Saharan Africa, and building upon her limited research in MENA countries—specifically in Lebanon and Sudan—this chapter seeks to identify relevant lessons for relatively nascent efforts at transitional justice in the region. While the literature and practice of transitional justice is relatively expansive and rich, having developed quickly over the past thirty years, there remain many gaps, which scholars have sought to fill with both qualitative and quantitative research. However, despite this research, debates remain unresolved as to whether transitional justice has any effect at all on immediate goals, such as bringing perpetrators to justice, or more attenuated goals, such as democratization and improved human rights records.[3]

This chapter argues that despite extensive research in transitional justice, there are significant gaps in knowledge. These gaps are clustered into four categories, with examples from around the world, with implications for countries in the Middle East and North Africa. These include: 1. How to assess impact? 2. Who is demanding transitional justice/what is the grass-roots view? 3. Does the institutional design of transitional justice measures affect desired outcomes? 4. Should transitional justice measures be expanded, particularly to address questions of economic rights and/or harm?

Within these four categories, this chapter seeks to address a range of important questions which should be considered by researchers, or by those seeking to create or assess transitional justice mechanisms. These include: What is the goal/what is transitional justice being invoked for? What are our benchmarks for success? Can we measure/assess them, and if so how? Are the mechanisms proposed or used reasonably designed to address the goals enunciated for transitional justice, or could they conceivably be?

Often, decisions about the creation of transitional justice mechanisms, and the assessments and critiques which follow, fail to take these questions into consideration sufficiently. However, clearly identifying what we do and don't know, how we might fill informational gaps, and where we may have unrealistic expectations about what transitional justice can do, is more than academic. It is also a matter of contemporary policy and programming as actors in international organizations, bilateral development organizations, and national and international NGOs seek to develop knowledge-based policies in complex transitional situations. Thus this chapter seeks both to identify those knowledge gaps and questions, and to draw out some lessons and implications from comparative research in a range of locations across the world.

First, however, a clarification is in order. Transitional justice is now the dominant term for a field of study and practice that can encompass prosecutions, commissions of inquiry, apologies, and many more processes to do with human rights abuses per se, as well as related activities such as rule of law and security sector promotion; and, as discussed below, its expansion has been significant. However, the two words in the term are themselves vague or contestable, which matters because this affects how one defines the parameters of transitional justice. This, however, is something on which the voluminous literature has seldom ruminated, much less converged. First, the term transitional is problematic, because increasingly mechanisms have been introduced in countries which have not undergone a significant change (such as democratization, or war termination). Thus the International Criminal Court (ICC) has been utilized in the context of significant violent conflict and varying degrees of polity change, in countries such as Sudan, the Democratic Republic of Congo, and Libya. In Morocco, the creation of a truth commission took place without a significant change in the state or ruling elite, but rather was initiated by a new king replacing his father; the commission in Bahrain took place in the context of no political transition; in Egypt, Aziz suggests, the elite reshuffled rather than any revolutionary change occurring, and constraints on the judiciary limited justice and the possibility of a genuine transition.[4]

It is unclear whether transitional justice must take place in the context of a transition, and if so what features must define such a transition, and how one can ascertain that they were definitely present. This is particularly salient in the MENA region, where questions of accountability have been raised for some time, but have been framed as transitional justice in the wake of the Arab Spring uprisings.[5] Further, the diversity of post-Arab Spring justice processes requires close attention, as in some instances leaders were removed and/or tried (Egypt and Tunisia), even as other key figures remained in power and used transitional justice processes not to signal transition but to control state-building processes.[6] Further, in Tunisia, similar to many states globally, there was a debate over the appropriate temporal scope of any transitional justice efforts—for abuses during the uprising only, or for longer periods of time.[7] In other states, the leaders endured but instituted some transitional justice mechanisms, as in Bahrain.[8] And in others uprisings were followed by violent conflict, with or without any justice mechanisms being invoked for human rights violations, such as in Syria or Libya.

The concept of justice is one that has been debated by political philosophers for millennia, but is often rather underdefined in the context of transitional justice. Must it mean prosecutions only, or other modes of judicial accountability? Or should it also entail forms of accountability such as truth-telling, apologies, and so on? Transitional justice processes, as we see below, have generally been treated as encompassing both judicial and non-judicial measures. However, there have been quite vigorous debates about the relative value of particular mechanisms as "justice," and in particular strong arguments regarding the place of non-judicial "traditional" justice, or memorialization. These debates may be further stretched by the idea that transitional justice can include memorialization through martyrdom (not ordinarily characterized as transitional justice) as in Algeria and Tunisia, or modes of accountability that can effectively generate vetting such as "political exclusion" in Tunisia and Libya.[9] We may also need to query whether the term "justice" applies at all in the context of show trials, selective trials, and punitive vetting processes. As Boduszyński and Wierda observe, political isolation legislation in Libya was punitive, and human rights organizations within the country viewed it as divisive. As Waltz notes: "[t]ransitional justice need not be linked to the modern concept of human rights" and may be used for political consolidation, the punishment of rivals, and sealing the past.[10] And indeed, even where specific human rights are invoked in transitional justice processes, as in Morocco's commission of inquiry, they are focused in many cases on grave abuses, and do not address questions of economic rights or political participation, with Tunisia's transitional justice legislation of 2014 constituting an exception.[11]

I turn now to the four key areas in which we do not yet have sufficiently robust knowledge about transitional justice.

Impact/Assessment

There has been a great deal of attention in recent years to the impact of transitional justice measures, which has taken a variety of forms ranging from impact assessment, monitoring and evaluation, to discussions of "legacy." Some of this comes from an increasingly critical strain of scholarship in transitional justice, where one or another mechanism is regularly denounced as a failure because it fails to meet a range of goals. Some comes from trends amongst donors and policy programmers, where the need for evidence-based programming and assessment is considered ever more important, particularly given the cost of such mechanisms and the limits to donor budgets. But to take just one example, a special issue of the leading journal in the field, the *International Journal of Transitional Justice* (*IJTJ*) in 2010, was devoted to assessing transitional justice, and a wide array of benchmarks and methods were outlined.[12] But many of the pieces utilized such different benchmarks or goals to assess transitional justice, and different methodologies, that systematic analysis of the "impact" writ large of transitional justice based on the findings of these diverse articles would not be possible. This is not a criticism of the special issue, but rather a reflection of the diversity of approaches in the literature more generally. Arguably, prior to debating what effects transitional justice mechanisms have, it is essential to be clear about what the mechanisms are expected to do and why. Thus it is important to be clear about the benchmarks against which the mechanisms are to be judged. The chapter turns to this question next before taking up the methodological challenges of analyzing impact.

Benchmarks/goals

In order to assess the efficacy or impact of transitional justice, we need to be clear what benchmarks we are setting for mechanisms, why we have set them, and whether they are realistic. To continue with the previous example, in the special issue of *IJTJ*, authors variously considered state-level effects, the role of outreach, views of rule of law in the wake of transitional justice processes, and victim perceptions. Some pieces challenged the role of evaluation, others the limited role of positivist methodologies, others still recognized the danger of utopian expectations of transitional justice mechanisms.[13] These pieces variously queried goals, research methods, and in some cases analyzed through the lens of different actors. All of these approaches might be valid, but in considering what lessons can be learned from past practice for new entrants to transitional justice practice, it is particularly worth considering what the major benchmarks or goals for transitional justice often are, what we still do not know, and how we might refine our research to assess current practice and advise practitioners more effectively. Numerous goals have been attributed to transitional justice practice by practitioners themselves, by scholars, and by recipient communities. The goals are not only significant but ever-expanding, and some analysts have insisted that the goals of transitional justice are internally irreconcilable, but several goals are particularly common in the literature: retribution, deterrence, the needs of victims, and societal needs.[14]

Retributive justice

One of the key goals of criminal justice, whether domestic or international, is retribution. This goal, as distinct from revenge, is about punishing wrongdoing: it is deemed a necessary response because a crime has been committed. Here we may expect that we should be able to assess the efficacy if not the impact of criminal trials: we may inquire if a crime has been committed, whether a properly conducted investigation identified an accused person or persons, and whether a proper trial was conducted. The benchmark should not be convictions per se, as a proper retributive process in a liberal democratic state should also entail due process, and thus the possibility of acquittal for substantive or procedural reasons. In such domestic legal systems, criminal trials are relatively well-designed to prosecute accused persons, and frequently result in penalties being imposed for crimes committed. However, even in ideal-type domestic contexts, many crimes, including serious crimes, go unpunished, and people are wrongly convicted. The limits of retributive justice are perhaps far more evident in the context of transitional or international criminal justice. This is the case first and foremost because the scale of such crimes and the number of possible perpetrators is so large that not all crimes could be investigated or perpetrators prosecuted, even given a robust police and criminal justice system.

Countries that have experienced mass atrocities seldom have such systems in place. International criminal tribunals do not have the resources or expertise to prosecute more than a handful of accused persons, often initially only those in relatively junior positions, although the goal is often ultimately to target "those who bear the greatest responsibility." The result is that many crimes committed in the context of mass violence are not prosecuted, which would appear to be a "failure" of retributive justice, although scholars have not been able to quantify this. All international criminal tribunals have been criticized for prosecuting too few persons. So too have domestic trials, which in Argentina for example targeted the leaders of the military junta and one stratum of military officials at the end of their rule in 1983 (convicting but then pardoning many). This left other perpetrators living amongst communities which they had harmed until trials were initiated in Spain in 2003 and in Argentina in 2012.[15] Given the limited number of prosecutions, however, other questions arise, which partly speak to the limited nature of retribution in transitional situations, but which also result in critiques which may undermine the legitimacy of prosecutions and related institutions. These questions include: Are the "right" people being prosecuted? And are they being prosecuted for the "right" crimes? For example, the prosecutions of former President Alberto Fujimori in Peru were originally "only" for corruption, not the serious atrocities of which he was also accused. Former Egyptian President

Hosni Mubarak's 2012 conviction for his role in the killing of hundreds of protesters was overturned on appeal, and he was never tried for other alleged crimes during his three decades in power; it is possible that his 2014 embezzlement conviction will be the only one for which he remains imprisoned. The ICC has been criticized for its approach to prosecuting Thomas Lubanga Dyilo for crimes in the DRC, on the grounds that he was a low-level rebel operative, and for prosecuting him for the crime of recruiting child soldiers, rather than for other war crimes of which he might have been accused.

Implicit or explicit in these criticisms are questions that extend beyond simple demands for retributive justice, to broader expectations about the impact of accountability upon victims, societies, and in deterring potential perpetrators. We thus need to consider carefully what we actually expect transitional justice to deliver in terms of retributive justice, and how extensive we can expect its effects to be in violent or transitional contexts. As scholars we might then need to think more carefully about how to assess the efficacy of retributive processes. Many other goals are often placed upon transitional justice beyond retribution, such as deterrence, serving victims' needs, educating society, and so on. It is to these that the chapter turns next.

Deterrence

In both domestic and international criminal justice, trials are often expected not only to punish the guilty, but also to deter future crimes. This is reflected in the preamble to the Rome Statute of the ICC, which refers to a determination "to put an end to impunity for the perpetrators of these crimes and thus to contribute to the prevention of such crimes."[16] There is however little evidence that international trials have contributed to deterrence, and there is some reason to be skeptical of the capacity of relatively limited trials to change the calculus of potential perpetrators.[17] Some of the questions we should ask include: does the prospect of prosecutions or other non-juridical penalty deter those who would commit atrocities? But there is a methodological problem: How would we know if deterrence worked? Even if we were confronted with someone who confessed to being a would-be genocidaire, and said they were deterred by the ICC or by the prospect of prosecution elsewhere, should we believe them? Could we rely on large-scale surveys, rather than individual accounts? Or should we, realistically, ever expect transitional justice to deter? Given the challenges of proving that deterrence works even in domestic criminal systems with greater capacities and greater probability that a perpetrator will be caught or prosecuted, there is reason to be skeptical that very limited international criminal trials will create sufficient risks to deter potential perpetrators.

Victim-centered justice

Many advocates of transitional justice and international criminal justice increasingly insist that processes should be victim-centered. This has taken the form of the promotion of the concepts of the right to the "truth," and the right to "remedy" and "reparation."[18] The rationale for victim-centered approaches are myriad, including repairing harms done to victims through material reparations, vindication for those who suffered psychological harm and/or social exclusion through moral reparations, and promotion of reconciliation within communities and between victims and perpetrators. A wide range of mechanisms are utilized, including the increased participation of victims in trial processes, truth-telling settings, memorials, apologies, traditional rituals, and reparations and restitution.[19]

However, what are the actual effects of such mechanisms—do they achieve any of these putative goals? This is an area where there is a great deal of uncertainty, although not for lack of research. Clearly, mass atrocities and state repression generate a significant number of victims, and they have needs and demands which should be addressed. If the goal is to address the demands and needs of victims, what is it that they need and want, and how do we know? Clearly, they want many different things, and what they want and how they voice it changes over time, and changes by location. In some contexts, significant survey data are available, but this may still obscure minority preferences, and in many cases self-appointed victims' groups may not be representative, with the effects on women and minorities being particularly problematic. For example, in many societies, women who receive reparations may either choose to hand them over to male relatives or be coerced into doing so.[20] Who the victims are and how they may be understood to have suffered is also disputed, and this affects how they are treated and understood in transitional justice processes. As Gray and Coonan observe in this volume, while much of transitional justice is about public victimhood, much of the harm caused to women may take place in the private realm. Examples include Tunisia, where women who challenged the regime, as well as female relatives of those incarcerated by the regime, suffered harassment in the home, sexual assault, as well as state-imposed impediments to taking up work or caring for their children.

Transitional justice processes, whether truth commissions or reparations, often do not take account of the specific types of harms experienced by women, nor offer modalities of restorative or retributive justice which may suit their demands. They may also treat women as "secondary" victims only, seeing them as casualties of the state's targeting of relatives, rather than recognizing that they are directly targeted.[21]

Assuming preferences and goals can be identified, what are they and how are they to be addressed? Is the goal to restore victims to societies where they may have been ostracized and blamed for their own victimization? Is it to provide material reparations to address physical harm or loss of property or livelihood, or moral compensation? In Brazil, the reparations process for a period of time compensated some persons significantly more for loss of earnings and pensions than individuals who had been detained and tortured, and was not surprisingly subject to a great deal of criticism.[22] Debates continue amongst scholars, practitioners, and victims groups about what the most appropriate forms are of either material or moral reparations. Are memorials which list the names of victims, memorials which convert former sites of torture and abuse, or commissions of inquiry most appropriate? Are victims satisfied with commission reports, such as that of the Rettig commission in Chile, which name victims and the circumstances in which they were disappeared or killed but do not name perpetrators? Nearly twenty years after that report was issued, the debate is still ongoing in Chile.[23] Memorialization can also take an informal, non-state-driven fashion, as in Egypt, where much dissemination of images and memories occurred virtually, distributed by citizens.[24]

At the Extraordinary Chambers in Cambodia, victims can participate with their own legal representation, which is also permitted in a more limited way in the ICC, but there is no evidence that victims' demands are in some sense "more satisfied." Indeed, there is evidence that some victims are frustrated because their expectations have been raised by inclusion in such processes.[25] In Guatemala, relatives of those disappeared and killed once said they wanted to know only where the bodies were buried, but have since revised their expectations to demand prosecutions. It is often unclear what victims want or how to satisfy them because of this diversity, which makes it a real challenge to assess subsequently whether any specific transitional justice mechanism "works." And furthermore, which needs and demands can realistically be addressed specifically by transitional justice measures? Which may require something else—sustained humanitarian or development assistance, or systematic legal, constitutional, or land reform, to target long-standing discrimination? Are there ways in which we as scholars and practitioners might answer these complex questions better? If so how, bearing in mind that every context is different and there is no one-size-fits-all prescription?

Further, in the MENA region there may be modalities of transitional justice which relate to broader discussions about victim-centered justice but are not framed as such. As DeGeorges discusses with reference to Algeria, Morocco, and Tunisia, martyrdom needs to be understood as a transitional justice concept, best perhaps placed within discussions of memorialization and restorative justice, although not necessarily of victimhood or victims' needs (indeed, the concept of the martyr evokes the opposite of victimhood). However, the concept of martyr itself divides people in divided societies, according to DeGeorges, along the lines of factions, generations, and ideologies. Further, the frequently state-sponsored cult of martyrs has the effect of preventing significant state change while challenging a few elites. Thus a relatively region-specific practice which may be construed as transitional justice has a unique focus on a few as heroes and does not attend to those usually categorized as victims, and tends not to promote transition.[26]

Societal effects

Transitional justice measures face particularly heavy, often unrealistic, demands that they effect social change in a variety of ways. These include, most notably, that they have educational effects, that they promote democracy, rule of law, human rights, and that they promote reconciliation.

Transitional justice measures are often expected not only to educate people about what has gone before, but also to promote norms of non-repetition, and demonstrate how conflicts should be managed. In this sense, they are expected to have pedagogic effects, often through a degree of public spectacle, whether a trial or truth commission, and potentially through memorials or even textbook projects.[27] The idea is that individuals and societies who had been active in, complicit with, or ignorant of past abuses would recognize not only that these abuses occurred but also that they were wrong, and therefore alter beliefs and behavior patterns. In order to assess whether this in fact occurs, one would have to examine whether transitional justice measures are linked to increased evidence of awareness of atrocities and rights, or attitudinal changes. Demonstrating such a link would be challenging enough, but measuring any effect would be even harder. And again, we must ask ourselves which if any transitional justice measures are well-suited to the task: Trials? Commissions of inquiry? Reparations? Memorials? Removal of those tainted from public office? In Tunisia, for example, transitional justice was expected to play an important role by removing certain political elites through criminal trials or vetting. In Libya, vetting or political exclusion may have been used as collective punishment, violating due process and human rights standards, perpetuating political divides, and creating obstacles to justice.[28]

Transitional justice measures are also often expected to contribute to state or societal transformations, through promoting the rule of law, democracy, and human rights. They may even, as in Tunisia, be part of efforts to engage in state-building, and get caught in political divisions.[29] In Morocco, the recommendations of the truth commission included commitments to certain international legal standards, and some of these were implemented, such as explicit domestic legislation to prohibit torture; subsequent reforms in the wake of further pressure included a new constitution providing for further human rights protections.[30] For programmers in the field and increasingly for researchers, this is a particularly critical demand, linking transitional justice to goals sought more generally by development actors and peace-builders, with a presumption of a positive correlation.[31] This makes some sense, intuitively, as transitional justice mechanisms seek to respond to the abuses that came about largely as part of the failures of democracy, rule of law, or human rights protection. But what do we know? And if we don't know, how would we go about analyzing these connections? There are significant methodological challenges.

Methodological problems in assessing impact

Methodologically, it is very difficult to demonstrate causation in social scientific inquiry, and the study of transitional justice is no exception, despite academic and policy demands for evidence of impact.[32] Statistical analyses show some positive correlation between specific transitional justice measures and improvements in democracy and human rights records, particularly when several measures are used.[33] However, as Waltz points out in this volume, despite the extensive development of quantitative measures to assess human rights efficacy, limitations in coding mean that there is reason for caution in using them to analyze developments.[34] Further, there are limits to what can be inferred, as these findings show correlations rather than causation. Other causes may be more significant. In complex conflict-affected or transitional states, the international peacekeeping or peace-building missions and bilateral assistance—which may themselves target rule of law, democracy promotion, and human rights—may shape outcomes more than transitional justice measures.[35] Indeed, transitional justice activities nearly always now operate alongside international peace and development activities, and in many cases are tightly linked to them, so disentangling any effects would be extremely difficult.[36] It may also be that we are searching for causation in the wrong direction: it could be that improved rule of law, democratization, or human rights commitments by the state facilitate pursuing accountability. Accountability processes such as trials may have limited effects on democratization or rule of law, or even negative effects, or be derailed by political elites.[37] Determining the direction of causality, if there is any, is important for policy-makers, who might either choose to delay accountability processes until foundations are in place, or alternatively might hope that accountability mechanisms which conform to the principles of the rule of law help promote the wider rule of law in a country.

The evidence seems to be contradictory. For example, while countries such as Argentina held trials at the time of transition from authoritarianism, those were fraught, and pardons ultimately imposed, yet the country democratized and is not only prosecuting cases relating to abuses committed during the Dirty War period of 1977–83. On the other hand, Sri Lanka had limited prosecutions of state security officials who committed abuses in the country's long-running civil war, as well as several truth commissions, and yet state abuses escalated in that conflict while the country became less democratic.[38] In Chile, despite several commissions of inquiry, myriad memorials, and ongoing trials, human rights advocates express concern that the result has been an understanding of human rights which is limited to abuses committed during the dictatorship, precluding recognition of abuses being committed by the democratic state.[39] In Kenya, investigations were initiated by the ICC against six people for post-election violence in 2008, and two of those individuals were subsequently elected President and Deputy President; again, democratic space has been constricted.[40]

Beyond large-N correlations or individual country studies, how might we investigate the effects of transitional justice processes? This is a difficult task. As part of a large comparative project on the impact of transitional justice measures on democratic institution-building right, this is what I am seeking to do, through process-tracing.[41] Process-tracing is a common methodological tool in qualitative research, which involves a close analysis of primary and secondary documentation, and frequently interviews, to examine the pathways through which policies may change and decisions may be taken. In my research, similar to much process-tracing, I engage in structured, focused case comparisons. This is an approach which can help to test mid-range theory, even if its predictive value is admittedly limited, and can be critical in theory-building, as leading proponents such as Alexander George have explained.[42] Through the use of process-tracing, one might hope not only to examine if transitional justice measures affect key goals, but if so, how they do it, and identify more effectively which mechanisms might be better suited to address which goals.

Finally, transitional justice measures are often expected to promote reconciliation. This is one of the most frequently cited goals of transitional justice advocates, and many commissions of inquiry are termed truth and reconciliation commissions to highlight this core goal. However, scholars and practitioners alike are often unclear about what they mean here—do they mean basic coexistence, or the creation or return of genuine affinity amongst and within communities?[43] Does this also mean a change in relations between victims and perpetrators? Who decides what processes are used and who should participate, and is that participation genuine and voluntary?[44] And how would we "know" that people are reconciled, or that any transitional justice process caused it? Do we know because people answer survey questions in ways that suggest that resentments are no longer at the surface? Do we know because they say they approve of a specific mechanism, such as a truth commission? And are there some transitional justice mechanisms that might not be suited to this goal? For example, trials target a small number of accused and are adversarial processes—should we expect them to support reconciliation? Certainly from my research in Sierra Leone, the Special Court is viewed not as a promoter of reconciliation in many communities but rather as a remote, elite-based, internationally-driven institution.

Clearer criteria for what constitutes reconciliation, which can be empirically assessed, would help scholars to examine whether, and if so how, certain transitional justice measures work in specific contexts. They might also help to identify risks in promoting some measures, such as cynicism, coercion, and bias. For example, some scholars of Rwanda have argued strongly that *gacaca*, a traditional measure modified to respond to the genocide, often failed to promote reconciliation and was in some cases used coercively.[45] Authoritarian leaders who left office in Latin America in the 1980s often invoked reconciliation, while putting in place amnesties to shield themselves and allies from future prosecution. However, bilateral donors, the United Nations (UN), international NGOs and some donor and transitional states devote considerable resources to promotion of reconciliation, particularly through commissions of inquiry, so a greater precision about the effects of such processes on reconciliation would undoubtedly help guide policy-makers.

Demand/the view 'from below'

While the questions of impact and efficacy continue to be the most salient ones for scholars and practitioners of transitional justice alike, there are several other arenas in which, arguably, not enough is understood. The next is that of demand: who actually seeks transitional justice, and what is it they want? This is often framed in terms of transitional justice "from below," or local ownership. Transitional justice has come under fire, alongside the peace-building operations it increasingly accompanies, for being internationally-driven, and not locally owned or suited to local culture.[46] Certainly, many transitional justice processes have been internationally run, or funded, or are hybrids with contested and complex local participation. For example, the Extraordinary Chambers in the Courts of Cambodia, a hybrid tribunal with international and domestic judges, and international and domestic co-prosecutors, has been marked by contestation between internal and international staff and judges, even as the court has been expected to address the needs and demands of a large number of victims.[47]

At the same time, there may be myriad voices from victim and civil society groups calling for different types of justice and accountability. Thus there may be significant disagreements about what justice means for different periods of time and specific events or crimes, or for what it means for different victim groups, and there will be visions of who constitutes a perpetrator and why. Thus simply developing processes will not suffice. In Tunisia, this became visible in debates about the temporal scope of justice, and the content of political exclusion laws.[48]

Furthermore, there are cultural objections, arguments that retributive justice is not the process by which specific communities have traditionally handled conflicts. Thus some Acholi leaders in northern Uganda issued complaints about the ICC interfering not only in the peace process, but promoting a type of justice unfamiliar to their communities. Some Sierra Leoneans who participated in the Truth and Reconciliation Commission felt that it was too legalistic, and did not reflect how people in that society handled treatment of past harms. The perceived disconnect between the commission and local practices may also have hampered its utility in promoting concepts of human rights and law in the post-conflict peace-building process.

The challenge is not one of simply gathering evidence, but of identifying the right questions to ask, and who should be empowered to answer the questions. Acholi leaders purporting to speak for all northerners in Uganda were not empowered to speak for the non-Acholi, and there was dissent even within Acholi communities. Local practices are also not static but change over time, and may be disrupted by extensive periods of conflict and state repression. At the same time, not all transitional justice processes are internationally driven. Many early processes in Latin America in the 1980s, particularly in Chile, Argentina, and Brazil, were driven by domestic human rights advocates and lawyers, often with the indifference of the international community and in some cases opposition not only by domestic elites but external states. Further, there were clear debates amongst internal rights advocates as well as affected communities about appropriate goals and tactics.

Nonetheless, we still do not know enough about what communities, or specific individuals, "really" want, and this is difficult to get at. There are increasingly refined surveys, and these do help to map what significant portions of the population of a country may think, or want, although these have some technical and methodological issues. However, we are still not very good at understanding what specific communities want, both in terms of goals and execution of transitional justice, and whether what they want is feasible (or even desirable). We may also need to bear in mind that in some cases local communities want simple revenge or mob justice. Or that locally recognized practices of justice also involve violations of international human rights standards. Is this something transitional justice processes should deliver?[49]

Institutional design

While many practitioners do work closely on the design of transitional justice institutions, creating templates and toolkits, questions abound as to which elements matter, why, and how. These matter for scholars and practitioners alike, given that the mere presence or absence of a particular mechanism is unlikely to yield good or bad results; rather its mandate, structure, and content may matter, given the range of goals it is expected to serve. While there is a range of design questions which might be raised, I note just three here.

Participation

Debates abound at the policy level and in academic research regarding who should be included in transitional justice processes, and how. As discussed above, the turn to heightened emphasis on victim-centered approaches to justice has meant increased emphasis on and demand for victim participation in court proceedings, including providing them with legal representation to act in court. This is a step beyond the more common expectation that victims will have the opportunity to testify in truth commission hearings. However, while heightened victim participation seems to be the trend, there are notable exceptions, such as the Lessons Learned and Reconciliation Commission (LLRC) in Sri Lanka, which was not clearly designed to manage extensive victim testimony.

Debates also abound about the importance of participation or absence of high-level perpetrators, whether government or non-state perpetrators. Does their presence signal a transition and their absence the opposite? Or should the effects of their participation depend upon whether they offer specific confessions or apologies, or upon how it is they arrive before an institution? For example, many former members of the apartheid regime in South Africa testified and confessed the bare minimum but did not apologize, and similar complaints were made in relation to the truth commission process in Sierra Leone.[50] In Morocco, the commission of inquiry established in 2004 relied upon testimony of victims and relatives, rather than alleged perpetrators, but there was at the same time a reform process for the security sector. In Tunisia DeGeorges observes that members of the security sector were reluctant to engage with the Bouderbala commission.[51] Whether commissions of inquiry should name the names of perpetrators or have public hearings continues to be a matter of debate in countries which have long since completed these processes. Frequently these are pragmatic decisions, rather than normatively-driven ones.[52] In many cases those prosecuted, such as Slobodan Milošević or Charles Taylor, are present against their wills and use the courtroom not only to challenge the legitimacy of the courts but to speak to their hardliner bases. Does it matter who participates, and how?

However, even as we engage in technical refinement and seek greater participation, we still do not seem to know how or whether different modes of participation matter, and therefore what types of institutional design matter in particular contexts.

Distance and accessibility

International courts and transnational justice processes have been subject to the criticism that they are distant and foreign and inaccessible to the affected societies and victims. They have also been criticized because their language and style can be inaccessible.[53] Hybrid tribunals, victim participation, and outreach offices are all an attempt to rectify this, but it is not clear that we have convincing evidence that any of these really address distance and accessibility problems.[54] Again this is not a simple academic criticism: it matters for practitioners if the effect is that mechanisms cannot be expected to meet key goals. This is, at the moment, less salient for MENA region countries, given the current status of ICC cases in Sudan and Libya, as high-profile accused such as President Omar al-Bashir and Saif Al-Islam Gaddafi are not in custody.[55]

Process–output relations

Identifying lessons of institutional design is complicated by the fact that many institutions which have been subject to significant criticism, often for good reason, for their mandates, members, and modes of operation, nonetheless produce at least some outputs which might be considered positive. There is insufficient research about how often this is the case, and if so what it means. For example, the LLRC in Sri Lanka was singularly non-consultative, taking testimony largely from urban elites of the ethnic majority and not from victims.[56] Yet the recommendations are considered stronger than expected in the circumstances.[57] The Truth and Reconciliation Commission in Sierra Leone was riddled with scandals, and again produced a report that many consider a strong one for its analysis of the causes of the conflict and identification of necessary reforms. The Truth, Justice and Reconciliation Commission in Kenya was widely criticized for its mandate and for its chair, whom many former truth commission chairs in Africa called upon to resign, as he had been minister of the interior for part of the time analyzed by the commission and was accused of responsibility for at least one massacre. The commission produced a relatively strong report, albeit one compromised by late revisions in relation to historical land grabbing.[58] The International Criminal Tribunal for Rwanda and to a lesser degree the International Criminal Tribunal for the Former Yugoslavia experienced significant corruption scandals, but are recognized as having produced very important jurisprudence on a range of issues, particularly relating to sexual violence as a war crime, crime against humanity, and genocide.[59] Or, as Waltz suggests, the reverse may occur: a robust process with rather limited effect. She argues that in Morocco, despite extensive public hearings, the commission of inquiry could not challenge an embedded culture of impunity, and failed to make any recommendations regarding prosecutions. On the other hand, Fakhro notes the structural limitations of the Moroccan commission: it did not have a judicial mandate, nor was it allowed to reveal the names of perpetrators, and those who testified were also not allowed to reveal perpetrators' names.[60]

Transitional justice mechanisms are judged by both the operation of the processes and their results; more analysis is needed on the effects of institutional design and process on desired outcomes.

Economic rights and development[61]

Finally, the appropriate scope of transitional justice is highly contested. This is particularly salient in relation to the role that transitional justice can or should play in economic matters. Increasingly, there are calls for transitional justice to serve goals of distributive justice/economic equality, of development needs, and of a range of social justice and equality issues including gender and youth justice. Some of these may clearly relate to harms inflicted during a conflict or period of repression, whether sexual assault or displacement from home and property. However, some of them are about rectifying much wider social inequalities which pre-date the conflict, although they may have helped to stoke it. Where should we draw the line? There is a lively debate on this issue, with former ICTY prosecutor Louise Arbour and others advocating that transitional justice should include social and economic rights, not least on the grounds that violations of economic rights both enable abuses and can promote violent conflict. However, the director of Human Rights Watch, Kenneth Roth, argues that this is beyond their institutional focus because violations and protection of such rights can be so difficult to define.[62] How can we decide what the scope should be? And is it determined by principle or pragmatism, e.g. what a state or its international donors can afford or are willing to dedicate? Transitional justice has increasingly also been linked to responses to corruption, either because corruption cases appear easier to try in the first instance than human rights cases, or because of the intimate link between the crimes by overlapping sets of perpetrators. Corruption is not traditionally considered a transitional justice matter, but many trials of former leaders also accused of serious human rights violations have focused on corruption, such as that of Mubarak. Tunisia's 2014 transitional justice legislation included economic crimes and corruption, as well as electoral fraud and forced migration.[63] Should corruption be considered a crime to be tried in transition alongside gross violations of bodily integrity? Inclusion of such crimes might well address a wider range of victims' demands and societal concerns, but also strain limited resources for accountability.

Continuing research questions

The continuing gaps in knowledge identified here point to the need for further research, relevant not only to countries with long histories of transitional justice, but also potentially to countries in the MENA region, which have only pursued or considered pursuing transitional justice measures relatively recently. Further, the gaps and lessons from elsewhere may inform proposals for transitional justice in the region, as well as give reason for caution. We have ample examples of situations in which transitional justice has not "worked," and highly contested claims based on both qualitative and quantitative research regarding where transitional justice "works." Sadly, perhaps the only point on which analysts agree is also a somewhat familiar trope: there is no one-size-fits-all solution. While true, this is also a truism, that is to say, it repeats what we know rather than helps to direct us. Thus, as I suggest next, more targeted research is needed in several areas; however, in specific situations, we can also ask more targeted questions in planning transitional justice interventions.

In summary, this chapter has discussed four areas in which there is quite vibrant research, but in which there are not yet satisfactory answers, which matter not just for academics but in very practical ways for policy-makers and affected communities:

1. Impact: what are we looking for, how should we measure it, and are we asking the right things of transitional justice measures?
2. Demand and the "view from below": who is promoting transitional justice, what is it they want, and are we sufficiently attentive to what those more directly affected want (and if so do we know what that is)?
3. Design: Are we setting up transitional justice institutions correctly?
4. Content: should the remit of transitional justice be broader than its traditional scope, dealing with severe violations of civil and political rights, and harm to bodily integrity?

Implications and policy questions

While there are clearly no simple prescriptions for transitional justice, and every country in every region has a distinct history with distinct demands and opportunities, there are a number of implications that could help inform those considering developing such processes in the MENA region. They build upon the four research questions above, but involve contextually-based knowledge and reflection. From the above, it should be clear that there is still much to be learned about what transitional justice does and does not do. However, comparative analysis can identify challenges and issues that have arisen in diverse countries, and help to identify questions that scholars and practitioners should utilize in considering transitional justice activities in emergent situations. This can assist in developing processes that suit a particular country far more than simply importing models or toolkits from elsewhere.

This means, for example, considering what the demand for transitional justice is, before mechanisms are designed. This entails a number of questions, which affect what might be preferable options.

1. What are the goals being demanded, and who is demanding them: the international community, state leaders, opposition politicians, rebel leaders, victims, NGO leaders, community leaders? Why are they demanding them? These questions matter because who is making the demands will affect the legitimacy and durability of any decisions taken.

2. In countries with similar arrays of demands, what has been tried, and what have been their apparent successes and failures? Here, although each country has its own trajectory, lessons may yet be learned from those experiences. For example, despite expectations that trials of high-level officials would result in army rebellion, Argentina tried top junta members and remained intact, albeit while pardoning those convicted. However, in common with Chile and several other countries, it has renewed prosecution efforts a significant time after the transition. Their experiences in prosecutions and amnesties/pardons, similar to their and other experiences in commissions of inquiry, lustration, and reparations might be informative if carefully applied to current MENA situations.

3. What are the constraints, politically or in security terms, which may shape options for transitional justice, or the design of mechanisms, and can lessons be learned from countries with similar experiences? As discussed above regarding Argentina, the expectation that prosecutions may disrupt democratization can be overstated; at the same time commissions of inquiry which do not allow the naming of perpetrators or testimony of victims or affected communities may not achieve intended goals. Thus, it is important to look closely at experiences of countries with analogous experiences of political

violence, and places with similar demands from affected communities, in considering what types of mechanisms might be suitable.

4. In short, rather than simply transferring mechanisms or presumptively successful models, can we identify similar traits, even amongst otherwise quite different countries, which shape transitional justice demands and options, such that we can learn from successes and failures in very different countries?

Such approaches would require more complex and sustained cross-regional comparisons, including in countries which are undergoing rapid transitional political processes, but could enable more refined policy choices about justice.

3

LINKING TRANSITIONAL JUSTICE
AND HUMAN RIGHTS

Susan Waltz

Introduction

It is often assumed that a primary purpose of transitional justice processes is to improve human rights, such that the two are inextricably entwined. I begin this chapter, though, with the proposition that such assumptions must be discarded, or at least set aside, if we are to consider the *relationship* between processes of transitional justice and any eventual impact on a state's human rights performance. Viewed abstractly, transitional justice is a neutral policy instrument; it is a political device that can be used for several purposes, some at odds with the others. Some elements of civil society may hope for an improvement in human rights, but political leaders endorsing or promoting the idea of transitional justice may simply want to mark a political moment or consolidate a regime transition—or punish rivals and seal away an unpalatable past. Transitional justice need not be linked to the modern concept of human rights, and indeed, scholars have referred back as far as ancient Greece to understand the workings of judicial processes intended to mark a political transition.[1]

In the contemporary period, transitional justice mechanisms have proliferated and have taken many forms, including lustration, truth commissions, trials and reparations.

The multiple forms of transitional justice are one important factor responsible for differential effects on subsequent human rights practice, but not the only one. The motivation and capacity of those in power after a political transition also shape the outcome of transitional justice processes. Authorities can support a judicial process with sincere intention to reveal truths and prosecute wrongdoing, but alternatively they can simply go through the motions, hoping to placate domestic or international critics and move on. Even officials who are not committed to reform or enhancing human rights may find some merit in a process of transitional justice that distances them from their predecessors and weakens or eliminates political rivals. In sum, many different motivations may lead to endorsement of a transitional justice policy, and there are accordingly good reasons to be skeptical that the outcome will favor human rights. As Jack Donnelly has observed, "Respecting human rights is extremely inconvenient for a government, even in the best of circumstances. And the less pure the motives of those in power, the more irksome human rights appear."[2]

With that sobering reminder and with a focus on the Middle East region, this essay addresses four distinct but related concerns that require attention when considering the probability that a process of transitional justice will improve human rights outcomes. The first of these relates to the identification of rights that are likely to be affected by a transitional justice process. While human rights advocates and professionals might see this as a straightforward matter, given the development of human rights standards over the past fifty years, vast gaps between professional orientations and popular perceptions and emphases can lead to very different expectations about the impact of transitional justice processes. This is particularly important in the context of the Arab Spring uprisings, which in some countries were driven by concerns about economic injustice that do not perfectly align with a mainstream human rights framework. The first section of this chapter will therefore deal with the question of which rights, and whose rights, are likely to be affected by a transitional justice process. The following sections address three additional challenges that complicate efforts to gauge the impact of transitional justice on a state's human rights performance. These include the difficulties of dismantling a culture of impunity that encourages those in positions of authority to regard themselves as above the law; the challenge of institutional reform in the judicial and security sectors; and the troublesome question of how to observe and potentially measure the extent of any change in human rights performance.

To illustrate the nature of the challenges that may confound efforts to improve human rights and to observe meaningful changes, I will draw on recent experiences from Morocco and Tunisia, and to a lesser extent Egypt. Defined broadly, there have been a surprising number of transitional justice initiatives in the Middle East over the past fifteen years.[3] To date, however, Morocco is the only country in the region to have completed a robust transitional justice process, and it went through quite a number of phases spanning several years. From 2004–5 onward, its Equity and Reconciliation Commission (*Instance Equité et Réconciliation*, IER) investigated some 20,000 cases of human rights abuse. Morocco's experience unfolded in the context of a royal transition, as Mohammed VI sought to consolidate his hold on the monarchy, but popular sentiments at the time were not unlike those that surfaced throughout the region a few years later to fuel the Arab Spring uprisings. In Egypt, of course, uprisings convulsed the country for several months in 2011, and a decision to try President Mubarak for corruption and ordering excessive force against demonstrators was taken swiftly, though three years later Mubarak and several of his associates were acquitted of most charges.[4] In the meantime Mubarak's successor, Mohammed Morsi, was arrested and awaits trial, and former military leader General Abdel Fattah el-Sisi has been elected president. Tunisia, on the other hand, is proceeding with efforts to carry out a transitional justice process. In December 2013 the National Constituent Assembly approved a comprehensive transitional justice law and within the year a newly established Truth and Dignity Commission began its work. But Tunisia has also seen important changes in its political landscape, including the 2014 resignation of the Islamist government and the subsequent election of elder statesman Beji Caid Essebsi as the country's president. How far the Truth and Dignity Commission will go in pursuing its broad mandate remains uncertain.

The very range of experiences with transitional justice within the region— and indeed, across the world—signals the need for caution about predictions of either short-term or long-term outcomes in particular cases. The following sections of this chapter focus attention on four issues recurrent in discussions of transitional justice and human rights. Together they establish the fault lines of a human rights analysis and suggest benchmarks for evaluating the human rights impact of transitional justice initiatives.

Which rights, whose rights?

Over the past several decades human rights have frequently served as an effective frame for mobilizing political support. But the popularity of this frame does not ensure a universal understanding of the term "human rights" or shed light on how it might be related to other concepts, like social justice and human dignity. Because different discourse communities may have different concerns in mind, it is important to clarify which rights, and whose rights, might beneficially be addressed by a transitional justice process. This is arguably an important consideration in any political transition, but it is of particular relevance in the Middle East, where adherents of political Islam have shown some ambivalence toward universal representations of human rights.[5]

Within the international community as well as among international and regional human rights advocates, universal human rights principles are defined and established by the International Bill of Human Rights (IBHR). The IBHR is comprised of three fundamental instruments: the 1948 Universal Declaration of Human Rights (UDHR), the 1966 International Covenant on Social, Economic and Cultural Rights (ICESCR), and the 1966 International Covenant on Civil and Political Rights (ICCPR). These instruments were negotiated within the United Nations (UN) system over a period of twenty years (1946–66), and the two covenants have been ratified by more than 160 UN member states, including a dozen countries from the Arab Middle East. They are complemented by a series of additional UN treaties and standards, the corpus of international humanitarian law (pertaining to situations of conflict), and a number of multilateral regional human rights treaties.

The IBHR covers a wide range of subject matter, from due process rights and prohibitions on torture and slavery to gender equality, the right to work, education, health, housing, and social security. Given this range, it is not surprising that conversations about what constitutes an improvement in human rights performance soon stall. While at one level all rights embedded in global treaties can be seen as having equal status, processes of transitional justice have tended to focus on a set of core rights related to individual security and physical integrity. These include most notably the protection against extra-judicial executions and political assassinations, torture, enforced disappearances, rape, genocide and enslavement. Transgression of these fundamental rights is understood to constitute *grave* or *serious* violations of human rights, and when such transgression is widespread or systematic, these assaults are considered crimes against humanity.[6]

Unfortunately, it is not difficult to find examples of these practices in the Arab Middle East. Syria, most notably, has been accused by UN human rights officials of gross violations of human rights and crimes against humanity.[7] Similar charges can be levied against the Ba'athist regime of Saddam Hussein in Iraq, though like Saddam Hussein himself, many of those responsible at high levels have been imprisoned or executed. Algeria has not publicly accounted for some 7,000 individuals who were forcibly disappeared between 1992 and 1998 in the context of its civil war, and in Libya collective punishment and forced displacement by militia groups have been added to the record of political killings, disappearances, and torture during Gaddafi's tenure (1969–2011). Fallen regimes in Egypt and Tunisia had instituted torture, and after evaluating available evidence, Human Rights Watch has concluded that the systematic and widespread killing of at least 1,150 demonstrators by Egyptian security forces in July and August 2013 probably amounts to crimes against humanity.[8]

For good reason, truth commissions and post-conflict tribunals have focused on such grave violations of fundamental human rights. Not only are these abuses life-threatening, but the secrecy that enshrouds them begs for truth. A willingness and ability to confront such abuses is one test for the integrity of a transitional justice process, and it is to Morocco's credit that its Equity and Reconciliation Commission (*Instance Equité et Réconciliation*, IER) was empowered to hear—and broadcast on public television—testimonies about human rights violations from 1956 to 1999, known as the "years of lead." Through the work of the IER, Moroccan citizens were invited to confront a recent past that included clandestine torture centers and previously unacknowledged prisons, where several hundred people had been sequestered for more than a decade and from which some never emerged.

Grave violations of human rights require attention and redress, but physical integrity rights are not the only set of rights that merit scrutiny in the context of transitional justice. Table 1 elaborates a broad array of rights relevant to processes of transitional justice, offering commentary on the nature of these rights and the population most affected by their abuse. From this broader perspective it is noteworthy that grave violations of human rights are shocking primarily because of their severity and systematic nature, not necessarily because of the large numbers of citizens directly affected.[9] As the general population begins to focus on injustices that have touched their own lives, concern for a broad range of *dignity rights* may rise to prominence. In addition to the serious abuse of physical integrity rights, most states in the region have a poor record with regard to elemental rights pertaining to social and economic welfare and the right to participate in the polity, including the exercise of voice and assembly. In some cases, corruption in the public sector may impinge on the ability of citizens to earn a living or access public goods (such as education or healthcare), while police harassment, fines and jail terms may be used to quash organizations and criticism. For many women in the region, routine and ubiquitous discrimination on grounds of gender is experienced as an assault on human dignity. The abuse of dignity rights affects large numbers of people, and for that reason human rights reform must touch on these rights, if it is to be recognized by the population at large. Tunisia's 2013 transitional justice law is exemplary in this regard, covering both fundamental and dignity rights. It specifically directs attention to grave violations of internationally recognized rights (including rape and torture), and it also authorizes a special judicial chamber to hear cases that relate to electoral fraud, economic crimes, corruption, and forced migration.[10]

In addition to addressing the grave abuse of fundamental rights and more widespread abuses of dignity rights, transitional justice processes must attend to another set of concerns, related to reparations and civil status and identified in Table 1 as *restorative rights*. These rights include the need to compensate survivors who have been abused, and ensure their civil and political rights are restored. As indirect victims of human rights abuses, family members of those who have died or disappeared may also have a personal need to know what happened to their loved ones, a need that may include clarification of their own civil status, as a widow or surviving heir for example. This aspect of transitional justice practice has developed rapidly since the late 1990s, when first Theo Van Boven and then Cherif Bassiouni—both well-known legal experts with extensive knowledge of human rights law and practice—were asked by the UN Commission on Human Rights to help compile guidelines on the right to restitution and rehabilitation following gross human rights violations.[11] In recent years their foundational work has been further elaborated and disseminated by the International Center for Transitional Justice (ICTJ), which on its own and in collaboration with the UN has developed materials to assist governments with reparations programs.[12] Morocco's IER is one of several truth commissions that have worked with ICTJ to devise appropriate reparations programs, including a small number of community-based projects.[13] Tunisia's new law on transitional justice, likewise, anticipates reparation payments.

In recent years, the understanding of specific human rights concerns that should be addressed through transitional justice mechanisms has evolved considerably. In the early 1990s advocates tended to place exclusive emphasis on redress for the abuse of fundamental, physical integrity rights and concordant due process rights. Today they are more likely to urge that attention be spread across all four classes of human rights identified in Table 1. If the ultimate goal of a transitional justice process is to combat a culture of impunity, as discussed in the next section, grave assaults on fundamental rights must be a focal point of proceedings. And if justice is to be served, the rights of the accused must likewise be respected. These are essential elements of a transitional justice process. But a more comprehensive approach to human rights, to the extent it is carried out, has potential to address the grinding indignities experienced by the largest number of people and provide the general population with a stake in the process. A comprehensive approach also promises to provide relief for individuals who live in civil ambiguity because a loved one's fate is unknown. In considering the potential impact of transitional justice processes on human rights, it is important to keep all these categories of rights in mind, and all the constituencies affected by their abuse, because each set of concerns points to very specific, and different, potential remedies.

Ending impunity

For international human rights advocates, the most central concern in the domain of transitional justice is establishing that perpetrators of grave human rights violations are held accountable for their actions, including those taken at the policy level. *Impunity* is the term for the practice of allowing heinous crimes to go unremarked and perpetrators unpunished. The UN formally defines impunity as "the impossibility, de jure or de facto, of bringing the perpetrators of violations to account—whether in criminal, civil, administrative or disciplinary proceedings—since they are not subject to any inquiry that might lead to their being accused, arrested, tried and, if found guilty, sentenced to appropriate penalties, and to making reparations to their victims."[14] In the case of political assassinations, impunity literally means getting away with murder.

At the heart of the impunity issue is the moral code and compass of a given society, and the degree to which these align with international human rights standards. As a matter of principle, prominent international human rights organizations have opposed measures of immunity or forgiveness in response to human rights abuses, arguing that such policies minimize the wrongdoing and effectively promote a culture of impunity.[15] Without denigrating efforts

Table 1: Differentiating human rights claims

	Nature of human rights abuse	Population affected	Potential remedy
Fundamental human rights, including the right to personal security and physical integrity	Political killings (including genocide); torture; enforced disappearances; political killings; enslavement; political imprisonment for speech and association	In most cases, relatively small numbers, including active political opponents. In cases of genocide or civil conflict the numbers may be large	Release (of those wrongfully imprisoned); public acknowledgement of wrongdoing; punishment of wrongdoers (and reparations; see restorative rights)
Due process rights	Includes right of the accused to legal representation and to a fair trial	Alleged perpetrators and collaborators	Provisions for legal counsel and judicial independence
Dignity rights, including rights that pertain to social welfare and ability to participate in the polity	Includes government's failure to provide access to services supporting social and economic rights, but may also include economic blacklisting, denial of due process, and prohibitions placed on civil society organizations and political participation. May be facilitated or exacerbated by corruption	Involves the largest number of people.	Welfare policies and community development projects. Policies to curtail corruption and possible punishment of public officials, including lustration
Restorative rights, including the right to rehabilitation, civil status and the right to know	Includes public denial of human rights abuse and deliberate withholding or concealment of information that would clarify status of surviving family members. Family members of human rights victims may be forced to live in penury, with limited access to social services due to ambiguous civil status	Family members and associates of those affected by abuse of fundamental rights (often a relatively small number of people), as well as the survivors themselves	Acknowledgement of wrongs and wrongdoing; restoration of civil rights through clarification of civil status

to restore peace and heal social and political rifts, they have argued the need for judicial accountability. In their view, the decision to disregard heinous abuses from the past is fundamentally incompatible with a commitment to protect human rights. These arguments are not propelled by a desire for retribution, but are rather made with the intention of condemning grave abuses unequivocally and preventing their recurrence.

From a human rights perspective, then, the main test of a transitional justice mechanism is its likely impact on a culture of impunity. This concern is so central that in the 1990s many human rights advocates were wary of truth commissions, fearing that they would serve as a substitute for prosecution, and thus indirectly promote impunity. As South Africa was setting up its Truth and Reconciliation Commission, for example, Amnesty International criticized the law's amnesty provisions, concerned that by exempting certain human rights abusers from prosecution, they might help perpetuate rather than eradicate human rights violations.[16] With the accumulation of experience, however, positions have matured and the current consensus is that transitional justice often involves multiple phases, with truth commissions and prosecutions representing complementary aspects of the process.[17]

There remains a concern, nevertheless, that truth commissions or panels of inquiry will be used by those in power not so much to establish the truth as part of a comprehensive transitional justice process, but as a means of covering up the unsavory past and avoiding further political obligations to establish accountability.[18] The case of El Salvador is sometimes raised in this regard, where vigilante groups with the self-proclaimed purpose of eradicating criminal elements through "social cleansing" emerged soon after the Salvadoran parliament approved a sweeping amnesty law in 1993. One of these, the *Sombra Negra* ("Black Shadow"), adopted practices of torture and assassination reminiscent of El Salvador's notorious civil war death squads. *Sombra Negra* operated with unofficial approval from the new, civilian-controlled and supposedly apolitical National Civilian Police, and it was thought to include several former members of the Salvadoran military who had been subject to lustration policies.[19] While *Sombra Negra* has faded from the news in recent years, the culture of impunity continues in El Salvador, with environmental activists and others finding little protection from vigilante groups.[20]

In 2004, an independent study commissioned by the UN Human Rights Commission (UNHRC) focused on three aspects of transitional justice processes crucial to combating impunity: the establishment of truth, including the *right* to truth; the administration of justice, including prosecution of gross human rights violations; and the right to reparations. Law professor Diane Orentlicher was asked to identify best practices to assist states in strengthening their own domestic capacity to combat impunity.[21] In preparing the report, Orentlicher reviewed international case law and comments from several UN member states. Her conclusions and recommendations emphasize the importance of a comprehensive strategy, cautioning that efforts to redress past injustices may fall short without effective policies to combat impunity.[22] The most far-reaching of the study's recommendations (and arguably the most controversial) are its wholesale rejection of amnesty provisions that shield authorities from prosecution and its assertion that governments hold an obligation to open their records for scrutiny.

While a comprehensive strategy is no doubt ideal, it may be politically unfeasible, or deemed too risky to venture; particularly when transitions are fragile and supporters of the ousted regime retain influence.[23] Jose Zalaquett wrote the introduction to the 1993 report of the Chilean Truth Commission, in which he sympathetically described the numerous political and legal constraints faced by Chile's Aylwin government, and the calculus involved in devising a sustainable transitional justice policy.[24] In the late 1990s, Elin Skaar conducted a study investigating the preferences of new and democratic governments about transitional justice policy, focusing in particular on the choice between truth commissions and prosecution. With some notable but readily explained exceptions, she found that the likelihood of a new government deciding to prosecute perpetrators from the previous regime diminished significantly when members of the *ancien régime* maintained political influence. Truth commissions, a less robust policy choice, were a more likely outcome when the strength of demands from the public for justice were counterbalanced by demands from the remnants of the outgoing regime for amnesty.[25] Skaar noted that government policy with regard to transitional justice is not static, however, and indeed many governments in Latin America have begun to abrogate previous promises of amnesty in what Sikkink has called the "justice cascade."[26]

In many ways the Moroccan experience illustrates the evolutionary nature of transitional justice programs, even though prosecutions have not been pursued in Morocco (nor indeed have perpetrators been publicly named).[27] In response to criticism at home and abroad, in the early 1990s King Hassan II initiated some political reforms and began closing down the country's clandestine detention facilities. He vowed to "turn the page" on human rights complaints, and though he did not follow up with any policies to address past abuses, he did approve the creation of a reparations panel just weeks before his death in 1998.[28] Upon accession to the throne, Hassan II's son Mohammed VI lost little time in setting up a mechanism to review indemnity claims, but the hasty initiative quickly backfired. The indemnity panel rapidly addressed some 6,000 claims, but it provoked an immediate backlash for excluding many categories of victims and for requiring silence from those who did receive pay-offs. Public protest ultimately led to consultation and collaboration with the International Center for Transitional Justice (ICTJ), and the creation of the IER in January 2004. After two years of public hearings, the IER issued its final report in late 2005, and responsibility for implementing recommendations was transferred to the Advisory Council on Human Rights (CCDH). In 2007 the CCDH reported that some $193 million had been committed as compensation to 23,676 individual victims of human rights abuse.[29] The ICTJ later reported that as of 2011, communal reparations programs were still in their initial phase and the IER's legal and institutional reform recommendations remained in embryonic form.[30]

Unfortunately the Moroccan case also illustrates the challenges of addressing a culture of impunity. Although it held hearings across the country and took decisions on nearly 17,000 cases, the IER did not make any recommendations about prosecutions, and it was widely believed that some high-level security officials who had been responsible for abuses in previous decades continued to serve. The IER sought to guarantee that such serious human rights violations would not be repeated, and called for a national strategy to fight impunity. In the meantime, however, old practices continued in the distant territory of Western Sahara, and in Morocco's interior hinterlands there was also a resurgence. After bombings shook the city of Casablanca in 2003, police rounded up between 2,000 and 5,000 individuals.[31] Even as the IER was holding its hearings, many were being taken to a secret detention center at Temara, where at least some were tortured and made to sign confessions.[32] In 2003 Amnesty International and Human Rights Watch noted that reports of torture were up sharply after several years of significant decrease.[33]

The challenge of institutional reform in the judicial and security sectors

If from a human rights perspective the main concern during a time of political transition is to dismantle and discourage a culture of impunity, one of the more demanding tasks is to nudge forward the reform of structures that gave rise to abuse in the first place. It is sobering but important to recognize that some patterns and practices of abuse may be sufficiently common as to be ingrained, and expected if not accepted. Where patterns of patrimonial and neo-patrimonial culture afford authorities a sense of personal power and entitlement, inculcating respect for rule of law and fundamental human rights is a formidable task.[34] Structural reform is particularly difficult because the structures themselves tend to be inscrutable and involve vested interests. Even where a government is ready to risk adverse publicity and prosecute egregious offenders, it may not be willing to undertake full structural reform.

Structurally speaking, the two governmental domains with the greatest implications for human rights performance are the security sector and the judicial system. In both cases, the issue is Janus-faced, in that while these two sectors are crucial for addressing the problem of serious human rights abuse, they are also typically an important component of the problem. Throughout the Middle East, as elsewhere, the security sector is an important bulwark of the authoritarian regime. The judiciary has been its accomplice, upholding the powers of the regime and denying appeals from its victims. Together they have helped transform abstract political power into the reality of repression. Other components of a system of government—parliament, the bureaucracy, interest groups—may also shore up an authoritarian or corporatist state, but the apparatus of repression depends most heavily on collaboration from security forces and the judicial sectors. Understanding just how these two key sectors contribute to the practice of political repression is an essential element in the analysis of an effective transitional justice process.

In authoritarian states the security sector dominates politics, and in some Middle Eastern countries it is a power unto itself. The Algerian historian Mohamed Harbi often quipped that while most states have an army, in Algeria, the army has a state. In addition to controlling the mechanisms of coercion, in several Middle Eastern countries—including Egypt as well as Algeria—the military possesses or controls factories and agricultural estates. With access to means of production and income, as well as control over instruments of coercion, security forces are afforded an impressive measure of independence. Analysts must exercise caution, however, for this sector is not necessarily monolithic, and there are important variations across the region. In some countries the military dominates; in others it is the national police and intelligence forces under auspices of an Interior Ministry or under direct control of an autocrat, whether president or monarch. The Syrian and Egyptian militaries, for example, have directly intervened in national politics, whereas in Saddam Hussein's Iraq, the Ba'athist paramilitary unit responsible for repression of regime opponents operated outside the military chain of command and reported directly to the president.

The Tunisian case illustrates some of the structural complexities and political nuances. Unlike many countries in the region, Tunisia's political culture does not privilege the military, and since independence the military has been under civilian control. Until recently, in fact, active duty military personnel were not permitted to vote. The military did ultimately enter the fray of the Jasmine Revolution in 2011, but it quickly returned to its barracks. General Rachid Ammar's decision not to fire on demonstrators is widely seen as a pivotal moment in the uprising, ultimately forcing President Ben Ali to flee. This restraint won the military respect and praise, but it did not become an impetus for military involvement in politics. Rather, so great was trust in the army's neutrality that its forces were charged with guaranteeing security in Tunisia's first openly contested election, delivering materials for polling stations and transporting ballots for counting. The high esteem accorded to the Tunisian *military* does not however extend across the entire security sector. From the late 1960s until recently, Tunisia's National Security Force (*Sûreté National*, SN) was largely responsible for the arrest and detention of political opponents, and many have claimed they were tortured while detained in the SN cells of the Interior Ministry, in central Tunis.[35] The SN included two special forces, the Public Order Brigade and the plain clothes Office of Territorial Security, which together with the National Guard fell under the aegis of the Interior Ministry. Ben Ali, who had begun his career in the army but developed a specialty in military intelligence, intermittently served as director of the SN from 1977 to 1986. During that time his powers expanded considerably, and he briefly served as Interior Minister before ousting President Habib Bourguiba in the bloodless coup of 1987. As president from 1987 to 2011, he was thus in a unique position to oversee and assess activities carried out under the aegis of the Interior Ministry.

The structure of the judiciary can also be complicated. In readily imaginable ways, the judiciary can serve as an accomplice to repressive, authoritarian governments. To begin with, laws themselves may restrict liberties or may fail to provide protection for individuals; and beyond that, judges may interpret laws in ways that do not favor political opponents qua defendants. Even where lawyers are able to build cases for their clients and judges have a measure of independence, corruption and patronage may minimize the independence of the judiciary. The integrity of the entire judiciary is called into question when a judge can credibly sentence hundreds of people to death in abbreviated judicial proceedings, as recently occurred in Egypt.[36]

In addition to concerns about the law and its application, jurisdictional questions may figure as important structural elements. For adjudicating cases that are deemed to touch on state security, authoritarian governments frequently depend on special courts that follow their own rules, and often lie beyond the control of a Justice Ministry. Recently, for example, Egypt's President Sisi has decreed that all public infrastructure should be considered under the jurisdiction of military courts, paving the way for defendants accused of committing a crime on public property to be tried in military courts.[37] An analysis of the justice sector must include not only civilian courts controlled by a Justice Ministry, but also any military or special security courts that may hold formal jurisdiction over accused perpetrators (or be in position to review accusations of abuse of authority). The fact that many such perpetrators lie beyond the reach of civilian courts helps foster a culture of impunity. Part of the challenge of assessing torture in Morocco, for example, is that after centralized torture stations like Casablanca's notorious Derb Moulay Cherif[38] were closed down in the mid-1990s, reports of torture at *local* police stations increased.[39] And when fresh allegations about torture spread after 2002, attention turned to Temara, the seat of a domestic intelligence agency attached to the Interior Ministry and known as the DGST. In theory, the DGST does not have authority to arrest or detain, as Moroccan law assigns exclusive responsibility for arrests and pre-trial detention to the judicial police under supervision of the Justice Ministry. In practice, however, human rights organizations have found numerous cases where arrests were made by plain clothes police (rather than uniformed judicial police) and the accused were incarcerated in a clandestine detention center for several weeks before a court hearing and transfer to a prison facility. Presumably these acts have been carried out by the DSGT. Because the DGST is not part of the judicial police, however, its actions go unsupervised by the Justice Ministry.[40]

Bringing structural change to each of these sectors alone is a daunting task, but comprehensive change that covers the complete security spectrum and its interface with the judiciary is an even greater challenge. For reform of the security sector, a central challenge is that even where a full political transition takes place, many or most of the military security personnel will necessarily remain in place. Even where purges or lustration policies are applied at the level of national leadership, abusive practices may continue at lower and/or local levels. In situations where there is no real political transition, the problems and challenges are only compounded. For an individual at risk of torture or clandestine imprisonment amounting to disappearance, the best legal protection is likely to be some form of habeas corpus, in situations where courts have sufficient power to subpoena the state. In some cases, legal reform limiting the amount of time or excluding the use of evidence collected under torture could afford some protection. Bringing security forces under control of a civilian oversight board is considered a crucial step in reform. But where civilians are not accustomed to such authority, and security forces are not accustomed to ceding it to civilians, the learning curve is very steep.

Observing changes in human rights performance

The final issue concerns how one gauges the effectiveness of a transitional justice process and its specific impact on human rights. In whatever form they take, processes of transitional justice are a matter of public policy, policy that many hope will improve future human rights performance. Like all public policies they are subject to scrutiny of the questions "How well do they work?" and "How do we know?" Neither of these questions is simple, but they point to different complexities. The collective wisdom is that transitional justice processes are most likely to produce salutary effects on human rights practice where commitment is genuine, public support strong, and countervailing forces unable to undermine the process—and where truth can be known, justice served, reparations made, and structural reforms enacted. Even where these conditions are indicated, though, the process is likely to be lengthy and results unlikely to be fully appreciated until significant time has passed.

Supporters of transitional justice advocate policies with greatest potential for successful outcomes, however those are seen, but consideration must also be given to the relative costs of different options, and the balance of potential gains against potential costs. One of the more sobering realizations after a decade of experience was that the cost of international tribunals could be exorbitant in terms of both time and money—and still yield few verdicts. In general, trials are more expensive than truth commissions, and this reality may guide some choices. Reparations may also be subject to such logic, particularly where national budgets are under strain.[41] At the other end of the spectrum, a blanket amnesty nominally acknowledges past abuses but requires no additional action. It may be particularly attractive to authorities as a policy option, though, particularly if domestic pressure for transitional justice is weak or absent. Elster has noted the trade-offs that countries must face when resources are scarce and the costs of a transitional justice process are to be borne domestically. Politicians no doubt find it more appealing to engage in "forward looking tasks" like constitutional reform or economic investment, rather than the "backward tasks" of trials and purges.[42]

The second question concerns evidence and methodology. Questions about measurement and the longer-term effects of transitional justice processes have only recently been explored by social scientists and results are inconclusive.[43] As noted in the introduction to this essay, there is no reason to expect that any particular transitional justice process will automatically and *sui generis* improve human rights performance, and the issue only becomes more complicated when allowance is made for placing emphasis on different sets of rights. How then can we know if a transitional justice process has had any impact on human rights? Answers to such questions require a means of assessing human rights performance and changes over time.

To meet that challenge, scholars in recent years have developed quantitative measures intended to assess human rights performance. The best known of these are the Cingrinelli-Richards Human Rights Data Project (CIRI Index)[44] and the Political Terrorism Scale (PTS),[45] both of which are derived from interpretations of reports produced by the US State Department and Amnesty International, guided by formal coding manuals. Since two recent studies have used these indices to estimate the impact of transitional justice mechanisms on human rights performance,[46] some scrutiny of them is warranted. As the review of the data concerning Morocco below demonstrates, there are good reasons to be skeptical of claims that the indices are reliable for use in longitudinal studies, that is to assess *changes* in human rights performance over time. This is a serious reservation and itself warrants explanation.

To assess the coding reliability of both measures, for this chapter I set out to replicate the CIRI codings for Morocco, reviewing thirty years of AI and US State Department reports and individually scoring annual entries according to instructions in the detailed CIRI coding manual. Why Morocco? Morocco is a good test case because its human rights situation has been exceptionally well documented by AI and the State Department over the thirty-year period covered by the CIRI index, and the patterns of human rights abuse alleged by AI but denied by the Moroccan government were ultimately corroborated by Morocco's truth commission.[47] It is also worth noting that the data cover most of the period known as the "years of lead," and a period of political reform that began with the accession of Mohammed VI to the throne in 1998.

Both the CIRI index and the PTS use rigorous methodology, and in both cases authors have made their datasets publicly available, in addition to publishing scholarly articles explaining their construction.[48] The CIRI measure is "an internationally-comparable baseline for broad comparative work" comprising four separate scales, assessing the prevalence of torture, enforced disappearances, political killings, and political imprisonment. The composite measure is known as the Physical Integrity Index (PHYSINT) and it is often taken as a measure of serious human rights violations. (Each of the four scales is scored 0–2, and the range on the composite physical integrity index is thus 0–8, with 8 being the "best" human rights score and 0 reflecting the worst human rights performance.) The PTS is a somewhat simpler measure spanning a 5-point range, with a score of 1 representing countries under a secure rule of law and 5 indicating countries where terror has spread to the entire population. It comes in two versions: PTS-s, derived from readings of State Department reports; and PTS-a, derived from AI's annual country commentary. (Each measure has advantages and disadvantages, which have been discussed in the scholarly literature but are not often discussed outside specialist circles).[49]

To replicate scores for Morocco, I began with the CIRI index, as the CIRI coding manual is quite detailed and offers explicit instructions for resolving problems that typically arise. Because it is explicitly intended as a measure of human rights performance, the CIRI index has also been a central metric in quantitative studies observing the impact of truth commissions. The results of my efforts against CIRI's own coding can be seen in graphic form in Figure 1.

For some years, the discrepancies are quite striking. In only five years were my codes identical to CIRI codes, and in eleven of the thirty years my codes deviated from CIRI's by two or more points. Consequently, the trend lines are dramatically divergent. One shows a trend toward general improvement, and the other graphs a continuing pattern of ups and downs over thirty years, implying no substantive change. *Both trend lines are based on the same data and follow the same coding rules.* As shown in Figure 2, the independently derived CIRI scores track the PTS scores[50] somewhat more closely than the actual CIRI scores, but the PTS scores vary so little over the thirty-year period that any change in human rights performance is difficult to detect.

Several factors explain the differences, some of which commonly arise in coding schemes and some of which are more unique to the CIRI dataset—but both of which have implications for interpreting change in human rights records and the impact of transitional justice processes. To begin with the more unique problems, it is frequently the case in human rights research that pertinent information does not become available until after the human rights violations take place, sometimes many years after the fact. The CIRI manual

Figure 1: Alternative scoring on CIRI Physical Integrity (Human Rights) Index, Morocco 1981–2011

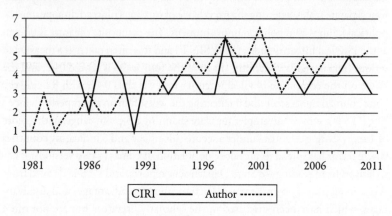

deals with this issue appropriately, by instructing coders to record scores that reflect *only* the information pertinent to the particular year being coded (to avoid double counting), and notes that previous years' scores will be revised to accommodate information as it becomes available.[51] The PTS scores do not appear to benefit from such corrections, which introduces a source of error in that measure. For this system to work in the fullest sense, however, there needs to be a more or less continuous review of human rights reports (from Amnesty, the State Department, or whatever source) in order to maintain the veridicality of the ratings.

Figure 2: Morocco: Alternative scoring of Human Rights Performance, 1981–2011

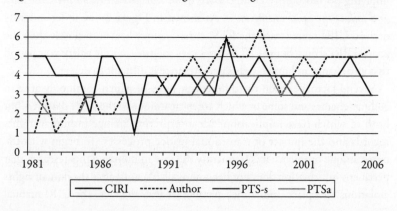

To provide a straightforward but detailed illustration of the problem in the case of Morocco, consider the representation of "Tazmamert deaths" in the scores on political killings from 1981 to 1990, listed in Table 1. In this category CIRI includes "political and other extrajudicial killings and arbitrary or unlawful deprivation of life," and coders are instructed to include deaths resulting from torture (as prisoners were in custody of the government or its agents at time of death). We now know that during the night of 7 August 1973, 58 military prisoners were transferred from Kenitra Central Prison to the secret detention center of Tazmamert, in the foothills of the Atlas Mountains. Over the next eighteen years, prisoners were confined to tiny cells in near-total darkness, in which more than thirty of them perished from disease, malnourishment, and exposure—most of them long after the expiration of their sentences.[52] For nearly two decades, Moroccan dissidents and international human rights groups pressed for information about this shadowy prison, but Moroccan officials steadfastly denied even the existence of Tazmamert. But by 1992 international pressure mounted to the point that the government was forced to acknowledge the king's "secret garden," and it released the surviving prisoners, soon after razing the clandestine facility (which had been hidden inside a military complex). Tazmamert was effectively a modern-day dungeon. Because its secrets were not revealed until many years had elapsed, the CIRI scores capture its horrors as a discreet event (deaths) that transpired in one or two arbitrarily identified years rather than as excruciating abuse drawn out over nearly two decades. In regression analyses, such distortions in the input data risk producing misleading results.

Table 2: Comparison of scores on CIRI Political Killings Scale, 1981–1990

Year	CIRI original score*	Replication score*	Comments
1981	2	0	Reflects discovery in 2005 of a mass grave from 1981 Casablanca demonstrations; 3 known deaths at Tazmamert.
1982	2	1	1 known death at Tazmamert, revealed in 1992; also 7 possible deaths from attacks on students (AI unable to confirm).
1983	2	1	2 known deaths at Tazmamert, revealed in 1992. (Also, General Dlimi died in mysterious circumstances; later revealed that he was plotting a *coup d'état*).

1984	2	1	2 known deaths at Tazmamert, revealed in 1992; in 2008 remains found at Nador were also linked to 1984 police abuse.
1985	2	1	In 1991 report, AI indicates that it has raised a 1985 case of death in detention due to torture with officials (Tahini).
1986	1	1	1 known death at Tazmamert, revealed in 1992. For this particular year, the original CIRI score is not easily explained, as neither the State Department nor AI reports mention any political killings in 1986. Coincidentally, however, this was the first year that Amnesty International mentioned that some twenty deaths were known to have taken place at Tazmamert since 1974.
1987	2	1	AI and State Department both note a possible death from torture in Tetouan, but government denies. In 1991 report, AI indicates that it has raised this case with Moroccan officials.
1988	2	1	1989 State Department report also indicates there were 12 cases of death in custody due to torture in the previous year (1988). Coincidentally, 1988 saw the creation of a new domestic human rights organization, the Moroccan Organization of Human Rights (OMDH). One of OMDH's first projects was to list suspect deaths in detention.
1989	2	1	2 known deaths at Tazmamert, revealed in 1992. Several more deaths in custody due to torture, reported by both State Department and AI.
1990	0	1	1 death at Tazmamert (a suicide), and 3–5 deaths in detention reported by State Department and AI. The original CIRI score is probably explained by AI's report that 29 individuals were known to have died at Tazmamert—but as noted above, these deaths had occurred in earlier years.

* 2 is the highest and "best" score; 0 is the lowest and "worst" score, reserved for 50 or more deaths per year from extrajudicial executions or unlawful deprivation of life, including deaths from abuse in custody.

Integration of post hoc information about the deaths at Tazmamert is not the only problem with CIRI scores on the physical integrity index, for the thirty years covered by the dataset. Given that the Moroccan Truth Commission addressed nearly 17,000 cases, it is very likely that scrutiny of these records would lead to more changes in the scores on individual deaths and torture.[53] But in addition to the challenge of integrating information that becomes available subsequently, CIRI codes are affected by the way in which human rights violations involving enforced disappearances, political imprisonment, and the excessive use of force against demonstrators are understood and reported. Notable year-to-year coding discrepancies may result from different coders interpreting similar information in different ways or from the judgment calls they make about ambiguous data.[54] Furthermore, the evolving concerns, practices, definitions, and information sources reflected in the coding sources (i.e. State Department reports and AI's annual report) inevitably vary over time and thus affect the year-to-year consistency of the CIRI coding.

The devil, of course, resides in such details, and in the end an independent replication of coding for the CIRI Physical Integrity Index presents a very different picture of Morocco's human rights record than does the original CIRI coding. That finding is significant on its own, but takes on additional weight in light of similar findings by other scholars (primarily with regard to Argentina, El Salvador, Guatemala, Peru, and other Latin American countries).[55] To be clear, the main problem is not the quality of the coding or the failure to conceptualize human rights problems adequately. Rather, the main problem is that human rights sensibilities change over time and the reports from which data are "mined" are not intended for the task and in many ways are not suitable to it. Clark and Sikkink refer to this as an "information effect," noting that choice of data, artifacts, methods of data collection, and the information environment within which human rights violations take place all potentially affect the ability to understand how levels of violations have evolved over time.[56] The US State Department reports depend heavily on information that comes to US attention (including reports by Amnesty, Human Rights Watch, and local non-governmental organizations) and Amnesty's own research is guided by a sense of urgency, available resources, and priorities for advocacy work. Neither source purports to provide the basis for quantitative assessment (and for many years Amnesty International has specifically cautioned against using its annual reports for comparative assessments of country performance).[57] Clark and Sikkink urge researchers to be on the lookout for an information effect, because "greater awareness coupled with more information can make a phenomenon seem more frequent when its empirical frequency has not actually risen."[58] In particular, they note a tendency to under-report human rights improvements, which is particularly pronounced with the CIRI index.[59]

This phenomenon may, in fact, explain the contradictions found by Wiebelhaus-Brahm in a comparative study of the effects of truth commissions. In four carefully and systematically analyzed case studies, Wiebelhaus-Brahm established that truth commissions had some discernable positive impact on human rights, but his nomothetic approach using both CIRI and PTS as dependent variables in a much larger sample actually yielded a negative correlation between truth commissions and human rights performance. He attempted to reconcile the contradictions by focusing on the nature of the inquiries and his choice of cases, but it might have been wiser to question the CIRI and PTS measures themselves.[60] As Hayner has observed, it is difficult to ensure that nuanced contextual issues are fully reflected in measures used to evaluate the impact of truth commissions, and for better or worse the study of transitional justice mechanisms will need to continue to focus on qualitative, case-specific comparisons in order to understand their dynamics, possibilities, and limitations.[61] The process-tracing methodology outlined by Sriram in Chapter 2 of this volume is one promising approach. It may prove particularly useful in the contemporary Middle East, where political transitions are absent or incomplete and thus many assumptions about the nature of transitional justice mechanisms do not apply.

Conclusion

The four considerations highlighted in this chapter emphasize the challenges involved in efforts to assess or anticipate the effects of a transitional justice process on human rights performance. As several recent surveys of the literature have noted, the proliferation of truth commissions and other instruments of transitional justice over the past two decades have provided welcome research opportunities to compare and evaluate the effects of confronting past abuses. A host of factors, however, impede firm conclusions.[62] Different sets of rights, different levels of concern about a culture of impunity, varying levels of attention to structural reform, and different approaches to benchmarking all contribute to variations in the design of comparative studies—and consequently, to variations in their conclusions. Moreover, policy decisions about transitional justice mechanisms themselves are highly contingent on circumstances. Differences in political context and developments, the choice of transitional justice mechanisms (or whether to pursue the past at all), and challenges of tracing the unique effects of transitional justice in a highly dynamic political environment combine to make strict comparisons unrealistic.

These constraints notwithstanding, some limited observations about the effects of transitional justice processes on human rights performance are possible. Most importantly, case studies on truth commissions and other mechanisms suggest that transitional justice can have a salutary impact on human rights, even if it does not affect democratization processes or other political developments. The overall chances of positive effect are increased where political conditions are most hospitable, and the adopted transitional justice mechanisms are most comprehensive.

In the contemporary Middle East, Tunisia comes closest to meeting these tests and offers the most likely prospect of a productive transitional justice process, contributing to future protection of human rights. The Arab Spring uprisings began in Tunisia in 2011, and though protests spread throughout the region, Tunisia alone has experienced a democratic transition. Tunisia's political transition has generally been inclusive, and the transitional justice process mapped out in recent legislation is robust, focusing primarily on gathering truth but also leaving openings for prosecution. With respect to the concerns outlined in this chapter, the legislative framework of Tunisia's transitional justice process addresses dignity rights as well as personal integrity rights; it anticipates reparations and paves the way for prosecutions, curbing impunity. Despite the setbacks and political upsets discussed by Lamont in Chapter 5 of this volume, some structural reforms are already in place, and others are anticipated to emerge from the transitional justice process. The attention to a range of details and best practices not only enhances the probability of a successful process, but it permits scholars to observe and track the process as it unfolds, in preparation for an eventual assessment.

There is thus room for some optimism with respect to Tunisia's transitional justice process and its potential impact on future human rights performance; but there are also good reasons for caution. Some twenty-five years ago, Tunisia's new president Zine El Abidine Ben Ali created a Ministry of Human Rights and appointed members of the Tunisian League of Human Rights to his ministerial cabinet, marking a transition from the autocratic rule of the deposed Habib Bourguiba. At that time Tunisian human rights advocates were optimistic about the prospects for improvement in human rights. It was not long, though, before their hopes were dashed. In the early 1990s, at a time when liberalizing reforms seemed within grasp, the rise of an armed Islamist movement in neighboring Algeria dampened popular enthusiasm for expanding human rights protection in Tunisia and provided the Ben Ali government with a pretext for reversing course. In today's context, resurgent security concerns in the region could well shift political energy away from the processes of transitional justice.

If the Tunisian process falters, the Moroccan experience will then stand as the region's best effort to address past abuses and promote human rights through a transitional justice mechanism. Although Morocco's transitional justice process made no effort to address a broad range of socio-economic rights, it did permit a public inventory of the most serious human rights abuses of preceding decades, and provided reparation payments in recognition of the many grave injuries that had been suffered. At the same time, however, by stopping short of prosecutions and even public shaming, it failed to upend a culture of impunity. Not surprisingly, when national security issues gained prominence after 2003, the old patterns resurfaced, despite legal reforms intended to prevent human rights violations. Morocco's experience with transitional justice does demonstrate the potential for a genuine if limited process of transitional justice in the Middle East region; all the same, the manifest limitations of that process have left many Moroccans with the impression that it was primarily for the benefit of international observers, and its long-term effects are uncertain.

This chapter must therefore end on a cautionary note. Even in the most propitious circumstances, wresting durable improvements to human rights is a formidable task and a significant achievement. By its nature, human rights change requires a commitment to broadly democratic values and a willingness to reconsider and reform existing power structures—from those in power. Political transitions offer opportunities, but they also carry risks. There can thus be no guarantee that transitional justice efforts in the Middle East will succeed in improving human rights, or even that new cohorts of political leaders will devote their own energies to that end. What can be certain is that without effort, improvement will remain elusive.

4

FOR THE SAKE OF PEACE OR JUSTICE?

TRUTH, ACCOUNTABILITY, AND AMNESTY IN THE MIDDLE EAST

Ibrahim Fraihat and *Bill Hess*

Introduction

In the wake of the Arab Spring uprisings, Tunisia, Libya, and Yemen are grappling with how to respond to the human rights violations that their former dictators perpetrated during their decades in power. In such transitional contexts, the choice that governments have has often been presented as a binary one: to pursue either peace or justice. In this dichotomy, peace usually means stability and the absence of violence, or "negative peace"; this as opposed to broader national reconciliation and social harmony, which would constitute a "positive" peace.[1] Justice, meanwhile, implies the prosecution and potential punishment of human rights violators through a fair legal process. There has been an underlying assumption that these two goals are difficult, if not impossible, to realize simultaneously. Such a conclusion seems logical. If a government pursues justice for past crimes, those whom it prosecutes are unlikely to keep the peace; but if it takes a lax approach to holding human rights violators accountable in the hope of maintaining stability, victims are unlikely to see justice served. This chapter will examine whether this traditional peace versus justice dichotomy is a credible one in the Middle East.

To achieve peace or justice following extensive human rights abuses, governments often employ transitional justice mechanisms. Three of the most prominent mechanisms are granting amnesties, pursuing accountability, and undertaking truth-seeking efforts. The purpose of this chapter is to analyze how Middle Eastern states have applied these three mechanisms, and whether their application has contributed to peace and justice. To do so, we first undertake a historical assessment of the most robust pre-Arab Spring examples of Middle Eastern governments implementing each of these mechanisms. Our case studies are the amnesties that Algeria granted during 1995–2006, Iraq's pursuit of accountability following the 2003 American overthrow of Saddam Hussein, and Morocco's 2004–5 truth commission. Based on these case studies, we make three interrelated arguments. First, we find that Middle Eastern governments' use of amnesty, accountability, and truth-seeking has not made meaningful contributions to peace or justice. We argue that this is because the governments' implementation of single-mechanism approaches in the purported pursuit of either peace or justice has instead perpetuated instability, injustice, or both. We argue further that this is not merely the result of ignorance or incompetence, but of Middle Eastern governments using transitional justice mechanisms primarily to preserve or consolidate their power, not to increase peace or justice.

This chapter proceeds with a brief review of the debates surrounding amnesty, accountability, and truth-seeking measures, and how they can contribute to peace and justice. We then consider how these debates relate to the Middle East, and examine the aforementioned case studies. Having drawn lessons from the experiences of Algeria, Iraq, and Morocco, we will apply them to the ongoing cases of Yemen, Libya, and Tunisia. Relying on a series of interviews conducted in the three countries in 2012 and 2013, we conclude with some observations about how the approach each has taken to transitional justice thus far has impacted on its political transition. We ultimately find that for amnesty, accountability, and truth-seeking to have a positive impact in the region, its governments will need to embrace more balanced, holistic transitional justice approaches to their pursuit of peace and justice.

Amnesty, accountability, and truth-seeking

The world's states implemented amnesties more frequently than any other transitional justice mechanism between 1970 and 2007.[2] While critics of amnesty tend to focus on its broadest manifestations, known as blanket amnesties, amnesties are actually quite diverse in form, varying in their timing, scope, and implementation. The most compelling argument for using amnesties to promote stability is that they can be essential to ending conflicts, or preventing their resumption, thereby saving lives and probably preventing additional human rights abuses. Offers of amnesty can help get parties to the negotiating table, and be valuable bargaining chips once there.[3] Andrew Reiter recently found that "when extended as part of a peace process—granted during negotiations, as part of an actual peace agreement, or passed shortly after a comprehensive agreement is signed—amnesties correlate highly with lasting peace."[4] Snyder and Vinjamuri contend that since amnesties make political bargains between competing stakeholders possible, they thus create the conditions necessary for justice norms and the rule of law to take hold.[5] Finally, others note that amnesty is simply the cheaper, easier option, an important consideration for transitioning or conflict-torn states that often have limited resources.[6]

The principal criticisms of amnesty are that it is illegal, that it encourages a culture of impunity by eroding the rule of law, and that it deprives victims of justice. As argued by Diane Orentlicher and others, states are obligated to prosecute gross human rights violations under international law, which would seem to place amnesty on thin legal ground.[7] Many scholars and practitioners, however, have offered counters to these criticisms of amnesty. Mark Freeman and Max Pensky argue that "the status of amnesty under international law is truly unsettled,"[8] and Freeman finds that in the face of an urgent and grave situation, carefully crafted amnesties are legally justified.[9] He and others have criticized international law as being too inflexible with regard to amnesties, failing to allow for realistic situations where prosecutions may lead to additional violence and loss of life.[10]

Accountability in the form of trials was states' second most commonly used transitional justice mechanism between 1970 and 2007.[11] Justice and accountability are favored by human rights groups and the United Nations, as reflected by the gradual increase in the types of crimes that states are legally bound to prosecute under international law, and the establishment of the International Criminal Court and special tribunals to undertake such prosecutions. Juan Mendez argued in 1997 that a state's obligations under international law in the aftermath of human rights abuses had come to include investigating, prosecuting, and punishing the perpetrators; disclosing all reliable information about their crimes; compensating the victims; and removing perpetrators from positions of authority.[12] Proponents of accountability have also argued that it serves to deter future human rights abuses and restore or reinforce the rule of law.[13] Diane Orentlicher calls criminal punishment "the most effective insurance against future repression" and warns strenuously against the "harmful effects of impunity."[14] Mendez adds that accountability is useful for signifying to society that rule-breaking will not be tolerated, and that trials are the most effective method of drawing a distinction between individual and collective guilt.[15]

Critics of accountability raise a variety of objections, including that trying and punishing human rights violators has not proven to be an effective deterrent of future crimes, a point even Mendez concedes.[16] Amsutz finds that a focus on accountability neglects victim rehabilitation and relationship restoration, underestimates context and the role of institutions, tends to focus on low-level individuals rather than leaders, and diverts scarce resources from other urgent societal needs.[17] As alluded to earlier, scholars and activists express concern that prosecuting abusers who still enjoy some power, or at least influence, can disrupt what may be a tenuous peace.[18] Indeed, former regime elements in Bosnia, Chile, Argentina, and Uruguay challenged the successor system when faced with prosecution.[19] Analysts have also cautioned that accountability is prone to politicization, which can lead to a mockery of justice if a state uses it to make a larger point or settle scores.[20] Acknowledging such concerns, Mendez calls for "a sober and realistic view of political constraints in proposing accountability measures."[21]

A third transitional justice mechanism, truth-seeking, gained prominence in the 1990s. As summarized by David Mendeloff, proponents of truth-seeking claim that it supports both peace and justice by encouraging social healing and reconciliation, aiding institutional reform, helping to promote democracy, and pre-empting as well as deterring future atrocities.[22] In theory, at least, truth commissions can establish accountability by identifying the perpetrators of past crimes, but avoid destabilizing a state by stopping short of trials. For some, not using the information gleaned in truth-seeking efforts is a drawback. Priscilla Hayner recounts that when truth commissions first emerged, there was a suspicion that they would make judicial justice less likely or be used "to avoid more serious accountability."[23] Indeed, there exists a "truth versus justice" debate alongside the "peace versus justice" one. Another major critique of truth-seeking efforts is that their theoretical contributions to peace and justice have not been proven.[24] Klaus Bachmann analyzed eighteen truth and reconciliation commissions and found that only three made significant contributions to reconciliation in their countries.[25]

For some, truth commissions are a useful compromise between draconian applications of accountability and blanket amnesties. This idea of trying to strike a balance between accountability and amnesty in response to human rights violations has begun to gain traction in the transitional justice community. However, the difficulty of proving impact is a criticism to which amnesty and accountability have also been subject. This may slowly be changing. In a recent effort, Tricia Olsen, Leigh Payne, and Andrew Reiter assembled the Transitional Justice Data Base, which attempts to capture every instance of amnesties, trials, truth commissions, reparations, and lustration worldwide between 1970 and 2007. This data set has aided some preliminary empirical studies. The same authors conducted one such study, examining whether there was a relationship between the use of amnesties, trials, truth commissions, or any combination thereof, and a country's democracy and human rights ratings, as assigned by Polity and Freedom House. As Susan Waltz demonstrates in Chapter 3 of this volume, these scores must be used only with healthy skepticism, but the study's results are nonetheless interesting. Olsen, Payne, and Reiter find that only the use of both amnesty and trials, with or without a truth commission, have correlated to an improvement in democracy and human rights. Their findings suggest that neither amnesties nor trials, when used separately, have an impact in either direction, while the exclusive use of a truth commission may actually hurt democracy and human rights.[26] While democracy and human rights do not directly equate to peace and justice, this analysis certainly lends support to proponents of using holistic or hybrid transitional justice approaches to respond to human rights violations.

Peace or justice in the Middle East

While Middle Eastern regimes have frequently tried or pardoned political opponents, the region has relatively limited experience with substantive implementations of transitional justice mechanisms. As this chapter is an attempt to understand how the use of amnesty, accountability, and truth-seeking has impacted on peace and justice in the Middle East, we have chosen to analyze the most robust pre-Arab Spring application of each mechanism. These applications, as is true of most, if not all, of the region's limited pre-Arab Spring experience with transitional justice, entailed governments employing single-mechanism approaches. During and after Algeria's civil war, its military-backed regime granted a series of amnesties, purportedly in the pursuit of peace and reconciliation, but eschewed an accountability component. Following the American invasion of Iraq, the transitional authorities and new government tried and punished members of the former regime and ruling party in the name of justice, without incorporating any sort of amnesty. In the Middle East's only substantive truth commission to date, Morocco investigated decades' worth of state repression under the pretense of making national reconciliation possible, but did not connect the effort to accountability or amnesty measures.

Algeria grants amnesties, pursues amnesia

The Middle East's most significant experience with amnesty came during and after Algeria's brutal civil war, fought from 1991 until 2002, between the military regime and Islamist militants, most notably the Armée Islamique du Salut (AIS) and the Groupement Islamique Armée (GIA). In 1995, Algeria's military government used an amnesty offer as an attempt to thin the militants' ranks. The regime passed a law that allowed repentant Islamist militants and their supporters to submit to the government in return for amnesty, unless they were guilty of major offenses.[27] The regime's use of amnesty to disarm individual militants rather than to bargain with their leaders indicates that the government's goal was not a negotiated peace, but rather a military victory. Indeed, the amnesty measure may have convinced some militants to lay down their arms, but it did not result in peace. The government reported that it received 6,000 submissions in response to the amnesty law, but the war continued unabated and the violence actually increased in 1997 and 1998 before tapering off.[28]

Algeria's second implementation of an amnesty provision also failed to produce peace. In 1999, after the conflict had finally begun to wane and the AIS and other militant groups had declared a truce, the new military-backed president, Abdelaziz Bouteflika, emphasized the importance of "drawing a line under the past" to help Algerians reconcile and move forward.[29] Accordingly, Bouteflika's government enacted the Civil Harmony Law. It offered amnesty to militants who would surrender, fully disclose their crimes, and had not—as verified by probation committees—killed, maimed, raped, or bombed a public place. The war-weary nation heartily endorsed the law in a referendum.[30] Shortly after the six-month application window closed, government officials told Amnesty International that about 4,500 militants had applied for amnesty. The probation committees proved to be suspiciously lax, as only around 350 of those militants, less than 8 percent, were apparently prosecuted for the unpardoned serious crimes.[31] Then, in 2000, Algeria supplemented the Civil Harmony Law with a measure granting a blanket amnesty to militants whose groups had agreed to disband.[32] The security forces and other state agents, which had also been implicated in the war's atrocities, continued to enjoy de facto immunity. The various amnesties and their implementation demonstrated how willing Algeria's regime was to sacrifice justice in the hopes of consolidating its military victory and achieving stability. Despite these efforts, the reduced level of violence continued.

In 2005, three years after the civil war finally ended, Algeria's regime confirmed its commitment to using amnesty—and only amnesty—to deal with the human rights violations that had occurred. Bouteflika enacted the Charter for Peace and National Reconciliation renewing the 1999 amnesty provision even though the government estimated that only about 1,000 militants were still actively resisting. The Charter also offered amnesty to those militants who had surrendered after the earlier provision's deadline or were serving a conflict-related prison sentence.[33] The charter was confirmed by a referendum, but controversially.[34] Unlike in 1999, there was substantive opposition, particularly from victims, their families, and human rights activists who rejected the idea of forgiving "throat-cutters" and the continued lack of provisions for truth and justice.[35] Moreover, whereas the earlier amnesty provisions had merely shunned the pursuit of truth and justice, the Charter actively inhibited it. The charter made questioning the past a political offense, and its enabling legislation, which was not publicly voted on, debated, or even circulated prior to its adoption, explicitly provided security forces with blanket immunity from prosecution.[36]

The amnesty measures outlined above reduced the number of militants opposing the government and may deserve some credit for Algeria's civil war not resuming, but the regime can only claim, at best, a negative peace. This is because of both the substance and implementation of the amnesty measures, and the failure to balance them with any semblance of accountability. Despite the regime's reliance on amnesty measures, it was either unable or unwilling to use them to reach a peace agreement with its military opponents, or a compromise with its primary opponent, the influential Front Islamique du Salut (FIS). Instead, the regime used amnesty measures as another weapon with which to isolate and undercut its opponents. The Charter actually banned the FIS from political life, perpetuating the underlying political conflict that was the root cause of the civil war.[37] Meanwhile, the GIA, though weakened and cornered at the end of the civil war, has experienced a renaissance as part of al-Qaeda in the Islamic Maghreb, and continues to carry out periodic high-profile attacks throughout Algeria.[38]

Ultimately, the Bouteflika regime's amnesty-only approach not only struggled to bring about peace, but also risked undermining the reconciliation that it was purportedly intended to facilitate. This single-mechanism approach also completely rejected justice in favor of stability, with unfortunate results. As scholars have cautioned, the lack of accountability for either militants or the military after years of atrocities reinforced a culture of impunity and left large portions of the population, especially victims, disgruntled. Unable to rely on state-administered justice, and without reason to fear it, some victims took matters into their own hands, committing acts of revenge.[39]

While Algeria's amnesties undermined justice, they were remarkably consistent in strengthening the regime's position. The 1995 and 1999 amnesties removed opponents from the battlefield, increasing the military's likelihood of victory. In 2005, with victory won and military supremacy assured, the Charter gave the military immunity from prosecution and removed the regime's primary challenger from the political scene. It seems that, ultimately, the Algerian regime's primary goal in using amnesty was neither peace nor justice, but the consolidation of its power.

Iraq aims for accountability, inhibits justice

After the United States led an invasion of Iraq and overthrew Saddam Hussein in 2003, it had to decide how to respond to the 35-year legacy of massive human rights violations he left behind. Thousands had been executed, hundreds of thousands were missing, displaced, or exiled, and hundreds of towns and villages had been destroyed.[40] The Bush administration, which was eager to turn Iraq into a liberal democracy that embraced the rule of law, and to see Hussein pay for his crimes, opted to implement accountability in the pursuit of justice. Accordingly, one of the priorities of the Coalition Provisional Authority (CPA) that governed during the transitional period was to track down and prosecute Hussein and his lieutenants. More controversially, the CPA, led by Paul Bremer, also decided to pursue a policy of de-Ba'athification. These decisions and their application ultimately undermined justice and stoked further conflict.

The CPA's implementation of accountability quickly ran into several of the potential issues that scholars have identified. First, Iraq in this chaotic transitional phase did not have the capacity to undertake such high-profile, politically charged, and technically complicated trials. The CPA created the Iraq Special Tribunal specifically to try top regime members for gross human rights violations.[41] Human rights organizations criticized the tribunal for failing to ensure that its judges and prosecutors were sufficiently experienced and able to maintain their independence and impartiality, and that their concerns were warranted.[42] The court struggled to find qualified staff, and some of the tribunal members had a poor grasp of international humanitarian law and admitted feeling stuck between international and Iraqi opinion.[43] Nonetheless, Saddam Hussein's trial for murder and other crimes that had occurred during a 1982 attack on a Shi'ite village got underway in October 2005. After a lengthy trial, the tribunal convicted Hussein and two co-defendants in November 2006, sentencing them to death. Saddam Hussein being put on trial for his crimes— a first for an Arab leader—was certainly significant, and signaled that justice might be possible in Iraq. Unfortunately, the numerous shortcomings of the tribunal and Hussein's trial began to erode any such optimism. When Iraq's Shi'ite-dominated government hanged Hussein, a Sunni, on a high Muslim holy day (30 December 2006), it revealed that the justice it was pursuing was of a sectarian, "victor's" nature. This was reinforced when a video of Hussein's final moments revealed that his executioners taunted him by chanting "Moqtada," the name of a Shi'ite rival, and did not allow him to finish his prayers prior to hanging him.[44] Rather than helping to establish the rule of law, Hussein's trial and execution, by becoming politicized, had made a mockery of justice.

For all their faults, the trials did serve the purpose of singling out individuals as responsible for specific atrocities. The CPA's policy of de-Ba'athification, however, was one of collective punishment. In May 2003, CPA Order No. 1 removed those in the top four ranks of the Ba'ath party; and any Ba'ath party member who was in the top three levels of management of Iraq's civil service was removed from their position and banned from holding such positions in the future. CPA Order No. 2 disbanded Iraq's military, security, and intelligence services.[45] These orders were implemented aggressively by Iraq's Higher National De-Ba'athification Commission (HNDC), chaired by Ahmad Chalabi, an exiled Iraqi who had the ear of the White House in the run-up to the invasion.[46] The HNDC enjoyed wide latitude, and an aide later called it a "government within a government" because of its broad mandate and plentiful resources.[47] Estimates as to how many civil servants were purged as a result of de-Ba'athification range as high as 2 million.[48]

In a mirror image of Algeria, the case of Iraq demonstrates the dangers of pursuing accountability in an uncompromising fashion. In Iraq, the CPA's accountability measures were intended to establish justice, but instead perpetuated new injustices that exacerbated the divisions that existed under Hussein, made peace and reconciliation unlikely, and encouraged retribution. It is hardly surprising that Iraq's Shi'ite and Kurdish constituencies, after suffering for decades under Hussein, were inclined toward vindictiveness. The United States, as a party to the conflict, chose to pursue the prosecution of Hussein and the dismantling of his party over insisting on a fair trial and just vetting procedures, even though it hoped to instill respect for the rule of law. Iraq's bloody sectarian conflict continues to this day, and the violence spiked once again in 2014 with the advance of the Islamic State in Iraq and al-Sham, or ISIS. Many of the group's military commanders are former Ba'athist Iraqi officers who were purged in 2003 and later imprisoned.[49] As in Algeria, Iraq's transitional justice approach has benefited those domestic actors that supported its implementation. Iraq's Shia continue to enjoy a dominant political position in Baghdad, while Iraq's Kurds have been able to claim unprecedented autonomy, to their economic benefit.

Morocco delves into its "years of lead"

In 2004, years before the Arab Spring, Morocco became the first country in the Arab world to establish a truth commission. Atypically, Morocco's truth-seeking experiment did not occur in the wake of a conflict or regime change, but as part of a gradual, top-down liberalization that had begun in the 1990s as a response to the new, post-Cold War international environment and external pressure.[50] Shortly after King Mohammed VI assumed the throne in 1999 following his father's death, newly empowered human rights groups pushed for a broad truth commission to investigate human rights violations committed by the state between 1956 and 1999, a period which Moroccans commonly refer to as the "years of lead." The king consented, and he established the Equity and Reconciliation Commission (ERC) in January 2004.[51] The commission, though notable, would not lead to reconciliation or contribute to justice. It would, however, reduce domestic pressure on the regime and improve its international image.

The ERC's mandate was to investigate and establish the truth about the years of lead, provide a comprehensive report of the violations, and recommend how to compensate the victims, memorialize the abuses, and prevent such abuses from recurring. In inaugurating the commission, the king emphasized that the ERC would serve to "'close the file'" on past human rights violations and resolve outstanding issues through extra-judicial means.[52] This focus on extra-judicial means indicated that the truth-seeking effort would not contribute to accountability for perpetrators or justice for victims. The ERC's final report established the state's involvement in a variety of "gross human rights violations," finding that hundreds of missing or "disappeared" persons had been killed by the government's disproportionate use of force or had died in arbitrary detention, often after being tortured.[53] Despite these damning revelations, the report boasted that Morocco had "opted for the path of peaceful reconciliation, justice and equity to face the past violations. It chose reconciliatory justice over an accusatory justice, and historical truth over judicial truth. Indeed, such kind of justice cannot be dealt with in courtrooms but only in the public space..."[54] The king went further, labeling the commission's work as "a sign of collective pardon."[55] Blanket amnesty or immunity would have been more accurate terms, as none of the perpetrators was even publicly identified, much less prosecuted. Indeed, in the case of Morocco, scholars who warned that states might employ truth-seeking efforts to avoid accountability were vindicated.

Clearly, the ERC was not undertaken for the sake of justice, and it also failed to produce the other aforementioned potential truth-seeking benefits, such as social healing and reconciliation, institutional reform, and preventing future atrocities. By employing truth-seeking as a single-mechanism approach rather than coupling it with accountability or formal amnesty measures, Morocco's regime lessened the prospects of reconciliation. Many victims and their families have found it difficult to embrace reconciliation when the institutions and individuals that abused them have not only escaped any sort of reform or prosecution, but remain in place. The ERC did, as mandated, propose reforms and other actions to strengthen the rule of law and fight impunity. The commission even recommended that the prime minister issue a public apology for the state's abuses and that Morocco adopt a memory policy. The king directed the country's Advisory Council on Human Rights to implement the recommendations, but the government ultimately did not follow through.[56] Nearly ten years after the ERC finished its work, Morocco's regime has yet to apologize to the victims, ratify additional international human rights conventions, or make the reforms the commission deemed necessary to prevent future abuses. Instead, human rights violations have continued, and in the aftermath of the latest bout of political unrest during the Arab Spring, political repression is reportedly on the rise once again.[57]

Morocco's early, pre-Arab Spring experiment in transitional justice failed to engender reconciliation, establish justice, or improve the country's human rights climate, but it certainly benefited the king. The ERC was clearly significant. Priscilla Hayner lists it as one of the five strongest truth commissions ever undertaken, because it was well funded, well staffed, and had a reasonable amount of time to complete its work.[58] The ERC functioned for 20 months and reviewed over 22,000 cases alleging abuses. It interviewed victims, families, and officials and collected information from public archives, hospitals, non-governmental organizations, and other sources. The ERC also held seven public, televised hearings during which victims spoke about disappearances, arbitrary arrests, reprisals against relatives, unfair trials, torture, and rapes.[59] One commentator called the public testimonies "a watershed in the political history of modern-day Morocco."[60] The ERC's efforts produced a few tangible results, most notably that the government paid various reparations to victims and their families, including $85 million, medical care, and vocational training.[61] Due to all these factors, the commission helped Morocco to improve its human rights image, and, more specifically, the king to burnish his credentials as an enlightened reformer intent on modernizing his country. The king was even able to co-opt key regime opponents by placing them in charge of the ERC, thereby reducing domestic challenges to his rule. The king, it appears, was willing to reveal some truths to strengthen his power.

In the Middle East, neither peace nor justice

There are three major takeaways from the pre-Arab Spring case studies above. The first is that historically when Middle Eastern states have implemented amnesty, accountability, or truth-seeking mechanisms, it has not led to peace or justice. Second, that shortcoming is because these states' use of single-mechanism approaches to pursue either peace or justice has undermined the realization of either. Lastly, it appears that when Middle Eastern regimes implement transitional justice mechanisms, the goals of peace and justice are secondary to those of regime security.

In Algeria, Bouteflika and the military sought peace, but were unwilling to entertain even a modicum of justice. Its repeated amnesties became insulting to the victims of the civil war, in addition to the militants, and began to make peace less likely. Tensions along the same lines remain to this day, but Bouteflika was re-elected in April 2014 and the generals still enjoy extensive power. For the regime, amnesty was an effective tool. In Iraq, because the CPA wanted to ensure that the Ba'ath party, which it seemed to view as an existential threat, did not stage a comeback, it prioritized justice over reconciliation and allowed accountability processes to become vengeful. Justice was often perverted, and peace became even less feasible. Chalabi and others took advantage of this to carry out retribution against political and sectarian opponents. Iraq has yet to recover, but the Ba'ath party was forced underground, at least temporarily, and Iraq's Sunni population remains effectively marginalized, even with the ousting of Nouri al-Maliki and attemts to form a unified response to the threat of ISIS. Morocco's regime permitted a truth-seeking effort in the name of reconciliation, but much like Algeria, it refused to allow any justice for victims, leaving many Moroccans' frustrations to fester. But since Mohammed VI allowed prominent rights activists to head up the truth commission on his terms, he simultaneously co-opted several influential regime critics, appeased at least part of the population, and improved his reputation with the international community. Clearly, in assessing any application of transitional justice mechanisms, whether in the Middle East or elsewhere, it is essential to consider who is driving the process and their motives. In each case examined above, the parties that selected and implemented the transitional justice measures enjoyed huge advantages in political power that enabled them to dictate favorable terms. If the Middle East is to make any progress in using amnesty, accountability, and truth-seeking to realize peace or justice, a good first step would be inclusive, representative governments that actually prioritize those goals. Which brings us to the Arab Spring.

Striving for peace and justice after the Arab Spring

Five years after the Arab Spring started, Yemen, Libya, and Tunisia continue to struggle with their political transitions. The challenges, which are plentiful, include establishing some semblance of security, reviving stagnant economies, writing new constitutions, and undertaking significant reforms. The countries also share decades-long histories of systematic, pervasive human rights violations perpetrated by repressive dictators and their regimes. To their credit, the transitional governments in all three countries have actively decided to address at least some of these abuses rather than ignoring them. That is where the similarities end, however, as each country has thus far taken very different approaches to redress their painful legacies.

Yemen's limited response to past abuses thus far has featured amnesty most prominently. Protests against the continued rule of Yemen's long-time dictator, President Ali Abdullah Saleh, erupted in January 2011 on the heels of uprisings in Tunisia and Egypt. As the demonstrations grew over the following month, portions of Yemen's military and several influential tribes elected to back the opposition. These defections from Saleh's power base limited his flexibility in cracking down on the demonstrations, as excessive escalation may have started an all-out civil war. Instead, Yemen experienced a lengthy stalemate with both sides refusing each other's proposals for resolving the situation. In November, Saleh, after multiple refusals, finally signed a deal brokered by the Gulf Cooperation Council (GCC), in which he agreed to step down in exchange for immunity from prosecution. Saleh turned power over to his vice president, Abd Rabbu Mansour Hadi, in February 2012, and Yemen embarked on a difficult transition process.[62]

This was about as clear a case as one could find of sacrificing justice in order to keep the peace. Following the GCC deal, the threat of civil war quickly abated, probably saving the already destitute, conflict-riven country from further immediate suffering. As a result, the deal enjoyed praise and support from the United Nations, which helped hammer it out, and much of the international community. Some Yemenis, too, were jubilant to see Saleh deposed without massive bloodshed. The peace that was realized, though, has proved to be fragile and short-lived, in part because Saleh, his immunity secured, has shown no interest in fading quietly into the background. In a shortcoming that Snyder and Vinjamuri warn against, the GCC initiative required Saleh to leave office, but not politics.[63] He has continued to lead his ruling political party, the General People's Congress (GPC), and many Yemenis and international observers believe that Saleh is working with the Houthi rebels that overran the capital in September 2014, paralyzing the country's transition and threatening to bring down his successor. One Yemeni said that Saleh "is like a ghost. You don't see him but you certainly feel his presence."[64]

Yemen has also been slow to prosecute human rights violators who do not necessarily enjoy immunity. Although President Hadi decreed in September 2012 that an independent commission of inquiry would be established to investigate the violence that occurred during the 2011 uprising, no such commission has been formed.[65] Proceedings began that same month against 78 suspects of a deadly attack on 18 March 2011 against protesters, but little progress has been made and none of the high level suspects is in custody.[66]

Yemen's extensive, ten-month National Dialogue Conference included a transitional justice working group, but a transitional justice law is still being debated. If such a law is passed, it may include a truth-seeking mechanism, but as of December 2014 no such effort had begun. Unsurprisingly, representatives of groups that suffered at the hands of the regime think that Yemen should pursue "justice to reach reconciliation," while the GPC and its allies are advocating "non-judiciary justice," a term that evokes Morocco's truth commission.[67] The vice chairman of the GPC parliamentary bloc, Yaser al-Awadi, defended his party's position, saying that "Yemen's political legacy shows that reconciliation was built on burying the truth, not openness. In the past, there was a victorious party and a defeated one. This time, both parties are equals, with no victorious and no defeated. This makes it more necessary for the two parties to move on and look toward the future, not the past."[68] Most of Yemen's other major political parties, including the Islamist Islah party, seem to agree, and have shown little to no interest in truth-seeking and accountability despite allying against Saleh during the revolution. As a Yemeni journalist explained, "The past was created by all of Yemen's political parties and it is not in their interest to go back to it."[69] Similarly, Yemeni activist Mahmoud Nasher acknowledged that a "complete departure from the past regime cannot be implemented, as the leaders of the transition in Yemen were part of that regime."[70]

If the GPC, Islah, and other well-established parties are able to reassert control over the government, Yemen is most likely to follow in the footsteps of Algeria by granting amnesties, shunning justice, and avoiding any investigation of past atrocities. If Yemen moves forward with a unity government that includes the Houthis and the newly empowered, youth-dominated political actors that led the revolution against Saleh, a compromise would be necessary, perhaps along the lines of Morocco's approach. Reparations reportedly feature prominently in Yemen's draft transitional justice law, which was developed by a politically diverse group.[71] Continued instability makes it unlikely that Yemen will be able to decide upon and implement a coherent transitional justice approach in the near future. Even if Yemen were to decide on an approach that included accountability, that same instability and the state's extreme poverty would make implementation extremely difficult, just as Libya is discovering.

Libya, which is discussed more fully in Mieczysław P. Boduszyński and Marieke Wierda's Chapter 8 in this volume, has thus far responded to past human rights abuses predominantly by pursuing accountability, which has sometimes become vengeful. This path was set in part by the nature of Libya's transition, as Gaddafi was deposed through an internationally-backed, armed rebellion. This mirrored the overthrow of Saddam Hussein in Iraq, though without any foreign actor playing a dominant role on the ground, and left the conflict's victors free to impose their will. For Gaddafi, that meant that he was unable to strike a deal like Saleh, and was instead forced to try to hide, like Hussein. When Gaddafi was found, however, he was summarily executed rather than being detained and prosecuted. Libya's original transitional government had made quite clear its intent to prosecute most other regime figures, including Gaddafi's family members. It is also quite clear, however, that conflict-wracked Libya, with two governments claiming power, does not have anywhere near the level of stability or capabilities needed to carry out a large number of political trials in a competent fashion. Unsurprisingly, then, Libya's pursuit of accountability has thus far been halting and flawed.

As of December 2014, over 200 senior former regime figures were being held for prosecution. Court proceedings have started for a number of them, including former prime minister al-Baghdadi al-Mahmoudi, former foreign minister Abd al-Ati al-Obaidi, and former spy chief Abdullah al-Sanousi, but few if any of the cases have progressed to the trial stage. Meanwhile, many of the other figures are being detained in prisons that are administered by local authorities, militias, or tribes, not Libya's internationally recognized government, which has been unable to assert control over the detentions and judicial proceedings. Perhaps the most glaring example is that the local military council of Zentan has, since November 2011, repeatedly refused to hand over one of Gaddafi's sons, Saif al-Islam, to the central government. Due to its concerns over Libya's ability to conduct a fair trial, the ICC has demanded al-Islam's extradition and rejected Tripoli's request to try him internally. Al-Islam's trial in Zentan has been suspended, and in December 2014 the ICC referred the issue to the UN Security Council.[72] Allegations of torture in militia-run detention centers have also caused international concern.[73] As a result, Tunisia's decision to extradite al-Mahmoudi was extremely controversial.[74]

Judicial capacity is also an issue, as it was in Iraq. Libya's justice system was thoroughly corrupted under the former regime and is in dire need of fundamental reform; some revolutionaries have even insisted that the judiciary be purged before any trials take place. A former militia leader who actively opposed Gaddafi even prior to the revolution pointed out that

> the judge who sentenced me to death during Gaddafi's reign is still a practicing judge. How can I trust this judge or the judiciary that employs him? I need to see new, honest judges who deliver justice to those who suffered and to those who committed crimes. That's when I'll feel confident that Libya is moving into a new era of justice and fairness. Then I'll be able to forgive and reconcile.[75]

In another similarity with Iraq, Libya's drive for accountability has gone well beyond trying former regime members. After a contentious debate, some of Libya's revolutionaries surrounded parliament, pressuring the General National Congress to adopt the Political Isolation Law (PIL) on 5 May 2013. The law purged anyone who held high-ranking positions at any point during the Gaddafi regime, including ministers, police chiefs, and student union heads, banning them from public office and other select positions for ten years.[76] While many pushing for the law genuinely believed that it was needed to "protect the revolution and ensure the new state is cleansed of the corrupt former regime elements," there were also less noble motives at work, among them political self-interest.[77] Some of Libya's political actors have used the PIL to exclude rival politicians who had long ago defected from Gaddafi's regime, such as Mahmoud Jibril, who served as the head of the Libyan opposition's interim government for much of 2011. According to Muhammad Toumi, a GNC member and leader of the National Front for the Salvation of Libya, this was justified:

> There's no such thing as defection from the old regime. It was just a smart reading by some former regime officials; they read the political map well and realized the regime was at its end. They jumped from the sinking boat to a new one. Political isolation, therefore, is a must.[78]

Others, however, expressed concern. Libyan law professor al-Hadi Bu Hamra warned that "political isolation is a program that could undermine the core of national reconciliation and split Libyan society in half... It's the opposite of transitional justice."[79] Shortly after the law was passed, the UN's Special Envoy to Libya at that time, Tarek Mitri, stated that the PIL's "criteria for exclusion are arbitrary, far-reaching, at times vague, and are likely to violate the civil and political rights of large numbers of individuals."[80] Much as in Iraq, Libya's pursuit of justice has itself become unjust. The imbalance in Libya's approach was confirmed by its one amnesty measure: in May 2012, the transitional government passed a law granting immunity for crimes committed while "promoting or protecting the revolution."[81]

Reminiscent of Iraq's de-Ba'athification law, Libya's pursuit of justice has had a negative effect on peace by deepening divisions between segments of society. A tribal leader expressed his frustration in January 2013:

> We're doing our best to contribute to the rebuilding of Libya. We don't want to keep being treated as Qaddafi loyalists; those of us who helped Qaddafi don't represent our tribe. We're reaching out to our fellow Libyans to build a new country. But if we continue to be excluded, we'll be left with only one option: looking for

those who are also excluded and building new coalitions among the marginalized. We will be forced to fight back. Permanent exclusion is not an option for us.[82]

This is the scenario that seems to be playing out now, with the emergence of former general Khalifa Haftar, who returned to Libya in 2011 to fight alongside the rebels against Gaddafi, but is nonetheless banned from a formal government role by the PIL. Since May 2014, Haftar has been carrying out what he calls "Operation Dignity," originally challenging both the central government and Islamist militias. He has enjoyed a large degree of support from militias, cities, and tribes that Libya's accountability measures have marginalized, and eventually earned the backing of the internationally recognized government.[83]

Libya's aggressive pursuit of justice is neither the only nor the primary reason that its transition is faltering. The large, oil-rich and tribal country was always going to be difficult to govern after the loosening of Gaddafi's iron fist, and it was awash with militias and violence prior to the enactment of the Political Isolation Law. Nonetheless, it seems that Libya's use of accountability has merely added one more conflict driver to an already complex web, rather than bringing justice for victims, deterring future crimes, or instilling the rule of law.

Tunisia, seemingly increasingly every day, has been the exception to the Arab Spring, and this includes how it has chosen to deal with the crimes of its former regime. As detailed in Christopher Lamont's Chapter 5 in this volume, Tunisia has thus far performed within the context of a broad transitional justice framework that was drafted in part by civil society groups, and informed by the country's national dialogue. Even as Ben Ali fled Tunis on 14 January 2011, Tunisia's security forces had begun taking steps toward holding him and his associates and family members accountable for the crimes they had committed while in power. Within days, 33 members of Ben Ali's extended family were arrested, as well as Rafik Belhaj, the former interior minister whom many blamed for the violent police crackdown during the uprising. The army and justice department were directed to gather and preserve evidence for investigating the former regime.[84] In addition, Tunisian authorities banned several hundred people suspected of corruption from traveling outside the country, and the National Constituent Assembly (NCA) froze the assets of 114 businessmen pending further investigation.[85]

While Tunisia's transitional government took several important, decisive steps in the immediate aftermath of Ben Ali's fall to make effective prosecutions possible, it did not rush to carry them out. Instead, it decided that Tunisia's response to the prior regime's human rights violations should be determined by an inclusive, consultative process. Civil society representatives led a national dialogue specifically addressing the issue of transitional justice. Khaled Kashier explained,

> We met constantly. We debated all aspects of transitional justice such as truth seeking, lustration laws, compensation, etc. We brought in international experts and heard their recommendations; we met with the victims and their families in many districts in Tunisia. We all came from different organizations in Tunisia and represented over 70 civil society organizations.[86]

Tunisia's NCA passed the resulting transitional justice law in December 2013. The law calls for the creation of a Truth and Dignity Commission and tackles accountability, vetting, institutional reform, reparations, and national reconciliation.[87] The Truth and Dignity Commission began its four-year term in June 2014, and was mandated to investigate gross human rights violations committed by the state since 1 July 1955.[88]

Some have been frustrated with the slow pace of progress in these areas, particularly because it has allowed Ben Ali supporters to remain politically active. As Mohamed Ben Aisa, a law professor at Tunisia University, put it: "They did not apologize to the Tunisian people, they are not being prosecuted, but instead they are now invited to the national dialogue table!"[89] More importantly, however, Tunisia has yet to sacrifice peace or justice. It has dealt with its fair share of tensions, but the government has avoided exacerbating them thus far. Like Libya, it considered an isolation law, but ultimately decided against it. One NCA member from Tunisia's Islamist Ennahda party, which dominated the transitional period, explained,

> We don't believe in exclusion. Practicing politics is a constitutional right for all Tunisians regardless of their political orientation. Those who committed human rights violations should be dealt with through the courts. Anyone who does not have violations must be included in the political process, not excluded. Exclusion laws can also lead to counter-revolution among other possible negative outcomes.[90]

Conclusion

The Middle East's contemporary experiences with transitional justice have both reinforced the lessons drawn from the historical cases and introduced new ones. Once again, states that attempt to pursue either peace through amnesty or justice through accountability, while ignoring the other, are suffering from conflict and continued injustices. In Yemen, the immunity granted to Saleh and his lieutenants has not only kept them from being prosecuted for years of abuses, but also allowed them to maintain significant influence in the country, which they have used to destabilize its transition. The GCC deal differed from Algeria's CPNR in that it removed Saleh from the presidency, but in a similar outcome many Yemenis' grievances remain unaddressed and frustration with the central government persists. Libya, as alluded to above, is replicating Iraq's aggressive pursuit of victor's justice. Just as in Iraq, this strategy is feeding into civil conflict and has done little to establish the rule of law.

Once again, key stakeholders in each country are attempting to use transitional justice mechanisms to strengthen their own political positions. In Yemen, the revolution and defections from the regime meant that Saleh was no longer able to rule effectively, but his power base was still strong enough that he could dictate the terms of his departure, even in the face of regional and international pressure. In Libya, vindictive and opportunistic revolutionaries used force to ensure that many of their political opponents would be purged, enabling them to expand their power. Tunisia's case was a bit more interesting in this regard, as Ennahda had a healthy plurality in the transitional government and probably could have imposed a transitional justice policy that gave it further advantages over its political rivals, perhaps including a political isolation law. Instead, in the face of significant popular pressure, it decided to defer to an inclusive process and avoided alienating potential spoilers and large swathes of the population.

The cases of Yemen, Libya, and Tunisia also shed further light on how external actors can impact on a state's implementation of transitional justice. In Yemen, the GCC and particularly Saudi Arabia intervened during the revolution in an attempt to preserve short-term stability in a strategically important neighboring country. They accordingly applied enough pressure to force Saleh ultimately to step down, but stopped short of forcing him from Yemen's political scene, and then resumed supporting its preferred factions rather than the country's political transition.[91] The United Nations and Western powers did a bit more, facilitating the national dialogue and helping to restructure government institutions, but these efforts, especially those of the United States, were often poorly coordinated and narrowly focused on self-interested priorities such as counter-terrorism.[92] In Libya, a number of Arab and Western nations played major military roles in helping rebels to overthrow Gaddafi, but those who stayed seriously involved afterwards focused much more on supporting favored proxies than institution-building. Tunisia, once again being the exception, seems to be the one situation where external actors played a constructive role, as non-governmental organizations such as the International

Center for Transitional Justice helped to shape the government's relevant policy. When it is nations that get involved, however, it appears that, much like the domestic stakeholders, they tend to support approaches that will most benefit themselves and their allies, rather than seeking out the best long-term option for the state at large.

Peace and justice are by no means easy aspirations to realize, especially in the aftermath of civil conflict, regime change, or both. Transitional justice mechanisms like accountability efforts and amnesties can help, but not if they are applied in a completely imbalanced manner and merely to serve the interests of a regime or subset of stakeholders. The lack of accountable leadership and inclusive politics in the Middle East has allowed its regimes to pursue many supposedly altruistic policies that ultimately do not benefit, and sometimes even harm, their populations. Such has been the history of transitional justice in the Middle East. This continues to be the case after the Arab Spring, except in Tunisia, which provides a glimmer of hope. Tunisia's hard work is just getting started, but its inclusive approach and willingness to consider all its options patiently—rather than immediately pursuing only either accountability or amnesty—may give it a chance to enjoy the best of both.

5

THE SCOPE AND BOUNDARIES OF
TRANSITIONAL JUSTICE IN THE ARAB SPRING

Christopher K. Lamont

Introduction

Since the beginning of what has become popularly known as the Arab Spring, there has been a renewed interest in transitional justice in the Arab world among both scholars and practitioners.[1] Prior to 2011, the Middle East and North Africa (MENA) region was largely absent from studies of transitional justice, despite the fact that the region witnessed no absence of violent conflict, political transitions, or even transitional justice mechanisms.[2] Instead transitional justice, as a field of scholarship and practice, draws heavily upon the Latin American, sub-Saharan African, post-communist European, former Yugoslav, and Asian experiences.[3] To be sure, when reflecting upon transitional justice demands in the Arab Middle East, it is important to be aware that our engagement with the Arab Spring is through the lens of a field that has not engaged on a sustained basis with Arab experiences. It also draws heavily upon international legal frameworks, such as international humanitarian law and international human rights law, which can be limiting in the sense that it underplays concepts of social justice deeply rooted in Islamic political thought,[4] but also potentially illuminating as it can provide an insight into contestations over the ownership of justice among local domestic actors.

As a field of law, transitional justice has drawn upon a post-Second World War move toward the international and domestic prosecutions of systemic human rights violations and violations of the laws of armed conflict. Engagement with transitional justice on the part of political scientists, on the contrary, draws upon case studies from the aforementioned regions, to conceptualize transitional justice principally in two ways. It is either theorized as a by-product of domestically negotiated political transitions, with variations argued to correspond to the balance of power between incoming and outgoing elites, or points to international diffusion of norms and ideas to explain justice outcomes.[5]

Transitional justice processes in states directly affected by the Arab Spring remain in their infancy, and therefore this contribution's focus will be on the negotiation of transitional justice in the MENA region in order to understand some of the most salient sites of contestation in transitional justice debates. It will thus help us to reflect on the nature of transitional justice in the Arab world, by exploring how Tunisia in particular, and other Arab states more broadly, responded to demands for justice voiced by protesters in 2011. Because Tunisia is perhaps more advanced in its post-Arab Spring transitional justice process than other Arab states, this contribution will take Tunisia as a case study through which lessons for understanding transitional justice in the region can be derived. Fieldwork for this chapter was carried out over eleven fieldwork trips to Tunisia between 2012 and 2014.[6] It will argue, in part, that contestations of legitimacy, and ownership of transitional justice processes, are products of the negotiated origins of transitional justice. Negotiation here is not defined exclusively as negotiation between outgoing and incoming elites, but rather negotiation among transitional elites and in some cases external actors, as to the targets, time frame, content, and scope of transitional justice. It is these negotiations among transitional elites over the boundaries and scope of transitional justice that highlight wider contestations over state identity. This contribution illustrates that in the Arab world, transitional justice demands voiced by political actors constitute attempts to deal concurrently with the legacy of past abuses and advance (in many cases) hitherto marginalized political projects, which have the potential for radical transformation of political orders established decades ago. The transformative potential of transitional justice in the Arab context has resulted in contestations over the content and scope of justice measures, with political actors attempting to mold transitional justice policies in a manner that reflects their own preferred narratives of the past and visions of the future.

Transitional justice, the Arab Spring, and political transitions

Tunisia provides an illustrative case study from which lessons can be drawn for transitional justice processes elsewhere in the Middle East and North Africa. Tunisia's attempts to deal with the legacy of the past have resulted in a wide range of transitional justice initiatives, which have been advanced by actors with competing demands in relation to the scope and content of these initiatives.[7] With the establishment of its Truth and Dignity Commission on 6 June 2014, the ratification of the Organic Law on Establishing and Organizing Transitional Justice on 13 December 2013, the holding of a national dialogue on transitional justice under the auspices of Tunisia's Ministry for Human Rights and Transitional Justice from April to October 2012, and the establishment of investigative commissions, Tunisia has undertaken a concerted effort to respond to demands voiced by protesters in December 2010 and January 2011.

Nevertheless, it would be misleading to interpret Tunisia's relatively swift ratification of a law on transitional justice, and the establishment of its Truth and Dignity Commission, as suggestive of a broad consensus on the scope and content of transitional justice in Tunisia.[8] Indeed, even in the context of a relatively homogenous Arab state with a cohesive national identity, significant cleavages have emerged during the negotiation of transitional justice over the past three years. In order to understand these cleavages, it is instructive to map transitional justice across three transitions that Tunisia experienced from 2011 until 2014, the period of time under study in this contribution.

Paradoxically, Tunisia's transitional justice process started before President Zine al-Abidine Ben Ali's departure for exile on 14 January 2011. Indeed, it was Ben Ali who, in his final address to the nation, called for the creation of three commissions that were to address human rights abuses, corruption, and political reform. Ben Ali's address set the course for Tunisia's nascent transitional justice process for the months that followed his departure from office. And it was offered in an attempt to placate demonstrators, rather than initiate a deeper reform of state institutions. Therefore, it is not surprising that the narrow and limited transitional justice mechanisms established in the weeks following Ben Ali's departure contrasted heavily with Tunisia's Organic Law on Establishing and Organizing Transitional Justice, ratified on 13 December

2013. This contrast highlights how the contested boundaries and scope of transitional justice in the context of Arab Spring transitions are derived from political contestations that seek to define or redefine state identity. Furthermore, as will be discussed below, the creation and later dismantling of a dedicated government ministry for human rights and transitional justice also illustrates the broader political salience of transitional justice for political transformations unfolding across the Arab Middle East.[9] Indeed, Ennahdha made the passage of its draft law on transitional justice a condition for the party's voluntary withdrawal from government, while opposition parties, which boycotted Tunisia's National Constituent Assembly at the time of the law's adoption, never reconciled themselves to the transitional justice law.[10] This contribution uses Tunisia to argue that transitional justice in the Arab Middle East takes place within the context of contested state-building projects, and thus it is less a means of dealing with past abuses and more a means of constructing a *usable past* on the part of political parties engaged in state-building processes.[11]

Transitional justice, while often described in legalist terms and approached from the perspective of a globalizing rule of law project, cannot be divorced from contested state-building political projects in the Middle East and North Africa. Tunisia's political cleavages are illustrative of this.[12] In Tunisia alone, Destourians and Islamists, not to mention Marxists and Arab nationalists, advance starkly contrasting state-building projects that do not share many of the liberalizing assumptions embedded in democratic transition frameworks.[13]

Transitional justice can recalibrate the trajectory of political transitions in two ways. The first is through its potential role in excluding political actors from the transitional process, through either criminal trials of former elites or the political exclusion of elites in the form of lustration and vetting legislation. The latter, as noted in Boduszyński and Wierda's Chapter 8, was used in Libya to remove from political life anyone who was deemed to have been a public official under Gaddafi. The second path through which transitional justice can recalibrate the trajectory of transition is through its symbolic function in recasting narratives of statehood and legitimacy, or through the construction of a shared usable past. Defined by Grzymala-Busse as "the historical record of party accomplishments to which the elites can point, and the public perceptions of this record—the repertoire of shared political references," I argue the concept of usable pasts is helpful in illuminating how transitional justice debates and processes have played out during Tunisia's contested political transition.[14]

When looking at Tunisia, post-transition reconfigurations of governing coalitions are useful in dividing Tunisia's transitional justice process into three phases. The first phase, which I have referred to as interim justice, characterized transitional justice in the immediate aftermath of the revolution, which preceded Tunisia's first post-transition elections in October 2011. The second phase saw a consolidation of these ad hoc processes, and their centralization into a ministry of transitional justice under Ennahdha. The third phase saw a retreat from transitional justice and the dissolution of the ministry as a technocratic government assumed power.

Table 1: Three phases of Tunisia's transition and transitional justice

	Phase I	Phase II	Phase III
Time frame	14 January 2011– 23 October 2011	23 October 2011 –29 January 2014	29 January 2014– 23 October 2014
Governing coalition/ authority	Interim governments of Mohamed Ghannouchi & Beji Caid Essebsi; Ben Achour Commission	Ennahdha-led "Troika" coalition in the National Constituent Assembly	Mehdi Jomaa's technocratic non-party coalition in the National Constituent Assembly
Transitional justice measures	Commission on Corruption and Human Rights Abuses	Ministry of Human Rights and Transitional Justice; National Dialogue on Transitional Justice; Law on Transitional Justice	Commission on Truth and Dignity; Human Rights Courts

Antecedents: Tunisia under Zine al-Abidine Ben Ali

On 7 November 1987, Zine al-Abidine Ben Ali became Tunisia's second post-independence president. Ben Ali assumed power through a non-violent coup in which he deposed Habib Bourguiba, who had ruled since 1956.[15] Bourguiba, Tunisia's first president, was sole leader of the Destourian or Constitutional movement, who presided over a deeply autocratic regime.

Political pluralism was obliterated in the young Tunisian state through the repression of opponents within the Destourian movement, Marxists, and nascent pan-Arab nationalists.[16] Although at the time of the 2011 Tunisian revolution protesters demanded the "*dégagement*" of Ben Ali and his ruling party, the *Rassemblement Constitutionnel Démocratique* (RCD), it was Ben Ali's predecessor Bourguiba who first established Tunisia as an authoritarian single-party state, forging state institutions in the image of his modernist secular Destourian ideology.[17] Thus, Bourguiba left Tunisia with a dual legacy of authoritarianism and secular modernism, a political legacy which Destourian successor parties have continued to embrace. In fact, the two pillars of Bourguiba's modernist secular legacy that have been reclaimed by post-2011 revolution Destourian movements are the promotion of public education and the Personal Status Code, which protected women's rights.[18] More recently, in the context of campaigning for the November 2014 presidential elections, Destourians have attempted to position authoritarian stability against the turbulence of transition.[19] Furthermore, the privileging of the secular state over Islam that was later challenged by Tunisia's emergent Islamist movements.[20] Indeed, contemporary secular parties, such as Nida Tounes, continue to object to a renegotiation of this equilibrium that would allow for a greater space for religion in public life.

With Bourguiba's authoritarianism under stress in the 1980s from increasingly assertive opposition movements, chief among them a growing Islamist opposition movement united under the banner of the Islamic Tendency Movement, Ben Ali sought to characterize his 1987 coup as constituting a break from Tunisia's authoritarian past, reaching out to formerly repressed groups, including Islamists, in a brief period of apparent liberalization. At this time there was a hope that Ben Ali's coup would herald a break from Bourguiba's authoritarianism.[21] To be sure, this view was not entirely unwarranted. Ben Ali amnestied thousands of political prisoners, abolished the practice of holding the office of presidency for life, ratified the United Nations convention against torture, and even entered into a dialogue with Islamists, which he had previously been tasked with repressing as Bourguiba's minister of interior.[22] Ben Ali also established a new ruling party, the RCD.

At the same time, Ben Ali sought to assume the mantle of leadership of the Destourian political tradition and maintain the appearance of secular nationalist continuity. This brief flirtation with liberalisation was quickly followed by a prolonged period of intense repression, which saw the RCD establish near total control of not just the state apparatus, but also the economy and media.[23]

Nevertheless, despite these early moves to liberalize, Ben Ali proved well placed to act as a catalyst for Tunisia's transformation into one of the world's most repressive states. As Bourguiba's former minister of interior, Ben Ali built his career within repressive security apparatuses that the violent repression of domestic opponents. Among these was the Islamic Tendency Movement, a forerunner to Ennahdha, and a collection of political movements which later formed the post-revolution Popular Front, a Marxist–nationalist coalition of parties.[24] In the aftermath of the 14 January 2011 revolution, Ennahdha would emphasize its victimhood at the hands of Bourguiba and Ben Ali, as Islamists became the primary target of state repression.[25]

In the context of the above, Tunisia's 2011 transition raised immediate questions as to the extent to which the state would be transformed in the aftermath of Ben Ali's ousting. Would the 2011 transition constitute a complete break from Tunisia's post-independence Destourian tradition and the 1959 Constitution, or would a transition be effected under the Constitution?

Throughout Tunisia's three phases of transition,[26] transitional justice draft laws and the debates they generated set contested boundaries for transitional justice measures. In many cases domestic political actors which embraced Destourianism feared that transitional justice constitutes a vehicle for dismantling the Destourian state.[27] The next part of this contribution reflects on the expanding boundaries of transitional justice.

Phase I: Transition and limiting the scope of justice

On the eve of the wave of nationwide demonstrations that brought about Ben Ali's removal from office, the RCD exercised near total control of the public sphere; however, there remained multiple sites of resistance and regime contestation that had emerged during his 23-year rule.[28] Of course, while Tunisia's experience might prove instructive for single-party states in the Arab world, it is important to recall that Tunisia did not experience a state of armed conflict. Thus, while conflicts in Libya and Syria produced hundreds of thousands of conflict-related victims at the point of regime transition and reinforced identity lines in divided societies, Tunisia was faced with confronting the legacy of long-term repression. In the case of Tunisia, this legacy spanned decades and included both bodily harm and economic abuses.[29] In addition, it should also be noted that the Tunisian military never played a dominant role in national politics, to the extent that can be observed elsewhere, such as in Egypt. These factors meant that salient political contestations took place within the

National Constituent Assembly (NCA), among Tunisia's political parties with the involvement of labor unions, and not between the military and the executive as in Egypt, or between armed militias and nascent political institutions as in Libya.

During Phase I of Tunisia's transition, the country experienced two critical political transformations. The first occurred on 14 January when President Ben Ali fled Tunisia into exile in Saudi Arabia. However, despite the dramatic images that followed Ben Ali's ousting, the RCD elite sought to limit the extent of change to the departure of the president. Ben Ali's prime minister Mohamed Ghannouchi, a senior RCD functionary who served as prime minister from 1999 until 2011, attempted to move into the office of the presidency and form a new government.[30] Ghannouchi sought to assume the vacated presidency under the terms of the 1959 Constitution and therefore limit the depth of political change by maintaining constitutional continuity with the Destourian state. Therefore, although Ghannouchi resigned from the discredited RCD ruling party on 18 January, and established a national unity government with representatives from opposition parties and civil society, he could not shed his association with the old regime, and was thus deemed unsuitable by those who took to the streets seeking a broader transition. As a result, in the days following Ben Ali's flight protesters returned to the streets to demand a withdrawal of senior RCDists from the transitional government.

In response to these demonstrations, on 27 February Ghannouchi resigned. His resignation marked the beginning of Tunisia's second political transition in a little over a month.[31] On 27 February another prominent political figure from Tunisia's past, Béji Caïd Essebsi, a former minister of interior under Bourguiba and a leading member of the Destourian movement, assumed leadership of Tunisia's transition. He would lead the country until National Constituent Assembly elections were held on 23 October 2011.

Under Essebsi, transitional justice addressed a narrow scope of demands related to human rights abuses and violence perpetrated during the revolution, as well as the Ben Ali family's corruption. While the Tunisian revolution did not mirror levels of violence witnessed elsewhere, Ben Ali's violent suppression of public protests produced over 300 fatalities and 2,000 injuries.[32] Despite the comparatively low fatality figures during the revolution itself, the focus on accounting for past human rights abuses was nevertheless limited to 28 days that followed Bouazizi's act of self-immolation.[33]

The Commission for the Investigation of Truth and Abuses was the first investigative body established to account for human rights abuses committed under Ben Ali. In addition, with Ben Ali and his wife Leila Trabelsi absconding to Saudi Arabia, both avoided the prospect of criminal accountability, except through largely symbolic *in absentia* trials, held later in 2011. In addition to the investigation of fatalities and injuries stemming from the revolution, two more commissions were established. One addressed graft and illegally acquired financial assets by the Ben Ali family, and the other addressed urgently needed political reforms in order to set out a framework for Tunisia's transitional process. In sum, Phase I of Tunisia's transition was characterized by narrow responses adopting a restricted temporal and material scope that limited attempts to account for past abuses to a narrow window, starting with the self-immolation of Bouazizi in December 2010. These early justice initiatives constituted improvised responses on the part of transitional elites, wary of attempts to broaden the scope of transitional justice to include a wider set of abuses perpetrated under Bourguiba and Ben Ali in an attempt to preserve Destourian continuity. As such, even at this early stage, competing transitional justice demands were increasingly viewed as constituting contested political projects aimed at recasting the Tunisian state in the aftermath of revolution.

As mentioned earlier, attempts to restrict the scope of justice measures often reflect instrumental attempts to secure regime survival. In January 2011, in an attempt to placate demonstrators, Ben Ali delivered a televised address in which he promised to hold accountable those individuals responsible for acts of violence against protesters. During this address, aimed at promising concessions so as to maintain his hold on power, he pledged to establish three investigative commissions: a commission for the investigation of corruption, a commission for the investigation of human rights abuses, and a commission for political reform.[34] The second would later become the aforementioned Commission for the Investigation of Truth and Abuses. It is therefore not surprising that his immediate successors, many of whom held positions of influence under either Bourguiba or Ben Ali, established commissions which were limited in scope and mandate.[35]

In addition to the three investigative commissions, two of which were explicitly tasked with the investigation of past abuses—both bodily harm and financial—criminal prosecutions were also initiated against former regime elites alleged to be responsible for acts of violence against protesters from 17 December 2010 until 14 January 2011 and acts of corruption. These proceedings took place before any substantial effort to reform Tunisia's judiciary took place, but nonetheless delivered convictions against a former minister of interior, and a handful of heads of Tunisia's anti-terrorist and special police units directly implicated. However, some of these convictions would later be overturned on appeal. The most prominent of these trials was held in June 2012 before the Le Kef Military Tribunal, which sentenced Ben Ali to life in prison *in absentia* for the killings of protesters. In a separate trial held in 2011, Ben Ali and his wife were convicted of financial crimes that included the embezzlement of public funds. These convictions resulted in 35-year prison sentences.[36]

During Phase I early financial compensation programs were also created for families of martyrs and those injured in the revolution. Within Tunisia, these payments provoked significant debate as there were no clear criteria for making a determination as to whether or not an individual's injury was the result of revolutionary activity, and rumors abounded of individuals who had committed criminal acts such as looting benefiting from these programs.[37] Human Rights Watch also noted the lack of criteria for determining whether or not an individual had been injured by the state while participating in the revolution, or criteria that would establish the level of financial compensation of each victim.[38]

At this time, the question of the political exclusion of former regime officials was debated, in the context of the ratification of an electoral law to enable Tunisia's first post-Ben Ali elections. Tunisia's first steps toward restricting the political participation of former regime officials were taken in the form of electoral laws that established the legal framework for Tunisia's National Constituent Assembly (NCA), which was the legislative body tasked with guiding Tunisia's constitution drafting process. It is important to note here that these laws were relatively narrow in temporal scope, in that they only applied to individuals for activities or positions held under the Ben Ali regime and not under Bourguiba.

The body tasked with implementing political exclusion in Tunisia was the High Independent Authority for Elections (ISIE), which was established through Decree Law 27. This law also contained Tunisia's first legal prohibitions on the political participation of former regime officials. It banned anyone who had held a senior function within the RCD during the past ten years, or had called for the re-election of Ben Ali in 2014 from serving on ISIE. In turn ISIE was the body that drafted the electoral law for Tunisia's NCA elections, which excluded former RCD officials from standing in elections or membership in political parties. Article 15 of the NCA electoral law excluded three categories of individuals. These categories included former ministers within Ben Ali governments, with the exception of those who served as ministers but did not belong to the RCD, persons who held positions of responsibility within the RCD, and persons who publicly called for Ben Ali's re-election in 2014. The first two categories of excluded persons were excluded on the grounds of affiliation with the Ben Ali regime alone, while the last category was more ambiguous because some individuals claimed they were unknowing *munachidine*, or "those who implored" in Tunisian Arabic, because their names were added to endorsement lists without their knowledge.[39]

Table 2: Phase I—Transitional justice: Time frame, scope and boundaries

Transitional justice measures	Mandate	Time frame
Commission for the Investigation of Truth and Human Rights Abuses	To investigate killings and injuries carried out by security forces	10 December 2010– 14 January 2011
Fact Finding Commission on Corruption and Embezzlement	To investigate graft and corruption under Ben Ali	7 November 1987en;14 January 2011
Political exclusion	Exclude former RCD officials and Ben Ali supporters from contesting NCA elections	7 November 1987– 14 January 2011
Financial compensation	Provide financial compensation for those injured or for families of those killed during the revolution	10 December 2010– 14 January 2011

In sum, during the months following 14 January, transitional justice measures were adopted with a narrow temporal mandate and limited scope. As Table 2 highlights, from investigative commissions to political exclusion, transitional justice measures focused on abuses carried out in the context of the Tunisian revolution itself, or in relation to financial crimes from a broader time frame that spanned the scope of the Ben Ali regime.[40]

In fact, for Essebsi, and later Nida Tounes, a narrow time frame and scope for transitional justice measures were essential for a Destourian attempt to recover a usable past, defined by Grzymala-Busse as a shared historical record and reference points between the party and wider public, in the aftermath of the collapse of the discredited RCD under Ben Ali. For Destourians, the restriction of accountability measures to Ben Ali's inner circle meant that the movement could continue to reproduce the modernist narrative of the Destourian movement, which emphasized its more progressive characteristics, such as the provision of public education and the protection of women's rights.

Phase II: Expanding the boundaries and scope of transitional justice

During the second phase, Tunisia witnessed the expansion of transitional justice in both time frame and scope through a national dialogue on transitional justice to include a wider set of crimes and include the Bourguiba era. During this phase it was not surprising that Destourians continued to express a preference for a narrower temporal scope for transitional justice measures, which would maintain a focus on the Ben Ali regime. On the other hand Ennahdha, which includes within its ranks numerous victims of rights abuses spanning both the Bourguiba and Ben Ali regimes, strongly advocated a broader temporal mandate. This position was also echoed by political parties within the leftist Popular Front, which were subjected to repression under Bourguiba.[41]

On 23 October 2011, Ennahdha's triumph in Tunisia's first national post-Ben Ali elections marked the beginning of a process of widening the temporal scope of transitional justice. Ennahdha initially sought to invite parties elected to the newly formed NCA into a national unity government, but in the end it entered into a coalition government with two smaller secular parties: the Congrès pour la République (CPR) and Ettakatol. Under this coalition government, known as the Troika, Ennahdha was first faced with the task of ratifying an interim constitution that would serve as a framework for governance, while the NCA carried out the process of drafting a constitution. Following the ratification of an interim constitution, the Law on the Interim Organisation of Public Powers of Tunisia known colloquially as the "little constitution," the NCA elected an interim president, Moncef Marzouki, a long-time human rights advocate from the CPR. Marzouki in turn appointed Hamadi Jebali from Ennahdha to form a government, which was presented to the NCA on 24 December. With long-time opposition movements assuming power, the limited justice measures adopted under Essebsi would find themselves subsumed by a concerted effort to broaden transitional justice measures to place Tunisia's entire history as an independent state under the lens of extraordinary justice measures.

Throughout Phase II, Ennahdha worked to advance a coherent transitional justice program, embracing it as a means of symbolically breaking with the past. Even within its first party program, drafted after the revolution, Ennahdha made explicit the movement's commitment to transitional justice. The program stated: "The Ennahdha movement proposes to Tunisians to establish a political system that eradicates the roots of dictatorship."[42] Here it is important to point out that, just as neo-Destourian parties such as Nida Tounes sought to reclaim elements of Tunisia's Destourian past, so too did Ennahdha seek to create a usable past centered on the movement's experience of having been the primary target of repression under Ben Ali. Beya Jouadi, an Ennahdha deputy in the NCA, noted that while other political groups also suffered, such as Marxists, it was Islamists who had the greatest number of victims of state repression within their ranks.[43]

In line with this commitment, Ennahdha took the step of establishing a dedicated ministry for transitional justice. Tunisia's Ministry of Human Rights and Transitional Justice was established on 19 January 2012, and became the epicenter of transitional justice planning under the NCA government. This was essential for Ennahdha, because it viewed the unreformed judiciary and courts as incapable of being entrusted with a coordinating role in the transitional justice process.[44] It also ensured that the earlier investigative commission report on abuses during the revolution, which was truncated by a narrow temporal mandate, would not be the last word on transitional justice.

Ennahdha's Minister of Human Rights and Transitional Justice, Samir Dilou, himself a former political prisoner, quickly placed the new ministry at the core of transitional justice policy-making and debates.[45] However, with Ennahdha strongly committed to advancing transitional justice, secular parties began to accuse Ennahdha of instrumentalizing transitional justice in order to weaken political opponents, particularly those parties which embraced Tunisia's Destourian tradition such as Nida Tounes. In response to these allegations, Dilou claimed that the ministry's role was not to impose Ennahdha's vision of transitional justice, but instead he argued that the role of the ministry focused on coordinating and facilitating communication between the different stakeholders in government and civil society.[46] Nevertheless, Dilou used his ministerial platform to make explicit his opposition to ex-RCD members returning to government.[47]

The Ministry of Human Rights and Transitional Justice effectively launched Tunisia's official transitional justice process in a national seminar on 14 April 2012, held in coordination with international stakeholders such as the UNDP and ICTJ, who would both assume significant roles in terms of providing technical assistance. Illustrative of the broad consensus within the governing Troika on transitional justice was the attendance of Tunisia's "three presidencies": the President of the Republic Moncef Marzouki, the President of the National Constituent Assembly Mostafa Ben Jafaar, and the Prime Minister Hamadi Jebali.

Tunisia's National Dialogue and law on transitional justice

Tunisia's National Dialogue on transitional justice was launched just weeks after, and marked the beginning of a national consultation that sought to solicit the input of broad sections of Tunisian society in a draft transitional justice law. However, rather than bringing about consensus, the law on transitional justice that emerged from the National Dialogue further highlighted a deepening of the Destourian–Islamist divide among domestic proponents of transitional justice. While the National Dialogue sought to advance transitional justice through a national consultation, Ennahdha pushed forward demands for justice that would place both the Ben Ali and Bourguiba eras under the scope of extraordinary justice measures. Indeed, the question of whether or not to include historic abuses dating back to 1955, alongside more immediate abuses perpetrated over the course of December 2010 and January 2011, as well as the question of whether or not to include the post-revolutionary period, provoked significant debate among Tunisia's political parties in parallel to the National Dialogue process.

In an attempt to bundle together the divergent, and at times competing demands voiced through Tunisia's National Dialogue, Samir Dilou established a technical commission to oversee the national consultation. This commission was established as an independent body, in order to grant it a measure of independence, and address mounting criticisms that the Ennahdha-led coalition government, or the Troika, was agenda-setting transitional justice debates.[48]

The technical commission's duties were relatively broad and included the organization of the National Dialogue and public consultations, selecting members of sectorial committees for the National Dialogue, recording the results of the Dialogue, drafting a final report, and finally preparing the draft law on transitional justice. In relation to national consultations on transitional justice, these were carried out from 16 September until 7 October 2012 by six regional commissions.[49]

The Organic Law on Transitional Justice that emerged from the National Dialogue was ratified in the context of a major political crisis, in which the

Ennahdha-led Troika government was confronted with the prospect of voluntarily relinquishing power; this following the assassination of two prominent Popular Front politicians. This political crisis marked the continuation of a concerted effort on the part of opposition parties to question the legitimacy of the Troika's governance during the prolonged constitution-drafting process. As part of the political deal that saw Ennahdha vacate government for a technocratic government, the party secured the ratification of Samir Dilou's draft law on transitional justice. This subjects Tunisia's entire modern history as an independent state to transitional justice through a 70-article-long piece of legislation. However, its passage remains a subject of controversy as the law was adopted at a time when opposition parties were boycotting the NCA.

On 13 December 2014, Tunisia's NCA adopted the Organic Law on Establishing and Organizing Transitional Justice,[50] which set out a comprehensive package of transitional justice mechanisms and established the Truth and Dignity Commission, which is mandated to carry out a number of tasks related to establishing a factual record of past abuses as stipulated in article 39 of the Organic Law. The Commission's tasks also include the referral of cases to a new specialized human rights court for prosecution. It is also entrusted with the establishment of a separate committee for the vetting of state institutions. The specialized judicial chamber is expected to hear cases related to gross human rights abuses, including deliberate killings, rape, and any form of sexual violence, torture, enforced disappearances, and executions without fair trial guarantees.[51] Furthermore, in addition to the human rights court's authority to initiate criminal cases stemming from abuses carried out under the previous regimes, it also has the crucial authority to re-open cases that have already been prosecuted. The transitional justice law also commits the state to undertaking a vetting process that will target the entire state administration.

Importantly, the Organic Law sets 1 July 1955 as its start date, and covers the period of time until the ratification of the law on 13 December 2014. The latter date potentially allows the commission to explore episodes of violence that have marred Tunisia's transition in the aftermath of the 14 January revolution; however, according to Ennahdha, the expectation is that the commission will focus most of its efforts on the 1990s.[52]

In short, for Ennahdha, but also leftist parties which now make up the Popular Front, it was important that the Organic Law extended back to before the establishment of the Tunisian Republic, so as to include crimes committed under both Bourguiba and Ben Ali. Meanwhile, those parties which draw upon Tunisia's Destourian tradition were insistent that the commission also investigate human rights abuses that were alleged to have occurred in the post-revolution period, while resisting attempts to delve too deeply into the pre-Ben Ali period.[53]

Table 3: Phase II—Scope and boundaries of transitional justice

Transitional justice measures	Mandate	Time frame
Ministry of Human Rights and Transitional Justice	Coordinate transitional justice measures	1955—2011
National Dialogue on Transitional Justice	National consultation on transitional justice	1955—2011
Organic Law on Transitional Justice	Establish legal framework and institutions to pursue transitional justice	1955—2013

Phase III: Narrow or broad justice?

Although the Ministry for Human Rights and Transitional Justice saw itself incorporated into the Ministry of Justice, the Organic Law did establish what is arguably the Ministry's successor organization, the Truth and Dignity Commission, which has a mandate to oversee transitional justice. This is defined by the Organic Law as:

> an integrated process of mechanisms and methods used to understand and deal with past human rights violations by revealing their truths, and holding those responsible accountable, providing reparations for the victims and restituting them in order to achieve national reconciliation, preserve and document the collective memory, guarantee the non-recurrence of such violations and transition from an authoritarian state to a democratic system which contributes to consolidating the system of human rights.[54]

With commissioners appointed in 2014, the Truth and Dignity Commission has already found itself at the focal point of contestation for Nida Tounes, which argues that the law on transitional justice should be revised to narrow the commission's power[55] or be outright withdrawn[56]. Political exclusion debates also continued to cast a shadow over transitional justice processes, as strong demands were advanced within the NCA to exclude RCD members and sympathizers from post-Ben Ali politics. In fact, Ennahdha's deputy speaker of the NCA, Meherzia Labidi, voiced a strong objection to political exclusion on the grounds that it was a hallmark of the

Ben Ali regime, which had banned Ennahdha. Labidi also pointed to Libya's political isolation law, noting that "exclusion will lead the country to war in Libya."[57]

In May 2014, Tunisia took a step back from electoral exclusion when the NCA failed to adopt a political exclusion clause within the electoral law authorizing national elections. Article 167 would have banned former RCD elites from participation in Tunisia's 2014 elections. The rejection, in a closely contested vote, saw the CPR and Ettatakol support political exclusion. The vote, however, divided Ennahdha. In short, the rejection of the political exclusion clause signaled a retreat from exclusionary politics. The result was that RCD successor parties, such as Moubadara, were permitted to contest Tunisia's parliamentary and presidential elections in October and November 2014.

Table 4: Phase III—Transitional justice scope and boundaries

Transitional justice measures	Mandate	Time frame
Commission for Truth and Dignity	To investigate bodily harm and financial abuses carried out under Bourguiba and Ben Ali	1 July 1955– 13 December 2013
Political exclusion	None—law not ratified	None

Conclusions

The fall of Ben Ali in January 2011 ushered in a period of rapid political change within Tunisia, and also acted as a catalyst for popular revolts elsewhere in the Middle East and North Africa, which either challenged or toppled authoritarian regimes that had hitherto been seen as resistant to democratization. As transitional justice scholars and practitioners attempt to understand demands for justice in the context of Arab Spring transitions, Tunisia can serve as an illustrative case study, given how far its transition process has advanced from 2011 until 2014.

While transitional justice in Tunisia was initially characterized by a number of narrow attempts to address the legacy of a wide array of past abuses, ranging from civil and political rights abuses to acts of corruption, it later became embedded in a national dialogue that sought to translate transitional justice demands into a comprehensive piece of legislation that would guide the overall process.

Nevertheless, while Tunisia's national dialogue resulted in a draft law on transitional justice that was presented to the Ministry and the NCA government in October 2012, it was only ratified in December 2013. Transitional justice debates in Tunisia remain politically discordant, as Tunisian elites seek to renegotiate the identity of the new post-Ben Ali state. It is within this context that the temporal boundaries of transitional justice have expanded since the revolution. The first investigative commission to examine human rights abuses was mandated to investigate only abuses that took place after 17 December 2010. Today, many Tunisians, in particular Ennahdha, express a preference for transitional justice mechanisms that explore abuses dating back even before the founding of the modern Tunisian state in 1956.

These debates over the temporal boundaries of transitional justice reflect divergent perspectives on Tunisia's modern history and the secular state. In the context of an emergent post-authoritarian political system, these debates also play out in the context of heated electoral competition. As an opposition movement that was the target of extreme repression by the state, it is not surprising that Ennahdha's leadership—many of whom were victims of long-term detention and torture—has embraced transitional justice as a means of deconstructing the modernist narratives of Bourguiba and Ben Ali. For Ennahdha, the suffering of its membership constitutes a core component of the party's *usable past*.

In Tunisia, transitional justice has become perhaps one of the most divisive questions that emerged from the January 2011 revolution, with ongoing contestations over the temporal mandates of investigative bodies, criminal prosecutions, dismissals, and the limits of political exclusion. And as political actors in the Middle East and North Africa attempt to carve out usable pasts in the aftermath of violent upheavals, the scope and boundaries of transitional justice will do much more than set the parameters of the periods of time subjected to extraordinary justice, but will also constitute the main site of contestation for post-revolutionary legitimacy.

PART II

TRANSITIONAL JUSTICE EXPERIENCES IN THE MENA REGION

COMPARATIVE LESSONS

6

REFRAMING GENDER NARRATIVES THROUGH TRANSITIONAL JUSTICE IN THE MAGHREB

Doris H. Gray and *Terry C. Coonan*

"And thus we have made you a just community that you will be witnesses over the people and the Messenger will be a witness over you."[1]

In recent decades, the field of transitional justice has addressed how states that are moving from war to peace or from authoritarian rule to democracy can best come to terms with legacies of mass abuse.[2] Truth commissions are an integral part of transitional justice processes that also include criminal justice, in the form of pursuing former perpetrators at various levels, reparations, financial, medical, psycho-social, and institutional reform. In isolation, these mechanisms are limited in their effectiveness, but as a combined effort they may lead to reconciliation, justice, forgiveness, and a rescuing of history.[3] Commentators have noted that few truth commissions to date have adequately addressed gender, and in particular the full impact of systemic human rights violations suffered by women under authoritarian regimes.[4] Tunisia, in its ongoing transition from authoritarian rule, is the latest of a number of states that must now confront this challenge.

This chapter focuses on one mechanism currently employed in the Tunisian transitional justice endeavor—that of its national truth commission, and in particular the role of women therein. The chapter examines the gender complexities of the transitional justice task facing Tunisia, and the need to incorporate fully the broader experiences of repression suffered by Tunisian women in the country's truth commission endeavor. The chapter is based on more than ninety personal interviews conducted from 2011 to 2014. Interviewees were selected based on dossiers collected by the Tunisian Ministry of Human Rights and Transitional Justice, human and women's rights organizations, and newly formed victim's rights associations. Effort was made to include women from various parts of the country, in order to avoid focusing only on the capital city of Tunis. The views represented in the following are representative of women who were victims of state-sanctioned repression during the Ben Ali era, regardless of their particular political or religious views or their socio-economic status.

Tunisia is the first Arab Muslim majority country thus far to embark on a genuine transitional justice process: after the overthrow of the regime of Zine el Abidine Ben Ali on 14 January 2011, an event that sparked uprisings throughout North Africa and the Middle East. Since the Tunisian uprising, there have been a number of important milestones.[5] Tunisia held its first free and democratic elections in October 2011, won by the Islamist Ennahda (Renaissance) party. In December 2013, the National Constituent Assembly (NCA) passed the Draft Organic Law on the Organization of Transitional Justice, providing the roadmap by which justice and accountability would be pursued in Tunisia.[5] In October 2014, Tunisia held its second free and democratic elections in which Ennahda lost the majority of votes and the more secular Nidaa Tunis party took the lead. Presidential elections were held a month later. The International Center for Transitional Justice (ICTJ), headquartered in New York, praised the transitional justice law as one that sets out a comprehensive approach for addressing past human rights abuses. In January 2014 the NCA adopted a new constitution, and in May 2014 the NCA approved all fifteen members of a Truth and Dignity Commission (*Instance Verité et Dignité* or IVD), whose task is to account for almost six decades of human rights violations.

On 9 June 2014, Tunisia reached yet another milestone when it formally launched its Truth and Dignity Commission. The 2013 Draft Organic Law tasks the commission with addressing reparations, accountability, institutional reform, vetting, and national reconciliation. The law specifically calls for the creation of a Fund for the Dignity and Rehabilitation of Victims of Tyranny (Article 41), and for special chambers with trained judges to deal with cases of human rights violations (Article 8). Violations against women and children are at the core of issues to be addressed by the Truth and Dignity Commission (Article 4).

These are milestones in a country that has no democratic tradition, a country that passed from French colonial rule to two dictatorships: first Habib Bourguiba (1959–87) and then Zine el Abedine Ben Ali (1987–2011), who deposed Bourguiba in a bloodless coup in 1987 and ruled until his own overthrow in 2011. Given the post-uprising situations in neighboring Libya and also Egypt, Tunisia has no contemporary role model in the Arab Muslim world to follow, and therefore developments in this country are important for the wider MENA region.

Women's rights in Tunisia

Among the most hotly debated topics since the fall of the Ben Ali regime are national identity, and with that the status of women. The issue of women's rights is at the political frontline in post-revolution identity politics. Despite the apparent contradictions between Islamists and more secular feminist approaches, both sides share a common desire to recoup ownership of the women's rights agenda. The issue of Islam versus secularism framed the post-revolution public discourse, as well as the question of women's status, and subsequently became fully politicized. Two of the main justifications of the Ben Ali regime, and the reasons for continued Western support, were Tunisia's exemplary status of women's rights—unparalleled in the MENA region—and the fact that Islamists, successfully portrayed within and outside Tunisia as akin to terrorists, were either in jail or in exile. The Tunisian Personal Status Code of 1956 is one of the most progressive in the Arab world, and has served as an example for neighboring Algeria and Morocco.

Women and transitional justice

Why is it necessary to focus on the gender dimensions of transitional justice? Does this not further divide a society that is already struggling to rebuild after a regime change? The answer to these questions is manifold: transitional justice, as justice in general, reflects cultural norms. Therefore, transitional justice mechanisms can challenge conventional gender norms and in so doing make a vital contribution to the construction of a more gender-egalitarian society.

There are certain unique aspects to the state-sanctioned persecution of political opponents in Tunisia. Under the previous authoritarian regime, many of the so-called "secular" elite supported the repression of the Islamist opposition by subscribing to the regime narrative that successfully portrayed Ennahda members as terrorists, and further depicted female Islamists as anti-modern ideologues intent on rolling back women's rights.[6]

Even though the persecution and repression of women who opposed the regime was similar to the treatment accorded to male opponents, there were distinct differences as well. As a result, Tunisia must now address several decades of gendered human rights abuses. Transitional justice most often addresses human rights violations and crimes perpetrated in public social spaces, whereas persecution and human rights violations committed in private social spaces are often not addressed with the same vigor. Tunisian women were often victims of violations that occurred in private spaces, such as harassment in the home, harassment of children, and invasion of their home by authorities, especially in the absence of men who were imprisoned. The system of *pointage* disproportionately affected women. *Pointage*, a French term that loosely translates as "tallying," required women who were relatives of incarcerated political opponents or who were previously jailed themselves for their political or religious convictions to report to the Ministry of the Interior in the capital city of Tunis several times a week, or to local police stations up to five times a day. This requirement made it impossible to hold a proper job or to take care of children adequately. Recalling this time, Najet Ichawi said: "When I was released from jail, the officer told me: Now you go from the little prison to the big prison that is our country."[7]

Wives of Tunisian political prisoners assumed traditional male roles by becoming heads of households, in effect single mothers, in an Arab Muslim country where single motherhood carries a particular stigma. This led to social isolation in a culture that thrives on community. The women's plight was compounded by economic persecution: political opponents were not allowed to continue their university studies, return to their previous positions, or hold state jobs, and employers were harassed when hiring known regime opponents. Many women were pressured either by police or their own families to divorce their husbands so as to end the police surveillance, persecution, forced unemployment, and harassment. Some succumbed, while others remained steadfast against all odds. All this made it extremely hard for women to provide for themselves or their children. It often rendered women dependent on other family members, who were themselves frequently struggling to make ends meet. This resulted in tensions that often led to various forms of domestic violence. Experts call this "a system of crime gradation at play in the transitional justice discourses."[8] Wassila Zoghlami, the current Ennahda Executive Member in charge of Women and Family, recalled:

> Time stopped for sixteen years and the clock started ticking again when my husband was released from prison. I had spent days, months, years, searching for him. Often I feared he was dead because the police would move him from prison to prison all over the country without telling me where he was. So I would travel all day with my food basket to one prison only to find out when I got to the gate that he had been moved to a prison in another town.[9]

Transitional justice generally addresses violations during a set time period in the past; however, for women, there is often no significant delineation between past and present. Men—and women—who come home after spending years or decades in prison return to their families with mental and physical problems that do not allow for a smooth re-integration into "normal" family life. Men often need to reassert their masculinity, a process that imposes a great burden on wives and mothers. According to Meherzia Ben Abed:

> Both my husband and I were in prison. Our marriage ultimately did not survive, we could not shake the trauma of violence and it became part of our life after prison. We carried that contagious prison poison within us. Unlike many other women, I am not ashamed to talk about this, I think of myself as a survivor of many forms of violence. When I was arrested, they took my two-year-old son along with me to the jail and kept him in a cell adjacent to the one I was tortured in. He heard me screaming when I was tied up like a grilled chicken. I was pregnant at the time. The officers said they would beat the baby out of me. That they did. I was bleeding all over but they would not take me to a hospital until days later.[10]

Transitional justice needs to be restorative justice; it cannot merely address offenses against individuals, but must deal with systematic human rights violations of the types that divide families and communities. In the case of women, the larger issue of domestic violence and sexual harassment will have to be addressed as Ben Abed's case illustrates. This middle-aged woman agreed to meet in Douar Hicher, one of the impoverished, disenfranchised parts of Tunis. She was sitting on a tiny wooden chair in a kindergarten classroom with a naked light bulb dangling from the ceiling, because she felt this was the safest place in which to hold a frank conversation. At the time of her arrest, she had been an Ennahda group leader in Douar Hicher and adjoining Hay Ettadhamen, and knew that her activities could put her at risk. However, as these parts of Tunis have always been under-served by public services, akin to some French *banlieue* on the outskirts of Paris, she had felt that Ennahda's social service projects were a necessity. She continued her story: when the prison officers finally took her to a hospital, the doctors and other patients asked "What did she do?" To which her guards responded, "Overthrow the government." Ben Abed continued: "They looked incredulous and said 'What, she?' I was 26 at the time, of real small stature, not very educated, and from a poor part of town. I did not look like someone who could take on the powerful Ben Ali regime."[11]

Though the fate of female secular regime opponents is well documented, the oppression of female Ennahda members and sympathizers is much less so.[12] Amnesty International documented individual cases of female Islamist prisoners, and also reported on forced break-ups of families. However, much like other international human rights organizations, AI was prevented by the Tunisian government in the 1990s and beyond from collecting data and their staff were eventually barred from entering the country.[13] Some statistics of imprisonment rates in the Middle East and Arab world of 2004 state that Tunisia had the second highest imprisonment rate in the region after Israel.[14]

While the crackdown on so-called Islamists was a widely publicized political project, ostensibly in the pursuit of terrorists, the extent of torture and human rights violations is only slowly being revealed in the years after the uprising. Lesser forms of harassment were chronicled in state-owned media at the time. For example, President Ben Ali had ordered the repression of women who wore headscarves, especially between 1989 and 1992. In the middle of 2003, Ennahda members were again subjected to a campaign of harassment. Women were arrested, taken to local police headquarters, and ordered to remove their scarves. Many were subjected to blackmail as they tried to pursue their professions or their studies and were physically threatened, so as to drive home the lesson of state feminism that was government-sanctioned policy.[15] Safaa, a young woman who was a high school student at the time, remembers that when she started to put on the *hijab* at age fourteen she was taken to a police station in her native Nabeul and told that the pins that tied down her headscarf were considered "deadly weapons." She had to sign a document stating that she did not support a terrorist organization. Safaa said she signed with a false name for fear that her family would be tracked down and face possible imprisonment.

While young veiled Tunisian women were typically perceived as conservative on all levels, Hibou describes these women as embodying another political dimension, namely that they "constitute themselves as modern subjects, fully integrated into society" and present an "alternative form of modernity and feminine emancipation."[16] This is in sharp contrast to the assessment offered by the most prominent women's rights association, the Tunisian Association of Democratic Women (*Association Tunisienne des Femmes Démocrates*, ATFD) whose leaders and members believe that Ennahda women were and are determined to erode women's rights. They describe the Islamist women's ascent to power as a "devastating blow to progress." Regarding the approximate 550 dossiers of female former prisoners (out of 12,000 total) that the Ministry of Human Rights and Transitional Justice has thus far collected, Bakhta El Cadhi Jmour of ATFD says, "I am doubtful there have been that many women prisoners, plus torture and rape are crimes that leave no physical trace so it is impossible to verify these claims."[17]

It is certainly true that sexual violence is nearly impossible to prove years after the fact, and it is also possible that victims of state-sponsored sexual violence may not always describe accurately and exactly what happened to them. It is however unlikely that women, in particular Ennahda women for whom sexual morals are of paramount value, would make up accounts of rape. To the contrary, it is more likely that women will under-report sexual violence for fear of repercussions within their own families and out of shame. Priscilla Hayner, co-founder of the International Center of Transitional Justice (ICTJ) and one of the foremost experts on truth commissions, writes:

> This underreporting is due to a number of factors. In many cultures, rape carries a great deal of social stigma, embarrassment, and shame for the victim, and women are understandably uncomfortable providing testimony about sexual abuse in public hearings, or even private hearings if the details would then be published in a public report. There is also sometimes a general tendency by women to downplay their experiences, emphasizing instead the stories of the men in their families.[18]

While sexual abuse of men is widely known in Tunisia, in part because videos of men raped in prison were posted on the internet, it is commonly assumed that a heterosexual man cannot consent to a homosexual act. Inexplicably, there persists the suspicion that women subjected to sexual violence may actually have consented to the experience.

Transitional or permanent justice

In such gender-divided discourse, what women hear is "You are not a real victim." Sriram uses the term "post-atrocity justice" instead of transitional justice, because ideally the new form of justice will not be transitory but rather the beginning of a justice system that permanently conforms to international human rights standards.[19]

One of the goals of truth commissions is reconciliation. Yet, reconciliation lacks a clear definition, as there are no real benchmarks for measuring forgiveness—the living together of victims and victimizers. Because Tunisia is a small country with a relatively homogenous population of only ten million, victims and perpetrators live in close proximity and are likely to encounter one another. Several women reported in the interviews that they have seen or passed their former tormentors in the street.

Hence it is important to consider carefully how various transitional justice mechanisms can be linked together. Transitional justice refers to both judicial and non-judicial measures that together allow a country to move forward after a period of repression or violence. As Buckley-Zistel argues, the gendered dimensions of transitional justice were initially largely unrecognized and have remained under-researched. Furthermore, when gender and transitional justice are studied, it is often a single themed approach, in that women appear singularly as victims and not as perpetrators or as women who managed to survive successfully in an oppressive climate. Moreover, when women are typically characterized as victims, the emphasis is invariably on sexual violence, perpetuating stereotypical gender categories.

Hayner notes that "[t]he factor that will most fundamentally affect the kind of truth that a commission will document ... is the information management system it uses to collect, organize, and evaluate the huge amounts of information that may be available to it."[20] That is, information collected must not only chronicle what was done by whom to whom, but just as importantly why it happened. The task of the Tunisian Truth Commission at the point of this writing is to define its goals and develop data collection mechanisms. To this end, multiple training workshops have been organized, mostly with the help of international organizations, such as the International Center for Transitional Justice and also the German Konrad Adenauer Stiftung. Methodology needs to address the questions concerning "what kind of truth, and for whom." Hayner argues:

> Ultimately, these questions come down to what purpose a commission is intended to fill. A truth commission's goals may be multi-layered: to reach out to victims, to document and corroborate cases for reparations programs, to come to firm and irrefutable conclusions on controversial cases and patterns of abuse, to engage the country in a process of national healing, to contribute to justice, to write an accessible public report, to outline reforms, or to give victims a voice. Each of these goals may suggest a different approach to its work.[21]

Most women interviewed for this chapter expressed the view that the current transitional justice process should aim not only at dealing with past violations, but also address the issue of violence against women more broadly.

In addition to the above mentioned ICTJ, the United Nations Development Programme has also been involved in the Tunisian transitional justice project since the beginning. According to UNDP officials, post-revolution Tunisian governments came to realize that when states fail to protect citizens, it becomes an international issue. Filippo Di Carpegna of the UNDP office in Tunis refers to an unpublished survey in the Gafsa region concerning reparations already received by victims of the revolution, victims of the 2008 Gafsa uprisings, and victims of the Ben Ali regime. This survey found that financial compensation is not the primary goal of victims. Instead, there is great need for counseling, not a widespread practice in Tunisia, aiming at physical and mental healthcare, and reintegration into the workforce. The same unpublished survey further revealed an overarching desire on the part of victims to make past atrocities known to the wider Tunisian public.

In this regard, truth commissions also serve the vital goal of correcting a singular account of history, in the sense that for the first time since independence from France, multiple narratives of historical events can be heard. In fact, the findings of truth commissions can pave the way for a more accurate historical understanding of the past. Tunisians will have to confront and reconcile their differences when for decades they have been indoctrinated to think of themselves as one people; a people moreover that benefited from the most progressive legislation on women's rights in the Arab world. In reality, only a certain segment of the population benefited from those rights, namely those who towed the line either by wholehearted or at least expedient support of Ben Ali's dictatorship. Though Islamists were the greatest number of victims of state repression, according to Mullin, "the country as a whole was subject to everyday violence and repression of the state."[22] The fate of more secular regime opponents has been well chronicled and Sihem Bensedrine, one of the most well-known critics of Ben Ali, is now head of the Tunisian Truth Commission.

Religion and truth telling

More often than not, women are conditioned to accept violence, to be modest, to talk about the trials and tribulations of their husbands rather than their own. Women need to tell complex stories both of their victimization and of their resistance and survival.[23]

In studying the role of women in truth commissions in a variety of countries, Godwin Phelps observes:

If we recognize the central role that language plays in political oppression, how the use of language is appropriated from an oppressive regime's victims, then our traditional ways of thinking about revenge and retribution might be expanded. If a victim wants a balancing—an "accounting," to "get her own back," to "settle the score"—getting back the ability to use language for oneself might indeed be seen as a significant kind of retribution.[24]

Because the majority of female victims of Tunisian state violence were women with a strong religious orientation, the truth commission includes a religious scholar, Azzouz Chawali. Explaining the inclusion of a religious authority, Mohsen Sahbani of the Ministry of Human Rights and Transitional Justice points out the importance of Anglican bishop Desmond Tutu in the South African Truth and Reconciliation Commission, and the vital role that Catholic church leaders played in Latin American transitional justice efforts.[25] A member of the Truth and Dignity Commission explains the Islamic religious context that informs the Tunisian transitional justice mandate:

> The prophet was first and foremost a witness, a witness to the revelation and a witness to the world around him. The revelation came to right the wrongs in this world. Victims need to be true to the Islamic tradition of bearing witness. As well, perpetrators need to understand that to come forward and admit to their crimes is within the context of forgiveness. Though they must face justice in this world and be held accountable for their deeds, they will face peace for their souls if they own up to the wrongs they have committed and ask for forgiveness. Victims or perpetrator, almost all concerned are Muslims. The concept of forgiveness is very important in Islam, most of the ninety-nine names of God pertain to His grace, mercy and forgiveness.[26]

Though there are some high-profile cases of gendered abuse, it is important that the testimony of ordinary Tunisian women informs the transitional justice process. The ordeal of Ouidad Larayedh, wife of Ali Larayedh, former prime minister (2013–14) and Minister of the Interior (2011–12), is a case in point. Ali Larayedh has been an Ennahda member since 1981 and was president of its executive council. He was first arrested in 1987 at the end of Bourguiba's rule and sentenced to death. Briefly released when Ben Ali took power, he was rearrested in 1990 and imprisoned for fifteen years, thirteen of which were in isolation. Videos of him having (forced) sex with men were posted on the internet. His wife Ouidad was filmed being raped and the video was shown to her husband in an attempt to break his spirit. She has never spoken publicly about her torture and though her testimony would lend credibility to the procedure, it is not certain that she will do so before the Truth and Dignity Commission. Some senior Ennahda members agree with her continued silence, believing that if she were to testify, the transitional justice project could face even greater accusations from secular political parties and critics that it is a partisan Ennahda project. The challenge remains to convince ordinary Tunisians to come forward without encouragement from such prominent figures as Ouidad Larayedh. "It needs to become clear who the real feminists in this country were, namely those ordinary women who survived under tremendous hardship rather than those who espoused human and women's rights without any risk to themselves," one Ennahda member stated.

Najet Ichawi spent two years in prison and was briefly jailed together with secular women's rights activists. She therefore feels her testimony cannot be disputed in secular circles:

> This is a historic moment. But I feel the truth commissioners must visit women in their homes, they cannot expect that women will come out and testify. Even when those meetings are not public, in small towns, everyone will know what is going on and women will not want to be seen going into a building where there is a truth commission. For one, it will remind them of being in front of a tribunal that sentenced them in the first place and second, because they don't want everyone in town—and often not even their own families—to know what happened to them. They worked so hard to leave this cruel time behind; they worked on forgetting and building a new life. All this is in jeopardy if they testify. I did speak about my torture on TV once. I am tired of speaking about these events. But most importantly, my 16-year-old daughter asked me to stop. She has endured comments at school from classmates and teachers. She wants this to be behind us. She wants to lead a normal life now.[27]

During the interview with Najet—as with the above-mentioned Ben Abed—she declined to meet in any of the omnipresent street-side coffee shops in Tunis. Instead, she opted for a tiny, backstreet office that is used by a women's association. Wrestling with tears as she recounted her conflict about testifying or not:

> I may speak out again if for no other reason than to make sure that violence against women will no longer be tolerated. If men get away with this even after the revolution, there will be continued acceptance of violence against women. Police feel immune from prosecution and continue to harass and violate women with impunity. So now is the time to reveal all this and put an end to it once and for all. If men know there is no punishment for rape or violence against women, why should they stop? Saying "sorry" will not be enough.[28]

Najet Ichawi was one of those who benefited from a program that reinstated victims to their former jobs after the uprising, and she returned to her previous profession as a school teacher. Some of her colleagues resented that after sixteen years of absence she was given a rank and position as if she had never left. "I just looked at them and said: would you like to trade places with me? That was the end of that discussion."

New gender norms

Latin American feminists have coined the slogan: "Democracy in the country and in the home."[29] This maxim may well describe the task facing post-authoritarian Tunisia. As the country is in the process of moving from authoritarian rule to democracy, transitional justice is not just about law or justice, but about creating a new sense of gender norms; and in a broader sense, a new national identity. In this process, managing expectations is crucial. It will be important to see how the long-term operation of institutions and institutional reform efforts incorporate new gendered rules. Gender scholars are familiar with the fact that formal institutions may guarantee gender equality and rights for all, while informal gender constraints can simultaneously operate to undercut formal rules of equality and to "fill in" the institutional spaces where strict formal rules of equality are "absent or un(der)enforced."[30]

This was the case in Morocco, the only country in the Middle East North African (MENA) region that has undergone a transitional justice process with its Equity and Reconciliation Commission (ERC) in 2004. This commission, initiated by King Mohammed VI himself, addressed the so-called "years of lead" under his father King Hassan II. The ERC focused primarily on a narrow group of victims, namely men accused of having been involved with the attempted coup against King Hassan II in 19971 and 1972. It was a pre-Arab uprising experiment in transitional justice that did not follow regime change as is most often the case. With regards to women in that process, Dennerlein writes: "The official discourse on women and political violence is a cacophonous one with openings and closures at different levels."[31] Accounts of the ordeal of women did not follow a clear procedure, nor were their testimonies gathered in a manner that would allow for an unambiguous understanding of what happened. She describes the ERC as a "space of conflict and negotiation over the course of the politics of gender and the degree of its governmentalization, [that] expresses the multi-layered and ambivalent character of the current Moroccan situation."[32]

Given the evolution of human rights and international law concerning women's experiences, the definition of women's rights in transitional justice remains, according to O'Rourke, a "moving target." This is especially the case because women are not only primary victims, but more often than men they are often perceived and classified as secondary victims. This secondary victim classification mostly pertains to women who are persecuted and/or imprisoned on imputed grounds, i.e. because they are either wives, sisters, daughters, mothers, or otherwise related to men who are engaged in proscribed political or religious activities. "The strictures of the human rights canon reveal a web of public and private harms against women in the context of political violence." It is important to recognize that this web of gender-based harms poses particular challenges. "The image of the web is apt: the web describes the connections between different types of harms against women, identifying the relationship of public and private harms." However, Hend Bouziri, a leader of Tunissiet, one of the new post-revolution women's rights associations, notes that the term "secondary victim" is not appropriate in Tunisia, because the majority of female victims fall into that category. "These women suffered the most and for the longest duration of time. Also, they are the most vulnerable population today. Some have spoken publicly and as a result were harassed by former state security and threatened if they would not promise to return to silence."[33]

This reality of "forced silence" strongly suggests that one of the most important tasks facing the Truth and Dignity Commission will be to counter and indeed to "fill in" such gaps in the Tunisian national narrative. The blurred distinction between "primary" and "secondary" victims in the Tunisian experience of repression further suggests that the traditional "hierarchy of victimization" should be fundamentally challenged in the workings of the Truth and Dignity Commission.

Indeed, the experiences of previous national truth commissions in addressing gender and human rights violations should greatly inform the work that awaits the Tunisian commission. Whereas initial Latin American Truth Commissions in Argentina (1984) and Chile (1991) did not focus on gender as a critical element of truth-seeking, this changed considerably in truth commissions that followed. While their mandates were formally gender-neutral, truth commissions in South Africa (1998), Guatemala (1999), and Peru (2003) ultimately paid notable attention to gender.[34] By way of example, notwithstanding its lack of an explicit gender-based mandate, the Truth and Reconciliation Commission in South Africa employed a number of ad hoc strategies to address gendered human rights violations committed during the apartheid period. Such ad hoc efforts included women-only hearings, collective testimony by women without live television coverage, and trainings for commissioners on gender issues.[35]

A subsequent generation of Truth Commissions, including Sierra Leone (2004), Morocco (2004), Ghana (2005), East Timor (2005), and Liberia (2009) sought to go further, and explicitly included consideration of gender or sexual violence as part of their basic mandates. It is worth noting that simply including gender-based human rights violations in the purview of a truth commission mandate is not alone sufficient to capture such wrongs effectively. How a truth commission defines and prioritizes human rights violations is critically important, as is the methodology that the commission employs to solicit and categorize victim testimony.

General lessons learned from recent national truth commissions begin with the importance of recognizing that women's experiences of political violence have often been neglected in transitional justice approaches. In some cases such as South Africa, the mandate of the Truth and Reconciliation Commission to focus on "extraordinary offenses" and "gross human rights violations" (extrajudicial killings, custodial torture, and forced disappearances) served to marginalize the much more systemic and "ordinary" gender-based wrongs that many South African women endured during the apartheid era. In the case of the Peruvian Truth Commission, women's experiences of human rights violations were often reduced to instances of sexual violence, thereby marginalizing or excluding other harms they also suffered. And in numerous cases of statement-taking by a number of truth commissions, the phenomenon has been observed that many women instinctively testify not about offenses perpetrated against them, but rather about harms done to male family members.[36]

The Tunisian Truth and Dignity Commission is uniquely positioned to benefit from the evolving wisdom of the truth commissions that preceded it regarding gender concerns. To begin with, gender is explicitly included in the truth-seeking mandate of the Tunisian Commission. In the Draft Organic Law that comprises its mandate, the commission is tasked with investigating the particularity of human rights violations perpetrated against "elderly, women, children, those with special needs, and vulnerable groups of society" (Article 4). This concern extends to questions of reparation, where the commission is enjoined to exercise both individual and collective concern for these groups (Article 11). The Draft Organic Law, moreover, explicitly recognizes that "victims" shall include family members who were harmed as a result of their kinship to another victim (Article 10).

Perhaps most importantly, the Draft Organic Law mandates that the Truth and Dignity Commission investigate both gross human rights violations *and* systematic infringements of any human rights committed by the previous regime (Article 3). This mandate is as groundbreaking as it is comprehensive. Importantly, it empowers the Truth and Dignity Commission to consider not just "extraordinary" offenses of political violence, but also the many systematic "ordinary" ones that so deliberately targeted Tunisian women deemed to be opponents of the Ben Ali regime. Also significant is the fact that rape and any form of sexual violence are specifically enumerated by the Draft Organic Law as being among the "gross violations of human rights" that can be investigated and also prosecuted, thereby overcoming the public–private distinction that had defied the best efforts of many preceding truth commissions to impose accountability for gender-based violence.[37]

The experience of prior truth commissions also suggests that particular strategies and policies may be critical to the eventual success of the Tunisian Truth and Dignity Commission in responding to gendered human rights violations. To begin with, the Tunisian commission will benefit from proactive efforts to solicit the testimony of women who suffered violations at the hands of the former regime. Commentators have noted that numerous truth commissions have failed to actively seek out or facilitate the testimony of women who suffered at the hands of preceding regimes. Moreover, in light of the reticence demonstrated by women in South Africa and other nations to speak before truth commissions about their own suffering, Tunisian women should be encouraged to testify about wrongs that they themselves suffered, rather than those suffered by other (male) family members.[38]

In the procedural realm, the Tunisian Truth and Dignity Commission should likewise avail itself of the best gender-inclusive practices developed by preceding truth commissions. As was done in South Africa, Peru, Ghana, and Timor-Leste, there should be special provision made for female statement takers.[39] So too should there be an option for victims of gender-based violence to testify in women-only hearings or in-camera hearings, should they be more comfortable in such settings.[40] Innovations such as allowing women to offer public testimony with their faces covered (as was done in Nigeria) or utilizing distorted facial broadcast imaging (as was pioneered in Peru) can further protect the identities of women giving public testimony.

The transitional justice movement has also developed a growing consensus concerning problematic issues that often arise with regard to gender and truth commissions. While truth commissions need to be proactive and systemic in their assessment of gendered human rights violations, they should nonetheless resist depicting women primarily as victims of sexual violence or simply as victims in general. Commentators have lauded the ad hoc innovations introduced by the Truth and Reconciliation Commission in South Africa to accommodate the needs of female victims of political violence, but have nonetheless noted that the TRC revealed little about the experience of women under apartheid in roles other than victim. This is a cautionary tale from which the Tunisian Truth and Dignity Commission should learn.

Similarly, the commission should avoid the flawed dichotomy of portraying women as either "primary" or "secondary" victims of human rights violations, thereby obscuring the structural continuum of harms experienced by women under a repressive regime.[41] An essential approach for accurately capturing the broader experience of women victims is to disavow any public/private characterization of human rights violations and to focus instead on the continuities between "extraordinary" and "ordinary" violence.[42] This is especially important in the Tunisian context if the Truth and Dignity Commission is to portray accurately the harms suffered by women under the *pointage* system of the Ben Ali regime.

Another critical area of concern lies with the question of reparations. Commentators have noted how vitally important reparations are for repairing sexual violence.[43] Given the sexual violence experienced by numerous conservative Islamic women while imprisoned on political grounds in Tunisia, reparations may prove critical in facilitating their reintegration into their communities and the state. Sexual violence, however, should not be the sole or even threshold requirement for assessing eligibility for reparations. Rather, the design of reparations should be commensurate with the broader spectrum of gender-based harms suffered by Tunisian women (e.g. reparations could include restoring jobs and careers, or awarding scholarship benefits to allow the completion of interrupted academic degrees).

Finally, the Tunisian Truth and Dignity Commission should explore the potential for holding thematic national hearings focused on gendered human rights violations, emphasizing the need for new practices and new gender understandings in post-authoritarian Tunisia. It is here that one of the most important longitudinal impacts of a truth commission can lie: even beyond chronicling past human rights atrocities, the Truth and Dignity Commission can lay the groundwork for a new culture of gender-based rights in twenty-first-century Tunisia.

Scholarly analysis of political violence likewise yields insights that are relevant for Tunisia's Truth and Dignity Commission, especially as regards the relationship between political violence and violence against women.

O'Rourke identifies four aspects of political violence that exacerbate violence against women:

1. First, political violence has a negative impact on the state's capacity to prohibit, prevent and punish private harms against women.
2. Second, political violence gives rise to the militarization of everyday life, which erodes any notion of a private sphere for women free from the state's negative infringement of their bodily integrity. This manifests in sexualized harms to women political activists.
3. Third, ideologies in periods of political violence lead to the acute public regulation of women's private reproductive lives.
4. Fourth, women often enter the public sphere during periods of political violence on the basis of the private maternal role and the need to provide for one's family and community. However, recognition of the subversive potential of women's collective action results in the public political manipulation of women's organizing.[44]

All four of these factors have relevance to the Tunisian regime under Ben Ali, and its success in creating the perception that Tunisia was the one country in the Arab Muslim world that promoted gender equality. Repressive regimes exacerbate violence against women because when a state is pursuing political opponents, women cannot rely on its protective role. This was precisely the experience of female relatives of political prisoners in Tunisia, who could not rely on police protection in cases of violence. Quite to the contrary, these women often experienced harassment at the very hands of the police and state security personnel. Furthermore, given that sexual morality is of paramount importance to Islamist women, abusers could count on Ennahda women not reporting acts of sexual aggression or violence.

Should transitional justice mechanisms not address gender-specific violence, this kind of violence is likely to continue even after political transitions have taken place. Schäfer argues:

> The female body in particular is a central symbol-rich point of aggression in national, ethnic or religiously charged conflicts... The female body becomes politicized during times of conflict. Culturally formed identities and masculinities which define men as the protectors of women and children, are targeted when hurting women. Men are being shown that they are unable to protect their female family members.[45]

Tunisian women whose husbands were imprisoned for long periods of time recount that their men also struggle with a sense of personal failure for not having been able to provide for and protect their wives and families. As one woman said in the city of Bizerte: "I don't want my husband to find out about all the things I endured during his absence; this would just add to his many burdens."[46] The more common model of transitional justice today aims at making perpetrators accountable not only for state-sanctioned political violence, but also for breaches of economic, social, and cultural rights. This expansive notion of what constitutes human rights violations continues to shape the mandates and responsibilities of truth commissions, and has great relevance for Tunisia's Truth and Dignity Commission. The Tunisian women who for almost a generation endured state-sanctioned harassment, the crushing daily obligations of *pointage*, as well as sexual violence, should be seen not as secondary or "derivative" victims but rather as survivors of primary human rights violations committed by previous Tunisian regimes.

Managing expectations

In the Tunisian transitional justice endeavor, the issue of managing expectations will be crucial. Transitional justice is not a panacea. Comparative studies of transitional justice in numerous countries have revealed that justice, truth, and reparations are rather malleable. Various, disjointed court cases in Tunisia bear this out. Military courts tried several groups of defendants for the killing of protesters, and even sentenced Ben Ali *in absentia* to life in prison for complicity in murder under Article 32 of the penal code. Military courts also sentenced a minister of interior, Rafik Bel Haj Kacem, who held office at the time of the uprising, to a total of 27 years in prison, and sentenced twenty other senior officers to several years in prison for intentional homicide during the uprising. Although the trials appeared to respect the defendants' basic human rights and seemed to provide victims access to justice, several factors undermined the contribution of these trials. These included their failure to identify the direct perpetrators of the killings, an inadequate legal framework for prosecuting senior officers for command responsibility for crimes that their subordinates committed, and a lack of political will from the government to press for Ben Ali's extradition from Saudi Arabia.

Non-political female prisoners

Returning to the issue of truth commissions, Kawthar Ben Romdhane of Bizerte, who spent five years in prison and says she is still not sure if she will testify when the opportunity presents itself, reflects:

This is a period of my past that is hidden in my soul; I am still not quite sure how to do with this. I don't want the truth commission to become a disruptive force when what we need most is healing. Inside myself, I feel a lot of confusion I ask myself: is it possible to speak and hear the other side as well? Am I capable to forgive? I certainly don't want to be judged by mass media but because this process is so highly politicized, I am not sure I can really be heard.[47]

Though Kawthar feels largely vindicated by the revolution, and is happy that her former job as a schoolteacher was restored after she was banned from her profession for more than fifteen years, but she is concerned about an entirely different group of women. Like other women interviewed, she too chose not to meet in a café but in a children's playground, an indication that numerous former victims still do not feel comfortable in common public places where they might encounter their tormentors.

I know I was a political prisoner and not a common criminal. I knew my activities were forbidden and dangerous. Unlike the men, we were incarcerated with common criminals. I lived with women with whom I would never have socialized prior to my arrest. Prostitutes, women who stole; I got to know these women really well and they were subject to the some of the same torture and abuse as I. Who will speak for them? Under Ben Ali, people got imprisoned for any number of reasons. The police could target any woman. I saw women giving birth in prison and they gave up their children. The cycle of suffering and deprivation continues. Will it be possible to have transitional justice for them? There are not always clean lines between prisoners of conscience and common criminals, at least not in my experience with these women. I don't want to speak about my personal fate; we are all Tunisians and are connected in some way. Prison really did change me in so many ways. I am a different person now. Actually, Ennahda is a different movement because of our experience.[48]

Kawthar speaks mostly of the changes she experienced as a result of her prison experience. Some Ennahda women may not have been feminist by ideology, but became vocal women's rights advocates based on their experience. Assuming male roles of responsibility and surviving under tremendous pressure was not a choice, but became a reality imposed upon them. It is unlikely that these survivors will now assume subservient roles to men, nor— just as importantly—are they likely to be subservient to a state and government that so dismally failed them. However, the aforementioned Wassila Zoghlami emphasizes the ways in which she has remained unchanged, in particular concerning her views on gender equality and women's rights:

I have always believed in gender equality, my experience of hardship and suffering did influence my attitude on this subject. I could never have married a man who did not share the same view. But it is certainly possible that for some women the harshness of their experience transformed some of their attitudes. For me, feminism does not just mean that women should have a career; it is a way of life that influences the private sphere just as much. To me, equality is an Islamic principle and is in line with *maqasid*, the ultimate goal of the revelation.[49]

Just a few years after the revolution, the Tunisian transitional justice process is still at a nascent stage. The work of the Truth and Dignity Commission will constitute a crucial step in the larger Tunisian transitional justice process. The success of this truth commission will depend on the extent to which victims feel safe enough to come forward with their testimonies, and the degree to which the truth commission facilitates this. In addition to the task of soliciting and commemorating the voices of women victimized by the previous regime, the Tunisian Truth and Dignity Commission faces a larger responsibility: that of countering the "dominant truth" perpetuated by the Ben Ali regime that it was forward-thinking and progressive where women's rights were concerned. The voices of Islamist women in Tunisia say otherwise, and their voices demand acknowledgment in the new Tunisia.

Given the lively, contentious, and acrimonious discourse within Tunisia, there will surely be a plethora of voices, domestic and international, scholarly and populist, that will decry the work of the Truth Commission. Still, as Monia Brahim said: "We know the Arab world is watching us. Muslims are watching us; the world is watching us. Even if we don't get things right just now, I believe we deserve not only to be criticized but we deserve to be encouraged."[50]

Without question, the Truth and Dignity Commission, along with the people of Tunisia, deserve the full encouragement of the transitional justice movement and the larger international community in this vital historical moment. There is hope that the complex and hard-earned lessons of gender justice of recent decades will shape and inform not only Tunisia's truth commission but its future as a country as well.

7

MARTYRDOM IN NORTH AFRICA FOLLOWING THE ARAB SPRING AND THE PROCESS OF TRANSITIONAL JUSTICE

Thomas DeGeorges

Introduction

This chapter addresses the ways in which martyrdom has been deployed as part of a transitional justice process in the North African countries of Algeria, Morocco, and Tunisia. It argues that although martyrdom has deep cultural roots in the region's past (often connected to the related Islamic archetype of exceptional "friends of God"), references to martyrdom by the modern nation-states in the MENA region have sought to reinforce the state's legitimacy during times of political transition.[1] The success of such efforts, however, varies widely among the Maghreb countries. I will argue that a process of transitional justice that embeds the memory of martyrdom as an unalterable component of a country's political system, as in Algeria for example, via the creation of public spaces of memory and their repeated inclusion in public discourse, is a poor substitute for politics. In many ways, Algeria remains a bitterly divided society after the war of liberation (1954–62) and the period of civil unrest in the 1990s, because of the failures of a political system which overly venerates the dead instead of focusing on policies designed to improve the conditions of the living.

Morocco and Tunisia, however, have pursued more promising paths of reconciling societal divisions—whether colonial or post-colonial—by establishing truth commissions that recognize the sacrifices of victims of state violence without allowing martyrdom to overshadow other elements of the official historical narrative of the state. Although victims of injustice (usually at the hands of state institutions and actors) feature prominently in the historical narratives of all three countries, Morocco and Tunisia have exhibited a willingness to experiment with various transitional justice bodies in a way that *resolves* political divisions, rather than *exacerbates* them. This is in contrast to Algeria.

The concept of martyrdom may seem to have little utility initially in a transitional justice context, especially given the myriad ways in which it may be defined. In this paper, martyrdom will be used to refer to persons who are victims of political violence. Often, this violence will result in the confirmed death of the victim as a direct result of security forces. However, it will also be employed to refer to individuals who were victimized by unknown actors, as well as those victims whose fate remains uncertain due to lack of forensic evidence.[2]

Analyzing post-revolutionary Tunisia, it is interesting that the initial uprising that ousted Ben Ali from power was focused around the concept of martyrdom. The seminal event that is often associated with igniting the social and economic demands of the Tunisian people was the dramatic suicide of the Sidi Bou Zid fruit seller, Mohammed Bouazizi.[3] This desperate act was caught on cellphones and rapidly went viral within the region, acting as a symbol of the regime's injustice toward the "ordinary man."[4] Following his act of self-immolation, Bouazizi survived for a while longer in the burns unit of a Tunisian hospital. He was visited there by Ben Ali himself, thus elevating Bouazizi's status (albeit mute) as an interlocutor of sorts with the regime.

Following Bouazizi's death and the subsequent flight of Ben Ali and his family to Saudi Arabia, it might be expected that the young man's death would continue to inspire Tunisians. Instead, Bouazizi's sacrifice has been overshadowed by his family's controversial decision to leave Sidi Bou Zid to move to a wealthy suburb of the capital, Tunis. More recently, the deaths of Tunisian political leaders and soldiers have captivated public imagination. The killings of leftist political leaders Chokri Belaid and Mohammed Brahmi in 2013 sparked large street protests against the ruling government officials, and ultimately led to the resignation of two separate governments led by the Islamist Ennahda party.[5]

A challenge often encountered when studying and documenting martyrdom is, of course, how closely and accurately can the martyr's life be portrayed when, by definition, the last stage (death) eludes our experience. Given this limitation, to what extent can any post factum analysis or study of martyrdom provide answers to the questions of a martyr's ultimate intent and purpose? Didier Fassin, in his analysis of international aid organizations' documentation of trauma and martyrdom among Palestinian populations, offers a convincing exposition of how victim experience and testimony have been rendered by both conflict survivors and the bureaucratic institutions that aid them.[6] Of most relevance here is Fassin's contention that the experiences of victims or martyrs of violence in conflict societies are interpreted and defined by bureaucratic institutions that are inherently political, and which use firsthand testimony to support broader narratives of victim experience based in compassion or injustice.[7] During the twentieth century, Fassin argues that the increasing brutality of warfare created unprecedented numbers of first-hand witnesses, while the growing bureaucratization of society forced the "third parties" involved in assisting them to develop procedures and codes of conduct when documenting state criminality.[8] Although Fassin's statement below refers to humanitarian NGOs, it applies equally to the role that truth commissions have played:

> The second age of humanitarianism thus corresponds to the advent of the witness—not the witness who experienced the tragedy, but the one who assists the victims.

> Thus, it was in bearing witness that the aid missions were able to find meaning for their work: adopting a new role, psychiatrists and psychologists began to piece together personal observations and clinical anecdotes to condemn what they were witnessing. Thus fragments of narratives about humanitarian workers in the Palestinian Territories multiplied on websites and in journals aimed at donors, in the media and among the senior management of international institutions. In a remarkable inversion of the traditional witness figures, the *testis* was now speaking in the first person, taking the place of the *superstes*.[9]

It is the way that martyrdom is analyzed by external, bureaucratic actors (via the procedures of truth commissions) that makes its contribution to transitional justice so important. As Ruti Teitel implies in the following: "There are periods when shared notions of political truth and history are largely absent. In transition, the very foci of shared judgment that form the basis for a new social consensus are expected to emerge through the historical accountings."[10] By quantifying the number of martyrs and defining their individual experiences of victimhood, these truth commissions begin the transitional justice process of establishing a "new social consensus" as Teitel mentions above.

Given such high expectations in post-conflict societies, and the lack of "shared notions" regarding societal truths mentioned above, such commissions have set the stage for vastly different interpretations of the meaning and political significance of martyrdom, for future generations in the three countries under consideration.

Before exploring martyrdom's significance in the twentieth century, it is important to remember that acts of principled sacrifice have long played an important role in Islamic culture. To this end, a brief overview of earlier typologies of "saintly" individuals in Islamic civilization follows.

Martyrdom in North Africa in Historical Context

The martyr must have belief in one belief system and possess a willingness to defy another belief system. He or she will stand at the defining point where belief and unbelief meet... In this sense the martyr creates a boundary with his or her life that may or may not have been previously apparent.[11]

Since martyrs are victims of political violence, one of the ways that their stories become meaningful in the context of transitional justice processes is by establishing the *motivation* of the martyr when confronting power. It is by exploring the motivations of martyrs that transitional justice processes provide the living with lessons in justice. The concept of clashing belief systems and individual opposition to injustice has ancient and modern antecedents. Throughout Islamic history, the archetype of an "extraordinary" individual has been encapsulated in the concept of a "friend of God."[12] John Renard's work on the subject mentions the hagiographic accounts of the earliest saintly figures in Islam, whose deeds earned them respect and, at times, veneration. In both Sunni and Shi'a traditions, such holy men have been perceived as "closer" to God than ordinary mortals. The Shi'a tradition, however, more than the Sunni, emphasizes martyrdom as a crucial aspect in the hagiographic genre, especially when assessing the deeds of the Imams.

The echoes of such early beliefs of extraordinary individuals, and the hagiographic accounts that accompany them, continue to inform modern belief in martyrdom today. Although martyrdom has historically been identified with religious belief, it is possible to identify modern secular ideologies

(Marxism, nationalism, etc.) that provide the basis for martyrdom.[13] During the nineteenth century, Maghrebis confronted the violence of European colonialism. Beginning with the French conquest of Algeria in 1830, and continuing through the successive conquests of Tunisia (1881) and Morocco (1912), those who perished at the hands of European armies were often posthumously commemorated as "martyrs."[14]

Foreign occupation and the concomitant loss of sovereignty forged a sense of nationhood among Algerians, Moroccans, and Tunisians, which emphasized the collective over the individual. Repeated invocations of the "people" or *al-sha'ab* came to dominate nationalist discourses, personified by strong leaders such as Abd al-Qadir al-Jaza'iri, Sultan Mohammed ben Yousef of Morocco, and Habib Bourguiba of Tunisia.[15] As a result, the glorification of such "exceptional" individuals has parallels with the hagiographies of the earlier "friends of God" we have considered. Thus, supporters of the sultan of Morocco claimed to see his image reflected in the moon following his exile to Madagascar by French officials in 1953.[16] Likewise, Renard cites the creation of a "hagiographic" narrative around Bourguiba's life as a key part of his image as the "father figure" of Tunisia.[17]

The cases considered above reflect the deeds and exploits of relatively well-known and powerful figures. With few exceptions, early examples of "extraordinary" people include mainly those who wielded either political or religious authority. However, the forms of Arab nationalism that emerged under colonial rule relied heavily on mass mobilization of the population to confront the colonizers. As a result, the focus shifted from vaunting the achievements of a notable person to commemorating thousands, if not millions of "extraordinary" people: the martyrs. To reiterate, the rise of modern political parties in the MENA region, with their emphasis on mass recruitment, expanded the number of people whose deeds were considered "extraordinary," thus reinforcing the populist themes which the nationalists sought to convey.

As noted above in reference to the work of Didier Fassin, the Israeli-Palestinian conflict has long been analyzed through the prism of revolutionary martyrdom, in which nationalist themes are reflected rites designed to remember martyrs. Laleh Khalili notes the similar nationalist overtones of funerary customs surrounding Palestinian martyrs:

> Collective mourning and ecstatic celebrations of martyrdom both create a sense of community among the mourners, and the dead body appeals to observers' emotions of sympathy and fury and act as potent instruments of political mobilization... Funerary rituals serve a range of political functions: they legitimate and integrate organizations, reinforce group solidarities, and viscerally embed political beliefs.[18]

127

Prior to the American invasion of Iraq in 2003 and the Arab Spring of 2011, it was Palestine that framed how martyrdom in the MENA region was planned, executed, and commemorated.[19] The case of Algeria, by contrast, although in some ways pre-dating that of Palestine in terms of the arrival of Europeans (1830 as opposed to the 1880s), has received relatively less attention overall. Yet Khalili's observations about the various political interpretations of martyrdom are no less accurate for Algeria, which has a long history of integrating martyrs into the national psyche.

Algeria and the Cult of Martyrdom

The Algerian war of liberation (1954–62) concluded with the rise to power of the National Liberation Front (FLN). The FLN swiftly sought to legitimize its seizure of power by claiming to represent the will of hundreds of thousands of martyrs who died during the conflict. Was the adoption of martyrdom as a pillar of Algerian nationalism sufficient to end the recriminations and fall-out from the violent war of independence? Most scholars of Algeria would say no.[20] Instead of lessening the divisions in Algerian society, the glorification of martyrdom and the veneration of the dead have only deepened the political paralysis of the Algerian system over time. Far from "reconciling" Algerians with their colonial past, the cult of martyrdom has encouraged festering resentments against the French colonial regime. Worse, the failure to achieve justice for the martyrs (in the form of a clear accounting of the circumstances and conditions of their deaths, or in the form of an official apology from France) has sapped the legitimacy of the FLN government over the decades.[21] Indeed, the experience of the "dark decade" of the 1990s in Algeria only confirmed the inability of officially sanctioned martyrdom to act as an effective process of transitional justice. The FLN's focus on the sanctity of martyrs in Algeria backfired dramatically when armed Islamist opponents of the regime characterized those who fell in battle against government forces as martyrs. Thus, rather than promote a shared historical vision around which Algerians could coalesce politically, the focus on martyrdom provided a template for recurring conflict between "authentic" Algerians and "foreigners." The classification of "foreigner" could mean the French, when talking about the war of liberation, or secular ruling elites in Algeria when discussing the period of the "dark decade." This era was characterized by the annulment of an election widely expected to bring Islamists to power for the first time. In the ensuing chaos, an insurgency developed in many parts of the country, initially pitting radical Islamists against the army and the state. In this situation, as Luis Martinez argues, the archetypes of the liberation-era maquis were reinterpreted by "dark decade" combatants to justify their actions in the 1990s:[22]

> The experience of the [War of Liberation, 1954–62] maquis was one that produced an identity, that of the Moudjahid: in the war of liberation as in the current civil war (1998–2002), recognition of the status of guerilla came through exile from the city to the countryside... By giving prime importance to warlike values (courage, endurance, foresight and cunning), it turned the social hierarchy upside down, favoring newcomers without educational qualifications over the "educated" and "holders of qualifications" favored before; thus the maquis became the preferred arena for political brigands.[23]

The glorification of martyrdom thus leads not to political settlement in Algeria, but rather increases the perceived differences between factions, generations, and ideologies. The state-sponsored cult of martyrs has created a discourse in which any group can (and often does) present their political claims on the state by virtue of the sacrifices made by their members.[24] As I have argued elsewhere, these socio-political claims are strongly linked to the model of state development in the post-colonial era:

> A paradox of political movements and parties in the Arab world has been their willingness to challenge those in power without fundamentally rethinking the state's role in society. The protest movements involved in the Arab Spring (including the Casbah protests in Tunisia), therefore, have targeted a narrow governing elite that demonstrates conspiratorial, non-transparent statecraft, at the risk of ignoring more radical steps needed to break with the developmentalist and distributory model common throughout the Arab world. In short, protest and martyrdom are interpreted as strategies to seize control over the distributory mechanisms of the state. The merits and efficiency of the developmentalist model are rarely questioned.[25]

In such fraught political climates, the chances for reconciliation are remote and difficult to envision, even with the construction of transitional justice instruments such as Algeria's Ad Hoc Inquiry Commission in Charge of the Question of Disappearances which operated from September 2003 to March 2005. Carefully crafted by the Bouteflika administration, with the tacit support of the Algerian army, as an attempt to address the human rights violations that occurred during the period of the 1990s, the commission was restricted to investigating disappearances, torture, and unlawful deaths *without* identifying the perpetrators. In addition, no public report on the proceedings or findings was ever issued.[26]

Morocco: Royal dispensation as the key to transitional justice processes

Unlike Algeria, Moroccan history does not have a strong tradition of martyrdom. The country must also be differentiated from its North African neighbors as one of the few remaining monarchies in the region. As John Waterbury pointed out decades ago, the Moroccan monarch has survived the post-independence period by carving out an indispensable role as both commander in chief and "arbiter in chief" (adept at raising or lowering the profile of political parties in order to smooth the functioning of the government).[27] As mentioned earlier, the struggle for independence against the French and the ensuing exile of the Moroccan sultan did create the conditions for similar cultural expressions, albeit briefly. Likewise, the various colonial wars with France and Spain created the conditions for *mujāhidīn* ("freedom fighters") to emerge in both the northern and southern areas of the country. However, for the most part Moroccans have eschewed the formal moniker of "martyr" for those who are perceived to have died unjustly.

There are, however, periods in Morocco's recent history in which the state and its institutions acted in "illegitimate" if not "illegal" ways, resulting in the deaths or disappearances of innocent citizens. For much of the rule of King Hassan II (1961–99), critics of the government or the monarchy were subjected to arrest, arbitrary detention, and attacks on their human rights. This period of time, known popularly as the "years of lead," was every bit as traumatic for Moroccan citizens as the war of liberation and the "dark decade" was for their Algerian neighbors. Much like Algeria, official efforts to atone for the abuses of the "years of lead" were delayed until the death or exile of key state actors like King Hassan II and his former Interior Minister, Driss Basri, weakening the case for effective transitional justice.

Upon the death of Hassan II in 1999, his eldest son, Mohammad, acceded to the throne. Like the selection of Abdelaziz Bouteflika as the Algerian presidential candidate in 1999, Mohammad VI was viewed popularly as someone relatively untainted by the human rights abuses associated with his predecessor. One of the first acts of the new king was to fire his father's long-standing Minister of Interior, Driss Basri. This decision was well received, as Basri was one of the senior figures implicated in human rights violations during the period of Hassan II.

In 2004, the King established an Equity and Reconciliation Commission, whose mandate was to investigate possible human rights abuses during the period of the "years of lead," and apportion blame within the state institutions, *without* focusing on specific individuals implicated in human rights violations.[28] The commission conducted its work over a period of twelve months and took testimony from a variety of witnesses: those whose rights had been violated or relatives and close friends of victims. The Moroccan commission's results have been closely analyzed by scholars, notably Susan Slyomovics' work on the performance of human rights in the country.[29] As she points out, the inherent difficulty in achieving a measure of justice for those whose human rights have been violated lies in the conflicting demands of the state security apparatus and the abused individual:

> The muffled, secretive nature of prison and disappearance is in many ways opposed to the qualities that make for verbal performance in the public domain. Transmitting social and public knowledge calls for breaking the silences. Many cannot or will not do so...the public performance strategies [used by ordinary Moroccans] may be in the form of mock trials...indemnity hearings...and demands for truth commissions.[30]

Unlike in Algeria, however, the Moroccan state has taken concrete and public steps to try to mediate between the demands of institutions and the broader citizenry, thereby introducing concrete steps to prevent "disappearances" and other forms of martyrdom in the future. The first step was the public documentation of the proceedings of the Equity and Reconciliation Commission. A parallel, but no less important, process occurred in the reform of Morocco's security services and the way they interact with the public. As Jonathan Smolin points out, beginning in 2003, King Mohammad VI appears to have opted for a significant reform of security protocols for dealing with crime and community relations.[31] With the appointment of Hamidou Laanigri as head of the General Directorate of National Security, the king selected a reformer who attempted to move the Moroccan police toward a model of "community policing" (*shurtat al-qurb*), involving the installation of smaller police stations covering broader areas of urban geography. Although Smolin acknowledges the controversy surrounding the figure of Laanigri, who was removed from his post following accusations of corruption in 2006, and his "reformed" police forces, he concludes that "despite their failings, the GUS [Urban Security Units] did establish a bridge between the state and the public."[32]

Tunisia: Commemorating martyrs in post-revolutionary times
(between grass-roots protest and fact-finding commissions)

To most analysts of Tunisia, the revolution of 2011 came as a total surprise. Despite its ferocious suppression of political Islamist movements in Tunisia, the Ben Ali regime had maintained excellent relations with European powers and the United States. Although foreign representatives often complained about human rights abuses in Tunisia, and the concomitant lack of a competitive electoral environment, fears of terrorism in the region during the 1990s and on a global scale after 2001 limited the impact of such critiques.

The two decades spanning the 1990s and the 2000s witnessed respectable economic growth rates in Tunisia, fueled by key export sectors, hydrocarbons, and tourism. Astute observers of the country pointed out that much of the country's economic growth benefited communities along the coastal or "Sahel" region.[33] The Ben Ali years were historically, culturally, and economically important, and profited these densely populated urban areas. Foreign direct investment and ambitious planning projects were concentrated in the Sahel. The poorer interior of the country was largely bypassed by the national growth patterns to the extent that unemployment (as well as underemployment) rose steadily.[34] Infrastructure investments that might have helped reduce the isolation of the central and southern areas of the country were instead diverted to constructing an *autoroute* network focused on the Sahel urban centers. By the end of the 2000s, many regions of the interior were poorly served by public transport and struggled with inadequate and insufficient public services.

As many scholars of Tunisia had warned for decades, these economic imbalances were made worse by the lack of accountability throughout the political and bureaucratic system.[35] The rifts between Sahelian elites, their allies, and the majority of the population grew as economic liberalization, amidst the privatization of the state sector, disproportionately benefited Tunisia's wealthy and politically well connected. These growing economic disparities were not lost on the emerging generation of Tunisian internet activists. The effects of microcomputing technology soon led to the expansion of internet access and new forms of socialization in Tunisia by the mid-2000s. Blogging and later Facebook and YouTube became the platforms of choice for Tunisian internet users wishing to express their views about their society. Increasingly, Ben Ali's regime found itself forced to limit or censor access to the internet, especially during sensitive periods of elections or protests.

The global financial crisis of 2007–8 destabilized Tunisia (and other Arab countries) in subtle, but ultimately profound, ways. Although the crisis erupted in the United States, the sharp decline in global demand and the reduction in credit availability quickly mushroomed into a global phenomenon. Global equity markets fell, with an especially sharp drop in the values of "emerging market" equities. The economic liberalization programs of the preceding decades had promoted conspicuous consumption behavior among Third World elites, which proved difficult to sustain with the precipitous drop in value of several asset classes simultaneously (such as real estate and equities). With no viable political system to temper the predatory behavior of state elites and provide relief to communities reeling from higher unemployment, and the decline in revenues associated with key industries (such as mining and tourism), regional protest movements emerged between the years 2008 and 2011.

The context of the global financial crisis of 2007–8 provides the backdrop for the economic and social frustrations that erupted in December 2010 in what became known as the "Tunisian revolution." This series of spontaneous demonstrations which began in the marginalized interior governorates of the country quickly spread to major urban areas in the Sahel. A month after the initial demonstrations began in Sidi Bou Zid, President Zine al-Abidine Ben Ali fled the country for Jeddah, Saudi Arabia on 14 January 2011.

The months following the departure of Ben Ali saw the formation of several interim governments with varying representation of Bourguiba-era ministers, Ben Ali technocrats, and representatives of Tunisia's opposition groups. The challenges these governments faced were profound, ranging from the near collapse of the Tunisian economy to the steady disruptions and protests emanating from various groups within Tunisia's civil society.

Martyrdom as a protest strategy deployed by grass-roots groups

The presence of unpopular officials from the Ben Ali period in government ultimately doomed the first transitional governments after January 2011. Mohamed Ghannouchi, Ben Ali's former prime minister, governed uncertainly from 14 January through 27 February 2011, as the head of a transitional cabinet which contained several holdovers from the Ben Ali period. Immediately following the revolution itself, individuals and parties that had been marginalized, exiled, or outlawed formed ad hoc coalitions in opposition to Ghannouchi's government: the most of important of which were the Front of 14 January 2011 and the National Council for the Protection of the Revolution. Determined to replace Ghannouchi's government with a more popular alternative, these organizations benefited from popular grass-roots movements known collectively as the "Casbah protests" of late January and mid-February 2011. As Ghannouchi's unpopular government sought to establish elections for a new president, ordinary citizens from around the country organized "caravans of liberty" which set out for the capital, Tunis, to stage a massive sit-in in front of the prime minister's office in the Medina.

Many who participated in the first Casbah protests came prepared to press their claims on behalf of the victims and martyrs of the chaotic period during and after the revolution. Incensed by the inclusion of former Ben Ali officials in the key posts of prime minister, interior minister, and foreign minister among others, protesters organized caravans of vehicles from throughout the country which converged on the capital, Tunis, beginning on 23 January. Establishing a sit-in protest in front of the prime minister's office in the Casbah in Tunis, their numbers grew and inspired similar protests throughout the country. Visual records of these events clearly demonstrate the use of pictures and signs in honor of those who perished during the revolution.[36] By 27 January, a beleaguered Ghannouchi formed a new government in which all but a few of the former *Rassemblement Constitutionnel Démocratique* (RCD) members were purged.[37] The victory of what would subsequently be known as the "Casbah I" protests represented the continuing influence of popular sovereignty over the unelected transitional governments of the immediate post-Ben Ali period.

Frustrated by the slow pace of reform and the perceived continuity between the Ben Ali regime and the second Ghannouchi government, protesters revived the Casbah strategy in late February to demand new leadership untainted by Ben Ali or the RCD party. By 25 February, thousands of protesters once again besieged the prime minister's office in Tunis demanding Ghannouchi's ousting. As a result of what would subsequently be known as the "Casbah II" protests, Ghannouchi submitted his resignation on 27 February, paving the way for the transitional government of Beji Caid Essebsi from 7 March.

The Casbah protest movements remain important as models for the exercise of Tunisian popular sovereignty in the post-revolutionary period. In July 2011, smaller groups of protesters established a sit-in in the Human Rights Park on Mohammad V boulevard (sometimes referred to as "Casbah III"). Here too, martyrdom represented an important concept around which the protesters framed and articulated their demands for social and economic reforms. Although the demands and the participants in these demonstrations were multi-faceted, martyrs and their sacrifice did play a pivotal role in successfully pressing the protesters' demands. The martyrs become a "Rohrschach test" for those protesters who referred to their memory:

> Most [protesters] agreed with the proposition that martyrs and families were "owed" something by post-revolutionary Tunisia. In this way, protestors' comments echoed those made by the families of those who died in Gafsa and Radayef uprisings of 2008... Many protestors talked about this debt being repaid in terms of

societal changes that would install a more just society and a moral economy. Interestingly, as they talked, protestors were inclined to impute motivations and reasons for martyrdom. A Tunisian who lost his or her life in the revolution "wanted" to fix the bad hospitals, increase the SMIG, and lower inflation. Random and senseless violence is thus parsed in a way to have meaning for the wider community, providing the living with a blueprint for effective societal change.[38]

Martyrdom considered by transitional justice institutions: the Bouderbala Commission

If popular anger and frustration at the political transition process found expression in the Casbah movements following the revolution, many Tunisians looked to more formal and deliberative transitional justice institutions to frame their political and social grievances. Given the popular outrage over the rushed electoral schedule demanded by the 1959 constitution, the transitional government led by Ghannouchi (and later Beji Caid Essebsi) initiated a process that would elect a constituent assembly whose members would be charged with drafting a new constitution for the country. These elections were to be held provisionally in July 2011, although the date was later moved to 23 October 2011.

In an attempt to promote a sense of non-partisanship and effective transitional justice, the outgoing Ghannouchi government had proposed three independent commissions to investigate the actions of the former regime and propose a framework for constitutional reforms. The most important of these transitional justice bodies was the one led by renowned jurist Yadh ben Achour, to propose political and constitutional reforms. Two other important commissions were convened to investigate potential criminal actions committed by security forces during the revolution (led by Taufik Bouderbala, the former secretary general of the Tunisian League of Human Rights), as well as to investigate the amount and whereabouts of the Ben Ali family's vast fortune (led by Abdelfattah Omar).

The Bouderbala Commission commands the most interest for this chapter. Officially called the "National Committee to establish the facts of the crimes committed during the period from December 17, 2010 to the end of the Commission's mandate," it was established by an official decree of the transitional government led by Fouad Mebazaa on 18 February 2011. The committee's mandate involved pursuing evidence related to the confrontations between protesters and security forces during the period of the Tunisian revolution. To this end, the committee and its members were enjoined to pursue such evidence (in the form of written and oral testimony) throughout the country. The decree establishing the committee also empowered its members to access government records from the period, so as to conduct a thorough investigation into the ministerial and bureaucratic decisions that contributed to death and injury during this period. Confidentiality was guaranteed to all those who participated in giving testimony before the committee. Along with the Committee to Investigate Corruption, this committee successfully completed its mandate and issued a final report on the subject in 2013.

Like the Moroccan commission established to catalog the abuses of Hassan II's "years of lead," the report of the Bouderbala Commission was published and discussed publicly.[39] The commission members decided to extend their work until the eve of the first post-revolutionary elections held in October 2011. Over this period, they pursued information on approximately 2,500 cases of human rights violations committed; of these, over 300 cases dealt with the deaths of individuals and over 2,000 cases dealt with injuries.[40] One of the most refreshing aspects of the commission's final report is the introspection that its members engaged in over the challenges they faced in performing their herculean task in a post-revolutionary environment. The commissioners reflected upon the difficulties of their task, as well as the most significant challenges they faced in pursuing their mandate. The most perplexing was one of "mistaken identity": apparently many potential witnesses were wary of the commission since they confused its formation with a promise made by former President Ben Ali in his third and final speech to the nation on 13 January 2011.[41] Ben Ali had promised, among other things, to set up a commission to investigate the conduct of the security forces during the Arab Spring. However, this commission was never constituted due to the president's decision to abdicate and flee the country the day after the promise was made. The other misunderstanding appeared to be the assumption that the fact-finding commission was working hand in hand with the judiciary, and that its findings would point the finger at individual responsibility for violations of human rights committed during the revolution. As in the Algerian and Moroccan traditions, the committee members acknowledged that their mandate did not include prosecutorial or judicial powers.[42] Perhaps most serious of all of the difficulties encountered by the Bouderbala Commission was the reluctance and, at times, silence of key members of the security apparatus. To a degree, this was partially resolved by working out an agreement between the commissioners and the labor union responsible for the security forces, resulting in an increased level of cooperation between the commission and members of the security forces.

One of the more surprising conclusions of the commission was its inability to certify that government snipers (long a *bête noire* of the families of martyrs and the protesters) actually reported to an identifiable command-and-control structure within the security institutions.[43] What the commission did ascertain was that the forensic evidence on certain victims, as well as eyewitness testimony, pointed to the existence and actions of armed men on rooftops at various stages of the revolution. Perhaps most importantly, the commission states that in no circumstances did a lack of direct supervision authorize security forces to use snipers as a legal means of crowd control.[44]

The discussion of the situation of women and children in the report is especially well treated and with appropriate sensitivity.[45] The commission makes clear that although women account for a minority of the victims of the revolution, this in no way diminishes their bravery or courage during this time period. Rather, many women stepped forward to provide testimony on the deaths or injuries of male relatives or acquaintances. Further, the commission challenges its readers to confront accounts of sexual assaults or threats, which many female witnesses refused to pursue due to the dangers to their honor and family status.[46]

All in all, the commission's final report contrasts sharply with the portrayal of martyrs by the grass-roots protesters. In the place of polemic, the commission's members opted for a nuanced and sensitive analysis, based on months of research, during which eyewitness testimony and other evidence was gathered and analyzed.

The question remains, however, to what degree the starkly different (yet connected) views of both groups (protesters and transitional government bodies) can be reconciled. Despite the numerous press conferences which the commission members held during their study, it is noteworthy that not one member of the commission was actually selected from the grass-roots movements. To be sure, the commission repeatedly emphasized its neutrality vis-à-vis the political forces of the day. Thus, for all its benefits and strengths, the commission cannot be said to represent the entirety of Tunisian views on the subject of martyrdom.

Conclusion

In October 2011, Tunisians went to the polls in the first free and fair elections since independence in 1956. The Islamist party, Ennahda, won the plurality of the vote and reached a power-sharing arrangement with two other parties, which granted it the prime ministry. A major surprise was the unexpected strength of an obscure political party known as the "Popular Petition." Its leader, Hachmi Hamdi, originally came from Sidi Bou Zid, but had lived abroad in London for years. The diminished presidency went to long-time human rights activist Moncef Marzouki, while the post of speaker of the constituent assembly was assumed by another long-standing opponent of Ben Ali, Mustafa Ben Jaafar.[47]

The promises and hopes of many Tunisians remain unfulfilled five years after the popular uprising that unseated Ben Ali. Although the elections of 2011 returned a popularly elected constituent assembly, as well as a government whose members came from the parties with the most votes, external and domestic upheavals made long-term planning difficult. The Tunisian revolution led to similar uprisings in neighboring Arab countries in 2011, none of which was as successful as the initial Tunisian uprising in making a clear break with the past.

The revolutionary demands for free speech and freedom of movement are now being debated as the state struggles to contain salafist and jihadi groups who promote the establishment of a transnational Islamic "caliphate" to replace the nation-state in the Middle East. Influenced by such propaganda, thousands of Tunisians have attempted to infiltrate Syria to join the militants fighting to overthrow Bashar al-Assad there. Domestically, aggressive protests in universities over the freedom of religion and strike action in the southern mining regions have created a sense of political paralysis as the new constitution was being hammered out.

Despite this continuing turmoil, in January 2014 the Tunisian constituent assembly ratified the country's second constitution since independence in 1956. Constitutions in transitional states wrestle with a fundamental paradox, according to Ruti Teitel:

> Revolutionary periods and their aftermath are times of political flux and, as such, present tensions with constitutionalism, which is ordinarily considered to bind an enduring political order...transitional constitutions arise in a variety of processes, often playing multiple roles: serving conventional constitutions' purposes, as well as having other more radical purposes in transformative politics.[48]

Tunisia's efforts to replace the older constitution of 1959 thus served to "transform" politics, as Teitel argues. But there is a deeper level by which we may measure transitional justice in Tunisia following the revolution: that is, the desire to effect "historical justice."[49] The first paragraph of the preamble of the constitution states the following:

> We, the Tunisian people's representatives, members of the national constituent assembly, honoring the struggle of our people toward independence, state-building,

ending despotism by demanding the people's will for freedom and implementing the goals of the revolution of freedom and dignity (the revolution of 17 December 2010 to 14 January 2011) and *faithful to the blood of our innocent martyrs and to the sacrifices of Tunisians over the generations*, and ending oppression, fear and corruption.[50]

As much as revolutionary states look ahead, they cannot help but look behind. The goals of an as-yet nebulous future are measured by the need to right the concrete injustices of the past regime. If the constitution of 2014 was meant to mark the "beginning of the end" of the revolutionary period, the reference to martyrdom in the very first paragraph of the preamble indicates the obsession of many Tunisians with obtaining a measure of "historical justice":

> Historical accounts generated in transitional times are not somehow autonomous but build on antecedent, national narratives. The background of ongoing collective memory defines a society. Thus, the transitional truths are socially constructed within processes of collective memory. As societal practices in these periods reflect, the historical accountings are less foundational than transitional.[51]

In Tunisia's case, more so than in its North African francophone neighbors, the revolution has provided a nexus in which grass-roots protest movements, fact-finding commissions, constitutionalism, and historical revisionism are being deployed simultaneously to craft the post-revolutionary citizen. The success or failure of these methods will determine the future of both Tunisia and other societies throughout the MENA region.

8

POLITICAL EXCLUSION AND TRANSITIONAL JUSTICE

A CASE STUDY OF LIBYA

Mieczysław P. Boduszyński and *Marieke Wierda*[1]

Introduction

A Revolution is not a painless march to the gates of freedom and justice. It is a struggle between rage and hope, between the temptation to destroy and the desire to build. Its temperament is desperate. It is a tormented response to the past, to all that has happened, injustices recalled and unrecalled—for the memory of the Revolution reaches much further back than the memory of its protagonists.[2]

The Libyan revolution of 2011 initially generated much hope. When Gaddafi, who ruled the country ruthlessly and erratically for 42 years, was toppled by a broad coalition of rebels backed by NATO, Libyans had a rare opportunity to rebuild their state in accordance with the appeals to justice (*'adala*), freedom (*hurriyya*), and dignity (*karaama*), which had animated the revolution.

The chaos that characterizes Libya at the end of 2014 stands in stark contrast to the optimism that accompanied its transition early on. In many ways, post-

141

Gaddafi Libya appeared to be a country ripe for transitional justice. Unlike the revolutions in Tunisia and Egypt, where there was some kind of accommodation with remnants of the former regime, Libya's revolution was much more far-reaching, and thus the prospects for real accountability seemed greater since Libya's new rulers did not have to enter into any compromising "pacts" with former rulers. The previous regime and its affiliated structures fully collapsed. Many former regime figures were taken into custody. Moreover, the coalition that came together to fight Gaddafi was unusually broad and unified, compared, for example, to Syria's factitious opposition. Such unity, as well as Libya's rich traditions of mediation and reconciliation between tribes, could arguably have provided the basis for genuine transitional justice and post-conflict reconciliation. Instead, the country has succumbed to ever increasing levels of violence. The justice that exists is most often meted out in the form of extra-judicial violence and revenge against those deemed by revolutionary brigades to be collaborators of the former regime.

In this chapter, we focus on a highly exclusionary vetting measure passed by the transitional Libyan parliament in 2013. Ironically, those subjected to this measure have not been Gaddafi's henchmen, but revolutionary stalwarts. Less than two years after the fall of Gaddafi, many of the revolution's main protagonists found themselves excluded from political life owing to a draconian measure called the Political Isolation Law (hereafter PIL). The PIL excluded a number of the most prominent leaders of the uprising, among them Mahmud Jibril, Mustafa Abdel-Jalil, and Mohamed Magarief, all of whom once held senior positions in Gaddafi's regime but became key leaders in the National Transitional Council (NTC). Indeed, the paradox of transitional justice in Libya is that while revolutionary leaders and others have been excluded from public life, little else in terms of transitional justice has been delivered, either in the form of verdicts against senior former regime figures in custody or reparations measures for victims.

Why has the struggle for a broad and inclusive justice failed in Libya, replaced instead by a harsh form of political exclusion? Our chapter situates the PIL in a broader political—and now violent—struggle for legitimacy and power in the new Libya. The Libyan case provides a cautionary tale in terms of the dangers of pursuing transitional justice in the form of retributive purges without parallel measures that could heal divisions and promote reconciliation, such as truth telling or reparations for victims.

We proceed as follows. The first section places the Libyan PIL in context by defining and analyzing the trade-offs inherent in vetting, lustration, exclusion, and purging mechanisms as forms of transitional justice, with comparative examples from other transitional and post-conflict states. This section also reviews some of the theories that have been put forward to explain the political determinants of various transitional justice mechanisms. Finally, it outlines the provisions of the Libyan PIL. The third section outlines the legacies of the past that Libyans face in their pursuit of justice, showing how institutional collapse and weak statehood have created a climate of impunity and intense competition for resources and power among Libya's ubiquitous extra-state militias, and describes existing efforts to deal with these legacies through nascent transitional justice mechanisms. The fourth section argues that a climate of victor's justice and revolutionary legitimacy has prevailed in Libya, further complicating the delivery of justice by the extremely weak state. It shows, moreover, how the PIL rose to prominence in the context of intense post-Gaddafi battles between different political camps and notions of legitimacy and has contributed to the chaos that engulfs Libya three years after Gaddafi's demise. The conclusions consider the consequences of the law to date, and argue that the zero-sum politics of exclusion reflected in PIL hinder any kind of settlement, reconciliation, and lasting peace in post-Gaddafi Libya.

Vetting and the politics of transitional justice

Though less studied than other forms of transitional justice such as prosecutions, reparations, and truth commissions, vetting, exclusion, lustration, and purges have long been on the agendas of post-authoritarian and post-conflict states.[3] "Vetting" refers to "processes for assessing an individual's integrity as a means of determining his or her suitability for public employment."[4] Vetting processes typically screen individuals, including public employees or candidates for elected office to determine if prior conduct—engaging in human rights abuses or corruption, for instance—warrants their exclusion from public office.[5] Vetting usually focuses mainly on those institutions that played a role in human rights violations, such as the security and judicial sectors. "Exclusion" may entail either removing individuals deemed to be problematic from certain positions, or restricting them from seeking such positions. Vetting and exclusion must be distinguished from a "purge," which implies wholesale exclusion of individuals or categories of persons based on their mere association with the former regime. Classic examples of purges include de-Nazification in post-war Germany and de-Ba'athification in post-2003 Iraq. The term "lustration" is associated with measures carried out over the past twenty-five years in post-communist Eastern Europe. Lustration laws were designed to identify and keep operatives and collaborators of communist-era security services out of public life.

Vetting and exclusion laws vary according to their depth and breadth. Some laws focus only on former high-level decision-makers, seeing them as primarily responsible for abuses, while others reach further down the hierarchy, holding even low-level bureaucrats accountable for the execution of orders from above. Vetting laws also vary in terms of how far back they go in time when looking at an individual's past involvement with an authoritarian regime or in a conflict. Furthermore, such laws vary in how harshly they sanction individuals for collaboration. For instance, in the Czech Republic top communist officials and secret police operatives were banned from public life for ten years, while in Hungary functionaries were given the option of either resigning quietly or having their past roles clarified and publicized in order to retain their positions. Poland implemented a similar system to Hungary, under which past association with the communist regime did not automatically exclude a person from public service; only misrepresenting the nature of the collaboration did so. Thus, the Polish and Hungarian models provide affected personnel with the "opportunity to demonstrate that they are disassociating themselves from the old regime and are willing to play by the rules of the new regime."[6] Procedural and institutional choices must be made as well, also with consequences for fairness.[7] For instance, one body can be used to vet all institutions and individuals, or alternatively different bodies can be used to vet different sectors. Finally, there is wide variation in the duration of vetting processes. In Greece, vetting of former military junta members lasted only ten months, while in Poland the process continued for over six years.

The motivation for vetting and exclusion arises from a justifiable concern that elements of the former regime may pose a threat to new and fragile democracies, if allowed to remain in the state apparatus or in politics. They may also pose a hindrance to building trust in new state institutions. Putin's Russia is an example of this, with its large number of former Soviet-era KGB officials in positions of influence. Moreover, it is hard to imagine successful institutional transformation, also vital to democratization, in the absence of personnel reform. Thus, vetting laws can become a powerful tool for security sector reform. Moreover, since vetting processes are administrative in nature, they impose a lesser evidentiary burden than criminal prosecutions. Where criminal prosecutions are not possible, the exclusion of human rights abusers may provide some measure of justice and accountability. Exclusion also provides a measure of economic justice by removing former offenders from access to the largesse of the state. Finally, vetting and exclusion can help legitimize the new order in that those who rose up against the authoritarian regime will never feel that their revolution has succeeded as long as former elites remain in positions of influence. Thus, a transitional regime that includes figures from the *ancien régime* may suffer from a legitimacy deficit. As such, those who participated in the revolution are often among the most fervent proponents of vetting measures.

The dangers of vetting

Schwartz, writing about the experience of post-communist Eastern Europe, notes that vetting, exclusion, and lustration laws are fraught with ethical dilemmas and risks to individual rights:

> What kind of personal or organizational involvement in the abuses justifies lustration? Who indeed was truly 'innocent?' Can a lustration system operate fairly? Will it drain too much administrative or other talent from these societies? Will it produce some kind of 'witch hunt?'[8]

There are those who may have worked with the former regime, but gained nothing from that collaboration, nor engaged in any abuses. Thus, vetting laws need to be carefully crafted and implemented to ensure that the basic rights of those targeted by them are respected. In particular, a vetting process ought to comply with the minimum requirements of due process, and to the principle of non-discrimination.[9]

Besides imposing unfair, collective punishment on individuals by virtue of association rather than conduct, vetting laws also carry the risk of being used to settle political scores. This was what happened in Czechoslovakia in the early 1990s, and later, in the 2000s in Poland, where a right-wing government pushed lustration laws as a way to attack and eliminate the communist successor parties. It can also be used as a way to grab resources and secure sources of income and patronage. For example, in Croatia in the 1990s, a purge of ethnic Serb officials from the organs of the newly independent Croatian state (including state-owned companies) often came to resemble a rush for access to economic resources.[10] In the context of post-conflict states where one side has won a clear and undisputed victory (in contrast to those where there is a negotiated settlement, stalemate, or ambiguous result), there is a temptation for the victors to use vetting and exclusion laws to exact revenge on and sideline their former enemies.

Finally, vetting measures can exclude those with the critical skills needed to carry a delicate political and economic transition forward. Moreover, these elites were often the only ones with the political acumen, technical skills, and international connections needed to carry out certain reforms effectively. Former Slovak Prime Minister Jan Čarnogursky claimed that if lustration laws had been introduced in Slovakia in 1991, he would have had no one to run the government.[11] Similarly, the mass dismissal of teachers tied to the former East German regime in the 1990s did little good to the educational system.[12] The empirical analysis of Libya's PIL we offer below shows that the rush toward vetting unfortunately succumbed to all of these pitfalls.

Vetting and the politics of transition

The debates and processes leading to vetting, exclusion, lustration, and purges are inseparable from the politics of transition. In the 1970s and 1980s, as authoritarian regimes fell in Latin America, Africa, and Eastern Europe, opposition elites soon found that they had to balance the desire for vetting and lustration with the political constraints inherent in the absence of an all-out revolution, coup, or military victory. As Grodsky observes, "retributive measures, such as mass criminal trials, were frequently replaced with more lenient policies, including truth commissions and blanket amnesties."[13] In the context of negotiated transitions, it was hard, at least initially, to exclude those who were integral to the launching of a democratic transition: that is, former authoritarian elites. As Przeworski notes, authoritarian elites are unlikely to give up power in the absence of "guarantees."[14]

Thus, the early literature on transitional justice suggested that the possibilities for accountability are determined by the distribution of power among key actors—especially the outgoing authoritarians and ascendant oppositions—prevailing at the time of transition.[15] The basic argument in this literature is that the greater the strength of old elites vis-à-vis the new ones, the less likely we are to see criminal trials and other forms of retributive justice. In negotiated transitions such as Poland's, in which former elites demand amnesties in exchange for handing over power, justice, particularly in its most retributive forms, is diluted. In such cases, the campaign for justice has to be balanced against the potential of an authoritarian backlash and the need for stability. Although the authoritarian leaders are no longer in power, they may hold varying degrees of influence over the military and the political process, and therefore can pose significant threats to fragile democratic transitions. In negotiated cases where the former elites lead the transition, such as South Africa, restorative forms of transitional justice are more likely. And only in cases where the new elites have fully defeated their predecessors (of which Libya is an example), such as Rwanda, or in those where outside actors exercise power over the transition, such as Iraq, will we see criminal trials or purges of former rulers for human rights abuses.

Monika Nalepa argues that authoritarian elites are more likely to negotiate a handover of power when they know that their opponents—the democratic opposition—have their own "skeletons in the closet," or a history of collaboration with the former regime.[16] Grodsky argues that it is not only the relative power of incoming and outgoing elites that determines outcomes in all forms of transitional justice.[17] He shows that the will of elites to provide transitional justice is closely linked to their perceptions of the demands for and benefits of delivering justice and their institutional capacity to deliver it. Thus in Serbia, leaders have enabled prosecutions (i.e. handing over indicted war criminals to the International Criminal Tribunal for the Former Yugoslavia [ICTY]) when they calculated that it would enhance their political standing relative to accessing Western-conditioned aid, and in relation to the process of accession to the European Union (EU).

The literature on the balance-of-power determinants of transitional justice reminds us that political competition for power and resources is central, especially when it comes to the formulation of vetting and exclusion laws. Indeed, while such laws carry potentially desirable benefits for transitional justice, in practice they have also been misconceived, misused, and poorly implemented for political reasons. In some cases, such as de-Nazification in post-war Germany or lustration in post-communist Poland, such laws have been rushed or abandoned halfway. In some countries, vetting and exclusion laws turned into an effective witch-hunt, and failed to respect the rights of individuals, thereby delegitimizing the process and opening it up to external challenges. The actual process of exclusion has often failed to muster the will and resources to review individuals fairly and adequately, as the experience of electoral vetting in Afghanistan demonstrates.[18] In sum, transitional and post-conflict states that have adopted exclusion laws have had difficulties in implementing measures that are legitimate, objective, safeguard human rights, are governed by the rule of law, and based on individual responsibility. More often, exclusion has become embedded in competition for political power and resources, as the Libyan case starkly shows.

Vetting and exclusion in Libya

The pressure for vetting and excluding former Gaddafi regime figures in Libya was immediate and intense. As such, vetting laws were adopted soon after the fall of the old regime, starting with the establishment in the summer of 2012 of a High Commission on Integrity and Patriotism. The commission removed persons from public positions based on a wide range of criteria, and was able to exclude even elected members of the transitional parliament, the General National Congress (GNC).[19] Then, in May 2013, the GNC passed what was to become one of the most draconian vetting laws seen in any transitional country to date, the PIL (*qanun al-'azil assiyasi*), which threatened to exclude thousands of Libyans from participation in public life based on past involvement (no matter how minor) with the Gaddafi regime.

The PIL disqualifies anyone who held any of a wide range of positions in Gaddafi's state apparatus between 1 September 1969 and 23 October 2011. It lists twenty-two criteria by which persons can be excluded. Many of the fourteen criteria related to positions target high-level posts, but they also encompass lower levels such as local government officials, student union leaders, and businessmen who dealt with Gaddafi's family. Exclusion according to these criteria is based purely on the position held. The final eight criteria deal with conduct and ideology, such as anyone who "took a hostile position against the 17 February Revolution, either through actions, incitement, agreement or assistance," "became rich at the expense of the Libyan people," "used religious discourse to support ... the rule of Gaddafi," or those who "repeatedly glorified Gaddafi or his regime, or promoted the Green Book." By including so many criteria, the law exceeds even de-Ba'athification in Iraq, which was restricted to the top tiers of Ba'ath party officials.

Compromises such as exceptions for those who joined the revolution early were rejected at the last minute. Precious few provisions are based on conduct, and those that are lie dangerously open to interpretation. Those deemed to have met these criteria will be barred for ten years from holding legislative or executive posts at the national or local levels, judicial positions, diplomatic posts, or leadership positions in the security and military institutions. They will also be barred from serving in leadership positions in political parties or other political bodies, institutions of higher education, and media institutions.

Rather than contributing to institutional reform, the PIL has excluded a number of Libya's most experienced politicians and technocrats from senior positions, unable to contribute to the rebuilding of their country. Various human rights organizations inside and outside the country have rightly characterized this law as divisive and dangerous: it finds individuals guilty by association rather than conduct, and threatens to deepen further social divisions that are already profound in Libya.

The PIL, according to Article 5, is administered by a special Commission for Implementing the Political Isolation Law Standards, whose members must be Libyan nationals older than 35 years of age, with legal training but without political affiliation.[20] In practice, a number of the members of the Integrity and Patriotism Commission were re-appointed. Unlike its predecessor, the Integrity and Patriotism Commission, the Political and Administrative Isolation Law in Libya includes certain minimum due process guarantees, including the right to an oral hearing. Those affected by the law can also appeal against the decisions of the commission before the Supreme Court within ten days of notification. However, these due process guarantees do not ultimately redeem what is an arbitrary and unfair process.

The political isolation law is antithetical to transitional justice efforts, which ideally should respect human rights and promote reconciliation. The emphasis on political isolation calls into question whether the Libyan revolution was a revolution of principles that sought to promote freedom from oppression and respect for human rights, or whether it was simply a re-allocation of power to other groups vying for control of the state and its immense oil wealth. The subsequent section describes the background and political dynamics upon which broader forms of justice were hijacked by groups seeing narrow political exclusion.

Violent conflict, militias, and weak institutions

Confronting the legacy of violent conflict

Libya faces the dual challenge of confronting a legacy of a brutal and repressive dictatorship as well as dealing with a past and present civil war. In addition to the justice challenges that derive from the 2011 conflict, Libyans also face the challenge of learning the truth about and confronting human rights abuses committed by the former regime during forty years of Gaddafi's rule. One notable example is the massacre of political prisoners at Abu Salim prison in 1996. Human Rights Watch estimates that 1,270 people were summarily executed in one day at the prison.[21]

The 2011 conflict produced many additional crimes committed by both loyalists and rebels. While the National Transitional Council (NTC), the non-elected body formed in Benghazi during the revolution which governed Libya until August 2012, originally announced that as many as 40,000 Libyans died in the conflict, early in 2013 the subsequent, elected Libyan government declared that in actuality about 5,000–6,000 rebel fighters and a similar number of civilians had died, as well as 5,000 or so loyalist fighters. According to these government figures, 2,000 or so persons from both sides of the conflict remain missing.[22] There are also an estimated 35,000 internally displaced persons (IDPs) in Libya,[23] a large number of whom are ethnic Tawerghans, members of a racially distinct group of Libyans evicted from their town near Misrata in retaliation for allegedly carrying out atrocities including a rape campaign in Gaddafi's name, allegations which are yet to be substantiated.

While the civil war officially ended with the death of Gaddafi in October 2011, Libya never clearly pursued a post-conflict settlement. In the years since, many smaller-scale conflicts have continued. In 2013, over 600 Libyans were killed in various acts of violence. Multiple assassinations were carried out in Benghazi against perceived Gaddafi loyalists (known as *azlam* in Libya), but more recently also against a range of others, including human rights defenders. Others died as a result of tribal clashes, such as in the ongoing conflict in the south-eastern town of Kufra near the frontier with Chad, between the Zuwaya, an Arab tribe, and the Tebu, a group with ethnic ties to Chad and sub-Saharan Africa.[24] To the west, in Sebha, there were bloody battles between members of the Tebu and of the Awlad Suleiman tribes on a regular basis. Such tribal conflicts in post-Gaddafi Libya are based on complex factors, including perceived loyalty to the former regime and control of smuggling routes.

In mid-2014, these local conflicts expanded and threatened to divide the country in two. In mid-May, retired General Khalifa Haftar announced an armed campaign, "Operation Dignity" (*'Amaliat al-Karama)*, against the Shura Council of Benghazi Revolutionaries (SCBR), an alliance including *Ansar al-Shari'a* militia, Libya Shield units, and other armed groups in Benghazi. In mid-July 2014, the situation in Tripoli likewise spiraled into an all-out conflict between an alliance of armed groups primarily from the city of Misrata but also from other towns including al-Zawiya and Gheryan, and Tripoli-based armed groups known as "Operation Dawn" (*'Amaliyat al-Fajr*), who were fighting against the Zintan-affiliated *al-Qa'qa'* and *al-Sawai'q* armed groups allied with fighters from the Warshafana region west of Tripoli. The recent fighting gives rise to yet another series of human rights violations that Libyans will ultimately need to confront. The UN has published reports accusing all sides of committing war crimes, in particular indiscriminate shelling and attacks on civilian objects, unlawful killings, detentions, abductions, torture, and denial of access to adequate medical care.[25]

In terms of the literature and cases surveyed above, at first the Libyan conflict was a case of total victory by one side. While this suggested opportunities for accountability—no amnesties for former regime figures were ever on the table given their total defeat—it also fostered a climate of victor's justice and revolutionary legitimacy (described in the next section) which, in the context of a weak state and judicial institutions, conditioned calls for the most problematic kinds of vetting and exclusion.

Militias, weak statehood, and flawed justice

There is perhaps no legacy of the Libyan conflict with more negative consequences than the numerous militias and weapons that remained spread throughout the country following the formal end of hostilities. Militias increasingly organized into "hybrid" shadow state security structures, which transformed into ever changing coalitions. Some militias contain strong criminal elements that have turned to sabotage, extortion, blackmail, kidnapping, trafficking, and terrorism. Militias have consistently undermined the authority of the fledgling central government and its monopoly on the use of violence, making it comparable to Somalia or Afghanistan.

Militias have thrived in post-Gaddafi Libya's institutional and security vacuum. Besides quashing any civil society, Gaddafi also left behind few institutions. As Boduszyński and Pickard note: "Gaddafi did not merely run the old system—he *was* the system."[26] The state institutions that did exist barely functioned and were often undermined in ways that reflected Gaddafi's paranoia and his ideology of *jamahiriya*, a neologism that he coined to signal the supposed subordination of republicanism to direct popular rule. In fact, the only encompassing "institution" in Libya was Gaddafi himself, his family, and his circle of advisors. Despite the rhetoric of statelessness, state authority was punishingly strong and repressive.

The three years that followed the revolution were too short to make any real inroads on building state institutions. In the aftermath of the NATO intervention, there were no foreign peacekeeping troops, nor for that matter any "boots on the ground" as have been present in other post-conflict countries such as Bosnia and Herzegovina, East Timor, Kosovo, and Afghanistan. While the United Nations deployed a special political mission in Libya (UNSMIL) offering technical assistance and advice, and a number of Western embassies and aid agencies have programs to train political parties or build the capacity of civil society, the degree of international involvement followed a "light footprint" approach and was miniscule compared to other post-conflict cases. The reasons for the West's highly restrained approach were many: fatigue with failed nation-building experiments in Iraq and Afghanistan, economic recession in Europe and the US, and a belief that Libya had the means and resources to conduct its own state- and democracy-building projects.[27] There was also an acute sense that, in spite of the large reservoir of goodwill resulting from Western support of the revolution, Libyans were wary and even hostile to outside, and especially Western, interference in their transition, as we shall discuss in the section below.

Libya's legal and judicial system, already weak and paralyzed, has been constantly challenged by self-declared *thuwwar* who argue that it is dominated by corrupt and politicized Gaddafi-era judges. Prior to the law on political isolation, reforms of the judiciary, including vetting, had been suggested but not yet carried out. Additionally, around 8,000 conflict-related detainees have been in custody since October 2011, without access to a lawyer or judge, tarnishing Libya's post-revolution human rights record. While most detention facilities officially fall under the authority of the state, *thuwwar* continue to guard countless detainees. In certain facilities, torture and ill treatment of detainees are widespread.[28]

In the context of a weak state, justice delivery was repeatedly hampered and delayed, which undermined the building of confidence in the state. While Gaddafi's violent demise at the hands of Misratans in the desert near Sirte will not easily be forgotten, many senior figures of the former regime are currently on trial together before the Court of Assize in Tripoli. Included are Saif Al-Islam Gaddafi, the son and one-time heir-apparent of the "Brother Leader," held in the western mountain town of Zintan by militias; and Abdullah Al-Senussi, Gaddafi's former internal security chief and one of his most notorious henchmen. Both Saif Al-Islam and Abdullah Al-Senussi are also wanted by the International Criminal Court (ICC).

After the revolution, the Libyan government insisted that all suspects should be tried in Libya, with the Minister of Justice promising that these will adhere to international standards.[29] Yet Libyan prosecutors are bringing charges of "inciting civil war" or "disrupting national unity." Such political charges, which may incur the death penalty, risk associating the trials with revenge rather than justice, as they affirm the narrative of the 17 February revolution. A trial of the infamous Abu Selim massacre is also due to begin, involving as many as 100 co-accused. In September 2013, over 30 former regime members, including many of the senior officials, were brought to court to be charged and their trial is currently underway. Saif Al-Islam was linked to the proceedings via video-link, but after the conflict in Tripoli in the summer of 2014, he is no longer participating in the trial.

In May 2013, the Appeals Chamber of the ICC ruled that Libya is unable to carry out a trial against Saif because he is not in state custody. Two months later, the same chamber made a contrary ruling in the case of Abdullah Al-Senussi, deciding that the Libyan authorities could try him as he was in state custody. However, as of this writing, that facility is under the control of the Operation Dawn forces that have taken over Tripoli, forcing out the elected government, which has taken refuge in the eastern city of Tobruk. The ICC is currently contemplating whether it should re-open the Abdullah Al-Senussi case to decide whether he should not be tried in The Hague after all.

Trials are focused on perpetrators but not much has been done for victims of Gaddafi-era crimes in Libya. In moving toward reconciliation, the Libyan transition lacks a South African-style truth commission. A lackluster law on transitional justice passed in February 2012 remains largely unimplemented. A new version of the law proposes a more robust fact-finding mechanism with powers to look at crimes that occurred after the revolution, but again remained unimplemented due to the political turmoil. Compensation is handed out on an ad hoc basis, mostly to placate revolutionaries or martyrs. While those who were injured in the revolution were given medical treatment packages to travel abroad, or pensions for their disabilities, for almost two years nothing was done for the victims of the notorious Abu Salim prison massacre of 1996.[30] Furthermore, the portfolios of "missing persons" and "martyrs" were combined in a single ministry, reflecting the singular emphasis on those victims who fought with the revolutions.

Revolutionary legitimacy and the road to political isolation

The roots of the political isolation law in Libya lie in the dominance of revolutionary legitimacy, the most fervent champions of which are the armed rebels (*thuwwar*) operating in the aforementioned extra-state militias. Revolutionary legitimacy is based on the narrative of a heroic battle of liberation against a brutal tyrant, for which tens of thousands of courageous martyrs (*shuhada'*) gave their lives in the venerated 17 February revolution. The symbols of this revolution are ubiquitous in Libya (the new flag, or images of

Omar Al Mukhtar, a hero of the fight against Italian colonialism), while the idea that the revolution is under threat from Gaddafi sympathizers is widespread. As such, acts of revenge are common. Entire cities and regions associated with support for the former regime have been subject to marginalization or violence. The dogma of the Green Book, Gaddafi's rambling revolutionary treatise that every Libyan schoolchild had to read, has been replaced by the new dogma of the 17 February revolution, according to which the courageous *thuwwar* who liberated the country can do no wrong. Some Libyan political actors have gone so far as to say that the armed militias deserve as much legitimacy as elected leaders, given their role in Gaddafi's overthrow.[31] Appeals to revolutionary legitimacy also account for the sharp rivalry between Gaddafi-era reformists, who defected early and went on to play key roles in post-revolution governing bodies, and those who fought on the frontlines against the former regime. The former claim legitimacy by virtue of elections, international connections, or high-value technical skills, while the latter point to the sacrifices they made during the former regime and the revolution. Over time, those claiming revolutionary legitimacy have asserted themselves using the threat of violence to achieve their political aims and protect their privileges, which include immunity from prosecution for any abuses committed during or even after the 2011 conflict.[32] Standing up against revolutionary legitimacy is a tall order in the post-Gaddafi Libyan political climate. Any politician, journalist, or group that does so risks being branded a Gaddafi sympathizer and an enemy of the revolution. Media outlets and figures that have dared to stand up to the militias have been met with violence and kidnappings.

Armed militias have invoked revolutionary legitimacy to justify political isolation as well as various military operations. Both the conflict in Bani Walid in 2012,[33] and the conflict between Operation Dawn and Zintan in Warshafana in the summer of 2014 were depicted in those terms, with adherents to Operation Dawn claiming that they have to "finish" the revolution through their takeover of Tripoli airport and much of western Libya, and cleanse it from "regime remnants" (*azlam*).

Libyan Islamists also deployed revolutionary legitimacy as political cover in their relentless push for the harshly retributive PIL. The passage of this law was seminal in Libyan politics, as it showed that one group of political actors was determined to exclude another, even if it meant using extra-legal measures and violence to do so. The PIL's predecessor was the High Commission on Integrity and Patriotism, established in the summer of 2012. The commission removed persons from public positions based on a wide range of criteria, and was able to exclude even elected GNC members. Yet its processes remained opaque and inconsistent, and its decisions were never published. Predictably, the results were controversial and did little for reconciliation.[34] For example, the process excluded deputies from regions perceived to be pro-Gaddafi, such as Bani Walid, the Abu Salim district of Tripoli, and large parts of the south.[35] As a result, minority groups like the Tuareg were left entirely unrepresented.

While the Integrity and Patriotism process was already far-reaching, the idea that the revolution was being corrupted continued to gain traction, and calls for a process of "political isolation" persisted. A heated debate ensued, and it quickly became apparent that the negotiations on new criteria were focused largely on current politics rather than on an attempt to confront the past. The party with arguably the most to lose from political isolation was the National Forces Alliance (NFA), the liberal coalition that emerged strongest from the July 2012 GNC elections, and succeeded in forming a government. Many of its members were reformist technocrats in the Gaddafi regime who had joined the revolution early on.

However, the NFA made a strategic decision not to oppose the law, though its leader, Mahmud Jibril, who ran a state-affiliated economic reform agency under the former regime and then defected after the outbreak of revolution and went on to head the National Transitional Council, remained one of the law's most outspoken critics as well as its main target. Jibril spoke candidly about what he perceived as the law's real aims, which in his view are an effort to eliminate political rivals and grab coveted public sector jobs.[36]

By contrast, the Islamist parties such as the Justice and Construction Party (JCP) and the Salafi *Wafaa al-Shuhada'* bloc were strongly supportive, viewing the law as an opportunity to extend their influence. The Grand Mufti, Sadeq Al-Gheriani, was an outspoken supporter. Islamist politicians such as JCP leader Muhammad Suwwan and *al-Watan* party leader Abdulhakim Belhaj characterized their fervent support for the law in terms of "building the state" and "protecting the glorious revolution," describing political isolation as a "right."[37] Others characterized the redistribution of power and resources away from those affiliated with the former regime as a revolutionary right.[38] While many prominent Islamists risked being excluded under a criterion referring to "reconciliation with the former regime," this clause was deleted in the final draft.

Proponents of political isolation found support in militias willing to use force to achieve their aims. On 5 March 2013, armed protesters stormed the GNC and attempted to force members to sign the bill into law at gunpoint.[39] On 9 April, the GNC passed an amendment to the Interim Constitutional

Declaration aiming to "immunize" political isolation from constitutional challenges, on the grounds that it is discriminatory. On 5 May, the GNC finally voted to adopt the political isolation law by an overwhelming majority, albeit again under considerable pressure, including a militia siege of the Ministries of Foreign Affairs and Justice, involving the Supreme Revolutionaries Council and the Libya Revolutionaries Operations Room with a strong component from Misrata. It is said that circulars were placed on the seats of GNC members threatening those who dared oppose the law. In an ominous gesture, demonstrators carried coffins to the GNC: coffins that ostensibly represented martyrs, but perhaps also a symbolic warning.[40] All GNC members had to declare publicly whether they were for or against. In the end only a handful of GNC members dared to oppose the law.

The implications for Libya's current and future political landscape are extensive, even if the law is never fully implemented. UNSMIL advised the GNC before its passage that the law was overly broad, vague, and arbitrary, and risked violating the civil and political rights of many individuals. It subsequently publicly criticized the law.

In early June 2013, the judiciary went on strike, fearing that judges would be removed en masse. The Supreme Judicial Council proposed an amendment to the law to limit its potential application to the judiciary. While around 400 judges were moved to other posts, affecting the functioning of the courts, no further steps were taken so far as to remove judges altogether.

Similarly, the law was originally opposed by the army, which established its own Integrity and Reform Commission that expelled hundreds of senior officers.[41] Estimates of individuals that could be affected ranged from very conservative estimates of 2,000 by the commission itself, to Jibril's rather overblown estimate of 500,000.

By early July 2014, the total number of disqualified persons numbered 176 out of around 6,000 screened, including 41 candidates for the House of Representatives in July 2014. In the run-up to the elections for the Constitutional Drafting Assembly, around 700 candidates were screened and just eight were disqualified, seven of which managed to overturn these decisions in court. In the local council elections, out of around 1,000 candidates screened, only twenty were excluded, and seven managed to overturn the decision.

In spite of the amendment to the Constitutional Declaration to immunize the law from change, both certain individuals and the National Council for Civil Liberties and Human Rights have filed several challenges against it. The Constitutional Circuit of the Supreme Court heard these challenges on 18 February 2014, amidst demonstrations outside protesting against the session. The complainants argued that in substance the law violates the Constitutional Declaration, as well as Libya's international obligations, *shariah'* law, and the democratic process itself in that GNC members were not able to perform their functions independently. The next sessions of the court were postponed until 26 June 2014, by which time Tripoli had erupted into violence and it was not able to reconvene. In February 2015, the internationally-recognized HoR revoked the Political Isolation Law, while the Supreme Court's scheduled ruling on its constitutionality was postponed. However, the application of any ruling remained constrained so long as legitimacy was contested among several governing bodies.

However, the effect of the law may be wider than just removals. Its symbolic message remains, and often results in "self-exclusion" for those affected. Many of the employees of the Ministry of Foreign Affairs, aware that they are affected by the law, simply stopped coming to work. In the parliamentary elections of summer 2014, some of those implicated by the law decided not to run rather than subject themselves to the process. Some exiled Libyans have said that they decided not to return to Libya because of the law.[42] Most critically, the PIL underscores the zero-sum nature of post-Gaddafi Libyan politics in which compromise is rare and various parties, under threat of exclusion, are given little incentive to participate peacefully in the political process.

The House of Representatives, elected in summer 2014, let it be known that it intended to revisit the Political Isolation Law but has not yet done so. Unlike the General National Congress (GNC), which was perceived to be dominated by Islamists, the House of Representatives (HoR) (*majlis al nuab*) is perceived as leaning more toward the "liberal" politics of the National Forces Alliance. On 6 November 2014, the Supreme Court of Libya ruled that the constitutional amendment that allowed for the election of the HoR was unconstitutional, injecting more uncertainty and chaos into an already fragile situation. It is not clear whether the court acted under pressure from Libya Dawn militias, but its decision was the equivalent of a legal bombshell in an already highly polarized environment. In any case, the Supreme Court decision served to increase the divisions between the parties and created uncertainty as to whether the Supreme Court can play a constructive role in resolving outstanding disputes on the law.

Conclusion

The story of the path to PIL in post-Gaddafi Libya, and the parallel stories of the rise of revolutionary legitimacy and the politics of exclusion, are closely linked to the question of what the 17 February revolution represents. Was it, as the narrative linked to the revolutionaries themselves often insists, a triumph of ideals—a fight for freedom from oppression and respect for human rights—or an attempt to wrest power from one man and his circle of supporters so as to redistribute this power (and the country's substantial wealth) to others? The passage in May 2012 by the NTC of an amnesty for "acts of struggle committed by the Libyan people ... with the aim to topple the former regime" gives rise to fears that justice in Libya will remain one-sided and partial, quite literally a "victor's justice." The new transitional justice law, passed in October 2013, refers to the importance of "legal recognition of the justice of 17th February Revolution as a right of the Libyan people as well as the recognition of the corruption, tyranny and criminality of the former regime." While these sentiments reflect *l'esprit du temps* in Libya, ultimately persisting in such a one-sided view will form an impediment to genuine reconciliation.

Both sides in the current Libyan conflict are guilty of pursuing a zero-sum politics of exclusion, which leaves little room and incentive for compromise. General Khalifa Hifter, for instance, recently declared that the only way to deal with his Islamist opponents is to eliminate them entirely, a strategy employed by President Abdulfatah Al Sisi in neighboring Egypt. Such sentiments do little to foster a climate in which dialogue can take place and trust be built. The PIL is based on precisely the same approach, which aims to eliminate one's political opponents rather than build bridges of cooperation.

Libya's substantial natural resources intensify this competition. The Libyan state, with a pre-2011 per capita GDP of over $13,000, is among the richer transitional states in the world. This wealth, based on extensive hydrocarbon resources (Libya has the tenth largest proven oil reserves in the world), may be a major conflict driver. Since the oil sector is almost entirely in state hands, the stakes of political power are high. A recent report describes the conflict in Libya as "an intensively local affair, stemming from deeply entrenched patronage networks battling for economic resources and political power in a state afflicted by a gaping institutional vacuum and the absence of a central arbiter with a preponderance of force."[43] At the same time, Libya's rich economic resources also provide impetus to several regional players—Qatar, United Arab Emirates, Turkey, and others—who are fanning the flames of conflict with provision of arms or military equipment.

It is clear, then, that the clamor for political isolation was a major contributing factor to the current turmoil in Libya, and that it will need to be addressed as part of any comprehensive settlement in the country. Political isolation remains a major fault line between Operation Dawn and Operation Dignity. Operation Dawn in particular accuses Haftar and its enemies in Zintan and Warshafana of being *azlam*, or linked to the former regime, whereas the House of Representatives in Tobruq passed a resolution in August 2014 that refers to Operation Dawn as "terrorists." Reconciliation is sorely needed to bring both parties together, to reunite the political tracks and to embark on a much-needed national dialogue about Libya's future. The PIL had the effect of reducing space for political dialogue to resolve differences, making compromise impossible and increasingly turning Libyan politics into a zero-sum game. It also absorbed much energy and political capital that would have been more constructively devoted to other transitional justice options, ones focusing on victims, or strengthening of institutions. This is all in the context of little progress in a justice system that continues to be steeped in paralysis.

Ideally, Libyans would look to successful transitions such as South Africa's as exemplary for the way forward. In South Africa, the legacy of apartheid was confronted through a variety of measures including a progressive constitution and a Truth and Reconciliation Commission. Libya desperately needs a political formula for power-sharing that is based on inclusion, not exclusion. The "revolution" ought to promote principles of inclusion, human rights, and respect for the dignity of victims on all sides. The drafting of a new constitution, which is still proceeding in spite of the turmoil, provides another important opportunity to decide on the future form of the Libyan state, and to determine the fundaments of its society. The constitution will contain a section on "transitional measures," which is likely to include mechanisms that seek to address the past.

But transitional justice measures should not just be left to the Constitution. Libya needs a national dialogue that will formulate a new roadmap for the political transition. Such a dialogue should acknowledge that human rights violations have taken place on all sides, and then aim to heal divisions, build institutions, and dignify victims.

Finally, the justice sector in Libya will ultimately need to be reconstructed, including additional security being provided to the prisons and courts. Trials should be conducted fairly and focus on a limited number of former senior regime figures, or those who committed serious violations on either side. Investigations into serious crimes committed by *thuwwar*, particularly in the summer of 2014, are also necessary to ensure even-handed justice and to demonstrate that there will be no impunity for such acts going forward.

Eventually, the Political Isolation Law will need to be refocused to concentrate on those who deserve to be excluded based on past conduct (focusing on serious human rights violations or corruption) rather than just affiliation, while allowing those who did not commit violations to contribute meaningfully to the new Libya. This would assist in many areas, including in the re-establishment of an army, sorely needed in Libya's flailing security sector. It will also send a signal that there is room for all Libyans to contribute to rebuilding the country. The political process should seek to convert "revolutionary legitimacy" into democratic legitimacy, and should aim at dismantling Libya's numerous militias. Indigenous Libyan traditions of reconciliation at the local level, in combination with broad transitional justice measures mentioned above, could serve to promote a lasting solution to Libya's divisions and enable it finally to emerge from the shadows of its troubled history.

9

TRUTH AND FACT-FINDING
IN THE ARAB MONARCHIES

Elham Fakhro

Introduction

History is rife with examples of states and societies seeking justice for past crimes during periods of political transition. Indeed, the earliest known practice of transitional justice took place in 400 BC, during the reinstatement of democracy in the aftermath of an oligarchical coup in Athens. During such transitional moments, efforts at establishing accountability and restitution for past crimes fell within the exclusive domain of national criminal justice systems, which took up the task of enforcing retributive or restorative justice. Today, transitional justice practices are increasingly shaped by two contemporary trends. The first is the rise of an international human rights movement, which promotes a value-based system of rights independent from the framework of formal politics. Rather than drive change through traditional avenues of politics and ideology, this movement emphasizes the creation of legal and institutional mechanisms to improve the rule of law, good governance, and individual rights outside the framework of politics. Within post-conflict settings, this trend toward institutional creation has contributed to a growth in the number of judicial and quasi-judicial bodies, including specialized courts, tribunals, and fact-finding bodies. A second trend responsible for shaping the contemporary transitional justice movement is the tendency toward the replication of human rights institutions across state borders, or "institutional borrowing." This phenomenon is particularly true of the truth commission. Established mainly in Latin America to uncover the truth about past abuses during the third wave of democratization, truth commissions are increasingly being created within states undergoing different forms of transition, by governments seeking to achieve a variety of aims ranging from democratization to justice. Further complementing the rise of these institutions are specialized policy centers, dedicated toward disseminating knowledge and technical expertise of comparative transitional justice.

The institutionalization and globalization of transitional justice institutions has influenced the behavior of governments and political activists in Arab states. In Morocco, leftist opponents of the regime launched a campaign in 1999 calling on King Mohammed VI to create a truth commission to reveal the truth about forced disappearances taking place between the 1960s and 1980s, with the aim of establishing compensation and accountability for disappearances. Eager to improve the monarchy's image abroad and build new alliances with its leftist opponents against the rising threat of radical Islamism, King Mohammed VI launched a truth and reconciliation commission in 2004, declaring it part of a broader process of political liberalization and reform in the state. Inspired by the campaign in Morocco, political activists in Bahrain launched a similar campaign in the year 2000, to pressurize the new King Hamad bin Isa Al-Khalifa to create a truth commission to investigate claims of torture taking place during a 25-year period of unrest between 1975 and 2000. The government responded by dismissing these demands. As Arab Spring-inspired protests erupted in 2011, the monarchy in Bahrain faced renewed calls by opposition activists and Bahrain's international allies to establish accountability for the deaths of protesters that year. In this context, King Hamad created the Bahrain Independent Commission of Inquiry, promising to reveal the truth about events taking place during a two-month period of unrest.

The next section will describe events leading up to the establishment of truth and fact-finding commissions in Morocco and Bahrain, and assess whether these commissions have been effective in two areas: first, in fulfilling the terms of their mandates by shedding light on past human rights abuses;

and second, in spurring broader reforms related to the rule of law, including democratization and accountability.

Morocco

The "years of lead"

In December 1952, protests and riots erupted across Casablanca to denounce the assassination of prominent Tunisian labor activist Farhad Hached, purportedly by paramilitaries linked to the French government.[1] France and Spain had assumed a protectorate status over Morocco decades earlier, in 1912.[2] In response, the Resident General of Morocco outlawed the Moroccan Communist Party and the Istiqlal (Nationalist) Party, the leading opposition movements in the state. The following year, authorities exiled the popular Sultan Mohammed V to Corsica, replacing him with his distant cousin. Viewing the new sultan as a puppet leader, Nationalists and Marxists intensified their use of violent tactics against French authorities.[3] Facing an increasingly aggressive opposition movement in Morocco, and a deteriorating situation in Algeria, French authorities succumbed to populist pressures and returned the exiled Sultan to the country. Upon his return, the Sultan successfully negotiated the country's independence, taking steps to build a constitutional monarchy and a modern governmental apparatus. Widely revered as a champion of anti-imperialism and a symbol of Moroccan independence, the reign of Mohammed V lasted just six years, until his death in 1961.

Following the death of Mohammed V, his son Hassan II acceded to the throne. The new King pursued a pro-Western foreign policy, strengthening alliances with France and the United States, whose regional interests he vigorously promoted.[4] On this account, King Hassan II came to be seen as an enemy of nationalist and progressive forces, a reputation he maintained by suppressing and punishing all opposition activity. Indeed, between 1960 and the late 1980s, in the decades referred to by Moroccans as the "years of lead," security forces abducted, arrested, tortured, and forcibly disappeared leftist activists, trade unionists, Islamists, and a range of other individuals accused of mobilizing against the government. The crackdown was particularly severe against members of the leftist National Union of Popular Forces Party (UNFP), whose leader Mehdi Ben Barka was exiled to France and later forcibly disappeared. During this period of challenges, there were two coup attempts, the first carried out by a group of army officers at the King's

Palace in July 1971, and the second led by General Mohamed Oufkir in August 1972.[5]

As the struggle between Moroccan opposition forces and the government intensified, a separate territorial dispute played out along the country's southeastern borders. Although Morocco had gained independence from colonial rule in 1957, the territory of Western Sahara remained under the control of Spanish forces, amidst competing claims to the area by Morocco and Mauritania. A nationalist guerrilla insurgency by native inhabitants of the region, the nomadic Sahrawis, erupted during the early 1970s, driven by the Popular Front for the Liberation of Saguia el-Hamra and Rio de Oro (Polisario Front).[6] In November 1975, Spain agreed to withdraw from the territory and partition the region between Morocco and Mauritania. A ruling by the International Court of Justice in October of the same year legitimized claims of independence by Sahrawis, stating: "there existed no tie of territorial sovereignty between Western Sahara and the Kingdom of Morocco or the Mauritanian entity."[7] Amidst rising domestic tensions, and the need of a "sacred cause" to unify the nation,[8] the King of Morocco ordered the military annexation of two-thirds of Western Sahara, placing the Moroccan government in direct conflict with the Polisario Front.[9] Armed struggle broke out between Morocco and the Polisario Front between the years 1975 to 1991, during which the Polisario declared an independent state. The Moroccan government bombarded Sahrawi refugee camps in the region with napalm and white phosphorus, and arrested and abducted suspected Polisario rebels. Human rights organizations in Western Sahara accuse the government of causing the disappearance of 1,000–1,500 Sahrawis in the territory over the years 1975–90.[10]

Experimenting with reforms

By the late 1980s, Morocco began implementing structural adjustment programs imposed as part of loans granted to the state by international financial institutions, leading to a contraction in government funding of social and welfare programs. The retreat of the state in the economic sphere created a climate amenable to the growth of civil society organizations, paving the way for the proliferation of social, political, and human rights groups that demanded reforms. Amidst pressure from civil society, King Hassan II announced the creation of the royal Advisory Council on Human Rights (CCDH) in 1990, tasking the body with "resolving all outstanding human rights issues within six months."[11] The subsequent year, King Hassan II announced the closure of Tazmamart prison, a security complex that had become a symbol of torture and oppression.

As part of its mandate, the CCDH carried out the first public inquiry in Morocco into the fate of disappeared persons, concluding that a total of 112 Moroccans had been forcibly disappeared, of whom 56 had died. The CCDH did not identify the entities responsible for their disappearance, nor did it include any victims from the Western Sahara region in its investigation. Activists dismissed the numbers of disappeared released by the CCDH as widely under-representative, demanding a more thorough investigation.[12]

In 1993, the King announced the creation of a specialized Ministry of Human Rights, and ratified the United Nations Convention against Torture.[13] In a speech delivered on 8 July1994, King Hassan II promised to "turn the page definitively" on human rights abuses, and resolve the issue of political prisoners. During the years 1991–6, the King released hundreds of political prisoners,[14] and approved constitutional amendments expanding the parliament's powers to include the investigation of ministers.[15] In 1991, he also signed a ceasefire agreement with the Polisario Front, ending the military conflict but providing no resolution to the territorial dispute.

Following the death of King Hassan II in 1999, his son Mohammed VI acceded to the throne, pledging to address past human rights violations and ordering the formation of the Independent Arbitration Commission (IAC), tasked with allocating financial reparations to victims of human rights abuses that had taken place since 1956. The IAC received 5,127 applications for compensation within the four-month deadline that it established, earmarking $100 million in reparations to 7,700 victims and their descendants. It submitted its final report to King Mohamed VI in November 2003, but the King did not release its contents to the public.[16] The following year, the CCDH began to distribute preliminary compensation payments to Sahrawis who had been disappeared or detained, aimed at meeting their medical and financial needs.[17]

The establishment of the IAC did not quell opposition demands for a Truth and Reconciliation Commission. Instead, human rights advocates within mainland Morocco used its formation as an opportunity to demand the establishment of a parallel forum, capable of revealing the full truth about past abuses. Led by Driss Benzekri, a popular former Marxist activist who had spent seventeen years in detention under King Hassan II, a coalition of Islamists, human rights campaigners, and former army soldiers established the Moroccan Forum for Truth and Justice (*Forum Verité et Justice*, FVJ), a group dedicated to mobilizing public opinion in favor of a truth commission. Many members of the FVJ consisted of former leftist militants, some of who adopted the slogans of the human rights movement and developed ties with international human rights organizations, as a new means of continuing their struggle against the monarchy.[18] The FVJ organized activities across the country, holding demonstrations in front of former detention centers. It also distributed complaint forms to victims and their families, encouraging them to document details of past repression, and conducted joint advocacy activities with local human rights organizations.[19]

The Equity and Reconciliation Commission

On 16 May 2003, a series of suicide bombings erupted across Casablanca, killing 43 civilians. This was a powerful indicator of the growing threat of religious radicalism in Morocco. Increasingly aware of the need to build alliances against radical Islamist opponents and eager to promote his image abroad as a pro-democracy reformist, King Mohammed VI announced the creation of a truth commission, the Equity and Reconciliation Commission (*Instance Equité et Réconciliation*, IER, or ERC) in 2004.[20] In its written report to the United Nations Human Rights Committee, the government stated: "The appointment by King Mohammed VI of the Equity and Reconciliation Commission represents a decisive step towards completing the process of democratic transition in Morocco."[21]

The King appointed Driss Benzekri as President of the Commission. Thirteen of the commission's sixteen members were former regime opponents, including activists driven to exile and many who had spent decades in the regime's prisons. Most members of the FVJ agreed to cooperate with the body. Some on the far left, who had used the campaign for the truth commission as a means to de-legitimize the regime, deemed the prospect of entering into a compromise with the monarchy a betrayal of their cause, and refused to work with the new institution. Nonetheless, the IER represented the culmination of a national political compromise, between activists hoping that the establishment of a truth commission might spur wider democratization, reform, and accountability; and a monarchy eager to isolate its Islamist opponents, co-opt its historic opponents on the left, and improve its image abroad.

Evaluating the Equity and Reconciliation Commission

The following section will describe and assess the work of the IER. It will examine whether the commission was effective in generating human rights and institutional reforms through its recommendations.

On 10 April 2004, King Mohammed VI issued Decree no. 1.04.42, granting the IER a triple mandate to investigate unresolved cases of forced disappearances and arbitrary detention, determine the responsibility of state organs or any other party in carrying out abuses, and to rule conclusively on reparation requests pending before the Independent Arbitration Commission.[22] The decree also immediately ruled out the possibility that the IER might establish individual accountability, stipulating that "the IER is not a judicial body and will not determine individual responsibility."[23]

The commission adopted a broad interpretation of its mandate, examining crimes not specifically included in it, such as torture, ill-treatment, and deaths caused by excess use of force. It adopted a broad definition of forced disappearances, to include deaths in detention, and cases of persons who disappeared in unclear circumstances.[24] Its definition of torture was also expansive, including physical suffering, ill treatment, and psychological suffering, in line with international standards.[25] Some forms of human rights violations remained outside the scope of the commission, including the torture of persons taking place outside the detention system, arrests deemed "non-political," and violence against demonstrators.

As part of its investigations, the IER organized seven public hearings throughout Morocco, to allow victims the opportunity to publicize their suffering, restore their dignity, and preserve a common memory. It also held specialized thematic hearings on issues such as arbitrary detention, and organized public workshops, aired on state media.[26]

The commission delivered its final report to King Mohammed VI on 1 December 2005. The report provided a chronicle of human rights violations taking place at the hands of security forces, concluding that forced disappearances were practiced "against individuals and groups, sometimes in cases where victims had no affiliation to any political, communal, or union activity, and usually after individuals were abducted from their homes and placed in isolation." It estimated that 750 persons had been disappeared, and detailed abuses that took place regularly in places of detention including isolation, ill-feeding, and lack of hygiene. The report concluded that torture was the preferred method used by security agencies to interrogate detainees on political issues, through use of hanging, burning, and forcing individuals to drink polluted substances. It also concluded that many detainees were killed as a result of excess use of force by authorities.[27]

In fulfilling the terms of its mandate on reparations, the IER studied 20,046 requests for financial restitution, and allocated reparations on the basis of loss of employment, income, property, and to fulfill the aims of medical and moral rehabilitation, and social reinsertion. In the years after its conclusion, the CCDH assumed responsibility for distributing reparations, handing out $85 million in reparations to over 16,000 affected persons. Eleven regions that were reported to have suffered disproportionately under the earlier regimes were identified as part of city-specific reparations programs.[28]

The final element of the mandate, allowing the IER to determine the responsibility of state organs, was constrained by a provision that prohibited it from revealing the identities of state agents implicated in past abuses. As a result, the commission did not allow individuals testifying publicly to identify their abusers by name. Further, while the final report attributed responsibility for most cases of forced disappearance to state security agencies, it did not indicate which branches or individuals held responsibility, nor did it indicate the chain of command followed.[29] This had several repercussions: it prevented victims from providing a full narrative of past experiences, it hindered the potential of the state to cleanse its agencies of perpetrators of abuse or follow up with criminal prosecution, and it also meant that victims could not rely on evidence from the report to pursue criminal prosecutions or group actions against state agents implicated in abuses.[30] In an interview provided by Driss Benzekri to Human Rights Watch, Benzekri noted that the IER did provide the names of individuals identified as routine violators to the King, but it is unclear what action, if any, was taken against these individuals.

The Commission's ability to reveal a full record of past abuses was also constrained by the absence of subpoena powers in its mandate, depriving it from the authority to compel officials to testify at its hearings. Officials implicated in abuses were therefore under no obligation to respond publicly to allegations of wrongdoing or neglect taking place under their watch. Indeed, some former officials refused to testify before the commission, depriving it of vital sources of information.[31]

The final report also failed to address abuses taking place in Western Sahara, one of the most politically sensitive areas of the conflict and where Moroccan security forces carried out hundreds of forced disappearances. Nor were Sahrawis given the opportunity to air public testimonies in the same way as other parts of the country. For example, a public hearing scheduled for Western Sahara was canceled at short notice, purportedly due to security reasons.

Beyond truth-telling: implementing the recommendations made by the IEC

In addition to revealing past atrocities and ruling on reparation requests, the final report made recommendations to the Moroccan government, including further investigations into forced disappearances and deaths in detention. Proposed legislative reforms included ratification of the Rome Statute to grant the International Criminal Court jurisdiction over crimes committed in Morocco, and abolishing the death penalty. Other proposed reforms included embedding greater human rights protections in the Moroccan constitution, proposals for security sector reforms, and judicial reforms to grant the body responsible for appointing Supreme Court judges greater independence from the Ministry of Justice. The proposals also included developing a national strategy to tackle impunity, and improving human rights education and awareness.

In a speech delivered to mark the end of the commission's mandate, King Mohammed referred to its work as the continuation of the work begun by King Hassan II, and as a sign of collective pardon. He expressed sorrow towards victims of human rights violations, but stopped short of providing an official apology, and pledged that all of the report's recommendations would be implemented. In the aftermath of the report, Morocco announced legislative reforms to bring its laws into line with international human rights standards. These included penal code amendments that prohibit torture, and render evidence obtained under violence or duress as inadmissible in court. On 19 October 2006, Morocco lifted its reservation to Article 20 of the Convention against Torture, recognizing the competence of the Committee against Torture to pursue investigations in the state.[32] The government also implemented training programs for law enforcement personnel and prison guards. In February 2010, the King issued a royal high directive making the National Police an autonomous directorate, which aimed at improving the quality of recruits and reducing corruption. That year the government also announced that it arrested, prosecuted, or opened investigations into government authorities at all levels, for crimes including assault and bribery, although the government did not publish information on the number of convictions or punishments made.[33]

Crucially, the Moroccan government also granted the CCDH authority to continue the investigations begun by the IER. In 2010, the Advisory Council of Human Rights published a follow-up report, providing its conclusions into an investigation into forced disappearances and deaths in detention. The report addresses some of the shortcomings of the IER related to Western Sahara, for instance naming 938 victims of forced disappearances, both from mainland Morocco and from Western Sahara. The report provides further details on a number of these victims, including a list of 90 detainees who died in detention centers in the south-east of the country, and a list of 151 individuals who died in military bases in Western Sahara. The report also provides information about burial sites located inside prison complexes.[34]

In 2011, in the context of sweeping political upheaval taking place across the Arab world, King Mohammed VI held a referendum for a new constitution that passed with the approval of 98.5% of voters. The new constitution provides for further human rights reforms, including by criminalizing genocide and crimes against humanity. It also contains political reforms, requiring the King to appoint the Prime Minister from the largest party elected to parliament, broadens the authority of the parliament, and grants greater autonomy to local provinces to manage their internal affairs. It also recognizes Amazigh, the language spoken by its minority Berber population, as an official language of the state. That year, King Mohammed VI also announced the creation of a National Human Rights Council to replace the CCDH. The decree creating the council grants it power to "investigate any allegations of human rights violations, to summon people to give evidence in its investigations, and to act as an early warning mechanism to prevent human rights violations." It also grants the council authority to "visit detention centers and inspect prison conditions, establish regional authorities for protecting human rights, and examine means to bring legislations in line with international human rights treaties."[35]

In revealing a narrative of past abuses, distributing reparations, and outlining structural recommendations for change, the IER succeeded in fulfilling the terms of its mandate, and acting as a catalyst for reforms within mainland Morocco. Constraints within the commission's mandate, however, precluded the commission from assuming a broader role in generating accountability, a role that activists had hoped it might fulfill. In this area, the government has refused to investigate or prosecute individuals implicated in past crimes. Nor has the government ratified the Rome Statute, which would grant jurisdiction to the International Criminal Court to launch its own prosecutions. Further, the Commission's work has done little to alter the structure of political authority in the state, or the sweeping executive powers held by the King who retains veto power over most government decisions.[36] Established as part of a broader settlement between political activists and the monarchy, the IER therefore served the specific purposes outlined in its mandate, of addressing past abuses, providing compensation to victims of abuse, and providing recommendations to strengthen human rights protections in the state. The commission's inability to spur accountability in this context reflects not only the political limits of the truth commission as an institutional avenue for delivering broad goals such as accountability, but also the boundaries of political reform laid out by the monarchy, which permits acknowledgement of the past in a manner that does not threaten the authority of individuals or institutions currently in power.

The impact of the IER has been significantly weaker in Western Sahara, where a low-level conflict between the government and independence advocates continues. Sahrawi activists remain deeply critical of the IER, citing the region's exclusion from the city-specific reparations programs as evidence of the government's insincerity in tackling the root causes of the conflict. Critically, activists allege that the government continues to cause forcible disappearance of independence advocates in the region, including Souadou el-Garhi, who disappeared from the city of Layounne in 2008; Mohamed Boutaba'a, who disappeared from the city of Dakhla in 2011; and a group of fifteen young Sahrawis who have been missing since 2005.[37] In 2012, authorities indefinitely postponed the trials of twenty-three suspects implicated in the deaths of security forces during clashes in Layounne, the capital of Western Sahara. In a joint submission made by ten human rights groups in Western Sahara to Juan Mendez, the UN Special Rapporteur on Torture, activists claimed that ten of the twenty-three men held in custody were sexually assaulted and raped during their detention.[38] Activists also insist that the CCDH has not taken steps to investigate evidence of mass graves, despite providing the government with credible information about their existence.[39] In the context of an unresolved political conflict, the commission of inquiry could do little more than reveal some information about past abuses, namely a list of persons disappeared by the state. Its establishment alone could not compensate for the absence of a political settlement between government and independence advocates, nor could the creation of the IER spur reforms in the absence of such a settlement.

Bahrain

Post-independence

Bahrain gained independence from Great Britain on 15 August 1971. Sheikh Isa bin Salman Al Khalifa assumed the role of Emir, or head of state. The population of Bahrain is diverse in its ethnic and sectarian composition, consisting of Sunni tribes originating from the Arabian Peninsula (Arabs), Shi'a communities native to Bahrain (Baharna), communities of Persian descent (Ajam), and Sunni tribes with histories of migration between the Arabian Peninsula and Iran (Hawala). Political loyalties are not intrinsically tied to sectarian identity. Indeed, during the 1950s, opposition to the regime emerged primarily from Sunni adherents to Arab nationalism, belonging to large merchant families. Following the Iranian revolution in 1979, the government began increasingly to accuse groups of Shi'a who derive religious guidance from clerics in Iran and Iraq of sowing plots to overthrow the government. Members of the Baharna community in particular accuse the government of long-standing patterns of discrimination in access to economic benefits, and political marginalization.

Following independence in 1972, the Emir held elections for a constituent assembly, mandated to draft the country's first constitution.[40] The new constitution divided legislative authority between the Emir and a majority-elected parliament.[41] The parliament had authority to give advice and consent to laws proposed by the Council of Ministers, and to question individual ministers and withdraw confidence from all ministers except the Prime Minister.[42]

Bahrain held its first parliamentary elections in 1973, with leftists and Islamist candidates making the largest gains. During the first session, legislators engaged in vigorous debates, including over a new State Security Decree issued by the Emir in December 1974, which defined terrorism broadly and increased penalties for terror-related crimes. On 25 August, the Emir dissolved the parliament, citing its inability to cooperate with the government. Instead of holding new elections as mandated by the constitution, the Emir announced that the parliament would remain indefinitely dissolved. He also declared a state of national emergency, suspended constitutional articles dealing with the legislative powers of the parliament, and established a State Security Court to fast-track terrorist crimes, whose judgments were not subject to appeal.[43] The Emir also ratified the State Security Law, authorizing indefinite detention for "crimes harmful to the internal or external security of the state," and banned gatherings of more than five persons.

Bahrain remained under a state of emergency for the following twenty-five years. During this period, activists, mostly in villages across the country, participated in protests against the government, demanding the reinstatement of the parliament. In 1981, the government announced that it had foiled a coup attempt by the Islamic Front for the Liberation of Bahrain, which aimed to install a Shi'a cleric as the head of a theocratic state. In 1996, the government announced that it had foiled another terrorist plot by a group it claimed represented Hizbollah. Authorities brought many accused members of the organization to trial on charges of conspiring to overthrow the regime, and colluding with a foreign entity. In the following years, state security forces ramped up arrests of hundreds of mainly Shi'a villagers suspected of opposition activity. Activists during this period accused security services and particularly the General Director of Security, an ex-British superintendent named Ian Henderson, of ordering the torture and abuse of detainees.

A new leader and new reforms

In 1999, the Emir's son Hamad bin Isa Al Khalifa acceded to the throne, ushering in a period of widespread optimism by declaring his intent to transform Bahrain into a constitutional monarchy. The new Emir repealed the State Security Law, dissolved the State Security Courts, and passed an amnesty law providing immunity from persecution for officials and individuals accused of past crimes. Media and press freedoms were expanded, and for the first time women were granted the right to vote and run for public office, as numerous opposition leaders returned to the state from exile.

In 2001, the new Emir held a national referendum, calling on voters to endorse the National Action Charter, a document outlining his intent to return to constitutional rule. The document gained the approval of 98.4% of voters. But instead of reinstating the suspended constitution, the new King introduced a new constitution without public consultation. This document made important changes to the legislative and executive powers of the state. It diluted the powers of the elected chamber of parliament, by forcing it to share power with an upper consultative council, whose members were appointed by the King. The new constitution also stipulated that the head of the executive branch have the final say in the event of a deadlock between the two chambers. Although political parties remained banned, political societies and trade unions were allowed, leading to an expansion in political and civil society organizations.[44]

Amidst the new configuration of political actors, new leftist and Shi'a opposition societies came together in their rejection of the new constitution as void of popular legitimacy, and boycotted the first round of elections. Together, these groups insisted on the reinstatement of the 1971 constitution. They also protested a new electoral law, which they claimed divided electoral districts to favor pro-government candidates and encourage greater representation of Sunnis in parliament.

Growing discontent

Beginning in 2007, activists from six domestic NGOs and five opposition political parties began a campaign for the creation of a Truth and Reconciliation

Commission, to reveal the truth and establish accountability for past abuses. The group organized workshops highlighting the need for admission of historic responsibility by the state, demanding financial compensation for victims of torture from the previous era, and calling for the revocation of amnesty laws to allow charges to be brought against officials implicated in past abuses. Government representatives invited to the events dismissed the need for any investigations or prosecutions, stating that the new constitution embodied a spirit of reconciliation and that amnesty laws served to promote peaceful coexistence of all groups.

The Arab Spring and 2011

The advent of popular revolutions in Egypt and Tunisia emboldened opposition activists in Bahrain, re-energizing their calls for change. In early January 2011, an anonymous online group calling itself the February 14 Youth invited citizens to participate in a "day of rage," demanding political reforms.[45] The group chose the symbolic date of 14 February as marking the tenth anniversary of the National Action Charter and their disillusionment toward the reform process. The group also lamented nepotism and corruption, which they blamed for fueling economic mismanagement, misappropriation of the country's wealth, and the privatization of large swathes of public coast.[46]

On the day of the scheduled protests, dozens gathered across the country holding signs demanding change and chanting slogans for reform. Events escalated after security forces fatally shot a young protester in the backstreets of a central village, Sanabis. Hundreds gathered at his funeral the following day, where security forces shot and killed a second demonstrator. The events prompted further outrage, leading to thousands of demonstrators amassing at a central traffic junction, the Pearl Roundabout.[47]

In the early hours of 17 February, security forces raided the area, killing four demonstrators. These deaths led to a split within the opposition, between a coalition calling for constitutional reform, and increasingly radicalized youth groups, represented by the February 14 Youth, who demanded the end of the monarchy. In response to the deaths, representatives from the largest Shi'a opposition party (Al-Wefaq) announced their withdrawal from parliament, where they held nearly half of all seats.[48]

The following day the Crown Prince appeared on state television, expressing sorrow for the deaths, ordering the re-opening of the roundabout to protesters, and inviting opposition societies to enter into a national dialogue.

According to opposition sources, the head of Al-Wefaq insisted that he would only meet with the Crown Prince if the remaining opposition societies consented to the meeting, and on condition that the Crown Prince disclose the ceiling of reform measures that would be proposed in a future political discussion.[49] In the subsequent weeks, the Pearl Roundabout acted as a platform for individuals from a range of political backgrounds to voice calls for change.

In response to the growing power of the populist movement, a prominent Sunni cleric called for a rally to take place on 21 February 2011 at the country's largest Sunni mosque, under the banner of National Unity. At the rally, the cleric announced the establishment of a new organization for "those in society who have no political or institutional affiliation to express their opinion." In the following weeks, the group expanded to serve as a pro-government counter to the anti-government populist movement, attracting tens, and by some estimates hundreds, of thousands of followers.

Thereafter, rallies and demonstrations continued. General security in the country deteriorated as masked vigilantes exercised a growing presence across the country. As protests continued, the Crown Prince again invited opposition leaders on 13 March to enter into a dialogue with the regime. The following day, and before opposition societies delivered a reply to the Crown Prince, GCC Peninsula Shield forces entered Bahrain through its causeway with Saudi Arabia, signaling the advent of a security crackdown against opposition supporters. On 15 March, King Hamad issued Royal Decree no. 18, evoking a State of National Safety, which granted government authorities heightened powers and prerogatives, but whose parameters were largely undefined.[50] In the subsequent weeks, security forces arrested hundreds accused of participating in anti-government protests, amidst growing evidence of abuses taking place against suspected opposition sympathizers in the country's prisons and in villages across the country.

The Bahrain Independent Commission of Inquiry

On 8 May 2011, King Hamad lifted the state of national safety, citing a general improvement in the country's security. In July 2011, he announced the launch of a National Dialogue, to produce agreement between Bahrain's political factions. That month, he also issued Royal Decree no. 28, creating the Bahrain Independent Commission of Inquiry (BICI or "the commission"), authorizing it to "investigate and report on the events occurring in Bahrain in February and March 2011, and any subsequent consequences arising out of the aforementioned events, and to make such recommendations as it may deem appropriate." The decree appointed Egyptian–American international law expert Cherif Basiouni to head the commission, and granted it authority to access "all concerned government agencies, files, and records."[51] In addition to directing the commission to provide a narrative of the events that took place and the context in which they occurred, the decree also mandated the commission to investigate eight other areas, including:

> whether any violations of human rights norms had taken place during interactions between the public and the government, acts of violence taking place at the Salmaniya Hospital and the GCC Roundabout [two of the main sites of protest activity], instances of alleged police brutality or violence by demonstrators, the circumstances and appropriateness of arrests and detention, allegations of disappearances or torture, media harassment against demonstrators, unlawful demolition of religious structures, and the involvement of foreign forces or actors in events.[52]

While the BICI and Morocco's IER were both established as part of top-down processes of reform by monarchs, they are distinct in several respects. First, the BICI did not include opposition leaders in its ranks, and relied on a narrower temporal mandate, limiting investigations to events taking place over the course of a few months. This is in contrast to the decree of the IER which granted it the right to investigate events taking place over a 43-year period. Further, Morocco's commission was created in the aftermath of conflict, and as the government pursued a broader political settlement with its former opponents. The commission in Bahrain, by contrast, was established as the conflict remained unresolved, and as high-level opposition supporters remained in detention. Finally, Bahrain's commission was almost entirely the product of a top-down initiative, and not the result of sustained grass-roots pressure, as had been the case with the IER. Instead, opposition activists in Bahrain had largely focused their demands on political reform, and direct accountability for members of security forces accused of abuses against opposition supporters, rather than an investigation. Demands for a truth commission had mostly been voiced in the past as part of a movement to establish accountability for purported abuses taking place during the 1980s and 1990s. The creation of the commission came as a surprise, so much so that some opposition leaders doubted the sincerity of the investigative efforts, amidst rumors that it had been created not as a means to address internal abuses, but rather to placate international pressure on Bahrain to reverse its security crackdown. Nonetheless, the announcement also generated some optimism, amidst those within the government and civil society who saw it as a reconciliatory gesture from the monarchy, and hoped that its work could pave the way for reforms and a process of internal political reconciliation.

Evaluating the BICI

The following section will analyze the work of the BICI. It will examine the interpretative role played by the commission in understanding the terms of its mandate. It will then assess the ability of the commission to achieve its primary aim of uncovering past abuses. Finally it will examine the extent to which the commission's recommendations may have been effective in paving the way for broader political and human rights reforms.

Interpreting the mandate

The terms of the commission's mandate allowed it to investigate numerous forms of abuse, from torture and ill treatment, to the role of the media in targeting demonstrators. The commission also chose to investigate abuses not specifically listed in its decree, including prosecutions made in connection with freedom of expression, association and assembly, and allegations of forced disappearances. The commission also took steps to extend this mandate temporally, by referring to the years of unrest 1975–2000, noting that during that time "almost 40 people were reported to have been killed in disturbances that included obstructing roads, burning tires, and attacking police patrols" and that "most of these clashes occurred in less affluent Shi'a villages where allegations of arbitrary arrests, police brutality, and even torture, were widespread."[53]

Applying the mandate

The commission gathered evidence from sites across Bahrain and conducted interviews with detainees in prisons and hospitals. It also conducted thousands of interviews with members of the public who chose to approach the commission complaining of harm during the unrest. It obtained evidence from numerous sources, including official government records, opposition and government supporters, politicians, and civil society.

In a 503-page report released in November 2011, the commission provided a day-by-day breakdown of events taking place in February and March 2011. In instances where the commission found competing narratives of disputed events, it included multiple versions of those events, stating that it could not reach a definitive conclusion. The report also included information on political developments related to those events, including details of political negotiations that had taken place between the Crown Prince and opposition societies.

In its final report, the commission found evidence of many violations of basic human rights, including violations of the right to live, excess use of force by security forces to disperse demonstrations, and violations of the right to a free and fair trial by military courts that had allowed evidence extracted under torture. It also found violations of the right to freedom of expression and assembly, including against some 4,500 workers who were dismissed from their jobs for participating in union-backed strikes, held in solidarity with the protest movement.

The commission concluded that 13 civilians had died as a result of the disproportionate use of force by security forces, noting that security agencies acted beyond what was necessary in their use of firearms and crowd-dispersal techniques.[54] It also found that masked security forces systematically raided private homes during the state of national safety, committing theft and vandalism, intentionally breaking doors, and terrifying the occupants.[55] It also found that in many cases "women were asked to stand in their sleeping clothes, which did not adequately cover their bodies," and that "this practice also constitutes a violation of Muslim religious practices."[56] The final report also detailed the deaths of three members of the security forces and two expatriates at the hands of violent protesters, including a police officer who was run over by a vehicle at the roundabout on 15 March 2011.

The commission relied on a team of forensic medical experts to investigate claims of torture. Its final report attributed five deaths taking place in the custody of the Ministry of Interior to acts of torture, noting evidence of a "clear pattern of physical and psychological abuse in state custody," including against a group of thirteen prominent opposition leaders. The commission also provided detailed information of 60 cases of torture and mistreatment, verified by the forensic team, concluding that torture and abuse were aimed primarily at obtaining confessions from detainees, and that a lack of accountability within the security system lead to a "culture of impunity," which was implicitly condoned by judicial and prosecutorial personnel.[57]

The final report concluded that national television and print media made derogatory comments about opposition supporters and provided inflammatory coverage of events, but that these violations stopped short of constituting hate speech.[58] It also concluded that the Government of Bahrain demolished 30 Shi'a houses of worship during the unrest, 25 of which were in violation of existing zoning and permit laws. The commission noted that the government should have been aware that the timing of the demolitions at the height of political and social unrest would inflame tensions between the government and the Shi'a population.

Finally, the report found no discernible link between events occurring in Bahrain and the Islamic Republic of Iran, which had been blamed by the government as the main instigator of unrest.[59]

Implementing reforms

The BICI presented its report to King Hamad on 23 November 2011. In addition to providing a chronology and analysis of events, the report also included 26 recommendations for remedying human rights abuses and strengthening the rule of law. These included recommendations aimed at creating new institutions, such as a national commission tasked with implementing the report's recommendations, and an independent mechanism to determine the accountability of those in government who committed unlawful and negligent acts. Recommendations in the area of institutional reform called on the government to separate the office of the Inspector General from the Ministry of Interior, to allow it to receive and investigate complaints, and the revocation of the law enforcement capabilities of the National Security Agency, one of the main security agencies implicated in abuses. Recommendations related to the training of personnel included the development of training programs for security forces, and the training of judicial officials on eradicating torture and ill treatment. In the area of legislative reform, the commission proposed the enactment of requirements to compel the Attorney General to investigate all claims of torture. In the area of judicial reform, the commission recommended that the government transfer all convictions from the National Security Courts to civilian courts. It also urged the government to drop all charges for offenses involving political expression that did not advocate violence. Finally, recommendations in the area of restitution and compensation included proposals to compensate families of deceased victims in a manner commensurate with the gravity of their loss, and recommendations to ensure the reinstatement of dismissed workers. The final report also called on the government to consider rebuilding some of the demolished religious structures at its own expense.

As of 2015, the government claims that it has implemented most of the commission's recommendations, including by creating special training programs for security and judicial personnel, and revoking arrest powers of the National Security Agency and the dismissal of its chief in 2011. It also highlights its creation of a Special Investigations Unit in the office of the Public Prosecution,[60] and the creation of an Ombudsman's Office in the Ministry of Interior, tasked with receiving and investigating allegations of wrongdoing by security officials. In June 2014, the Ombudsman's Office released data claiming that it had investigated 242 complaints in 2014, of which 29 were referred to the Special Investigations Unit, and 15 to a specialized military court. According to these figures, twelve personnel from the Ministry of Interior, including officers, are currently facing criminal charges in connection with allegations of torture and police misconduct.[61] The government also states that it has implemented mandatory human rights courses for all students at the University of Bahrain, dropped all charges related to freedom of expression from activists, and created a tripartite commission made up of representatives of the International Labor Organization, the Ministry of Labor, and the General Federation of Bahrain Trade Unions, to reinstate dismissed employees. Finally, it states that it has launched a compensation program to award financial restitution to victims of the unrest.

Opposition activists insist that the reforms do not go far enough, highlighting the lack of accountability of high-level personnel, and the continued detention of the thirteen opposition leaders, including the head of Bahrain's largest leftist society. Lawyers representing youth accused of stirring unrest claim that while the judiciary has dropped charges related to freedom of expression in many cases, activists continue to face lengthy prison sentences for charges, including illegal assembly and insulting the regime. Lawyers also note that while the government did transfer all cases from military to civilian courts, the transfer of these cases has not resulted in new trials. Instead, it has led to a review of convictions based on evidence obtained from military courts, obtained in many cases under threats of duress and torture.[62] The General Federation of Bahrain Trade Unions, the largest union federation in the country, also notes that while many of the 4,500 employees dismissed at the height of the unrest have been returned to their positions, approximately 400 employees remain dismissed, and many have been forced to accept demotions in the workplace. Opposition activists are particularly critical of the ongoing impunity of high-level officials, and the absence of high-level prosecutions for past abuses. Indeed, to date, just a handful of low-level security personnel have been sentenced for crimes related to past abuses, with no individual above the rank of officer found guilty in a court of law.

Furthermore, opposition activists claim that although $26 million has been earmarked for a compensation fund, it remains unclear whether these funds have been distributed, and under what criteria.[63]

Critics also point to a wave of new restrictive legislation, which has had the effect of reversing the impact of any human rights reforms. These include a new law approved in February 2014 which imposes a jail sentence of up to seven years and a fine of up to $26,500 for "whoever has insulted, in any kind of public manner, the King of Bahrain, its flag, or its national emblem."[64] The National Assembly also approved an amendment to the Public Gathering Law, banning demonstrations near "hospitals, airports, embassies, consulates, economic, and lively places," and requiring protest organizers to provide up to $53,000 as a security deposit. Authorities have been granted discretion to reject permission for protests based on vague criteria, including those that might "harm the economic interests of the country."[65] New legislation under the Bahrain Workers' Trade Union Law also prohibits strikes against a long list of "vital and important facilities," and the law has also been amended to create pro-government trade union federations, while it grants authorities the power to decide which federation may engage in collective bargaining at the national level.[66] On 24 July 2014, new amendments to the Citizenship Law came into force, permitting the Ministry of Interior, with the approval of the cabinet, to strip citizenship of a person who "aids or is involved in the service of hostile state" or who "causes harm to the interests of the Kingdom or acts in a way that contravenes his duty of loyalty to it." To date, over one hundred individuals, including opposition supporters, have been stripped of their citizenship for "damaging the security of the state."[67]

A series of national dialogues initiated by the government did little to resolve the political crisis. The first round of dialogues, held in July 2011, included over 300 representatives from a broad range of interest groups, including business associations, social clubs, and journalists. Opposition groups withdrew from the talks just weeks later on grounds of under-representation.[68] A second round of dialogues launched in 2013 failed to produce an agreement on the mechanisms governing the dialogue process, or the methods through which any agreement reached might be implemented. In October 2013, opposition groups suspended their participation in the national dialogue following the arrest of a senior opposition leader on charges of inciting terrorism. The government formally ended the dialogues in January 2014, although behind the scenes negotiations are at times reported to be ongoing.[69] Low-level clashes between youths affiliated to the February 14 movement and security forces continue to take place in the backstreets of Shi'a villages, with occasional deaths of both demonstrators and security forces being reported.

In an interview with *Al-Monitor* in July 2014, Cherif Bassiouni assessed the government's progress in implementing the BICI recommendations, stating:

> The government has consistently carried out the implementation of the recommendations. What critics see is that these recommendations have been implemented on a piecemeal basis, so that its cumulative impact is not felt... The accountability mechanism leaves much to be desired. Cases of torture and deaths under torture have not been adequately investigated; they have not been adequately prosecuted. There are very fundamental social and economic issues involved in the Shiite population that need to be addressed. Upheaval is bound to increase unless we address the social and economic reasons... I have to say that the Minister of Interior in particular has really taken to heart the recommendations (by establishing) an ombudsman, a police professional practices office and the chief of police has been changed. Within the judiciary... the prosecutor is acting independently, the judiciary is acting independently and the minister of justice is acting independently. So it's difficult to say who is moving fast enough and effectively enough. And I think there is also a question of public credibility that the prosecutor's office does not have good credibility with the victims of the crimes... There's no doubt in my mind that the King and the Crown Prince, a number of people in government, like the Ministry of Interior, are committed to making progress.[70]

Conclusion

How effective are truth commissions that operate in the absence of democratization? What should these institutions be expected to achieve, and how important is the political environment in shaping their efficacy? The cases of Morocco's Equity and Reconciliation Commission and Bahrain's Independent Commission of Inquiry offer some insights into these questions and into the efficacy of institutional borrowing, more generally.

As with fact-finding bodies created in the aftermath of democratic transitions, these commissions operated within the context of political sensitivities and sometimes in the presence of outright prohibitions in their mandates preventing them from identifying individual responsibility for past abuses. As a result, investigations were limited to establishing general patterns of past abuse, and identifying victims of violations. While commissions would no doubt have been more effective had they been granted the ability to reveal the identities of the perpetrators of abuse, the acceptance of their narratives by the heads of state in Morocco and Bahrain, and implicit admission of governmental responsibility, also provides an important break with the past in states otherwise characterized by denial and deflection. The distribution of reparations, particularly in Morocco, also had symbolic and practical significance.

While both commissions emerged as remarkably successful in detailing general patterns of past abuses, their ability to act as catalysts for lasting reforms was successful only in instances where the conflict in question had come to an end, and where governments and opposition leaders had reached a political settlement. Within mainland Morocco, the creation of the IER came about in the aftermath of a broader process of reconciliation between the government and opposition actors, and following the establishment of a series of mechanisms intended to promote reform, notably the CCDH and IAC. The inclusion of former regime opponents within the commission was key in allowing it to gain symbolic significance and mark a new era of improved human rights practices in the state. Amidst a broader process of reconciliation, the country's human rights record did witness a substantial improvement from the past.

This is not the case with Bahrain or Western Sahara, where no settlement was reached between opposition actors and the government. In the case of Bahrain, the establishment of the fact-finding commission did not come about as part of a broader political deal, but rather in spite of it. Indeed, the commission conducted its operations as many political leaders remained imprisoned, and as opposition sympathizers vowed to continue the struggle against the government. The absence of local or opposition representation on the commission, while guaranteeing it independence, also had the effect of diluting the role it might have played as part of a broader mechanism of compromise between the government and opposition actors. In Western Sahara, the IER began its investigations while independence and anti-government sentiments remained high, and as human rights abuses remained ongoing. In that context, it is unsurprising that a commission of inquiry was able to achieve little more than reveal some patterns of past abuse.

In the final analysis, expectations by activists that a commission of inquiry could lead to accountability proved misplaced; nor are they catalysts for democratization, nor a substitute for political reconciliation, where these processes are absent. These limitations are reflected in much of the literature on truth commissions, which identify a fundamental trade-off in their operation between truth and accountability, as mechanisms of compromise between incoming and outgoing regimes. Where regimes remained unchanged, as in the cited examples, these institutions also reflect the extent of reform that regimes in power are willing to accept, which allow reflections on past abuses so long as doing so does not lead to criminal sanctions against those in power.

Ultimately, examining truth commissions operating under monarchies raises broader questions in the field of transitional justice. In the absence of objective or internationally agreed criteria for what constitutes a transition, or how these commissions should be assessed, how much should be expected from these bodies? Should they be understood as vehicles designed only to examine past abuses, or should they also be expected to deliver a basket of desirable aims designed to strengthen the rule of law, or promote democracy? As these institutions continue to proliferate across the globe, scholars and practitioners will need to take steps to improve assessment of their impact across these different settings, and identify their limitations within these contexts. What is evident is that an institutional form cannot act as a substitute for a political process, particularly when so much of the work of these commissions is both shaped by, and in response to, a set of local political circumstances.

PART III

KEY DIMENSIONS
OF TRANSITIONAL JUSTICE

LESSONS FROM EGYPT

10

"THE WALLS WILL NOT BE SILENT"

A CAUTIONARY TALE ABOUT TRANSITIONAL JUSTICE AND COLLECTIVE MEMORY IN EGYPT[1]

Judy Barsalou

Introduction

The application of transitional justice entered a new phase with the wave of uprisings that swept through the Arab world starting in 2010. In a region where authoritarian regimes have long prevailed and little justice has been available for their victims, the uprisings raise questions regarding Arab expectations about justice and accountability in politically dynamic settings, including when or how to implement transitional justice when the nature or extent of the transition is not yet clear. This chapter explores two primary questions: following the removal of President Hosni Mubarak in February 2011, to what extent has transitional justice been undertaken in post-Mubarak Egypt; and how have collective memory processes affected struggles to define the country? It examines the intellectual underpinnings and contested understandings of the goals of transitional justice, as viewed through the blurry lens of the

Egyptian "revolution," and it shares insights from fieldwork conducted in Egypt between November 2011 and March 2012, focused on the expectations and hopes articulated by some Egyptians during the first year following Mubarak's removal.

The chapter argues that elements of transitional justice were introduced by the transitional government operating under the Supreme Council of the Armed Forces (SCAF), but only after ongoing strikes and demonstrations exerted significant pressure for reform, which the government sought to relieve primarily by holding a limited number of public officials accountable for the previous regime's crimes. It exposes the disparate political agendas that emerged around the popularly named "25 January Revolution," and outlines varying expectations about the end goals of transitional justice.[2] For some, transitional justice represented the opportunity to foster sustainable democracy. For others, the primacy of socio-economic justice for Egypt's poor was the main point of transitional justice, not democracy. The chapter also argues that the arrival of international transitional justice experts, sharing lessons learned from other countries without engaging in Egypt's political realities, created pressure to implement transitional justice even before consensus about Egypt's political future had been forged. Finally, the chapter explores the scope of efforts by ordinary Egyptians to influence collective memory about the past, arguing that failure to recognize memorialization as a key element of transitional justice is both a risk and a lost opportunity.

Background: The emergence of transitional justice as a field of practice

Imagine that it is 1988. A group of human rights activists, lawyers, and social scientists have gathered at a conference in Wye, Maryland, organized by the Aspen Institute and funded by the Ford Foundation, to discuss challenges associated with promoting justice and accountability during times of political transition.[3] Some of those present have risked their lives opposing dictatorships in Latin America. In earlier times, they assumed that their work would be complete with the demise of those regimes. However, as complex transitions unfold in Brazil, Argentina, Uruguay, and Chile, the use of basic human rights strategies, namely, "shaming" (exposing rights abuses) and "blaming" (documenting who is responsible), no longer seem sufficient. Increasingly, activists and social scientists in this context perceive a distinction between classic human rights work and other activities designed to bolster fragile democracies. At the conference they explore challenges, opportunities, approaches, and goals aimed at facilitating the exit of authoritarian regimes and securing justice for victims and survivors.[4]

These early pioneers of transitional justice were conducting their discussions in an evolving intellectual climate. In the 1960s, a widely accepted explanation of why some countries had achieved democracy while others remained authoritarian was based on the argument that socio-economic development was a "precondition" of sustainable democracy.[5] Critics of structural theories of democratization began to articulate their views in the early 1970s. Notably, about a decade later, Guillermo O'Donnell and Philippe Schmitter argued that democracy is the outgrowth of choices and behaviors of political elites, rather than a reflection of a stage of development.[6] Using evidence from transitions in Argentina, Brazil, and Uruguay, amongst other countries, they emphasized the role of civil participation, public space, political identity, and, especially, bargains worked out by political elites. Importantly, they recognized these transitions as intensely political negotiations designed to facilitate the exit of dictators and make the fragile democracies that succeeded them more sustainable. In its early days, the emerging field of transitional justice reflected this evolution in thinking about how democracies were established and strengthened.

Later, in the 1990s, with the fall of the Soviet Union and the wave of "color" revolutions in Eastern Europe and Georgia, others theorized about the role of strategic non-violent action, which prioritized massive, organized civil society protests to bring down dictators.[7] On a practical level, organizations such as the International Center on Nonviolent Conflict (ICNC) and the United States Institute of Peace (USIP) funded and/or organized training workshops led by civil society activists. To these theorists and practitioners, conflict was a creative force to be channeled in positive ways by strategizing and waging a sort of non-violent war involving peaceful, mass civic action to initiate transitions to democracy.

Fast-forward twenty-three years to Tahrir Square on 25 January 2011: several thousand activists have chosen to honor the new Egyptian holiday, National Police Day, by breaking the law prohibiting gatherings or demonstrations involving five or more persons without a permit. In a tightly policed society, where trucks holding security forces are routinely parked next to universities, mosques, and other potential hotspots of protest, it is astonishing to see thousands streaming across Cairo to assemble in Tahrir Square. The security forces make the strategic error of blocking access to streets leading away from Tahrir, thereby increasing the demonstrators' mass by bottling them up in the square. Within days, the number of demonstrators increases dramatically after the regime shuts down access to the internet and mobile phone networks, and disrupts TV transmissions. This has the effect of encouraging previously passive and politically demotivated citizens to join the protests, if only to find out what is going on in the street. With bewildering speed, the demonstrations spread to major cities and rural villages throughout Egypt. Within 18 days it is "over": Mubarak has resigned and the SCAF, a body appointed by Mubarak and consisting of roughly two dozen senior military officers, has announced it is forming a transitional government. To many Egyptians, the stage appears to be set for a swift transition to democracy and social justice.

Transitional justice, collective memory, and trauma

The growing pool of international transitional justice practitioners and the explosion of academic literature make it is easy to forget that the field emerged scarcely two decades ago.[8] In fact, it is in its infancy and serious ambiguities remain at its heart. Does transitional justice work and, if so, under what conditions? Does it promote "reconciliation" or "social reconstruction," and what conditions are conducive to its success?[9] When survivors experience psychological trauma from their exposure to violence, how does that affect collective memory and the implementation of transitional justice? Scholars have explored these questions, but much work remains to be done.[10]

As transitional justice has grown as a field, interest in how national narratives about the past are constructed has increased. Memorialization was not discussed at the aforementioned conference in 1988.[11] Although not initially included in early definitions of transitional justice, memorialization and other memory projects are now considered to be part of the transitional justice "toolkit."[12] This relatively new focus on memorialization in transitional justice mirrors the emergence over the last century of the notion of "collective" memory, a term attributed to Hugo von Hofmannsthal in 1902, when he referred to "the dammed up force of our mysterious ancestors within us."[13] A landmark study in 1925 by French sociologist Maurice Halbwachs made an important distinction between writing history, which seeks truthful accounts of events through scholarship, and the formation of collective memory, which is based on socially constructing versions of history that piece together perspectives influenced by ethnic, religious, geographic, or other influences.[14]

The embrace of the notion that history *and* collective memory affect human understanding of the past has led to what David Berliner has called a "memory boom," in which a "vast number of scholars are currently occupied with research about memory," including political scientists who now study it as an independent variable affecting political outcomes.[15] There is a growing literature that focuses on how private mourning resulting from death or injury caused by violent conflict can evolve into public memorials designed to promote social solidarity and particular political agendas. Increasingly, memorialization is recognized as a tool to help societies become more peaceful and democratic, by embracing their difficult past and "moving on" in positive ways. Yet, in many settings, memorialization also has the opposite effect, sharpening political divisions and promoting conflict.

Seeking to establish the truth about violent conflict and repression through interpretation of memory is difficult, because it is an essentially political act that involves the simplification of complexity. Those who construct memorials embody an effort to "fixate an otherwise fluid and elusive strain of memory."[16] Creating opportunities for survivors of violent conflict to recount historical narratives is important for getting at the truth, although such narratives inevitably represent the perspective of the teller and can reinforce divides and fuel conflict. What is particularly challenging is to use memorialization to depict complex, multiple "truths," but without engaging in moral relativism that weighs, valorizes, or trivializes the harm experienced by one group against another. Professionals working in transitional justice grapple with the knowledge that "reality" is mediated by the observer's frame of reference, and that memory is fluid, elusive, non-linear, context-specific, and highly subject to manipulation.

In part, the incorporation of memorialization into the transitional justice toolkit is also based on the recognition that some individuals living in countries emerging from violent conflict experience post-traumatic stress disorder (PTSD). But does trauma displayed by individuals take on broader social dimensions in shaping collective memory, and how is it to be managed through transitional justice?[17] Psychiatrist Vamik Volkan argues that violence inflicted on a particular social or ethnic group can create, transform, or entrench group identity, fuel the emergence of a sense of group victimization and perpetuate conflict.[18] He suggests that so-called "chosen traumas," based on particularly significant or memorable events, are reshaped or glorified in their retelling by group members to subsequent generations. These "chosen traumas" become historical markers used to reify identity, justify revenge, or restore the honor of victims, and they contribute to keeping conflict alive by renewing and refreshing the feeling of victimization.

The role of trauma and how to address it remains controversial in transitional justice. Some practitioners staunchly reject efforts to "psycho-pathologize" or "medicalize" the understanding of social reconstruction by focusing on trauma, and prefer to identify sources of strength and resilience that can contribute to the rebuilding of "post-conflict" societies.[19] Controversy aside, common discourse about "healing" transitional societies through "reconciliation" suggests that many scholars and practitioners consciously or unconsciously embrace the psychological framing of transitional justice, even as evidence that it promotes healing or reconciliation remains elusive.

Two other related ambiguities about transitional justice are especially relevant to Egypt and other so-called Arab Spring countries, notably Tunisia, Yemen, Libya, Syria, and Bahrain. First, does transitional justice have a primary goal—such as easing transitions from authoritarianism to sustainable democracy and the ending of conflict—or is it more focused on human rights and promoting justice, including socio-economic rights, for victims and survivors? If the latter, is it correct to refer to measures undertaken in countries that remain undemocratic as "transitional justice"? The International Center for Transitional Justice notes that accountability measures associated with political transitions in Latin America and Eastern Europe in the late 1980s and early 1990s "were popularly called 'transitions to democracy'" and, as a result, the "new multidisciplinary field [was called] 'transitional justice.'" However, it also cautions that "each society should—indeed must—choose its own path."[20] Tricia Olsen, Leigh Payne, and Andrew Reiter address this issue in weighing what they call the "justice balance" that countries negotiate as they choose among different transitional justice mechanisms and political objectives.[21] Other authors in this volume address this issue, notably Chandra Lekha Sriram, who suggests changing the term "transitional justice" to "post-atrocity justice," when measures are implemented where no transition to democracy has occurred.[22] The scope and aims of transitional justice may be especially contested in settings where calls for distributive justice and achievement of social and economic rights by the poor are on the rise—a key demand and expectation expressed by demonstrators throughout the Egyptian uprising.

"Revolutionary" Egypt's political transition

Since Mubarak was removed from office, the country has passed through three distinct stages. The first was kicked off by the formation of a technocratic government overseen by the SCAF that governed the country between February and November 2011. The second stage began with the formation of the Muslim Brotherhood-dominated government brought to power by parliamentary elections held between November 2011 and January 2012, and the election in June 2012 of President Mohamed Morsi, a leader of the Brotherhood's Freedom and Justice Party. The third phase began with *Tamarrud* (Rebellion), a campaign that brought millions back onto the streets, calling for the resignation of the Morsi government after only one year in office. It precipitated a military coup that removed the Morsi government in July 2013 and led to the election of President Abdel Fatah el-Sisi a year later.[23] During all three periods, revolutionaries, including some Islamists, continued to push for real transformation of Egypt's social and political order, acting on their ever-present threat to deploy mass protests to challenge authority. But when it came to redefining the parameters of the new political system along democratic lines, they were consistently out-maneuvered by a diverse collective of forces, including remnants of the Mubarak regime, the intelligence, police, and military services, and Muslim Brotherhood leaders who struck their own political bargains with the military to facilitate their rise to power.

Arguably, what Egyptians called a "revolution" fell far short of that. The popularly named 25 January Revolution succeeded because it required consensus only on one issue: the removal from power of Mubarak and those closest to him.[24] Led by informal, nimble underground networks with no established offices, leaders, or political programs, the decentralized nature of the uprising made it difficult to suppress. The focus of young revolutionaries was not on forging consensus among diverse interests or groups, but on mobilizing Egyptians onto the streets.[25] Once that objective was achieved, and as discussions began about how to organize the transition, the SCAF struggled to identify leaders who could legitimately claim a link to the uprising *and* the ability to represent important constituencies. In the immediate weeks following Mubarak's removal, some high-profile youth activists declared their job done: they intended to leave negotiations to more seasoned politicians, whereupon a self-appointed group of prominent "wise men" presented itself. Because they were mostly older, economically privileged men, the group was neither representative of the youth activists nor the millions who had filled the streets, and it lacked the credibility to speak on their behalf.

Within months of the 18-day uprising, activists realized that achieving consensus on a minimal position—the removal of the head of state and his closest allies—had been the easy part. They needed to remain engaged in politics in order to negotiate who and what would replace it. Not surprisingly, secular political parties that sought to take on that challenge had poor showings in parliamentary elections in 2011 and 2012, because they were newly formed, divided, and inexperienced. The Muslim Brotherhood's Freedom and Justice Party and the Nour Party, which had longer- and better-established networks in local communities, simply out-campaigned them. Secular forces also failed to unify behind a single candidate in the 2012 presidential elections, while parliamentary and presidential elections demonstrated that the majority of Egyptians were betting on Islamist parties to lead the way to a better future. As time passed, however, those expecting Egypt's rapid transformation into a system that delivered social justice for the poor realized that the uprising had not destroyed what Egyptians came to call the "deep state"—the stubborn persistence of pre-existing, authoritarian, and unaccountable governing elites, well entrenched bureaucracies, and undemocratic behaviors left over from the Mubarak era and before.

While Egyptians adjusted their expectations, the term used to describe the uprising nonetheless survived. According to historian Joel Beinin:

> The "January 25 Revolution" has already taken place in Egyptian national historical memory along with the "1919 Revolution" and the "July 23 Revolution." Assigning dates to these events, whose significance in the modern history of Egypt is undeniable, is perhaps a necessary convenience. Calling them all "revolutions" emphasizes their popular character... However, this form of dating and naming also encourages historical misunderstandings and myth-making which do not serve the interests of Egypt's ninety-nine percent... The January 25 Revolution is not over. Rather, it has not occurred.[26]

One sign of this was that the military maintained its role, established over the past sixty years, as the dominant political institution. While revolutionaries' vision of social justice (*al 'adala al ijtima'iyya*) implied radical social and political change, the Islamists who came to power briefly appeared resigned to, if not comfortable with, the military's role, at least in the short term. Certainly the military's reputation as Egypt's savior was sorely tested between 2011 and 2013, but it was never debunked. Governmental mismanagement and inefficiency, along with security force impunity, reduced the military's popularity during the SCAF period, but it recovered substantially following the July 2013 coup. Overall, the military's position was strengthened as months of unrest unfolded. As Egyptians grew weary of chaos and feared the outbreak of civil war, they looked to the military to restore order.[27]

Applying transitional justice to Egypt

In post-Mubarak Egypt, the transitional government instituted a necessary but insufficient element of democracy—a reasonably credible set of referenda and elections that addressed next steps during the transition, and brought a new group of Islamist politicians to power. Moreover, under great pressure from ongoing demonstrations, strikes, formation of victims' groups, and media coverage, the government ushered in various elements of transitional justice. They included the following:

1) Key Mubarak regime figures were put on trial, along with some policemen accused of killing demonstrators or other crimes;
2) Various fact-finding commissions were organized to investigate killings that occurred during the uprising and at other significant events, such as massacres in Cairo's Maspero neighborhood in October 2011, and at the Port Said soccer stadium in February 2012;
3) The government launched the National Council of Care for the Revolution Martyrs' Families and Wounded to provide limited monetary compensation to some claimants, and it touted free medical care for all victims, along with medals and government jobs to wounded members of the armed forces;
4) The Ministry of Interior claimed in March 2011 that its State Security Intelligence branch was disbanded;
5) Seven months later, the government announced a "treachery law" (*qanoon al-ghadar*) to ban former leaders of Mubarak's National Democratic Party from public office;
6) Finally, the Constituent Assembly formed during the SCAF era was tasked with drafting a new constitution, a process completed by a constituent assembly convened by the subsequently elected Morsi government.

All of these efforts at transitional justice struggled to achieve credibility. When trials of Mubarak and his close associates were organized during the SCAF transition, the Ministry of Interior refused to cooperate with prosecutors seeking evidence of their involvement in alleged crimes. The proceedings stretched over months, and were notably short on decorum. While a few guilty verdicts were handed down, the vast majority of high officials and security force members responsible for the injury and death of demonstrators and other crimes were not held to account.[28] Meanwhile, nearly 12,000 Egyptian civilians were tried in military courts on charges relating to alleged violations of the penal code in areas either controlled by the military or at events at which a military officer was present. These trials typically lasted less than an hour, sometimes without benefit of legal counsel, and often resulted in long prison sentences.

None of the fact-finding bodies held public hearings or released their full findings. Tellingly, the conclusions of a commission empowered by President Morsi, which found police responsible for most of the deaths during the 25 January revolution, were leaked but not acted upon.[29] Rushed efforts by the SCAF to compensate victims and survivors failed, in part because of unclear guidelines regarding eligibility, and because the perpetrators were rarely held accountable for the acts leading to compensation. The announcement that the State Security Intelligence agency was dismantled and replaced by Egyptian Homeland Security left many wondering if only the name had changed. The treachery law was issued just days prior to parliamentary elections—too late to take effect—and in any case applied only to a limited number of Mubarak regime figures who had been charged in criminal courts of committing crimes.[30] The Supreme Constitutional Court subsequently ruled the law unconstitutional. Even constitutional drafting efforts disappointed many. The Islamists who dominated the 2012 Constituent Assembly that drafted the new constitution showed little sympathy for the views of secular party representatives, independent women, and religious and ethnic minorities, many of whom resigned from the assembly when it became clear that their perspectives would not be taken into account.

All the above pointed to the fact that those in control, whether during the SCAF transition or the Morsi government, were not deeply committed to democratic transformation. In a pact that emerged between the Muslim Brotherhood and the military, the latter accepted the former's rise to power on condition that they did not push for military trials or investigations into the military's extensive business operations, which benefit from government subsidies and prison labor. Some also remembered that the Muslim Brotherhood only joined the uprising belatedly, and were largely unresponsive to the poor's demands for social and economic justice once they achieved power. In short, throughout the transition, the reality was that the "powers that be," whether the *fulul* (remnants of the Mubarak regime), the Islamists voted into office, or the unreformed military and security services, were unresponsive to demonstrators' demands for *'aish hurriyya, al-'adala al-'ijtima'iyya'* (bread, freedom, social justice).

Instead, managing Egyptians' expectations became a major preoccupation for those in power. After all, the speed of the uprising that led to Mubarak's removal had caught everyone by surprise. As fear diminished of confronting what previously had appeared to be the unassailable Mubarak regime, it seemed to many only natural that other hated institutions of the state, especially the police force and intelligence services, would quickly succumb. Memories of millions of Egyptians from diverse backgrounds gathering in forbidden public spaces fed the impression that Egypt's transformation was imminent and inevitable. Intense media focus on the Arab Spring contributed to the early euphoria. During 24-hour coverage of what appeared to be a contagion of civil disobedience sweeping across multiple Arab counties, commentators engaged in breathless speculation about the imminent collapse of authoritarianism. The arrival of foreign experts within months of Mubarak's removal to advise on the implementation of transitional justice contributed to the sense that Egypt must be on the verge of democratic transformation.

The reality, however, is that revolutions are rare occurrences in history. When they do take hold, generally they unfold over many years or even decades, and are marked by intense conflict, violence, and chaos. Clearly Egypt, Tunisia, Yemen, and the other Arab Spring countries were unlikely to rewrite history and leap from authoritarianism to democracy overnight.[31] Egyptians' adjustment to that fact was gradual. As strikes and demonstrations stretched on months after Mubarak's removal, and the economy continued to suffer, Egyptians began asking themselves whether the "revolution" was truly worth it. Who was to blame for the mess that succeeded it? Was the military a positive or negative force for change? Did Egyptians have the stomach to continue prolonged, possibly violent conflict to dismantle the "deep state"? A year after Mubarak fell from power, patience was running out fast, as the struggle merely to survive intensified in a country where approximately 40 percent of the population lived on $2 per day or less.

Egyptian perspectives on transitional justice and the role of international actors

In Egypt, the term "transitional justice" (*al-'adala al-intiqaliyya*) has only recently made an appearance. Fieldwork conducted by the author in Egypt in the first year after the uprising revealed few respondents familiar with the term, and little knowledge of how other countries have addressed justice and accountability challenges during political transitions.[32] That research involved in-depth interviews with more than fifty mostly middle-class residents of Cairo, and a survey administered to a more diverse group of 169 Egyptians in Cairo and three outlying governorates. Table 1 in the Appendix contains details about how the sample was constructed. No substitute for a random, nationally representative sample, which was difficult to undertake given political conditions, this limited sample nonetheless provides suggestive insights into attitudes held by some Egyptians, and deserves further research.

When asked to cite relevant examples, respondents expressed strong interest in learning about other transitions, but scant knowledge. Those who did reference specific transitions were most likely to cite Tunisia, whose own uprising helped to spark Egypt's. Only one respondent cited Morocco's Equity and Reconciliation Commission, but was unfamiliar with the details. No one mentioned the ongoing Special Tribunal for Lebanon, relating to the assassination of former Prime Minister Rafiq Hariri, or Iraq's troubling experience with transitional justice following the 2003 US invasion. Several respondents were aware of South Africa's Truth and Reconciliation Commission, and described it as a possible model for Egypt.

So what expectations did Egyptians express early on in the transition? Our limited survey revealed that the frame of reference that Egyptians brought to trials of regime leaders reflected strongly held views about justice and accountability. The survey asked a series of questions designed to reveal attitudes about due process and the rule of law. Chart 1 in the Appendix displays mean scores for the whole sample. Overall, survey respondents supported due process and the rule of law as general principles. More precisely, they agreed with the statement that alleged wrongdoers have the right to defend themselves through trials, and they strongly endorsed the idea that all wrongdoers should be held accountable—not just those who crafted wrongful policies but also those who carried out their orders. Consistent with these reviews, the respondents generally did not support protection from prosecution in exchange for testimony, although there was relatively high disagreement among respondents on this question. Views on these issues did not differ significantly with respect to respondents' gender, age, place of residence, or religion. Working-class respondents, however, were much less supportive than middle-class respondents of the right of alleged wrongdoers to defend themselves through trials, and more likely to think that people who broke the law should be held accountable. These differences were statistically significant at $p < 0.0001$.[33]

What were Egyptians saying about the transition as it evolved over time? When Mubarak and his sons appeared in court for the first day of their opening trial, the country paused as millions gathered around televisions and radios to follow the proceedings. Commenting on the novelty of these appearances, an Egyptian human rights activist said: "We will never forget seeing Mubarak in court on the first day of the trial when he first responded to the question of whether he was present: '*Afandim, ana mawgud*' (Sir, I'm here)." She noted that this phrase was downloaded as a mobile phone ringtone more than 12,000 times within 24 hours.[34] An office manager also remembers the excitement of the moment: "On the first day of the [Mubarak] trial [in August 2011] I was on vacation in Sharm El Sheikh and 30 people gathered in one room [to watch the televised proceedings]. We couldn't believe the day would come when we saw Mubarak in court." He added: "Now [in January 2012] people have lost interest. We know the verdicts will be postponed."[35]

Why was this observer pessimistic about the value of the trials? Interviewees revealed that they were following the trials closely, but were increasingly disappointed as they progressed. Some expressed distrust of the forensic investigations associated with the trials, both because it became clear that the responsible authorities had limited forensic capacity *and* lacked independence. An arts manager asked:

> Why should police cooperate in protecting and investigating crime scenes when their own members are among the suspected perpetrators?" A filmmaker cautioned: "Rough and quick trials do not satisfy people. When you have a serious crime, you must have a serious process." An NGO training manager asserted: "Prosecutors don't inspire confidence that they are working seriously. I believed [in them] initially but my confidence is fading. The Ministry of Interior didn't cooperate in the [Mubarak trial] investigation because they are part of the old regime, and the old players are still in their positions.

Interestingly, optimism about Egypt's transition seemed to be conditioned by demographics. Our limited survey revealed that women were more pessimistic than men about the future ($p < 0.0001$), and older persons were significantly more optimistic than young persons (see Chart 2 in the Appendix). Notably, respondents who perceived the trials of major regime figures to have value were more optimistic about Egypt's future ($p < 0.001$).

In the immediate aftermath of the uprising, well-meaning donors funded workshops and conferences in Cairo for participants from Arab Spring countries to share lessons learned from other countries.[36] International experts and NGOs organized trainings and facilitated visits to post-conflict countries to help activists and political elites understand how transitional governments elsewhere had handled justice and accountability challenges. Enthusiastic development practitioners arrived in Egypt to lend a helping hand, some touting the benefits of "reconciliation," without considering how that might be achieved in the absence of credible criminal prosecutions or truth-telling processes.

What was wrong with this picture? The aforementioned had the positive impact of provoking media discussions in Egypt about transitional justice. But some of the international experts conveying best practice were unprepared to engage with Egyptian political realities. Meanwhile, circumstances in Egypt remained highly unsettled with respect to elements critical to transitional justice, which is conditioned by who is in power and how they define their interests. The presence or absence of basic security and the availability of institutional, professional, financial, and cultural resources also influence the implementation of transitional justice.[37] As international actors tried to kick-start a national conversation about transitional justice, newspapers were focused on deepening labor unrest and economic decline, faulty trials of former regime leaders, summary military trials of civilians, rising crime rates, surveillance and imprisonment of activists, security force impunity, and stringent restrictions on NGOs.

Collective memory processes in contemporary Egypt: The rush to remember

Decades of abusive government created memories that many hesitated to share publicly for fear of invoking governmental wrath. With Mubarak's removal, inhibitions relating to expressing opposition to the authorities and documenting the uprising were lowered. Seizing whatever tools lay closest to hand, millions pulled out their cameras, mobile phones, paintbrushes, and computers to create or capture memories. They recorded, collected, and widely disseminated memories of the uprising and the months that followed on Facebook, blogsites, and other virtual platforms.[38]

For some involved in these pursuits, the purpose was purely personal. They simply wanted a photograph capturing them with their friends at a demonstration. Initially, many of the memories collected represented the amazement and fear that ordinary Egyptians felt as they confronted the Mubarak regime, and realized their power to inhabit formerly forbidden public spaces and influence public life. As the death toll mounted, however, others displayed a conscious effort to use the power of images, words, and music to pursue a political agenda by honoring the injured, dead, and marginalized. An advisor to a presidential candidate in the 2012 election referenced this when she talked about the conservative backlash against women's participation in the public arena. Noting growing harassment and violence targeting women who joined demonstrations, and calls by Islamists for them to stay at home in traditional roles, she asserted: "Photos and videos from the January 25 Revolution prevent women from forgetting and remind men that they were present." Graffiti artists and cartoonists sought justice for murdered demonstrators by creating memorial images of the deceased on the walls of Mohammad Mahmud Street leading from Tahrir Square.[39] After the government white-washed them, one artist said: "This work embodied many things: the martyrs, the military regime and a people looking for freedom and democracy. It was the memory of a place that witnessed many important events."[40] This explo-sion of artistic activism was evident on the walls of virtually every town and village in Egypt. Ordinary Egyptians also recaptured public spaces by holding public events, notably a series of art festivals organized by *Al-Fan Midan* (Art is a Square).[41] They also did so by renaming schools, squares, and other physi-cal spaces.[42] In some cases, efforts to represent the past covered activities that took place well before the uprising. One such example was when demonstra-tors stormed police stations to capture documents documenting years of police abuse and torture, and then posted them on the internet.

Throughout the transition, demonstrators built physical memorials honor-ing the memory of victims. Perhaps the first collective effort of this type was a memorial constructed by demonstrators in Tahrir Square, immediately fol-lowing Mubarak's removal from power. The SCAF authorities swept it away within days.[43] In November 2013, without public discussion or consultation, the Mansour government erected two memorials: one in Tahrir Square to honor Egyptians killed during the 25 January uprising, and a second in Raba'a Al Adawiya Square honoring police and military forces—in a place where they previously massacred around 1,000 Morsi government supporters. A few days later, the filmmaker collective *Mosireen* (Insistent) issued a video of a police general dedicating the new Tahrir Square memorial and expressing condo-lences for fallen "martyrs." In the Mosireen video, his speech is juxtaposed against a backdrop of footage of attacks on demonstrators. Activists immedi-ately denounced both memorials as an attempt to appropriate history, while arguing that only three perpetrators had been held accountable since the ini-tial uprising began. The video ended with the words "*'u'a tinsa wi khallik fakir*" (never forget, always remember).[44]

Where did efforts to manage collective memory register on Egyptians' list of reform priorities? Our survey asked respondents to rank in order a list of activities that would "put Egypt on the right path." Respondents named insti-tutional reforms as the highest priority—security sector reform foremost, followed by judicial independence and constitutional reform (see Chart 3 in the Appendix). Strong support for strengthening judicial independence ech-oed a similar finding from a Pew Research Center poll, in which Egyptians ranked a "fair judiciary" as their second highest priority after "improved economic conditions."[45] Choices relating to addressing victims' needs through apologies and compensation, and to managing collective memory through preservation of documentary materials, museums, and memorials ranked lowest. Did this signal that the respondents were heartless or unconcerned about history? Not at all. Instead, it suggests that Egyptians suffered intensely from abuses committed by police and intelligence forces, and that they identified institutional reforms, rather than trials, a truth commission, or management of collective memory, as the most urgent priority. Illustrating the preoccupation with security sector reform, one women's rights activist said:

> If you don't have political connections you're vulnerable and everyone has a horrible sense of insecurity and the feeling that no one has any rights and could be picked up by the police at any time. Parents are always afraid of getting a phone call that a child has been arrested.

A prominent university professor, who described police brutality as a "trigger" of the uprising, agreed: "There was fear or realization that running into trouble with the police could happen to you: it was random, not political, and could happen to anyone. I came close to being abused once and could have been killed."

Official and unofficial efforts to rewrite history: The push to forget

Public officials and ordinary people alike have sought to influence collective memory by erasing older "versions" of history. In April 2011, the Ministry of Education announced that a committee would review and remove from elementary and junior high school textbooks positive representations of the Mubarak government, and prepare new chapters on the uprising for the 2012 school year.[46] Subsequent civics textbooks covered the goals and events of the uprising, but after the July 2013 coup they were subjected to further revision by acting President Adly Mansour's government. This time it was to remove what Minister of Education Mahmoud Abdulnassr described as "outrageous" rewrites characterizing Egypt as part of a broader Islamic caliphate.[47] Then the Muslim Brotherhood, even before their ascension to power, and to the consternation of activists and parties that disputed their facts, notably launched their own unofficial school curriculum that presented a contested version of the group's role in the uprising.[48]

Political parties and government officials were not the only ones trying to rewrite history. Ordinary people also sought to eradicate politically "incorrect" expressions, images, or texts. For example, the group 'Askar Kazaboon

(Lying Military) posted videos of security forces' assaults on civilians, and the Facebook campaign "Imsik Fulul" (Catch a Remnant) "outed" former Mubarak associates running in the 2011 parliamentary elections.[49] Countering these views, a video issued by a pro-SCAF group that called itself "Badr Team" encouraged Egyptian youth to erase graffiti to prevent "agents and traitors [from spreading] their violent ideologies against the police, the army and Egyptian traditions."[50]

Some Egyptians created new symbols and undertook activities explicitly designed to bridge social and political divides. During the initial uprising, thousands of demonstrators carried signs bearing a newly invented symbol—a combined cross and crescent—showing the unity of Muslims and Coptic Christians. In November 2011, Coptic marchers in Cairo expressed their deep connection to the county's historical roots through the adoption of symbols that link Muslim and Coptic Egyptians to a common Pharaonic past: the female marchers donned Pharaonic costumes and the men wore black T-shirts bearing the ankh, the well-recognized Egyptian symbol of eternal life. Common references in Egyptian discourse to *al Midan* (the Square) continued to evoke memories of mass demonstrations focused on changing Egypt's future. Artists and musicians constantly reminded Egyptians of their power to reconstruct the country on their own terms.

Conclusion

There are three lessons from this experience relevant to Egypt and beyond. First, as transitional justice becomes increasingly established internationally, it risks being regarded as a set of technical "fixes," as experts arrive to advise transitional governments and civil society activists on its different elements. As noted by participants in a meeting organized by Chatham House, international experts eager to provide advice risk the "standardization of transitional justice," although the "the essence of transitional justice is the 'local.'"[51] The same group noted that, across Arab Spring countries, "transitional justice was almost being used as a metric for the success of the revolution," promoting in some places the "tendency to rush into the adoption of transitional justice measures ahead of the emergence of any consensus on a political settlement."[52] These risks were obvious in post-Mubarak Egypt.

Clearly, the situation was complicated by Egypt's stalled or blocked transition to democracy, and by differing views about the goals of transitional justice held by those who desired deep change. Regarding the latter, for some the main goal of the uprising was to achieve social justice, defined by improving public services and raising the standard of living of the poor. Democracy was less important. Illustrative of this perspective were views expressed by Nasserites (proponents of the nationalist ideology articulated by President Gamal Abdul Nasser, himself a leader of an authoritarian regime established by military coup) at a meeting organized by the Ibn Khaldun Center for Development Studies. They argued that Nasser's government had achieved transitional justice through land reform, implying that a post-Mubarak government operating under unreformed security and military services could do the same.[53] For these young Egyptians, social justice trumped democracy, and the point of transitional justice was to achieve the former but not necessarily the latter. Aside from disagreement about the goals and application of transitional justice, this issue underscores a significant challenge for transitional justice: it generates expectations that it can and should address the socio-economic demands of victims whose loss of human dignity is rooted in inequality and poverty. But transitional justice theory and practice specifies no clear guidelines to satisfy such expectations, and its track record of promoting social justice is poor.[54]

Second, evolving conditions in Egypt underscore the need for in-depth research about how Egyptians view transitional justice. While preliminary findings suggest that many held strong values and well-reasoned expectations relating to justice and accountability in post-Mubarak Egypt, further research based on a national sample is essential, particularly because the unstable situation in Egypt since then may have caused many who participated in our survey to reconsider their views.[55] International transitional justice experts should be cautious if they presume to know what Egyptians want, especially in view of preliminary findings from that survey regarding attitudes about seeking remedies through international justice mechanisms if Egyptian courts fall short (see Chart 1). Even then, many of our respondents were skeptical that it is legitimate to seek justice outside Egypt if it is not accessible locally. Some interviewees used strong language to denounce any who might embrace this course of action: one university student said it would be "an act of treason" and another suggested it would "undermine the sovereignty of the Egyptian state." Since these attitudes were expressed in the first year following the uprising, Egyptians' negative views about international transitional justice may have intensified, spurred by the filing of a complaint at the International Criminal Court by the now-banned Muslim Brotherhood.

Third, access to digital technologies and the use of social media have radically democratized, and expanded the reach of, contributions made by ordinary people to collective memory processes. In Egypt, approximately a third of the population has regular access to the internet, while most now have mobile phones.[56] Rising levels of basic literacy and the spread of the 24-hour news cycles have improved access to information and contributed to the sense that the whole world is watching. Egypt has the highest number of Facebook users (16 million) in the Arab region and is ranked 17th worldwide.[57] In this context, both managing conflict relating to memorialization and shaping it as a tool to promote transitional justice and social reconstruction have become more challenging. Yet, these developments were not reflected in the agenda of the aforementioned conferences held in Cairo in 2011 and 2012. They focused on instigating criminal accountability, recovering looted assets, implementing lustration, and achieving security sector reforms—all vitally important, to be sure—but not on managing memorialization. The irony is that such processes were not in easy reach, given the strong grip of the "deep state," whereas memorials crafted by ordinary people in honor of victims and shaping collective memory about the past were immediately visible in the streets surrounding the conference halls. The failure to recognize the role that memorialization plays in influencing collective memory represents both a risk to future governments vulnerable to ongoing unrest, *and* a lost opportunity to promote social reconstruction through critical but inclusive narrations of the past.

Where does that leave transitional justice in Egypt? Clearly, it is stalled for the time being, especially since a military coup swept away the Morsi government and instituted President el-Sisi. Independent civil society activists and organizations, including Islamists and secular activists, are being sidelined by intimidation and imprisonment that in some ways exceeds repression experienced during Mubarak's thirty-year rule.[58] The rise of so-called Islamic groups fueling civil wars in Iraq and Syria, along with fears about the consequences of ongoing civil strife in Egypt, have provided the government with an excuse to suppress independent voices calling for justice and accountability. Under the circumstances, it is difficult to imagine progress on transitional justice, despite the existence of a largely inactive Ministry of Transitional Justice and National Reconciliation. But the story of Egypt's uprising has not yet ended. Memories of the 25 January Revolution lie just below the surface, and expectations of a better life are just around the corner.

Appendix
Table and Charts

Table 1: Summary of the survey sample[59]

Number	169 Egyptians
Gender	Male (59%); female (41%)
Age	15–29 (38%); 30–39 (25%); 40–49 (17%); 50–59 (11%); 60 and older (9%)
Last degree earned	Primary school (7%); secondary school (16%); secondary technical school (6%); technical diploma (13%); university degree (32%); postgraduate degree (26%)
Social class[60]	Working class (41.3%); middle and upper middle class (58.8%)
Religion[61]	Muslim (74%); Christian (15%); not possible to determine by name (11%)
Place of residence	Cairo: (82%); outside Cairo, primarily Menoufiya, Qalubiya and Helwan governorates (18%)

Chart 1: Attitudes about the rule of law

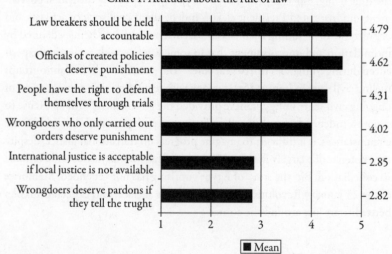

Strongly agree (=5), agree (=4), neither agree or disagree (=3), disagree (=2), Strongly disagree (=1)

Chart 2: Optimism about Egypt's future

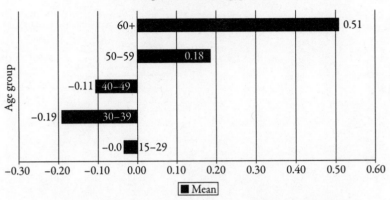

Optimism Scale (minus scores are pessimistic and positive scores optimistic)

Chart 3: Relative importance of interventions to put Egypt on the right path

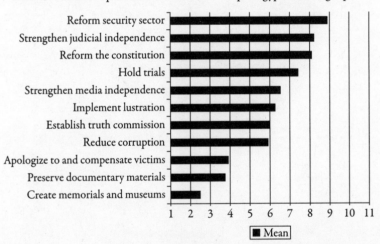

Most important (=11); Least important (=1)

11

THEATER OR TRANSITIONAL JUSTICE

REFORMING THE JUDICIARY IN EGYPT

Sahar Aziz[1]

When Egyptian courts sentenced over 1,000 defendants to death in the spring of 2014, and when former President Hosni Mubarak was months earlier acquitted of human rights violations despite decades of documented torture, serious questions arose about the independence of the judiciary.[2] Of all Egyptian institutions, the judiciary's history of resisting executive interference caused many to believe it to be the least likely to partake in such affronts to individual rights.[3] A closer look, however, reveals that Mubarak's efforts to curtail judicial independence successfully produced a conservative body whose top echelon supported the law and order narrative that facilitated the generals' return to rule.[4] As a result, legal reforms are unlikely to come from within the judiciary.

These cases, along with numerous others, exposed the degree to which the judiciary had been co-opted into the authoritarian patronage system. Mubarak's executive branch had apparently succeeded in its concerted efforts to quash the judicial independence movement that peaked in 2006, and reinforce the coalitions within the judiciary to ensure it remained a loyalist state institution. Thus, the conservative judiciary's response to the 25 January 2011 uprisings was part of a larger phenomenon that ultimately left the authoritarian regime untouched, but for a new president and his new elite inner circle.[5]

Taking stock of the past three tumultuous years in Egypt, it has become evident that transitional justice was illusory from the start. Mass protests that once had the potential to produce revolutionary changes to the political and economic system were prematurely co-opted to produce little more than a reshuffling of the elite coalition within the same authoritarian system.[6] The institutions constituting the "deep state" were deeply entrenched in a corrupt patronage system which, if overhauled, risked the liberty and livelihood of its top echelon.[7] Hence, the millions of Egyptians who marched into Tahrir Square were up against far more than a dictator and his cronies.

Analysts have been late in this realization, however. This is largely due to the dominant narrative in Western literature that Egypt's judiciary is relatively independent and its legal system is based on rule of law.[8] As discussed in more detail in the second and third sections, Egypt's legal system is a hybrid of "thin" rule of law and rule *by* law, resulting in a politically vulnerable and facially independent judiciary.[9] Rule of law assumes a separation between a society's politics and law, such that people are protected from political anarchy and arbitrariness through legal mechanisms that constrain government action.[10] In contrast, rule by law permits authoritarian regimes to employ ostensibly legalistic mechanisms such as elections, parliaments, and judiciaries to impose their mandates on the public. In Egypt, these mechanisms are set up to be easily reversible, should they produce outcomes that threaten the authoritarian regime's survival.[11] Egyptians' preference for endogenous transitional justice conducted by Egyptian courts, therefore, further jeopardized a meaningful assessment of the Mubarak regime.[12]

Specifically, the military's savvy use of law and the courts to consolidate its political and legal authority created the appearance of a transition after 25 January.[13] By arresting and charging key members of Hosni Mubarak's inner circle, including his sons, the military went through the motions of holding former Mubarak officials accountable, while cognizant that the Mubarak-hired Prosecutor General was likely to sabotage the cases.[14] Simultaneously, the military issued executive decrees and constitutional declarations that placed it above civilian control. This ultimately led to the current regime with former Field Marshall Abdel Fatah al-Sisi as president and a Defense Minister appointed by the military, not Egypt's president.[15] It also failed to hold Mubarak accountable for the torture, deaths, and other human rights violations over a thirty-year dictatorship.[16] In the end, the outcome of the people's uprising is a nation firmly in the grasp, both politically and legally, of its military—with the judiciary's blessing.

This chapter argues that transitional justice did not occur in Egypt following 2011 and stood little chance of occurring for three reasons. First, despite valiant efforts by revolutionary opposition groups that triggered the 25 January uprising, a political transition never materialized;[17] and without a political transition, transitional justice is improbable. Second, a conservative judiciary whose top echelon had been effectively co-opted by Mubarak's centralized executive played a key role in ensuring that no political transition could occur.[18] Finally, the different opposition groups calling for transitional justice, and in effect a political transition, diverged in their expectations of what that entailed.[19] Revolutionary groups including youth activists, labor activists, and progressives called for thick rule of law that would overhaul the legal system substantively, rather than only procedurally. As they chanted "The people want the fall of the regime," they demanded that government affirmatively improve the lives of Egyptians through distributive justice.[20] In contrast, established secular liberal opposition groups and the Muslim Brotherhood (MB) were satisfied with establishing thin rule of law that enforced procedural protections against everyone, including the political elite. The established opposition was focused on reforming the existing legal system rather than developing new structures to redress decades of political suppression and corruption. In the end, transitional justice proved elusive, denying many Egyptians a remedy for decades of tyranny under Mubarak.[21]

Discussions on transitional justice in Egypt presuppose a political transition. As I argued in a previous article, more than three years after Egypt's historic 25 January uprising, nothing may be farther from the truth.[22] In turn, this chapter focuses on the period between the 25 January uprising and Fall 2014 to examine why the judiciary impeded the political transition that is the prerequisite to transitional justice. Although Egypt's judiciary has been historically more independent than other state institutions, the circumscribed independence it fought to attain was stunted over the past decade due to the purposeful efforts of the Mubarak regime to counter a nascent judicial independence movement that reached its zenith in 2006. Whether by packing the court with police academy graduates trained to be loyal to the executive branch, employing carrot and sticks tactics to discipline independent-minded judges while rewarding compliant ones, or entrenching judges into a corrupt patronage system that sustained the authoritarian state,[23] Mubarak's regime created a judiciary incapable of delivering transitional justice to the millions of Egyptians who have been tortured, imprisoned, and denied basic social and economic rights for decades.[24] Even worse, members of the senior judicial leadership were either actively quashing the revolutionary forces or passively preventing a meaningful political transition from taking place.[25]

In analyzing why the courts failed to hold Mubarak-era officials seriously accountable, my first section begins by examining rule of law as a contested concept whose definition depends on the proponent's ideological leanings. The common fault line lies between proponents of thin and thick rule of law. Thin rule of law emphasizes procedural legal mechanisms and procedural due process as sufficient for producing transitional justice. Thick rule of law, by contrast, goes beyond procedural mechanisms to focus on producing substantive equality within a political system that is not necessarily liberal or capitalist.[26] Whether a country pursues thin or thick rule of law affects the types of transitional justice tools it adopts, such as reparations, truth and reconciliation commissions, amnesty, and criminal prosecutions. It also determines the broader political and socio-economic outcomes sought in the pursuit of transitional justice.

My second section proceeds to describe the restraints on Egypt's judiciary leading up to 25 January which contributed to its circumspect stance toward the uprising. The executive branch had put in place various structural mechanisms to restrain the judicial leadership from being led by judges acculturated and empowered to uphold the law irrespective of its impact on the executive's power.[27] Indeed, independent adjudication entailed prohibitively high costs to a judge's professional and personal life, including unfavorable judicial appointments, disparate disciplining and transfers, and denials of certain promotions. The Judicial Authority Law of 1972 (JAL) that governs the judiciary, coupled with informal coercive tactics, incentivize judicial self-censorship and voluntary compliance with executive branch expectations.[28]

Finally, my third section examines how Egypt's judiciary impeded the transitional process through its cooperation with the Supreme Council for the Armed Forces (SCAF) and defiance of Morsi. Specifically, the SCAF's constitutional declarations and executive decrees were consistently upheld as lawful, while the Morsi regime's actions were heavily scrutinized by a skeptical judiciary with an apparently obstructionist agenda. Indeed, the Supreme Constitutional Court issued decisions clearly aimed at handicapping a president from the long-distrusted MB.[29] Although the judiciary is not monolithic, a sufficient number of judges at the helm of a centralized governance structure, coupled with a power-ful and politicized prosecutor general, had vested interests in cooperating with the military–security apparatus to sabotage the young revolutionaries' reform efforts and prevent any systemic restructuring of the political and economic system. While it is clear that the 25 January revolutionary moment was stillborn, it remains to be seen whether Egypt's judiciary can be rejuvenated into a mean-ingfully independent institution, able to keep an over-reaching executive from perpetrating another protracted era of authoritarianism.

The role of law in Egypt's muted transition

During Egypt's 18-day uprising, the demand for "rule of law" was a common catchphrase by various stakeholders calling for the overthrow of the Mubarak regime. A broad coalition of opposition groups invoked rule of law as a means of obtaining their revolutionary demands for bread, freedom, and justice (*"aysh, horriya, wi adala"*). After Mubarak's overthrow, transitional justice became another slogan among international NGOs and Egyptian human rights groups.[30] Despite the common rhetoric, these hotly contested terms were defined differently depending on the proponent. For the youth revolu-tionaries, labor activists, and progressives, "bread, freedom and justice" entailed overhauling the political system. It entailed meaningful inclusion of the youth, poor, and other politically disadvantaged groups in decision-mak-ing processes in social and political institutions.[31] The revolutionary slogan also entailed that the state abandon crony capitalist policies that had enriched the elite while impoverishing tens of millions of Egyptians.[32] The youth revo-lutionaries called on the new government to embark on a socio-political program that would reallocate resources and wealth to the vast majority of Egyptians.[33] To address the decades of human rights violations, including state violence during the uprising itself, the revolutionaries demanded transitional justice primarily through criminal trials, with a few calling for a truth and reconciliation process.[34] Despite these calls for radical change and accounta-bility, the Egyptian judiciary held fast to its belief that the existing judicial structures were fully capable of holding Mubarak regime officials accountable for their past corruption and abuses.[35]

Although the more established opposition groups, including the liberals and MB, agreed that transitional justice was due, they preferred to tweak the existing legal system by enforcing laws that had historically been arbitrarily and selec-tively enforced, if at all, and focusing legal reforms on procedural mechanisms.[36]

By focusing on existing laws and electoral processes, the MB accepted the legitimacy of the old regime's legal system and institutions. These fundamental differences between the youth revolutionaries and the established opposition proved fatal for both camps, as the security–military apparatus was able to manipulate the fissures between them to retain control of the state, while leaving the legal and political system intact. Worth noting is each stakeholder's emphasis on law as a tool, among others, for furthering its agenda. As such, a brief examination of the role of law during transition is warranted.

To be sure, law is more than the sum of courts, legislators, police, prosecutors, and other institutions with a direct relationship to the law.[37] Law is a normative system based on particularized cultural norms and values. In communitarian societies, for example, law is emphatically not neutral but rather conforms to and enforces a certain way of life influenced by history, culture, and religion.[38] Adjudication, thus, is oriented toward achieving an outcome consistent with the community interest, and in the case of Egypt, in accordance with the principles of Islamic law.[39]

During transitional times, the role of law is further complicated as legal responses are both symbolic and performative of transition.[40] States experience disorder and legal instability that cannot be addressed through the formalism of thin rule of law.[41] Countries recovering from protracted conflict or revolutions experience normative shifts in their populations' understandings of justice and the role of law.[42] In Egypt, for instance, Nathan Brown aptly notes that its transition was "shaped by political contests among confused and confusing actors at a time when the basic rules of political life are unclear, constantly reshaped, and broken."[43] The conception of justice is partial and contextual as law is used to normatively construct the new political regime.[44]

Naturalist and positivist approaches to transitional justice also inform the different ways in which law may be employed to remedy past wrongs. The natural law approach argues that the role of law in transition is to redress evil perpetuated under past regimes. Because putative law under the former dictatorial regime lacked morality, it never constituted a valid legal regime. As such, violating the law of the oppressor is not only justified, but moral.[45] Universal conceptions of justice animate retributive or corrective justice, as do popular understandings of legality during the transitional phase.[46] Furthermore, naturalists are more inclined to critique liberal democratic conceptions of the rule of law for its excessive individualist orientation and formalism at the expense of social solidarity and harmony.[47] Under the naturalist approach, in times of political flux, leaders and institutions justify otherwise extra-legal acts as to produce the justice demanded by the people. Consequently, naturalists critique positivist approaches to rule of law programs for reinforcing the existing power structures that jeopardize delivering transitional justice.[48] The criteria for measuring progress go beyond simply the fairness of elections, stability of institutions, or economic development in evaluating burgeoning new democracies.[49] Instead, institutions of the former regime must be completely restructured and former regime leaders be removed to create a clean break from the past. Thus, the role of law is to transform the meaning of legality as part of a broader shift toward a more liberal regime.[50]

In contrast, positive law is composed of the orders of government, statutes, and judicial enactments. Positive law is detached from moral considerations. The positivist approach argues that preserving procedural regularity is a key priority for transition to democracy.[51] This view assumes that injustice under the previous regime was due not so much to unjust laws but failure to adjudicate them equally and in adherence to basic procedural rights. By divorcing questions of the legitimacy of law from the meta-rule-of-law value of due process, positivists believe that transitional justice responses to past tyranny lie in politics not law, thereby treating the two as neatly separated.[52]

The revolutionary youth from the start adopted a naturalist approach, calling for an overhaul of the political system and demanding socio-economic rights. In contrast, the SCAF and the Muslim Brotherhood invoked the naturalist or positivist approach, depending on their interests at a particular time. When the SCAF was in power, for example, it advocated positivist perspectives to justify thousands of military trials of civilians pointing to Mubarak-era laws that created a parallel judicial system for political cases.[53] But when naturalist arguments produced the desired political outcome, the military argued that revolutionary times called for revolutionary measures. For instance, the SCAF invoked such reasoning when unilaterally issuing a constitutional declaration on 30 March that went far beyond the public's mandate of the 11 March 2011 referendum.[54] The 63 new articles granted the SCAF sole discretion to convene a joint session of parliament. It also allowed the presidential election process to be delayed indefinitely without affecting the constitutional drafting process, thereby prolonging the SCAF's rule such that the generals could influence the constitution drafters and process. The 30 March declaration granted to SCAF both executive and legislative functions that authorized it to issue legislation, determine the state budget, appoint members to the lower house of parliament and ministers, and represent the state externally.[55] Weeks prior to Morsi's assumption of the presidency, the generals issued another constitutional decree in June 2012 that granted the SCAF more power than the office of the presidency.[56] When pressed on the dubious legal basis for issuing the declarations, the SCAF responded that revolutionary times called for unconventional acts to protect the public interest.[57] Meanwhile, if anyone challenged the SCAF's authority, the generals pointed to the law as a basis for their legitimacy.[58] And thus rule by law, rather than rule of law, was perpetuated to manipulate a so-called transitional process that produced minimal changes to the political and legal system.

Likewise, Morsi's administration justified his fatal constitutional declaration of November 2012 with natural law-based arguments that violating the law was justified to preserve democracy and stop former regime elements from sabotaging his regime.[59] Nine months later when the military deposed Morsi, the MB reversed course to make positivist arguments highlighting violations of the constitution and due process rights, among other legal violations, to argue that 3 July was a military coup.[60] This opportunistic conceptualization of the role of law during "revolutionary times" continued into Adly Mansour's military-backed government as thousands were killed, detained, and tortured in the crackdown against pro-Morsi supporters in Raba'a and Nahda squares in the summer of 2013.[61] Despite the ideological differences between various parties that have controlled Egypt since 25 January, they each defined the role of law on naturalist or positivist bases, depending on which approach was politically expedient. It quickly became apparent that law was the handmaiden of politics.

While a full accounting of the complex role of law in Egypt's stillbirth transition is beyond the scope of this chapter, one thing is clear: both the positivist and naturalist approaches emphasize the role of the judiciary in delivering transitional justice. The various stakeholders viewed an independent judiciary as a prerequisite for establishing rule of law, and by extension democracy.[62] But similar to rule of law, an independent judiciary is a contested concept that is purported to exist in both democratic and authoritarian regimes. The next section examines the role of courts in authoritarian states and the implications for Egypt.

The fragility of judicial independence in authoritarian states

In authoritarian regimes, courts play an important role in preserving the executive's grip on political and economic outputs. As such, persuading the international community that the judiciary is independent attracts foreign investment which expands the tax base and ultimately enriches the power elite.[63] For instance, Sadat established Egypt's Supreme Constitutional Court in 1979 primarily to gain the trust of foreign investors skeptical of Egypt's protection of private property.[64] Courts are also used to establish social controls, sideline political opponents, bolster a regime's claim to legal legitimacy, and resolve coordination problems among competing factions within the regime.[65]

Cognizant that authoritarianism constrains avenues for airing public grievances and invites corruption, the Egyptian regime used the judiciary as a mechanism to discipline the civil bureaucracy, curb government excesses, and allow for public venting. Administrative litigation generated an independent stream of information on bureaucratic misdeeds to the chief executive.[66] This allowed the executive to rein in the state bureaucracy at any sign of autonomy or excesses that threatened the chief executive's. Venting through the courts also diverted the public from partaking in political disputes, instead turning to litigation under a judiciary closely monitored by the executive.[67] Litigation, thus, took the place of mobilizing, organizing, and sustaining a political movement.[68] For instance, election fraud was addressed through high-profile cases challenging the constitutionality of election laws, resulting in the SCC striking down the laws and forcing the dissolution of the People's Assembly in 1987 and 1990. Similarly, civil society combatted the regime's use of libel laws to silence critical views through litigation that resulted in the SCC ordering amendments to the law in favor of freedom of expression.[69] A few years later in 1995, the Labor party successfully challenged the constitutionality of criminal provisions that imposed joint liability on heads of political parties, reporters, and editors-in-chief for alleged libel of public officials in party newspapers, thereby decreasing self-censorship.[70] By 1997, public interest litigation became the primary form through which civil society promoted reform.[71] Because political mobilization could ultimately topple a regime, Mubarak tolerated human and civil rights litigation as a controllable mechanism for venting public grievances.[72]

The following sections describe the various means of control exercised by the Egyptian executive and how this ultimately produced a conservative judiciary willing to cooperate, or look the other way, in the counter-revolutionary crackdown on pro-Morsi supporters and youth activists.[73] The first section argues that the prosecutor general has been the executive's gatekeeper who employs the criminal justice system to punish political opposition and reward loyalists. This practice continued after the 25 January uprising under the SCAF, Morsi, and Adly Mansour's military-backed interim government. It has yet to be determined if President Sisi can continue this practice now that the 2014 constitution grants the Supreme Judicial Council the authority to appoint the Prosecutor General for a term no longer than four years.[74] The second section argues that the fragility of judicial independence, as articulated in Tamir Moustafa's ground-breaking work on the Egyptian judiciary, was a key factor in transforming the judiciary into a conservative deep state institution suspicious of, if not outright opposed to, the demands of the revolutionaries. The third section shows how specific acts of judicial independence were swiftly quashed by the executive through legal and coercive measures, thereby sending a chilling warning to judges that the boundaries of their independence were circumscribed by the executive's core interests.

Egypt's Prosecutor General as gatekeeper

Authoritarian regimes govern through highly centralized rule under the tight grip of the chief executive. Egypt is no exception. Since the 1952 revolution, Egypt's president and his inner circle exercised centralized control over state organizations, including the judiciary.[75] An extensive patronage system allowed a select group of elites to manipulate state institutions to rely on the presidency both politically and financially.[76] As such, Mubarak continuously interfered in governmental portfolios, violated the autonomy of state institutions, and fortified his position in the system.[77] Parliament was merely a décor to mask the true authoritarian face of the regime to the international community.[78] As a result, state institutions were weak, apolitical, and unable to compete openly with each other or oppose the upper elites' prerogatives.[79] Instead, they served the interests of the central authority, even if it meant that the institution's mandate was compromised. Because the ruling elite in control of state institutions derived their power from the chief executive, anyone who challenged his power was quickly eliminated and replaced with a compliant member of the ranking elite.[80]

The centralized authoritarian system is deeply entrenched in a hierarchical patronage web that feeds at the top with each institution depoliticized and unable to raise any serious contest to the top executive. Paradoxically, this makes the president more dispensable because the system can quickly adapt to whoever takes the reins.[81] Should the executive unexpectedly be removed or die, executive elites can confront and overcome challenges to their rule by adapting without forcing the regime to collapse.[82] Thus, when Mubarak was forced out of office on 11 February 2011, General Tantawi was able to take on the role of chief executive with relative ease, after which he quickly got to work putting the military elite at the helm of a centralized system. As Joshua Stacher predicted, Egyptian ruling elites were able to shed Mubarak's inner circle of established figures and incorporate new elites from the military–security establishment.[83] Because current President al-Sisi is subject to the same fate, should he choose to push for radical reforms that jeopardize the deep state's economic and political interests, a peaceful transition to democracy is highly unlikely in the near term.

The Prosecutor General in Egypt is a key facilitator in the chief executive's centralized system of political control. Based on the French legal system, the position wields significant powers through life tenure combined with supervisory authority over a hierarchy of prosecutors across Egypt.[84] The President had constitutional authority to appoint the Prosecutor General until January 2014, when the constitution was amended to transfer appointment authority to the Supreme Judicial Council pursuant to Article 189.[85] It remains to be seen whether this significant change will impede the executive from unduly interfering with prosecutions or simply be manipulated through political or other legal means to subordinate the prosecutor's office to the president's prerogative. Similar to other French-based legal systems, all public prosecutors in Egypt are members of the judiciary, and most become sitting judges once they reach the age of thirty.[86] Prosecutors are required to swear the same oath as judges, protected from dismissal from their post without their consent, and prohibited from consulting on cases that conflict with their job, including political activities.[87] As members of the judiciary, prosecutors are also immune from prosecution.

Despite these protections and ethical obligations of impartiality, the Ministry of Justice has used its significant influence over career members of the public prosecution to politicize prosecutions.[88] Specifically, the ministry has the authority to appoint investigating judges, transfer prosecutors at its discretion, and discipline prosecutors.[89] These powers are used to select investigating judges in criminal cases whom the Minister of Justice knows holds views favorable to the prosecution.[90] Or the Ministry of Justice can withhold appointing an independent-minded judge to investigate alleged criminal acts by regime loyalists.[91] Because the investigating judge's report is considered as credible evidence in a trial, a biased selection process has adverse consequences to the defendant's right to a fair trial. Other reported abuses of power include "suggesting" to prosecutors that certain investigations should be dropped or started.[92] Should a prosecutor refuse to cooperate with the minister's request, he is likely to face retaliation through transfers to unattractive positions that are effectively demotions in quality of work and status.[93] The minister has mastered these unspoken rules such that he provides pretextual reasons when accused of undue politicization of judicial transfers.

The Prosecutor General's authorities allowed the Mubarak regime to maintain its authoritarian grip on the political system while proclaiming that Egypt respected the rule of law. For this reason, human rights advocates had long advocated for the judiciary, rather than the executive, to appoint the Prosecutor General, set term limits, and prohibit the Prosecutor General from serving on the Supreme Judicial Council where he has power to appoint and promote judges. The 25 January uprising provided the long-awaited political opening to implement these demands. To no one's surprise though, the SCAF declined to act.[94]

Indeed, when the SCAF took the reins of power, it immediately tasked the Mubarak-appointed Public Prosecutor, Abdel Meguid Mahmoud, with quashing the young revolutionaries' calls for substantive equality and thick rule of law. During his six-year tenure, Mahmoud was notorious for exploiting the prosecutor's office to detain, torture, and prosecute the regime's political opposition. Indeed, his reputation was so nefarious that his resignation was among the top demands voiced by the 25 January revolutionaries.[95] Nevertheless, his status as a member of the judiciary with life tenure offered the SCAF the pretext for retaining Mahmoud to transfer over 10,000 civilians to military courts.[96] As a result, from February 2011 to June 2012, thousands more civilians were tried in military courts than during the thirty years under Mubarak.[97] Military courts had jurisdiction to try any crime committed in a location operated by or for the military, including commercial places.[98] These courts were an effective mechanism for successful prosecution of dissidents, because all judges are military officers appointed by the Minister of Defense and the President for two-year renewable terms. Due to their institutional identity and legal training, military judges tend to defer to the military's position, making a conviction nearly guaranteed. Military judges also determine whether the offense occurred within their jurisdiction, the trials are held in secret, and there is no right to appeal.[99] Moreover, the president has discretion to decide if any crime under the Penal Code can be tried by a military court.[100]

The SCAF did not hesitate to abuse these powers to prosecute liberals, youth revolutionaries, labor rights activists, and other secular groups for criticizing the military's human rights abuses and failure to provide transitional justice to the millions of Egyptians who had suffered under Mubarak's brutal state security apparatus.[101] Meanwhile, Mubarak and his cronies were tried in conventional criminal courts with tighter evidentiary and procedural standards.[102] Despite tenacious protest, military trials of civilians were authorized under Egypt's 2014 constitution and continue to be used to prosecute political opposition.[103]

Adopting another aspect of the French legal system, criminal investigations in Egypt can be initiated by complaints by private citizens accepted by the prosecutor's office or *sua sponte* by the public prosecutors.[104] Before and after 25 January, Mahmoud abused his gatekeeping powers in determining which complaints to prosecute, the quality of the factual investigation, which prosecutors to assign to a case, and which judges to punish for criticizing the SCAF.[105] For example, three judges—Alaa Shawqi, Hassan El-Naggar, and Ashraf Nada— were investigated for allegedly insulting the military when they condemned military courts on television as lacking the due process rights provided by civilian courts.[106] Similarly, more civilians were charged with "insulting the military" than under Mubarak's thirty-year rule.[107] These cases, among others, offered further proof that Mahmoud's loyalties to the security–military apparatus fatally compromised the prosecutions of Mubarak and his cronies.[108]

Because the public's demand for the criminal prosecutions of Mubarak-era officials was too great to ignore,[109] Mahmoud had no choice but to charge them. However, he sabotaged the trials by assigning junior prosecutors to complex corruption cases, conducting poor investigations that could not withstand judicial scrutiny, and declining to prosecute police and security personnel accused of killing protesters.[110] As a result, Mubarak's conviction and life sentence for complicity in the killings of protesters during the 25 January uprisings were reversed on appeal, and on 29 November 2014 the charges were dismissed in their entirety.[111] The intense pressure in 2011–12 on the court of first instance to convict Mubarak, coupled with the fact that the judge presiding over the case was scheduled to retire after this case, thus having little to lose in issuing a conviction, probably explains the initial conviction.[112] Yet, only one police officer is serving a three-year sentence for shooting protesters during the bloody Mohamed Mahmoud protests in November 2011, during which over 51 protesters were killed in five days.[113] And only two police officers are serving time for the killing of at least 846 protesters in the protests of January 2011.[114] In the end, the public's overwhelming trust in the military at the time of Mubarak's ousting facilitated the SCAF's agenda, which was not much different than Mubarak's, with minimal public scrutiny.[115] The next section examines why judges became either complicit or powerless in the executive's obstructionism against transitional justice after 25 January.

Structuring Egyptian judicial self-restraint

Savvy authoritarians can constrain judicial activism without directly infringing on judicial autonomy.[116] In Egypt, the regime uses carrots and sticks to persuade the upper echelons of the courts to cooperate on high priority cases in exchange for maintaining some institutional autonomy.[117] Tamer Moustafa highlights four key strategies that Mubarak used to constrain judicial independence: 1) institutional incentives that promote judicial self-restraint; 2) incapacitating judicial support networks; 3) constraining access to justice; and 4) fragmented judicial systems.[118] This section focuses on the first strategy to argue that the judiciary that existed on 25 January was predisposed to reject revolutionary upheavals to the political system and revolutionary youth's calls for thick rule of law reforms.

The Mubarak regime employed various institutional and legal mechanisms to incentivize judicial self-restraint while disincentivizing judicial activism. These include the process for appointing judges, assigning judges to particular cases and courts, appointments to lucrative secondments in state institutions, and the use of military and other exceptional courts.[119] Some of these restraints have been removed since the 25 January uprising, while others remain in place.[120] For instance, until January 2014, the president had the legal authority to select both the Chief Justice on the Supreme Constitutional Court (SCC), who presides over the presidential election commission, and the Prosecutor General, who sits on the Supreme Judicial Council.[121] As of the writing of this chapter, the Minister of Justice appoints the presidents of the highest courts from among the judges at the appeals courts, some of whom also serve on the Supreme Judicial Council (SJC).[122] The SJC in turn selects all the prosecutors and most of the judges across the judiciary, thereby granting it significant powers over the administration of justice and judicial governance.[123] Through these various direct and indirect appointment powers, the executive is able to control senior judges who in turn restrain, discipline, or expel junior judges whose rulings threaten the executive.[124]

The Supreme Judicial Council (SJC) is the judiciary's governing body which, in theory, shields the judiciary from undue interference by the executive branch.[125] It was reinstated by Mubarak in 1984 after Nasser abolished it in 1969 as part of a broader assault on the judiciary, known as the Massacre of the

Judiciary.[126] Nasser dismissed over 200 judges, including senior judges on the Court of Cassation and prosecutors in various parts of the judicial system; he also created the Supreme Council of Judicial Organizations, to retain full control over judicial appointments.[127] The seven-member council comprises the Chief Justice of the Court of Cassation, the two most senior Vice Presidents of the Court of Cassation, the General Prosecutor, the Chief Judge of the Cairo Appellate Court, the Chief Judge of the Alexandria Appellate Court, and the Chief Judge of the Tanta Appellate Court.[128] Even though they are nominated by judicial bodies based on seniority, each judge who occupies these positions must be approved by either the Minister of Justice or the President.[129] Thus, in practice, the SJC's independence is compromised by the executive branch's powers to appoint the senior judges who comprise the SJC.[130]

The SJC has extensive powers in determining pay, promotion, and transfer of judges.[131] These powers can be used to reward or punish judges. For example, a judge whose rulings are consistently unfavorable to the regime may find himself transferred to a rural area in south Egypt far from his family and the conveniences of urban life.[132] Likewise, a judge up for promotion as chief of an appellate court may be passed up if the regime fears he will not exercise his authorities to protect the regime's core interests.[133] Such decisions more often originate from the Minister of Justice, and while the SJC has the authority to decline to approve the minister's decisions, it rarely does so because this could lead to political retaliation.[134]

The SJC's gatekeeper role caused Egypt's past presidents to take great interest in ensuring that those promoted to the SJC are either regime loyalists or at the very least not detractors.[135] Indeed, reformists have long accused the executive of making judicial appointments based on political considerations that would ensure a cooperative SJC, and in turn a cooperative judiciary vis-à-vis the regime's core interests. At the peak of the judicial independence movement in 2005–6, the reformist judges unsuccessfully sought to amend the JAL to change control over appointment of SJC judges from the Ministry of Justice to an election by judges.[136] The demand remains unmet until the present day.

The chief judge of each appellate court serves as another powerful gatekeeper position. He oversees case assignments in the courts of first instance and the appellate court within his district, thereby controlling which judge will preside over cases important to the regime.[137] Should the chief appellate judge select a judge known for his independence, the case outcome could jeopardize the regime's core interests. Although the chief judge is supposed to be selected through nomination by each appellate jurisdiction's general committee, meeting annually to decide on promotions and transfers, in practice the committee does not nominate a judge they know the Minister of Justice will reject—a power vested in him by the JAL.[138] Therefore, ambitious judges are careful not to be perceived as too independent by the executive, lest they be denied future opportunities for promotion.

Another powerful disciplining mechanism in the executive's toolbox is the committee that investigates judges' alleged ethical and legal violations. Despite the judiciary's requests to transfer it to the SJC, this investigative committee remains under the control of the Ministry of Justice.[139] As a result, the Minister of Justice has the authority to appoint the judge who heads the office, and in effect utilize the office to punish judges in the regular courts who go too far in challenging executive actions.[140] Some judges, for instance, have been pushed out of the judiciary as baseless investigations are used to harass and embarrass them. In exchange for closing the file and avoiding an adverse ruling, the Ministry of Justice calls for the judge's resignation.[141] Others are coerced to leave the country to limit their influence over other judges. A case in point is the referral of senior judges Mahmoud Mekki and Hisham Al-Bastawisi to internal disciplinary hearings after they publicly condemned vote-rigging and election irregularities in the 2005 parliamentary elections.[142] Although the disciplinary board found Mekki innocent while giving Al-Bastawisi a mild reprimand, the two judges left the country for Kuwait soon after, presumably under pressure from the regime.[143] The case sent a chilling message to judges who took their independence too earnestly.[144] At the moment, over sixty judges who condemned the deposition of Morsi as a military coup are being investigated and systematically purged from the judiciary.[145] The judges had signed a statement on 24 July 2013 in support of the sit-in at Al-Raba'a Al-Adawiya opposing the July 3 military coup.[146] Another sixteen judges, who call themselves "Judges for Egypt," have been expelled from the judiciary through disciplinary proceedings based on accusations that by declaring Morsi's victory before the official results were released they participated in politics in violation of the JAL.[147]

The executive uses three ways to coerce or persuade judges to engage in self-restraint in high-profile cases. First, judges are incentivized to impose harsh sentences against defendants in high-profile political cases in the hope of being rewarded with lucrative secondments to the Ministry of Justice, international organizations, or embassies abroad as special counselors.[148] For instance, the Ministry of Justice has been known to reward compliant judges with temporary transfers to non-judicial posts as governors or legal experts in government ministries where their monthly salaries are supplemented by up to 20,000 Egyptian pounds, which more than doubles an average judge's salary.[149] Similarly, the president must approve secondments to foreign governments, international organizations, or Egyptian embassies abroad.[150] Both the Ministry of Justice and the Supreme Judicial Council influence which judges are rewarded or denied such opportunities, and do so taking into consideration the judge's rulings on cases important to the regime.

Second, the judiciary is entrenched in Egypt's politics of patronage and clientalism.[151] Like other state institutions, the judiciary is wrought with nepotism. The appointment process is not fully meritocratic. Judges' sons and nephews often become judges, even if their academic records do not qualify them.[152] For instance, the International Bar Association Human Rights Institute reported that the president of the Tanta Court has twenty-one sons and nephews who are either judges or prosecutors, despite academic records that disqualified some of them from judicial appointment.[153] Upon appointment, judges benefit from special treatment arising from their fathers and uncles in the judiciary who lobby on their behalf in transfer requests, disbursement of fringe benefits, and promotions. For instance, the SJC is wary of approving disciplinary actions against the sons of special counselors or senior judges, is more sympathetic to their requests for leave of absence or secondments, and is likely to approve requests for court transfers.[154]

Third, the executive branch exercises significant influence in the vetting and initial hiring of judges. Domestic security forces collaborate with the Minister of Justice to vet judicial candidates thoroughly for any affiliations with the MB, political opposition groups, and criminal activities.[155] Anyone found to possess even the slightest anti-government leanings or have an extended family member associated with political opposition groups, particularly the MB, is often barred from entering the judiciary regardless of qualifications.[156] While some may argue that this produces a desirable apolitical judiciary, the objective is to exclude prospective judges who may exercise their role as neutral arbiters to the detriment of the executive's interests.[157]

Although the executive uses courts to advance the authoritarian regime's interests, courts sometimes transform into sites of political resistance.[158] The next section explores the episodes of judicial independence that laid the foundation for the 25 January uprising, prompting the executive to react by installing regime loyalists in senior judicial positions. With judicial regime loyalists strategically placed and a weakened reformist camp, the probability of judicially-led transitional justice after 25 January was slim from the start.

Bouts of judicial independence under Mubarak

Throughout its history, the Egyptian judiciary has struggled to combat executive interference in judicial affairs, election results, and case outcomes.[159] Such resistance has resulted in periods of executive curtailment of the judiciary's powers. Prior to the 1952 coup that brought General Gamal Abdel-Nasser to power, judges and lawyers represented prestigious professions that were at the frontlines of opposing foreign occupation and preserving rule of law.[160] With the nationalization of the economy and open access to higher education, lawyers' incomes plummeted and law students were no longer limited to the best and brightest.[161] The quality of lawyering and judging suffered. In addition, repressive laws intended to quash any traces of judicial independence restricted reform-oriented judges to applying subtle pressure for political reform at the margins; otherwise they risked retribution, should they impinge on the executive's political priorities.[162]

Nevertheless, on at least six occasions under Mubarak's reign, the Egyptian judiciary pushed for legal reforms that would bolster its institutional independence, and exercised its judicial review powers to challenge executive action. Starting in 1986, the first Judicial Conference produced resolutions calling for removal of the government's emergency laws and authoritarian legislation to foster democratization.[163] Five years later in 1991, under the leadership of Judge Yahya al-Rifa'i, the Judges' Club negotiated intensively with the Ministry of Justice to amend the JAL to disentangle judges from executive control.[164] For instance, the judges wanted to eliminate the Minister of Justice's authority to appoint and annually confirm chief judges to the Courts of First Instance, which effectively permitted him to remove chief judges who failed to manage these courts in a manner that protected the regime's core interests.[165] Likewise, the minister indirectly controlled these courts' general assemblies by virtue of his authority to endorse their decisions, without which such decisions were unenforceable.[166] At the top of the judicial hierarchy, judges sought to require that the majority of members on the Supreme Council for Justice be elected by the General Assemblies of the Court of Cassation and the Court of Appeal in Cairo, as opposed to appointed by the executive branch.[167] Ultimately, the judicial reform proposals sought to transfer the Justice Ministry's administrative supervision to the courts and the Supreme Council of Justice's supervision to judges elected by other judges.[168]

Although such efforts produced little by way of immediate changes in the law, they created political space for the Supreme Constitutional Court to issue dozens of opinions that expanded basic rights and reined in executive excesses, which in turn emboldened civil society to litigate against human rights violations.[169] Notably, the court did not dare strike down the emergency laws or military trials of civilians, as this could lead to its demise.[170] Nor did the court grant citizens the right to appeal against emergency or military court rulings to the regular courts.[171] However, the most transformative ruling came in 2000 when the SCC declared the constitution mandated that judges monitor all national elections, paving the way for the judiciary's boldest challenge of executive power in 2005–6.[172] After witnessing pervasive electoral fraud in the 2000 parliamentary elections, reform-minded judges in control of the Judges' Club formed a committee to investigate widespread fraud in the 2005 parliamentary elections. Following the lead of a young female judge in the Office of Administrative Prosecution, Noha Al-Zini, who publicly disclosed these violations, judges collected testimony from other judges who witnessed similar fraud to publish a judicial report denouncing the election abuses. The executive swiftly retaliated. The Supreme Judicial Council threatened to investigate any judges who spoke to the press about election fraud.[173] The Ministry of Justice suspended the annual subsidies it gave to all judges' clubs, which was a primary source of funding for judges' fringe benefits.[174]

The Judges' Club plays an important role in judges' lives because it controls which judges have access to scarce government resources, including apartments in Cairo at discounted prices, villas on the Mediterranean and Red Sea, subsidized car loans, and free medical care in the US or Europe for a judge and his family.[175] To the chagrin of the Mubarak regime, a group of reformist judges won the Judges' Club elections in 2001 under the leadership of Judge Zakaria Abdel Aziz.[176] In addition to mobilizing judges to demand electoral reforms, the Judges' Club pressured the executive to amend the JAL to give the judiciary more autonomy. In response, the Mubarak regime passed its own law to transfer the authority to distribute judicial fringe benefits from the Judges' Club to the Ministry of Justice. It also amended the Constitution to weaken substantially the role of judges in overseeing future elections.[177]

In retaliation, the Egyptian police attacked protesters, including judges engaged in a peaceful pro-reform sit-in in 2006 in front of the Judges' Club in Cairo.[178] Nearly 150 protesters were arrested on charges of supporting the judges.[179] Among those arrested was Dr Mohamed Morsi, who was portentously to become Egypt's first democratically elected president after the 25 January uprisings.[180] The following month, Mubarak instructed Judge Abo El-leil, Minister of Justice from 2014 to 2016, to refer two leading judges from the Judges' Club to disciplinary proceedings on pretextual charges of "insulting the judiciary," for allegedly defaming a fellow judge.[181] As the hearings were taking place, massive and well-equipped security forces surrounded the Judges' Club, the Court of Cassation, the journalists' syndicate, and the lawyers' syndicate.[182] This was a clear warning to judges and lawyers of the government's intent to crack down hard on anyone planning to challenge the regime's centralized grip on power.

Intent on crushing the judicial independence movement, the executive also employed administrative and legal means to change the Club's leadership to pro-regime judges.[183] In January 2007, the Ministry of Social Affairs announced that the Judges' Club should register as an association under the 2002 law on associations.[184] The move was aimed at bringing the Judges' Club under the administrative control of the executive and taming the judicial independence movement.[185] The confrontation culminated in Ahmed Al Zind retaking the Cairo Judges' Club in 2009, while some of the leading dissidents were "encouraged" to work outside the country or retire.[186] In the aftermath of the 25 January uprising, the staunchly pro-regime Judge Ahmed Al Zind galvanized members of the judiciary to join the deep state's confrontation with Mohamed Morsi's regime.[187] He actively called for aggressive prosecution of judges who participated in the independence movement of 2005–6. Currently, Al Zind is leading the charge within the judiciary to discipline and expel those judges who publicly condemned the ousting of Morsi as illegal.[188]

Fragmenting the judiciary is another tactic employed by the executive to incentivize cooperation and disincentivize independent adjudication on cases important to the regime. Specifically, Mubarak created special security courts to try national security-related cases, broadly to quash political dissidents belonging to the MB and other political Islamist groups. Paradoxically, because the executive was able to send politically sensitive cases to the auxiliary state security courts, the regular judiciary was granted significant autonomy.[189] In creating a fragmented judicial system, the executive retained control through non-tenured political appointments, heavily circumscribed due process rights, and the authority to order retrials if it wished.[190] As a result, the more independently the regular judiciary behaved, the more fragmented the judicial system.[191] By contrast, the more judges complied with executive agendas, the more the regime allowed political cases to remain within the regular courts' jurisdiction.[192] This explains, in part, why Adly Mansour's military-backed government permitted the ordinary judiciary to prosecute MB members, Morsi supporters that were not members of the MB, and youth revolutionaries. The senior judicial leadership's cooperation with the executive's crackdown, coupled with a critical mass of judges that distrusted the MB, transformed the judiciary into a political ally.[193]

To be sure, the Egyptian judiciary is in a difficult bind. On the one hand, it must be careful of how far it pushes back on executive policies in case of extermination, as occurred under Abdel Nasser in the Massacre of the Judiciary.[194] On the other hand, judges have an institutional interest in preserving the legitimacy of the judiciary so as to incentivize compliance with the law, preserve order, and bolster their status in society.[195] Some judges may find that while the auxiliary state security courts violate citizens' substantive and procedural due rights, the ordinary courts could join the citizenry in condemning such actions and thus claim clean hands. Other judges may find the judiciary's institutional interests lie in expansive jurisdiction, which keeps political cases within the ordinary courts and judges cooperating with executive political agendas.

A case in point is the Supreme Constitutional Court. Although it had been one of the only formal sites of meaningful resistance during the 1990s, by the time the 2005–6 judicial independence movement was underway, the SCC had been significantly emasculated.[196] Throughout much of the 1990s, the regime had tolerated the SCC's liberal rulings on social rights, due to the court's liberal rulings on economic reforms.[197] However, the SCC's seminal 2000 ruling mandating judicial oversight of elections went too far. With the slowing pace of the controversial economic reform program, the regime was less dependent on the SCC for favorable rulings.[198] Meanwhile, the court's expansion of social and political rights had emboldened civil society to leverage international pressure to demand systemic political reforms.[199] To curb this menacing trend, the president appointed Fathi Naguib in 2002 as chair of the SCC; he had previously been second in command at the Ministry of Justice.[200] With the unprecedented move of appointing a chair outside the SCC, Mubarak took back control of the court. Soon after taking office, Naguib packed the court with justices whose jurisprudence did not challenge the executive's power.[201] Within a short period, the SCC's liberal majority had been eliminated and the judicial independent movement had been weakened, producing a judiciary willing to support the state for the post-25 January counter-revolutionary measures.[202]

After decades of rampant nepotism and exclusion of anyone even remotely associated with or sympathetic to the MB, Egypt's judiciary had become a conservative institution suspicious of both the youth revolutionaries and the MB.[203] That the judges would suddenly transform into vanguards of transitional justice was improbable. Likewise, the prosecutors responsible for investigating the facts of prosecutions of Mubarak and his cronies were the same ones who for decades had propped up the Mubarak regime. Indeed, most judges were members of the same political elite that had benefited both financially and politically from the authoritarian state.[204] The next section analyzes the judiciary's role in the deep state's counter-revolutionary efforts, which ultimately led to a military coup on 3 July 2014 and the subsequent violent crackdown on all forms of political dissent.[205]

Judicial activism or counter-revolutionary compliance?

Despite the judiciary's relative autonomy as compared to other state institutions, the executive imposed sufficient constraints to produce a conservative judicial leadership with material interests in preserving the status quo.[206] Financial and status interests, coupled with deep anti-Brotherhood biases, caused members of the judiciary to forgive the past regime's transgressions as negligible compared to what many judges perceived was worse to come. Specifically, the revolutionary demands for judicial reforms would displace judges' sons and nephews from coveted judicial appointments, restrict judges from taking lucrative secondments in ministries, and potentially oust current senior judges from the highest courts. Calls for increased transparency in judicial governance would also expose the nepotism and corruption within the Judges' Club. It is thus no surprise that judicial institutions ultimately sided with the deep state in opposing revolutionary changes, including transitional justice, to the political system.[207]

Signs of this alignment became increasingly obvious as the MB Freedom and Justice Party (FJP) rose to power in parliament and successfully fielded Dr Mohamed Morsi as a presidential candidate.[208] A series of events heightened tensions to such an extent that the MB and the judiciary became locked into a war of attrition as transitional justice fell by the wayside.[209] This was further exacerbated by many judges' distrust of the MB, who for decades had been vilified as a secretive, menacing group with questionable national loyalties. When some FJP parliamentarians called for abolishing the SCC and transferring its authorities to the Court of Cassation, these suspicions were confirmed.[210] The SCC responded by issuing a far-reaching opinion on 14 June 2012, finding that the new election law passed by the SCAF was unconstitutional, thereby dissolving the FJP-dominated lower house just weeks before Morsi took office.[211] By leaving Morsi without a parliament, the court effectively emasculated the office of the presidency.

The revolutionary opposition accused the MB of engaging in the same cronyism as under Mubarak by installing MB loyalists into key government positions and institutions as part of a broader agenda to control the political system.[212] The Morsi regime's recommended reforms to the JAL only served to confirm those suspicions as the judiciary perceived the reforms as a direct assault on the judiciary. Specifically, mandatory retirement would be decreased from seventy to sixty years of age, consistent with other state institutions.[213] Because the Ministry of Justice's authority over judicial appointments was still in place, the thousands of vacancies arising from the new law would remove the most senior judges, who also tended to be the most loyal to the old regime, and replace them with judges vetted by the Morsi regime.[214] To pave the way for appointing practicing lawyers as judges, the Morsi regime sought to enforce Article 41 of the JAL that required a quarter of the judges in the courts of first instance to be selected from practicing lawyers.[215] If successful, Morsi would be the first president to enforce this provision. This sudden and large influx of judges had the potential to transform the judiciary's leanings and pave the way for additional Brotherhood-friendly judges in the future. For the security–military apparatus, this would have posed a serious threat to their plans to use the judiciary to weaken the Morsi presidency.[216]

Although the FJP's draft law maintained the Minister of Justice's authority to appoint judges to executive bodies, it limited the terms of secondments to once in a judge's career for up to four consecutive years.[217] Secondments were also limited to positions that required judicial or legal work only.[218] Article 44 of the draft law tightened the criteria for judicial employment in appointment or promotion to be "on the basis of competence, without favoritism or intercession and in line with the principles of efficiency and academic appropriateness," but kept final approval of judicial employment within the authority of the president of the republic.[219] The amendment was presumably intended to decrease the nepotism that nearly guaranteed that sitting judges would hire their sons and nephews, who were unlikely to be Brotherhood sympathizers. It also kept the final say of judicial appointments with the Brotherhood-dominated presidency.

The tensions between the FJP and the judiciary were most acute in relations with the SCC. The court viewed itself as the most prestigious judicial institution, which deserved its own section in the constitution and complete control over its budget and assignments, separate from other courts. Thus, when the FJP responded to judges' calls for salary increases, it proposed that all judges be paid at the same levels as the SCC justices. This was viewed as a direct economic threat, as well as a blow to the SCC's prestige.[220] If the rumors were true that the justices were significantly more highly paid than other judges, there would probably have to be a readjustment of salaries adverse to the SCC justices' salaries.

The Morsi-appointed constituent assembly further cut the number of SCC justices from eighteen to eleven, resulting in the removal of Justice Tehany Al Gibally, the most vocal critic of the MB and the only female justice.[221] Morsi's legal advisors defended the decision by claiming it to be a cost-saving measure which aligned the number of judges with those of other courts around the world.[222] Further weakening the SCC, the constituent assembly removed its *ex post* judicial review and limited it to *ex ante* review. As a result, once a law was passed, the SCC lost its jurisdiction to determine the law's constitutionality. This strategy proved fatal to Morsi's attempts to install a parliament during his first, and only, year as president, as the SCC repeatedly rejected drafts of the election law sent by the Shura Council.

Morsi's constitutional declaration of 22 November 2012 was his most controversial, and arguably signaled the death knell of his administration. In it, he imposed a new four-year term on the Prosecutor General, which authorized Morsi to replace Mubarak-appointed Abdel Meguid Mahmoud with Talaat Abdullah.[223] He also revoked the power of the SCC to declare parliament or the constituent assembly unconstitutional.[224] To ensure that the courts could not reverse his decisions, he placed his presidential decrees above judicial review altogether. This was perceived as a direct attack on judicial independence, which expanded Morsi's unpopularity beyond the top echelon of the judiciary to the entire judiciary.[225] The head of the Judges' Club, Ahmed Al Zind, rallied judges against Morsi's regime, calling for his removal.[226] Al Zind's political activities, arguably in violation of the JAL, made him a lightning rod in rallying the judiciary in support of the 3 July military coup.[227] Al Zind's loyalties to the former regime and animosity toward the 2005–6 judicial independence movement were well known, making him a powerful figure within internal judicial coalitions that supported the ousting of Morsi in July 2013.[228]

The Al-Zind coalition's agenda did not end with supporting the deposal of Morsi, however. Judges who had openly aligned themselves with the Morsi regime, whether by supporting his legal decrees or condemning the events of 3 July as a military coup, found themselves subjects of internal disciplinary investigations. Ironically, the same judges who had openly condemned Morsi as an incompetent president—a clearly political stance—were now accusing their colleagues of violating the JAL, prohibiting judges from engaging in politics. That disciplinary proceedings have been opened against these judges shows that the proceedings are aimed at punishing a judge's non-alignment with Al Zind, rather than being an objective determination that a particular judge violated the law.

By the end of summer 2014, it was clear that key members of the judicial leadership had actively supported the deep state and business elite in ousting Morsi and the MB from power. Meanwhile, the vast majority of judges kept quiet, either in agreement or out of fear, as they were all too familiar with the high price of betting on the losing side of a high stakes political game. And justifiably so, as the minority that spoke out against the military's takeover of the presidency through the proxy of the Chief Justice of the Supreme Constitutional Court are being purged from the judiciary.[229] Hence judicial activism was rewarded so long as it was in favor of the security–military apparatus—one of the bastions of the authoritarian state that was in control throughout Egypt's purported transitional period.

Conclusion

Notwithstanding the significant challenges facing the nation, Egypt's stillborn revolution was not necessarily a *fait accompli*. There were key points along the path from a decades-long dictatorship toward a democratic transition that could have changed the fate of its uprising. In hindsight, however, each crossroad became a lost opportunity to change the direction of the country wherein substantive equality enforced through thick rule of law could have provided meaningful opportunities for prosperity for all Egyptians, not just its small elite. From the SCAF's immediate ascendancy to power on 11 February 2011, to the MB's secret deal to protect the military's interests, to the SCAF's decision to forgo transitional justice beyond nominal prosecutions of top Mubarak officials, Egypt was being directed by a deeply rooted security–military apparatus intent on limiting the impact of the uprisings to merely switching out the elite coalition.

To the surprise of some Western analysts, Egypt's judiciary proved more counter-revolutionary than independent.[230] More than three years after Egypt's uprising, the judiciary has proven to be a formidable deep state institution, guarding its material interests in the status quo, even if it means betraying the rule of law. The judiciary serves the interests of powerful state actors, leaving little incentive for those actors to change their monopolistic and authoritarian practices.[231] This may be due to pressures by executive agencies that control judicial budgets,[232] economic incentives where judges benefit financially from the litigant's success,[233] or punitive measures taken against non-compliant judges in the form of transfers, investigations, or forced early retirement.[234] Its material interests in the status quo, particularly at the highest echelon, trumped any commitment there may have been to judicial independence and (thick) rule of law. Because transitional justice meant an overhaul of the existing patronage system that benefited sitting judges and their families, it was against their interests to support it.[235] In a country saddled with debt and high unemployment, giving up the status, fringe benefits, and potential for lucrative secondments amounted to economic suicide. This coupled with Mubarak's successful efforts in weakening the judicial independence movement of 2005–6 and co-opting the SCC, the judiciary was structurally incapable of taking the lead on a meaningful transitional justice process. In the end, Egypt's real revolution is yet to come. And when it does, a judiciary complicit in authoritarian practices may very well be among the targets of the people's rage.

12

SECURITY SECTOR REFORM
AND TRANSITIONAL JUSTICE AFTER
THE ARAB-MAJORITY UPRISINGS

THE CASE OF EGYPT

Omar Ashour and *Sherif Mohyeldeen*

The quest for justice and the Arab-majority uprisings

The "Arab-majority uprisings"[1] were principally sparked by the brutality of the security sectors in the countries where they occurred. In Tunisia, Mohammed Bouazizi's self-immolation, following an insult by a policewoman in December 2010, triggered the uprising. In Egypt, the June 2010 murder of internet activist Khaled Said by two policemen, followed by state-perpetrated violence during the fraudulent parliamentary elections of November–December 2010, set the uprising's context. In Libya, the arrest in February 2011 of Fathy Terbil—a human rights lawyer who had represented the families of the victims of the June 1996 Abu Selim prison massacre, in which more than 1,236 political prisoners were gunned down by Muammar Gaddafi's security forces—sparked that country's armed revolution. In Syria, abuses committed in March 2011 by Assad's security forces, which included the use of extreme violence against children and teenagers in Deraa, triggered the protests that ignited that country's ongoing armed uprising. In many ways, the Arab-majority uprisings were a region-wide reaction that was sparked by the violations committed by the security services and a quest for holding them accountable.[2] In the background, other variables were at play, including socio-economic inequalities, deprivation, and repressive authoritarianism and limited political freedoms.

Throughout the decades prior to the 2011 revolutions, many Arab security establishments behaved more like organized crime syndicates than professional security services. Concepts such as transitional justice, human rights, human security, democratic control, elected civilian oversight, and accountability were absent from the lexicons of Arab interior and defense ministries, and any attempts to introduce them meaningfully were met with repression. Egyptian activists unsurprisingly chose to stage the protests that initiated Egypt's uprising on 25 January, Egypt's National "Police Day," a state holiday intended to honor the security services.

But the confrontation with the security services did not end after toppling Mubarak on 11 February 2011. Activists realized that the regime had deeper roots. By March 2011 the accumulated grievances and legacy of brutality led to another confrontation between the pro-revolution forces and parts of the security sector, this time directly[3] with the State Security Investigations (SSI), the feared domestic intelligence services. On the evening of 5 March thousands of Egyptian protesters stormed a few of the SSI headquarters. Secret graveyards, medieval-like dungeons, files of political dissidents held for more than two decades, names of judges who helped fix elections and lists of informants—celebrities, religious figures, talk-show hosts, and opposition leaders—were all captured on camera and uploaded onto popular websites.[4] Torture rooms and equipment were captured on camera in every SSI building stormed by protesters. For average Egyptians, the sheer volume and graphic details of the released files were shocking. Although the unlawful detentions, kidnappings, disappearances, systematic torture, and rape perpetrated by the regime and its security forces have been documented over the last three decades, by both local and international human rights organizations, most media outlets would avoid addressing those taboos while Mubarak ruled and even afterwards.

As a result, security sector reform and transitional justice became immediate objectives of most revolutionary and reformist forces, regardless of ideological or political affiliation. Between 2011 and 2013, activists, scholars, parliamentarians, officials, non-governmental organizations (NGOs), and international governmental organizations (IGOs) proposed several initiatives aiming at security sector reform (SSR) and transitional justice (TJ). In early 2013, a five-phase, ten-year-long proposal was submitted by one of the co-authors of this chapter[5] to the Presidential Adviser on Security Issues, General Emad Hussein,[6] and the National Security and Foreign Affairs Committee of the Egyptian Upper House (Consultative Council), which is partly composed of retired army and police officers, among other parliamentarians. None of these initiatives reached an execution stage, due to various political, institutional, and bureaucratic hurdles. Following the military coup of July 2013, the probability of implementing any transitional justice or security sector reform initiatives became almost negligible.[7] The political will and material interests of the new military-dominated regime have not reconciled yet with reform processes. This was reflected in a widely disseminated lecture by General Abd al-Fattah al-Sisi to army commanders:

> What happened with the police in the last two years engendered a new environment. The police officer would stand with you [army officers] to a certain point. He can shoot, use bombs, tear gas, shotguns. But if someone dies, he may get tried. This [due process] should never happen again. And the protestors now [should] know it.[8]

Despite the gravity of the security violations and the intensity of the pro-democracy efforts, the January uprising in Egypt failed to bring about successful security sector reform and transitional justice processes. The question is "why?" This chapter takes an overview of some of the important TJ and SSR initiatives following the January uprising and attempts to explain the reasons behind their failure. It starts with a historical overview of the crises of transitional justice and the security sector in Egypt. It then analyzes the TJ and SSR proposed initiatives during the period 2011–13, and the reasons behind their failures. The chapter concludes with the ramifications of the failure of SSR processes, mainly in the case of Egypt.

Transitional justice in Egypt: A background

Transitional justice (TJ) is a concept incorporating political, economic, and social dimensions, in addition to communicative and institutional reformist ones. The concept "refers to the set of judicial and non-judicial measures that have been implemented by different countries in order to redress the legacies of massive human rights abuses. These measures include criminal prosecutions, truth commissions, reparations programs, and various kinds of institutional reforms."[9] The concept, and the processes based on it, are not a form of selective justice, but an approach to achieving justice in times of transition from conflict and/or state repression.

In the case of the Arab-majority uprisings, TJ was understood by many activists as a form of justice that targets the legacies and the figures of repressive authoritarian regimes after toppling them. This includes the questions of how to approach trials, amnesties, moral and financial compensation, institutional reforms, and, more generally, state–society relations. At the core of TJ is preventing the resurgence of repressive authoritarianism. Hence, security sector reform is critical for achieving TJ's objectives, especially in terms of institutional reforms.

The term "transitional justice" was relatively unknown in Egypt until the January uprising. Afterwards, the concept has been widely discussed on public and activists' forums. Many activists and politicians considered it a key indicator of the progress of reforms and, overall, democratization. As a result of the interest in the subject, the country has witnessed several TJ initiatives proposed by civil society and official actors since March 2011.

Since then, many revolutionary youth movements have been lobbying for a criminal justice process targeting officials who were involved in repressing activists, most notably members of the SSI and the Central Security Forces (CSF), both within the Ministry of Interior. The lobbying campaign included sit-ins, demonstrations, marches, and meetings with officials. The demand for TJ was reflected in the slogan "the rights of the martyrs," which featured in many pro-revolution activities. It was understood to mean the prosecution of security figures, accused of human rights abuses under successive regimes; and hence the process redeems the "rights" of the "martyrs."

The politicization, selectivity, and manipulation of the TJ process have been a significant feature in the Egyptian case. In Egypt, several parties have used the concept to get rid of, marginalize, or criminalize their political rivals. The most notable example is the case of the Muslim Brotherhood (MB) and their Freedom and Justice Party (FJP) following the 2013 coup. The group and the party are charged with terrorism, committing torture, mass murder, and even using "heavy, nuclear and chemical weapons" in their protests and sit-ins.[10] As a result of the December 2012 Ittihaddiyya clashes between the supporters and the opponents of President Mohammed Morsi, the latter is being tried with several of his advisers and aides for the deaths of two protesters. However, eight out of the ten victims of the Ittihaddiyya clashes are from Morsi's supporters and no one was charged or tried for their deaths—a small example of the selectivity and politicization of the prosecution office and the TJ process.

But the politicization of justice after the 2011 uprising started under the rule of Supreme Council of the Armed Forces (SCAF), February 2011 to June 2012. Under the Mubarak-appointed prosecutor general, Abdel Magid Mahmoud, several senior figures in Mubarak's regime were tried, but many others were left unquestioned. This served a political purpose. On the one hand, it defused popular discontent and even provided some popular support for the SCAF from unlikely candidates, such as various pro-revolution groups and pro-reform parties. On the other hand, the legal process did not affect any of the SCAF's key allies. For example, Ahmed Ezz, a prominent businessman in Egypt and a key ally of Gamal Mubarak, was placed on trial; whereas General Omar Suleiman, the head of the General Intelligence Directorate and Mubarak's vice president, was left unquestioned.

As a result of the selectivity and the politicization of due process, several activists, civil society organizations, and independent scholars and experts demanded fact-finding committees, whether national or international, compensation to the victims (regardless of political affiliation), trials for the ones accused (regardless of the official position and the military/security rank), and a reconciliation process. So far, no major steps have been taken to address such demands.[11]

The security sector in Egypt: A background

Security sector reform (SSR) can be described as "the transformation of the security system which includes all the actors, their roles, responsibilities and actions, so that it is managed and operated in a manner that is more consistent with democratic norms and sound principles of good governance, and thus contributes to a well-functioning security framework."[12] The philosophy behind SSR is partly rooted in human security: the idea that the primary objective of the security apparatus is the security of the individual citizen, not that of ruling regimes. It is an idea that contrasts distinctly with the reality in Egypt, where the daily threat for many law-abiding citizens prior to 2011 was the Egyptian security establishment itself.

Ideally, the reform process should embrace all branches of the security sector, from the armed forces to the customs authorities. The focus of this chapter, however, will be limited to the Ministries of Defense and Interior, which, in Egypt, include the high command of the army (Supreme Council of the Armed Forces), paramilitary forces (Central Security Forces), and domestic intelligence services (SSI, now renamed National Security Apparatus).

Two core objectives of SSR processes are critical in the case of Egypt:[13]

1) Establishment of effective governance, oversight, and accountability in the security system.
2) Improved delivery of security and justice services.[14]

To achieve those objectives, any comprehensive SSR process must involve a number of key initiatives, and Egypt was no exception. Demands included the improvement of oversight and accountability, whether internally, through the executive branch, through parliamentary oversight and legislation, or through the judiciary. Civil society actors, and indeed individual citizens, demanded to play a role in enhancing accountability through independent monitoring mechanisms (such as public complaints commissions, independent ombudsmen, and inspectors general).[15] A clear legal framework and mandate for the activities of the services, which integrates established human rights norms, was also of crucial importance and was among the demands of pro-reform. Within the security services themselves, there was a need for enhanced capacity-building through improved police training, staff development, and personnel policies. Successful SSR processes often emphasize decentralization and "civilianization" of the police force through measures such as ensuring civilian leadership, reforming ranking structures, and even changing uniforms. Ultimately, the security services must build a new, depoliticized identity, based on a strong professional and meritocratic culture, within a TJ framework.

Political repression

The security establishment's involvement in Egyptian politics has been well documented. Historically, the position of Interior Minister has been manipulated by different political forces. Following the 1919 revolution, Wafdist prime minister and liberal revolutionary leader Saad Zaghloul held the position in 1924 and used it against his political opponents. Following the military coup of 1952, Gamal Abdel Nasser held the position and kept it even when he became prime minister the following year.

Two major police sectors—State Security Investigations (SSI) and the Central Security Forces (CSF) sectors—have had significant impact on the Egyptian political scene. The predecessors of the SSI go back to pre-1952, when the "Political Bureau" was in charge of reporting and occasionally cracking down on dissidents. But there is no comparison between the influence of the SSI and that of the Political Bureau. After the July 1952 coup succeeded, the victorious "Free Officers" dissolved the Political Bureau, which had been reporting on them in the years prior. But once they faced political opposition and worker strikes in the industrial town of Kafr al-Dawar, they decided to re-establish a similar state security body, with the help of senior officers from the old Political Bureau. On 22 August 1952, only weeks following the July coup, the General Investigation Apparatus was established, to be renamed the General Administration of the State Security Investigations (SSI) in 1971, when Sadat took over. By the time of Mubarak's ascent to the presidency in 1981, the SSI had become the most powerful police sector in the country. It employed an estimated 100,000 individuals, and the influence and authority of its captains exceeded that of generals in other police, and even military, sectors. Even after Mubarak's removal on 11 February 2011, the behavior of the security reflected more continuity than change.[16] For example, the CSF, NSA, and other security apparatuses (including the Military Police and the Special Forces which operate under the Ministry of Defense) were involved in wide-scale repression campaigns that resulted in thousands of deaths and tens of thousands of injuries.[17] Under the SCAF, the most infamous of those happened in Maspero, mainly against Christian protesters (October 2011); in Mohammed Mahmoud Street, mainly against youth revolutionary groups (November 2011), near the Cabinet Building (December 2011), and the Abbassiyya district of Cairo (July 2011 and April 2012).[18] This is in addition to the responsibility of multiple security apparatuses for hundreds of torture cases, political detentions, and military tribunals for civilians between February 2011 and October 2012.[19] After the July 2013 military coup against President Morsi, the level of repression rose to another level. Constant repression and mass killings took place from 5 July 2013 onwards. But Egypt's worst massacre in modern history took place in Rab'a al-'Adawiyya Square on 14 August 2014. In less than ten hours, the death toll numbered 1,269 victims.[20] But this estimate is not incontrovertible, due to the difficulties of documentation. But the numbers of victims in this single episode undoubtedly exceed those of Muammar Gaddafi's two-day massacre in Abu Selim prison in June 1996 (1,236).[21] The Abu Zaabal prison massacre on 18 August 2014, in which 38 anti-coup political prisoners were gassed to death inside a prison transport van,[22] reflected a major crisis of impunity within the security sector. The four police officers accused of gassing the prisoners inside the van were all acquitted of "unintentional killing" charges in June 2014.[23]

Transitional justice initiatives in Egypt, 2011–13

One of the main obstacles to implementing the various TJ initiatives outlined below was the political will of the authorities, and the balance of power between the forces of change and forces of continuity. That has been the case since February 2011. TJ-relevant policies and acts were limited to nominal financial compensation provided to the victims of security forces' abuses and fact-finding commissions, whose reports were either partly or fully censored. This, however, did not prevent civil society actors, and pro-revolution activists and politicians, from pursuing and lobbying for further implementation of TJ-related policies. The following sections outline some of these initiatives under the SCAF, the presidency of Mohammed Morsi, and the post-coup authorities.

The interim rule of the Supreme Council of the Armed Forces (SCAF)

Under pressure, the SCAF had to take, and implement, several decisions that impacted on TJ efforts. After the removal of Mubarak on 11 February 2011, various pressure tactics were employed against the SCAF by pro-revolution activists to prosecute the former dictator and his two sons. Those tactics included mass demonstrations, marches, and limited but persistent sit-ins. All that led to the initiation of due processes against some of the most powerful figures in the Mubarak regime, including the latter himself. The list of defendants featured Habib al-Adly, the former Interior Minister, and several leading generals in the ministry, as well as Safwat Al-Sharif, the former Minister of Information and General Intelligence officer, among others.

While prosecuting the generals of the Ministry of Interior and Mubarak's neo-liberal business tycoons, the SCAF was protecting the military establishment. In 2011, it decreed law no. 45, by which the Code of Military Justice was amended to protect active and retired military personnel from accountability and prosecution in front of civilian courts. Even in the cases of corruption, graft, and illicit earnings, only military judges have the absolute jurisdiction on active and retired military personnel.

Under the SCAF, civilians tried before military tribunals were subjected to gross violations of human rights while in military custody. Some of these violations attracted international headlines, including the so-called "virginity tests." Unmarried female protesters in detention had to go through a virginity test to prove to the military that they were not prostitutes.[24] While civilian protesters faced military tribunals, Mubarak and many of his military and police generals were facing civilian proceedings. Human Rights Watch claimed: "Egypt's military leadership has not explained why young protesters are being tried before unfair military courts while former Mubarak officials are being tried for corruption and killing protesters before regular criminal courts. The generals' reliance on military trials threatens the rule of law by creating a parallel system that undermines Egypt's judiciary."[25]

The SCAF policies sparked multiple reactions from activists and civil society groups. "No Military Trials" emerged as one of the groups that challenged the military prosecution of civilians. Think tanks and academic experts also weighed in on the issue, with several proposed initiatives.[26] But most of the policy-relevant recommendations outlined by the activists and academic experts were ignored by the SCAF. The oft-repeated line of the military was that security can only be ensured by military trials and that these trials only target a few ex-convicts and criminal elements.[27]

The presidency of Mohammed Morsi

President Morsi began his short-lived term by establishing a fact-finding committee on 5 July 2012. Like the previous one under the SCAF, the objective of the committee was limited to "compiling data and evidences about the murder, the attempted murder, and the injuries of protestors in the entire republic."[28] The timeline suggested was from 25 January 2011 to 30 June 2012—the date on which authority was transferred from the SCAF to Egypt's first freely elected president.

In January 2013, the president received the committee's report after five months of investigations. But the conclusions and recommendations were kept classified.[29] Earlier in August 2012, the president made a daring move against the leadership of the SCAF by discharging Field Marshal Hussein Tantawi and his deputy General Sami Anan, a move that was welcomed by most of the pro-revolution youth forces. However, military violations continued, most notably in the form of military trials of civilians.[30]

As a result, the pressure of civil society groups for transitional justice continued under President Morsi. One of the creative initiatives was *Warakum bi al-Taqrir* (WBT, meaning "We are after you with the report"). It was endorsed by the National Community for Human Rights and Law, composed of lawyers, human rights activists, and the families of some of the victims. On the national level, WBT was lobbying for the public declaration of the conclusions and recommendations of the 2012 fact-finding committee.[31] On the international level, it cooperated with other local human rights organizations to bring one of the cases against the military in front of the African Commission on Human and Peoples' Rights.[32]

The gap between the soaring expectations of the presidency and its limited capacity and meagre achievements engendered an intense sense of frustration among many activists. This fed directly into the further politicization of human rights organizations, many of whom not only supported the July coup, but also made statements that support and glorify the campaign of repression the followed it.[33] One former human rights activist and academic called for turning mosques and schools into concentration camps for 750,000 alleged members of the Muslim Brotherhood.[34] As a result of their support, some of the pro-coup "human rights" figures were given official positions in the National Council for Human Rights (NCHR), a move that further complicated the national course of transitional justice.[35]

The post-coup authorities

On 3 July 2013, President Morsi was removed by the military. The generals appointed the head of the Supreme Constitutional Court, Adly Mansour, as interim president until presidential elections were held. The controversial elections were held in June 2014 and resulted in a landslide victory (96.9 percent) for General Abd al-Fattah al-Sisi, although he had publicly vowed not to rule when he led the coup a year earlier.

Under Mansour/al-Sisi rule, Egypt witnessed the largest systematic repression campaign in its modern history, conducted mainly by the security and the military forces. The most notorious event was the dispersals of the Rabʻaa al-Adawiyya and al-Nahda sit-ins, in which more than 1,000 protesters were killed in less than ten hours.[36] Human Rights Watch described the events as "likely to be considered a crime against humanity."[37]

Egypt's civilian judicial system has been suffering from politicization and limited independence since the 1952 coup and even earlier.[38] But it was further compromised during the Mansour/al-Sisi regime, as the politicized verdicts were consistent and unprecedented. Amnesty International described the post-coup judiciary in a report entitled a "Roadmap to Repression" as follows:

> The Egyptian authorities still use judicial harassment as a tool of repression, as it increasingly seems that the judicial proceedings taken against those who are perceived as political opponents or critics are politically motivated procedures that aim to punish the opponents and not to achieve justice. This worrying trend is manifested in selective justice in the cases chosen by public prosecution for investigation

and referral to trial. Instead of ensuring the accountability of security forces and its restrain, the authorities combated the activists asking for police reform and who criticized the Ministry of Interior.[39]

The selectivity and politicization of justice is also highlighted by the stark contrast between the failure of the public prosecution to conduct investigations with the police and the armed forces into the killing of more than 2,000 protesters since July 2013, on the one hand, and putting tens of thousands of protesters in custody pending further investigation, on the other hand. In return, "no criminal investigations were carried out regarding the excesses committed by security forces regarding the killing of hundreds of protestors during the dispersal of Raba'a and al-Nahda sit-ins."[40]

On the Ministry of Interior side, impunity continues. The ministry keeps on rejecting any independent investigation into alleged violations in the aftermath of the coup, or even the 2011 uprising. Brigadier-General Radi Abd al-Radi, the Director of Community Outreach, at the Human Rights Sector in the Ministry of Interior, said:

> We reject all of these charges. We are not a criminal suspect to be investigated in a transitional justice framework. We are a key actor aiming to achieve justice. Since the January revolution, the Ministry restructured itself and reformed and dealt with all of its previous mistakes. The Ministry is also working hard to show that it has changed. That is why we have established a new sector for Human Rights and Community Outreach. This is new thinking, with new mechanisms in dealing with the citizens. The duty of this sector is to protect the rights of the citizens and to secure them.[41]

In addition to the Human Rights Sector in the Ministry of Interior, a Ministry of Transitional Justice and National Reconciliation was established after the July coup. But like the Human Rights Sector, the Ministry did not initiate any serious measures to implement TJ or SSR. Amin El-Mahdy, the first Minister of Transitional Justice in Egypt's history, was appointed by the military. He declared in an interview that "there is no time for transitional justice."[42] Under El-Mahdy, there was no clear mandate for the ministry and its functions. The clarification of the ministry's mandate, the functions and the objectives, were introduced six months after its establishment.[43] The recently appointed Minister of TJ, Ibrahim El-Heneidy, stated that the current aim of the ministry was to create an "adequate atmosphere" for a "Transitional Justice Council" which should be established after the future parliamentary elections. El-Heneidy asserted that he "will be stronger and more able to carry out his duties in the Ministry" after the establishment of that council, but without clarification of why that is the case.[44]

"If you would like to kill an issue, establish a committee or a council for it," said one of the former MPs.[45] He was referring to a Mubarak-era tactic aimed at absorbing the energies and frustrations of the MPs by creating official institutional entities for unwelcomed proposals/issues. On the one hand, these entities serve as safe havens for "venting out." On the other hand, the levels of institutional and bureaucratic hurdles ensure that issues raised do not move beyond the discussion stage, and stay away from legislative and executive implantations. Given the level of violations, the functions of the Human Rights Sector and the Transitional Justice Ministry seem similar to those official bodies described by the MP as "killing the issue."

Security sector reform: attempts and failures

Starting from March 2011, Egypt saw more than fifteen security reform and transitional justice initiatives. While they vary significantly in seriousness, quality, and scope, none of them focused on the control of the armed forces. Instead, these initiatives have mainly targeted the internal security forces under the Ministry of Interior and were proposed by a varying spectrum of stakeholders in the SSR process: civil society groups, independent security experts and scholars, active and former police officers and their unofficial organizations, the Ministry of Interior, the parliament, and the presidency. This section considers some elements of important initiatives and reflects on the hurdles to their implementation in Egypt. The same hurdles are relevant to other countries of the Arab-majority uprising.

Security sector reform initiatives

As noted earlier, the police force was directed by Mubarak's regime to suppress the uprising, and incurred some heavy losses as a result. More than 95 police stations were burned during the eighteen days of the 2011 uprising, as well as more than 4,000 police vehicles. Additionally, officers and soldiers suffered from public animosity, physical and verbal attacks, reputation smearing and psychological pressures. "It is a broken army. More or less like the Egyptian army after the defeat of 1967," says Dr Muhammad Selim al-Awa, a former presidential candidate who discussed reforms with the former interior minister, General Mansour Issawi.[46] In reaction, both the Ministry of Interior and the mid-ranking police officers aimed for changes and various types of reforms.

After sacking the Mubarak-appointed government of Ahmad Shafiq and his interior minister, General Mahmoud Wagdy, the SCAF appointed a "reform-friendly" government on 3 March 2011, headed by Prime Minister Essam Sharaf. The newly appointed interior minister, Mansour Issawi, was a general who had retired fourteen years earlier, but he had a clean reputation and remained popular among officers. General Issawi was credited for some changes and reforms within the ministry. With the support of the SCAF, he disbanded the SSI and sacked or retired 505 lieutenant generals, 82 brigadier generals, and 82 colonels.[47]

Additionally, mid-ranking police officers formed several groups to push for internal reform: "we want to save face and tell our people that we neither sold them nor killed them; the traitor al-Adly and his gang did. Now the whole police force is paying the price for his policies," said Lieutenant Colonel Mohammed Salah, an officer commanding a CSF battalion and a member of the now defunct General Coalition of Police Officers (GCPO).[49] The GCPO emerged as the largest independent police officers' organization in Egypt following the uprising, but showed signs of collapsing in late 2012. It aimed to become an officially recognized police union with an elected leadership, and officially applied for that status in January 2012.[49] All of its known figures were reprimanded or punished by the Ministry of Interior at different periods between February 2011 and July 2013, most notably in the trial of two officers who were leading the police union foundation efforts, Lieutenant-Colonel Nabil Omar and Major Ashraf al-Banna. The initiatives proposed by the GCPO focused on cleansing the police force from corrupt generals, enhancing working conditions, training, media and public relations, and increasing salaries and pensions.

The short-lived (January–June 2012) Egyptian lower house (People's Assembly) was another institution that was expected to lobby strongly for an SSR process, before getting dissolved by the SCAF. It had an overwhelming majority which opposed the Mubarak regime and participated in the revolution. By the time the parliament was dissolved, it only made some amendments of a few articles in Law 109 (1971) which organized the police force (otherwise known as the Law of the Police Institution). Among the changes, the new version of the law removed the president as the head of the Supreme Council of the Police and amended articles related to two other issues (salary controls and the promotion of warrant officers). That was a major disappointment for some of the MPs and many of the pro-revolution activists. "We have more than 70 dead Egyptians in Port Said stadium and a group of generals running the Ministry of Interior like an organized crime syndicate. And all that the revolutionary parliament does is try to amend a few article on salaries and pensions," complained one of the MPs bitterly.[50] The Upper House of the Parliament (Consultative Council) also addressed SSR but without exceeding the discussion and deliberation phases between members of the National Security and Foreign Affairs Committee and independent experts.[51] The presidency, under Morsi, had similar activities, in which the presidential security advisor, General Emad Hussein, and other members of the presidential team in charge of the security files addressed and discussed the details of a ten-year initiative aiming to change the curricula, recruitments, standard operating procedures, and ultimately the behavior of the security services. In April 2013, the proposal was submitted to the Supreme Police Council, the highest executive authority in the police security structure, but none of the nineteen recommendations of the two-year-long first phase was implemented.[52]

Causes of SSR failure within a transition framework

Based on the experience of SSR initiatives and attempts in Egypt, eight major hurdles to successful SSR attempts were identified. The same hurdles apply to other Arab cases, in which Arab-majority uprisings succeeded in overthrowing despots, either by civil resistance or armed rebellion tactics. These are as follows:

1) **Extreme political polarization** between pro-change forces (whether reformists or revolutionaries) leading to the politicization of the SSR process as well as to political violence;
2) **Internal resistance** and spoiler games played by anti-reform factions within the security sector;
3) **Limited capacity and resources** of the newly elected governments;
4) **Weak democratic institutions** that failed to contain the political polarization and limit the political conflict to the institutional realms;
5) **Limited knowledge** and experience of SSR requirements among stakeholders;
6) **Limited pro-reform regional support**, mainly among democracies and pro-reform states;
7) **Aggressive anti-reform regional patrons**, mainly among repressive autocracies bent on maintaining the dominance of an authoritarian status quo in the region;
8) **Incomplete demobilization, disarmament, and reintegration (DDR)** (mainly in Libya and Yemen).

The extreme political polarization should not per se be a major hurdle to SSR. The diversity in the political spectrum, the heated debates, the intense arguments and the general difference of opinion should be celebrated as gains of the pro-democracy uprisings in Tunisia, Egypt, Libya, and Yemen. This freedom of opinion and expression should be aimed for in other Arab-majority countries. However, some of the ramifications of such polarization have negatively affected SSR processes. In all the aforementioned transitioning countries, political and criminal violence is cheap and effective and the risks of using violence are low. On the one hand, ministries of interior are responsible for defending elected state institutions, constantly under attack by various violent groups, including the groups affiliated with the losers in the electoral process or the losers from the whole transition process. On the other hand, if any of these protesters were killed or injured, the ministries of interior will be accused of brutality; add to that, the limited experience in non-lethal riot control tactics.[53] The other consequence of the extreme polarization is the politicization of the SSR process by rival politicians. On talk shows, political figures call for SSR and TJ to be implemented and for police brutality to end. At the same time, the same political figures praise security generals known for their support of brutal tactics, mainly when they crack down on their political rivals. As shown in other comparative cases, the unity of political forces on the very particular demands of de-politicizing the security sector and civilian control of the armed forces is key to the success of SSR, TJ, and overall democratization.

A second challenge is the strong resistance within the ranks of the Arab security sector to several critical elements of the reform process. Many of the Arab ministries of interior commanders perceive the reform process as only increasing the material capacities and the budgets of their respective institutions. Whereas this is a part of the process, exclusively aiming to enhance the performance of the sectors, other elements of SSR are usually unwelcomed and therefore blocked, especially in the Egyptian case. These elements include effective civilian oversight, procedures ensuring transparency, promotion criteria on a merit basis (as opposed to year of graduation), and even revisions of the police academies' curricula (although there is less resistance to that element compared to others).[54] Accountability in particular faces strong resistance.[55]

A third challenge is the limited capacity and resources. The post-revolution, democratically elected governments in Egypt, Libya, Yemen, and Tunisia are faced with serious economic challenges. In early 2013, Egypt's public debt exceeds EGP 1,310 billion (US$ 188 billion), or 85 percent of its GDP.[56] Though much lower public debts exist in Tunisia (15.8 percent of GDP) and Libya (4.2 percent of GDP),[57] their governments still suffer from limited resources to allocate to a thorough SSR process. The economic crisis in Egypt, however, did not prevent the SCAF from increasing police bonuses by 300 percent in the 2012 budget to "enhance the security performance."[58] It also did not prevent the post-coup al-Sisi regime from increasing the official budget of the Ministry of Interior to $4.1 billion and to buy 50,000 new pieces of weaponry.[59] There is limited public information on how such resources are spent and what the outcomes of such spending are. This undermines both transparency and accountability.

Two related challenges, the fourth and fifth, are the weak democratic institutions and the limited knowledge and experience of SSR requirements among many of the stakeholders in the process. In Egypt, the lower house of parliament (People's Assembly), elected following the revolution, was dissolved by the SCAF following a Constitutional Court verdict that deemed parts of the electoral law unconstitutional in June 2012. The Upper House (Consultative Council) was dissolved following the military coup of July 2013. What was clear in the dissolved lower and upper houses is the big gap between the revolutionary demands of eradicating torture, ending impunity, and reflecting transparency as against the limited knowledge of how to translate such demands into policies and procedures of SSR.[60] A general understanding of such limitations in Tunisia led the government and the Ministry of Interior to collaborate with an international organization and several SSR experts as early as July 2011.[61] In Egypt, similar attempts were foiled, most notably an attempt by the presidential establishment in the fall of 2013, seeking international assistance in SSR.

The sixth and seventh challenges listed above are quite straightforward. The seventh challenge is not that different from the European monarchies rallying to put an end to the French Revolution. In an attempt to defend a regional status quo whose main feature is authoritarianism, several regional actors did not perceive SSR and TJ processes, as well as any meaningful democratization process, as beneficial to their interests; more as threats to their regimes' security and stability. As a result, most of the pro-continuity forces in Egypt and other Arab uprising countries had strong, wealthy, and aggressive regional backers which bolstered their stances, morally, logistically, financially, as well as by intensive propaganda campaigns of deception and misinformation. On the other hand, most Western democracies and regional ones were hesitant to commit or to assist in a time-consuming, resource-draining, no-holds-barred conflict. This stance differed from the support granted to Eastern European transitions during the "third wave" of democratization, and thus weakened most pro-change and pro-reform Arab forces.

The future of security sector reform and transitional justice in Egypt

This chapter has provided an overview some of the important TJ and SSR initiatives in the aftermath of the January uprising. As outlined in the above sections, it has shown some of the main reasons behind the failures of these initiatives. The ramifications of that failure can be disastrous for the future of democratization in Egypt. On the one hand, reforming the security sector and achieving transitional justice were main objectives upheld by most of the pro-revolution forces in Egypt and the rest of the Arab-majority uprising countries. But on the other hand, after the 3 July 2013 coup, those objectives seem further away, even compared to the pre-uprising years. The gap between expectations and reality are reflected by the large numbers of protesters killed by the security forces between 2011 and 2014; the more than 40,000 detained and the arrest warrants issued in the aftermath of the coup; as well as by the over 18,000 injuries.[62] As opposed to TJ, a post-coup process of "legalizing repression" ensued. It featured a controversial protest law,[63] by which the new rulers aimed to control public protests; a series of collective death sentences;[64] and a resurgence of the notorious system of "secret prisons," most infamously al-Azuly military prison controlled by the military intelligence,[65] dubbed by some activists as the "Guantanamo of Egypt."

Between January 2011 and December 2013, nine fact-finding committees were formed to investigate major incidents of repression and human right violations, including massacres. The effect of these committees on the TJ process was limited, if not negligible, however. All of the reports produced were either partially or—the overwhelming majority—fully classified. Some of the committees were even dissolved before finishing their work, most notably the committees formed by the legislative authorities in Egypt represented by the upper chamber (Consultative Council) and the lower chamber (People's Assembly) of parliament. With such hurdles in the paths of fact-finding committees during Egypt's freest period since November 1954 (February 2011 to July 2013), the probability of implementing TJ or SSR processes in post-coup Egypt is limited. Perhaps one of the most critical indicators was a statement given by the former prime minister, Hazem al-Beblawi, who was appointed by the military following the coup. When a group of activists approached him in a meeting in July 2013 stressing the necessity of SSR, he replied by saying: "there is no time for reform during 'war.'"[66]

NOTES

1. INTRODUCTION: TRANSITIONAL JUSTICE IN THE MENA REGION

1. Alexandra Barahona de Brito, Carmen González Enríquez, and Paloma Aguilar, eds, *The Politics of Memory: Transitional justice in democratizing societies* (Oxford: Oxford University Press, 2001); Vesselin Popovski and Mónica Serrano, eds, *After Oppression: Transitional justice in Latin America and Eastern Europe* (Tokyo: United Nations University Press, 2012); Gary J. Bass, *Stay the Hand of Vengeance: The politics of war crimes tribunals* (Princeton, NJ: Princeton University Press, 2002).

2. Renée Jeffery and Hun Joon Kim, eds, *Transitional Justice in the Asia-Pacific* (Cambridge: Cambridge University Press, 2014).

3. See e.g. the special issue of the *International Journal of Transitional Justice* vol. 8, no. 3 (2014); Pablo de Greiff and Roger Duthie, eds, *Transitional Justice and Development: Making connections* (New York: Social Science Research Council, 2009); Dustin N. Sharp, ed., *Justice and Economic Violence in Transition* (Berlin: Springer, 2014); Chandra Lekha Sriram, Jemima García-Godos, Johanna Herman, and Olga Martin-Ortega, eds, *Transitional Justice and Peacebuilding on the Ground: Victims and excombatants* (London: Routledge, 2013).

4. United Nations, "The rule of law and transitional justice in conflict and post-conflict societies. Report of the Secretary-General," UN Doc. S/2004/616 (23 August 2004), para 8, elaborated by United Nations in "The rule of law and transitional justice in conflict and post-conflict societies. Report of the Secretary-General," UN Doc. S/2011/634 (12 October 2011); United Nations, "Guidance Note of the Secretary-General: United Nations Approach to Transitional Justice" (March 2010) at https://www.un.org/ruleoflaw/blog/document/the-rule-of-law-and-transitional-justice-in-conflict-and-post-conflict-societies-report-of-the-secretary-general/ (accessed 17 June 2016).

5. Neil J. Kritz, ed., *Transitional Justice* (3 vols.) (Washington, DC: United States Institute of Peace Press, 2005); Tricia D. Olsen, Leigh A. Payne, and Andrew G. Reiter, *Transitional Justice in Balance: Comparing processes, weighing efficacy* (Washington, DC: United States Institute of Peace Press, 1995).

6. Rosalind Shaw, Lars Waldorf, and Pierre Hazan, eds, *Localizing Transitional Justice: Interventions and priorities after mass violence* (Palo Alto, CA: Stanford University Press, 2010).

7. Robert Muggah, *Security and Post-Conflict Reconstruction: Dealing with fighters in the aftermath of war* (London: Routledge, 2009); Chandra Lekha Sriram and Johanna Herman, "DDR and transitional justice: bridging the divide?" *Conflict, Security, and Development* vol. 9, no. 4 (2009): 455–74.

8. Mark Freeman, *Necessary Evils: Amnesties and the search for justice* (Cambridge: Cambridge University Press, 2011).

9. Naomi Roht-Arriaza, *Impunity and Human Rights in International Law and Practice* (Oxford: Oxford University Press, 1995); Mark Osiel, *Mass Atrocity, Collective Memory and the Law* (New Brunswick, NJ: Transaction Publishers, 1999).

10. Martha Minow, *Between Vengeance and Forgiveness: Facing history after genocide and mass violence* (Boston, MA: Beacon Press, 2000); Priscilla Hayner, *Unspeakable Truths: Transitional justice and the challenge of truth commissions* (London: Routledge, 2011).

11. Alexander Mayer-Riekh and Pablo de Greiff, eds, *Justice as Prevention: Vetting public employees in transitional societies* (New York: Social Science Research Council, 2007).

12. Chandra Lekha Sriram, Olga Martin-Ortega, and Johanna Herman, eds, *Peacebuilding and Rule of Law in Africa: Just peace?* (London: Routledge, 2011).

13. Dustin N. Sharp, "Emancipating transitional justice from the bonds of the paradigmatic transition," *International Journal of Transitional Justice* (2014): 1–20, at http://ijtj.oxfordjournals.org/content/early/2014/12/02/ijtj.iju021.full.pdf+html (accessed 17 June 2016); Rodrigo Uprimny, "Transitional Justice Without Transition? Possible lessons from the use (and misuse) of transitional justice discourse in Colombia," Paper prepared for the international conference, Building a Future on Peace and Justice, Nuremberg, 25–27 June 2007, at http://www.peace-justice-conference.info/download/WS%205%20-%20expert%20paper%20-%20Uprimny.pdf

14. Sharp, ed., *Justice and Economic Violence in Transition*; Sriram, Martin-Ortega, and Herman, eds, *Peacebuilding and Rule of Law in Africa*; Christine Bell and Catherine O'Rourke, "Does feminism need a theory of transitional justice? An introductory essay," *International Journal of Transitional Justice* vol. 1, no. 1 (2007): 23–44.

2. TRANSITIONAL JUSTICE IN COMPARATIVE PERSPECTIVE: LESSONS FOR THE MIDDLE EAST

1. Ruti G. Teitel, *Transitional Justice* (Oxford: Oxford University Press, 2000); Chandra Lekha Sriram, *Confronting Past Human Rights Violations: Justice vs peace*

in times of transition (London: Frank Cass, 2004); Susanne Buckley-Zistel, Teresa Koloma Beck, Christian Braun, and Frederieke Mieth, eds, *Transitional Justice Theories* (London: Routledge, 2014); Chandra Lekha Sriram, Jemima García-Godos, Johanna Herman, and Olga Martin-Ortega, eds, *Transitional Justice and Peacebuilding on the Ground: Victims and excombatants* (London: Routledge, 2013); Dustin N. Sharp, ed., *Justice and Economic Violence in Transition* (New York: Springer, 2014).

2. Gary J. Bass, *Stay the Hand of Vengeance: The politics of war crimes tribunals* (Princeton, NJ: Princeton University Press, 2000); Alison Brysk, *The Politics of Human Rights in Argentina: Protest, change and democratization* (Palo Alto, CA: Stanford University Press, 1994).

3. Oskar N. T. Thoms, James Ron, and Roland Paris, "The effects of transitional justice mechanisms: A summary of empirical research findings and implications for analysts and practitioners" (Ottawa: CIPS working paper, 2008) at http://aix1.uottawa.ca/~rparis/CIPS_Transitional_Justice_April2008_ExecSummary.pdf (accessed 17 June 2016); Tricia D. Olsen, Leigh A. Payne, and Andrew G. Reiter, *Transitional Justice in Balance: Comparing processes, weighing efficacy* (Washington, DC: United States Institute of Peace, 2010); Kathryn Sikkink, *The Justice Cascade: How human rights prosecutions are changing world politics* (New York: Norton, 2011).

4. Elham Fakhro, "Truth and fact-finding in the Arab monarchies," Ch. 9 in this volume. Although the father of the incoming king had created a commission in 1990, this was of relatively limited effect; Sahar Aziz, "Theater or transitional justice: Reforming the judiciary in Egypt," Ch. 11 in this volume.

5. Christopher Lamont, "The scope and boundaries of transitional justice in the Arab Spring," Ch. 5 in this volume; Fakhro, "Truth and fact-finding in the Arab monarchies."

6. Lamont, "The scope and boundaries of transitional justice"; Susan Waltz, "Linking transitional justice and human rights," Ch. 3 in this volume.

7. Lamont, "The scope and boundaries of transitional justice."

8. Fakhro, "Truth and fact-finding in the Arab monarchies."

9. Lamont, "The scope and boundaries of transitional justice"; Mieczyslaw P. Boduszyński and Marieke Wierda, "Political exclusion and transitional justice: A case study of Libya," Ch. 8, and Thomas DeGeorges, "Martyrdom in North Africa following the Arab Spring and the process of transitional justice," Ch. 7 in this volume.

10. Waltz, "Linking transitional justice and human rights," opening paragraph.

11. Waltz, "Linking transitional justice and human rights."

12. Colleen Duggan, "Editorial Note," *International Journal of Transitional Justice* vol. 4 (2010): 315–28.

13. Geoff Dancy, "Impact assessment, not evaluation: Defining a limited role for pos-

itivism in the study of transitional justice"; Brandon Hamber, Liz Ševcenko, and Ereshnee Naidu, "Utopian dreams or practical possibilities? The challenges of evaluating the impact of memorialisation in societies in transition," *International Journal of Transitional Justice* vol. 4 (2010): 355–76 and 397–420.

14. Chandra Sriram, "Truth commissions and political theory: Tough moral choices in transitional situations," *Netherlands Quarterly of Human Rights* vol. 18 (2000): 471–92; Bronwyn A. Leebaw, "The Irreconcilable Goals of Transitional Justice," *Human Rights Quarterly* vol. 30, no. 1 (2008): 95–118.

15. Sriram, *Confronting Past Human Rights Violations*, pp. 107–26.

16. Payam Akhavan, "Beyond Impunity: Can International Criminal Justice Prevent Future Atrocities?" *American Journal of International Law* vol. 95, no. 1 (January 2001): 7–31.

17. Sriram, "Truth commissions and political theory."

18. United Nations General Assembly, "Basic Principles on the Right to a Remedy and Reparation for Victims of Gross Violations of International Human Rights Law and Serious Violations of International Humanitarian Law," UN Doc. A/RES/60/147 (21 March 2006); United Nations Economic and Social Council, "Promotion and Protection of Human Rights: Study on the right to the truth. Report of the United Nations High Commissioner for Human Rights," UN Doc. E/CN.4/2006/91 (8 February 2006).

19. Sriram, Garcia-Godos, Herman, and Martin-Ortega, eds, *Transitional Justice and Peacebuilding on the Ground*; Thorsten Bonacker and Christoph Safferling, eds, *Victims of International Crimes: An interdisciplinary discourse* (New York: Springer, 2013).

20. Ruth Rubio-Marin, ed., *The Gender of Reparations: Unsettling sexual hierarchies while redressing human rights violations* (Cambridge: Cambridge University Press, 2011).

21. Doris H. Gray and Terry C. Coonan, "Reframing Gender Narratives through Transitional Justice in the Maghreb," Ch. 6 in this volume; Rubio-Marin, ed., *The Gender of Reparations*.

22. Chandra Lekha Sriram's interviews in Rio de Janeiro and Brasilia, August 2013.

23. Chandra Lekha Sriram's interviews in Santiago, July 2014.

24. Judy Barsalou, "'The walls will not be silent': A cautionary tale about transitional justice and collective memory in Egypt," Ch. 10 in this volume.

25. Johanna Herman, "Local voices in Internationalised justice: The experience of civil parties at the Extraordinary Chambers in the Courts of Cambodia," CHRC Research Report (May 2014), at http://www.cambodiatribunal.org/wp-content/uploads/2014/06/UEL_JHermanReport_140530_Local_Voices_ECCC.pdf (accessed 17 June 2016).

26. DeGeorges, "Martyrdom in North Africa."

27. On pedagogic effects, see Mark Osiel, *Mass Atrocity, Collective Memory, and the Law* (New Brunswick, NJ: Transaction Books, 1999).

28. Boduszyński and Wierda, "Political exclusion and transitional justice."
29. Lamont, "The scope and boundaries of transitional justice."
30. Fakhro, "Truth and fact-finding in the Arab monarchies."
31. United Nations, "The rule of law and transitional justice in conflict and post-conflict societies. Report of the Secretary-General," UN Doc. S/2004/616 (23 August 2004); United Nations, "The rule of law and transitional justice in conflict and post-conflict societies. Report of the Secretary-General to the Security Council," UN Doc. S/2011/634 (12 October 2011); Chandra Lekha Sriram, Olga Martin-Ortega, and Johanna Herman, eds, *Peacebuilding and Rule of Law in Africa: Just peace?* (London: Routledge, 2011).
32. Duggan, "Editorial Note"; Dancy, "Impact assessment, not evaluation."
33. Olsen, Payne, and Reiter, *Transitional Justice in Balance.*
34. Waltz, "Linking transitional justice and human rights."
35. Olsen, Payne, and Reiter, *Transitional Justice in Balance*; Eric Wiebelhaus-Brahm, *Truth Commissions and Transitional Societies: The impact on human rights and democracy* (London: Routledge, 2010); Sikkink, *The Justice Cascade.*
36. Sriram, Martin-Ortega, and Herman, eds, *Peacebuilding and Rule of Law in Africa*; Chandra Lekha Sriram, "Justice as peace? Liberal peacebuilding and strategies of transitional justice," *Global Society* vol. 21, no. 4 (2007): 579–91.
37. Jelena Subotic, *Hijacked Justice: Dealing with the past in the Balkans* (Ithaca, NY: Cornell University Press, 2009); Lara J. Nettelfield, *Courting Democracy in Bosnia and Herzegovina: The Hague Tribunal's impact in a postwar state* (Cambridge: Cambridge University Press, 2010).
38. Chandra Lekha Sriram, "Sri Lanka: Atrocities, Accountabiltiy and the Decline of Rule of Law," in Renée Jeffery and Hun Joon Kim, eds, *Transitional Justice in the Asia-Pacific* (Cambridge: Cambridge University Press, 2014), pp. 61–86.
39. Sriram's interviews in Santiago.
40. Chandra Lekha Sriram's interviews in Nairobi and the Rift Valley, February and May 2014.
41. Website, project on the Impact of Transitional Justice Measures on Democratic Institution-building, www.tjdi.org (accessed 17 June 2016).
42. Alexander George and Andrew Bennett, *Case Studies and Theory Development in the Social Sciences* (Cambridge, MA: Massachusetts Institute of Technology Press, 2004).
43. Joanna R. Quinn, ed., *Reconciliation(s): Transitional justice in postconflict societies* (Montreal: McGill/Queens University Press, 2009).
44. Sriram and García-Godos, "Conclusions and considerations for practitioners," in Sriram, García-Godos, Herman, and Martin-Ortega, eds, *Transitional Justice and Peacebuilding on the Ground*, pp. 255–68.
45. Scott Straus and Lars Waldorf, eds, *Remaking Rwanda: State building and human rights after mass violence* (Madison, WI: University of Wisconsin Press, 2011).

Gacaca is a form of community justice utilizing lay judges to consider guilt and punishment of lower-level accused.

46. Patricia Lundy and Mark McGovern, "Whose Justice? Rethinking Transitional Justice from the Bottom Up," *Journal of Law and Society* vol. 3, no. 2 (2008): 265–92; Andrew B. Friedman, "Transitional justice and human rights: A framework for the protection of human rights," *Akron Law Review* vol. 46 (2013): 727; Roger MacGinty, "Gilding the lily? International support for indigenous and traditional peacebuilding," in Oliver P. Richmond, ed., *Palgrave Advances in Peacebuilding: Critical developments and approaches* (London: Palgrave, 2010), pp. 347–66.

47. Michelle Flash, "Investigations, Misconduct and Uncertainty in the ECCC Regarding Case 003," *Human Rights Brief* (5 September 2012) at http://hrbrief. org/2012/09/investigations-misconduct-and-uncertainty-in-the-eccc-regarding-case-003–8/ (accessed 1 December 2014).

48. Lamont, "The scope and boundaries of transitional justice."

49. Chandra Lekha Sriram, "Post-conflict justice and hybridity in peacebuilding: Resistance or cooptation?" in Oliver P. Richmond and Audra Mitchell, eds, *Hybrid Forms of Peace: From everyday agency to post-liberalism* (London: Palgrave, 2012), pp. 58–72.

50. Sriram, *Confronting Past Human Rights Violations*, pp. 147–70; Tim Kelsall, "Truth, lies, ritual: Preliminary reflections on the Truth and Reconciliation Commission in Sierra Leone," *Human Rights Quarterly* vol. 27, no. 2 (2005): 361–91.

51. DeGeorges, "Martyrdom in North Africa," observes that this is part of a broader tension between the abused individual and the state apparatus.

52. Sriram's interviews in Brazil and Chile.

53. Sriram, "Externalizing justice through universal jurisdiction: Problems and prospects," *Finnish Yearbook of International Law*, vol. 12 (2001): 53–77.

54. Jessica Lincoln, *Transitional Justice, Peace and Accountability: Outreach and the role of international courts after conflict* (London: Routledge, 2011).

55. For more information, see the website of the International Criminal Court, at www.icc-cpi.int

56. Website of the Lessons Learned and Reconciliation Commission, www.llrc.lk; Amnesty International, "When will they get justice? Failures of Sri Lanka's Lessons Learnt and Reconciliation Commission" (7 September 2011) at http://www. amnesty.org/en/library/info/ASA37/008/2011/en (accessed 17 June 2016).

57. Communications from civil society activists in Sri Lanka, not for attribution.

58. Sriram's interviews in Kenya.

59. Chandra Lekha Sriram, "International rule of law? Ethics and impartiality of legal officials in international criminal tribunals," and William A. Schabas, "Judicial ethics at the international criminal tribunals," in Vesselin Popovski, ed., *International*

Rule of Law and Professional Ethics (Oxon: Ashgate, 2014), pp. 171–88 and 189–206.

60. Waltz, "Linking transitional justice and human rights"; Fakhro, "Truth and fact-finding in the Arab monarchies."
61. See generally Sharp, ed., *Justice and Economic Violence in Transition*.
62. Sriram, "Economic violence and liberal peacebuilding," in Sharp, ed., *Justice and Economic Violence in Transition*, pp. 27–50.
63. Waltz, "Linking transitional justice and human rights."

3. LINKING TRANSITIONAL JUSTICE AND HUMAN RIGHTS

1. Jon Elster, *Closing the Books: Transitional Justice in Historical Perspective* (New York: Cambridge University Press, 2004).
2. Jack Donnelly, "International Human Rights: A Regime Analysis," *International Organization* vol. 40 (1986): 617.
3. These include Morocco's Equity and Reconciliation Commission of 2004–5, the 2011 Bahrain Independent Commission of Inquiry, the Ad Hoc Inquiry Commission in Charge of the Question of Disappearances in Algeria (2003–5), de-Ba'athification and trials before the Iraqi High Tribunal over the 2003–10 period; several Egyptian trials from 2012–14, including that of former president Hosni Mubarek; the continuing international Special Tribunal for Lebanon (established 2009), and the International Criminal Court's consideration of cases in Libya (with arrest warrants issued in 2011). In December 2013, the Tunisian parliament approved legislation mandating a comprehensive program of transitional justice, but as of 2015 a similar initiative in Yemen appears to have stalled.
4. "Egyptian court overturns Mubarak's graft conviction and orders retrial," *New York Times*, 13 January 2015, http://www.nytimes.com/2015/01/14/world/middlee-ast/hosni-mubarak-conviction-overturned.html?hp&action=click&pgtype=Ho mepage&module=first-column-region&region=top-news&WT.nav=top-news&_ r=0 (accessed 13 January 2015).
5. In 1981, a number of Islamic scholars promulgated an alternative to the UN's Universal Declaration of Human Rights (UHDR), titling it the Universal Islamic Declaration of Human Rights, http://www.alhewar.com/ISLAMDECL.html (accessed 21 August 2014). Several years later, the Islamic Conference of Foreign Ministers issued an alternative version, known as the Cairo Declaration on Human Rights in Islam, http://www1.umn.edu/humanrts/instree/cairodeclaration.html (accessed 21 August 2014). Both of these documents have been analyzed at some length by Ann Elizabeth Mayer in *Islam and Human Rights: Tradition and Politics*, 5th edn (Boulder, CO: Westview Press, 2013). Her analysis points up discrepancies between the English and Arabic versions of the UIDHR (76–8), and she argues that both of these initiatives are best understood as initiatives by political elites to

use religion and culture as devices to weaken international human rights law, rather than as representations of Islam's incompatibility with the international human rights standards (203). In any event, neither the UIDHR nor the Cairo Declaration has status in international treaty law, and repeated efforts by Iran and others to revise the UDHR have not found purchase within the UN. Nevertheless, taken collectively, such initiatives help shape the context for considering transitional justice efforts and the possibilities of human rights reform in the Middle East.

6. These particular rights are often considered *jus cogens*, or peremptory norms of international law. See Peter Malanczuk, excerpt from *Akehurst's Modern Introduction to International Law*, 7th edn, in Henry J. Steiner, Philip Alston, and Ryan Goodman, eds, *International Human Rights in Context: Law, Politics, Morals*, 3rd edn (Oxford: Oxford University Press, 2008), pp. 77–8; and American Law Institute, Restated (Third) *The Foreign Relations Law of the United States* (Vol. 2, 1987), in Steiner, Alston and Goodman, pp. 172–3.

7. See Independent International Commission of Inquiry on the Syrian Arab Republic, http://www.ohchr.org/EN/HRBodies/HRC/IICISyria/Pages/IndependentInternationalCommission.aspx (accessed 8 January 2015).

8. Human Rights Watch, "Egypt: Rab'a Killings Likely Crimes Against Humanity," http://www.hrw.org/news/2014/08/12/egypt-rab-killings-likely-crimes-against-humanity (accessed 8 January 2015).

9. In Morocco, for example, some 20,000 victims of grave human rights violations were identified by the IER, and while that number is shocking, it still represents a very small percentage in a country of 30 million.

10. République Tunisienne, Ministère des Droits de l'Homme et de la Justice Transitionnelle, *Loi organique relative à l'instauration de la justice transitionnelle et à son organization*, Chapitre III, "De la redevabilité et de la responsabilité pénale" (Tunis: Government of Tunisia, 2014).

11. In 2005 the UN General Assembly adopted the document they had drafted, "Basic Principles and Guidelines on the Right to a Remedy and Reparations for Victims of Gross Violations of International Human Rights Law and Serious Violations of International Humanitarian Law," http://www.ohchr.org/EN/Professional Interest/Pages/RemedyAndReparation.aspx (accessed 21 August 2014).

12. Pablo de Greiff, ed., *The Handbook of Reparations* (New York: Oxford University Press, 2008).

13. International Center for Transitional Justice (ICTJ), "The Rabat Report: The Concept and Challenges of Collective Reparations," http://www.ictj.org/sites/default/files/ICTJ-Morocco-Reparations-Report-2009-English.pdf (accessed 21 August 2014).

14. United Nations Economic and Social Council, "Updated Set of Principles for the Protection and Promotion of Human Rights Through Action to Combat

Impunity," Addendum to the Report of the Independent Expert to Update the Set of Principles to Combat Impunity, Diane Orentlicher" (ECOSOC, E/CN.4/2005/102/Add.1: 2005): 6.

15. Human Rights Watch, "Policy Statement on Accountability for Past Abuses," and Amnesty International, "Policy Statement on Impunity," in *Transitional Justice: How Emerging Democracies Reckon with Former Regimes*, vol. I, ed. Neil J. Kritz (Washington, DC: US Institute of Peace, 1995), pp. 217–18 and 219–21.

16. Amnesty International, "South Africa: Reforms Promise Solid Foundation for a New Society Based on Human Rights but Questions Remain on Other Issues," http://amnesty.org/en/library/info/AFR53/017/1995/en (accessed 21 August 2014).

17. Priscella B. Hayner, *Unspeakable Truths: Transitional Justice and the Challenge of Truth Commissions*, 2nd edn (New York: Routledge, 2011). See also Section I of Diane Orentlicher, "Independent Study on Best Practices, Including Recommendations, to Assist States in Strengthening Their Domestic Capacity to Combat All Aspects of Impunity," a report issued by the United Nations Economic and Social Council, "Promotion and Protection of Human Rights: Impunity," E/CN.4/2004/88.

18. To that end, the international non-governmental organization Impunity Watch was founded in the Netherlands, http://www.impunitywatch.org (accessed 21 August 2014).

19. Amnesty International, "El Salvador: The Spectre of Death Squads," http://www.amnesty.org/en/library/info/AMR29/015/1996 (accessed 21 August 2014); and Human Rights Watch, "El Salvador," https://www.hrw.org/reports/1996/WR96/Americas-05.htm (accessed 21 August 2014). See also Laura Pedraza Fariña, Spring Miller, and James L. Cavallaro, *No Place to Hide: Gang, State, and Clandestine Violence in El Salvador* (Cambridge, MA: Harvard University Press, 2010).

20. Robin Oisin Llewellyn, "El Salvador, Violence and Impunity," *Le Monde Diplomatique*, 11 February 2014, http://mondediplo.com/blogs/el-salvador-violence-and-impunity (accessed 21 August 2014).

21. Orentlicher was also asked to update and expand the existing Joinet Principles for combating impunity. Formally titled "Principles for the Protection and Promotion of Human Rights Through Action to Combat Impunity," the Joinet Principles were named after their principal author, Louis Joinet, member of the UN Sub-Commission on Human Rights.

22. "Measures that are well-conceived in their own terms have often produced disappointing results when other elements of an effective policy for combatting impunity are absent or have been poorly implemented." Orentlicher, "Independent Study," p. 4.

23. See Chandra Sriram, *Confronting Past Human Rights Violations: Justice vs peace in times of transition* (New York: Frank Cass, 2004), pp. 25–33, for a discussion of factors that affect choices available in times of transition.

24. Jose Zalaquett, "Introduction to the English Edition," in *Report of the Chilean National Commission on Truth and Reconciliation* (Washington, DC: US Institute of Peace), http://www.usip.org/sites/default/files/resources/collections/truth_commissions/Chile90-Report/Chile90-Report.pdf (accessed 21 August 2014). Zalaquett is uniquely positioned to comment on such challenges, as a specialist in international human rights law and a member of the Rettig Commission, but also having served in several leading roles within Amnesty International as well as having been briefly imprisoned during Chile's dirty war in the 1970s.

25. Elin Skaar, "Truth Commissions, Trials—Or Nothing? Policy Options in Democratic Transitions," *Third World Quarterly* vol. 20 (1999).

26. Kathyrn Sikkink, *The Justice Cascade: How Human Rights Prosecutions are Changing World Politics* (New York: W. W. Norton, 2011).

27. See Royaume de Maroc, *Instance Equité et Réconciliation*, http://www.ier.ma/rubrique.php3?id_rubrique=40&lang=en (accessed 21 August 2014); Susan Slyomovics, *The Performance of Human Rights in Morocco* (Philadelphia: University of Pennsylvania Press, 2005); Fadoua Loudiy, *Transitional Justice and Human Rights in Morocco* (New York: Routledge Press, 2014).

28. International Center for Transitional Justice (ICTJ), "Morocco," http://www.ictj.org/our-work/regions-and-countries/morocco (accessed 21 August 2014); and Human Rights Watch, "Morocco: Human Rights at a Crossroads," Section III, http://www.hrw.org/reports/2004/morocco1004/3.htm#_Toc84811760 (accessed 27 August 2014).

29. Middle East Online, "Morocco finishes compensation for rights victims," http://www.middle-east-online.com/english/?id=21644 (accessed 21 August 2014).

30. ICTJ, "The Rabat Report: The Concept and Challenges of Collective Reparations," http://www.ictj.org/sites/default/files/ICTJ-Morocco-Reparations-Report-2009-English.pdf (accessed 27 August 2014).

31. See Mohamed Saadi, *Le difficile chemin des droits de l'homme au Maroc: Dudéni à la reconnaissance* (Paris: L'Harmattan, 2009).

32. Amnesty International, "Morocco/Western Sahara: Torture in the 'Anti-Terrorism' Campaign: the Case of Temara Detention Center," http://www.amnesty.org/en/library/info/MDE29/004/2004/en (accessed 27 August 2014); Human Rights Watch, "Morocco: Human Rights at a Crossroads," Section IV, http://www.hrw.org/reports/2004/morocco1004/4.htm; Laila Mernissi, "Le Mouvement du 20 février au Maroc: vers une seconde indépendence?" *Revue Averroes*, http://revueaverroestest.files.wordpress.com/2011/08/art-mernissi-revue-averroc3a8s-n4-5-aoc3bbt2011.pdf (accessed 27 August 2014).

33. Human Rights Watch, *Morocco: Human Rights at a Crossroads*, Section IV, "Human Rights after the Casablanca Bombings," http://www.hrw.org/reports/2004/morocco1004/4.htm (accessed 21 August 2014); and Amnesty International, "Morocco/Western Sahara: Torture in the 'Anti-Terrorism' Campaign: the Case

of Temara Detention Center," http://amnesty.org/en/library/info/MDE29/004/2004/en (accessed 21 August 2014).

34. Gavin Maxwell's account of the House of Glaoua in the early twentieth century provides some insight into the extent to which checks and balances were absent in governance structures of Morocco's more remote provinces a hundred years ago: Gavin Maxwell, *Lords of the Atlas: The Rise and Fall of the House of Glaoua* (London: Eland Books, 2004). Hisham Shahrabi's classic work *Neopatriarchy: A Theory of Distorted Change in Arab Society* (New York: Oxford University Press, 1992) provides insight into the ways that patriarchal structures continue to shape and inform politics in the Middle East.

35. Susan E. Waltz, *Human Rights and Reform: Changing the Face of North African Politics* (Berkeley, CA: University of California Press, 1995), pp. 64–5. For more recent commentary on the structure and impact of the Tunisian security sector, see Mahmoud Ben Romdhane, *Tunisie: Etat, Economie et Société* (France: Sud Editions–Tunis, 2011), pp. 105–10.

36. Patrick Kingsley, "Egyptian judge sentences 720 men to death," *Guardian*, 28 April 2014, http://www.theguardian.com/world/2014/apr/28/egyptian-judge-sentences-720-men-death (accessed 21 August 2014).

37. "Egypt places civilian infrastructure under army jurisdiction," *Guardian*, http://www.theguardian.com/world/2014/oct/28/egypt-civilian-infrastructure-army-jurisdiction-miltary-court (accessed 9 January 2015).

38. See Jaouad Mdidech, *La chambre noire, ou, Derb Moulay Chérif* (Casablanca: Editions Eddif, 2000).

39. See for example Amnesty International's annual report covering 1997 and its 1999 report "Morocco/Western Sahara: 'Turning the Page': Achievements and Obstacles," MDE 29/01/99.

40. Human Rights Watch, "Section IV. Human Rights after the Casablanca Bombings"; and Amnesty International, "Morocco/Western Sahara: Torture in the 'Anti-Terrorism' Campaign."

41. Tricia D. Olsen, Leigh Payne, and Andrew Reiter, *Transitional Justice in Balance: Comparing Processes, Weighing Efficacy* (Washington, DC: United States Institute of Peace, 2010), pp. 61–72.

42. Elster, *Closing the Books*, p. 213.

43. Tricia D. Olsen, Leigh A. Payne, Andrew G. Reiter, and Eric Wiebelhaus-Brahm, "When Truth Commissions Improve Human Rights," *International Journal of Transitional Justice* vol. 4 (2010): 457–76.

44. CIRI Human Rights Data Project, http://www.humanrightsdata.com (accessed 24 August 2014).

45. Political Terror Scale, http://www.politicalterrorscale.org (accessed 24 August 2014).

46. Eric Wiebelhaus-Brahm, *Truth Commissions and Transitional Societies: The impact*

on human rights and democracy (New York: Routledge, 2010); and Olsen, Payne, and Reiter, Transitional Justice in Balance.

47. State Department annual country reports for the period are available online and in (US) federal depository libraries. Amnesty International published numerous reports on various aspects of Morocco's human rights performance during the period. All are available online at http://amnesty.org

48. Documentation related to the Cingranelli–Richards scale is available at the CIRI Human Rights Data Project, http://www.humanrightsdata.com (accessed 24 August 2014). Information about the PTS can be found at Political Terror Scale, http://www.politicalterrorscale.org (accessed 24 August 2014). See also David L. Cingranelli and David L. Richards, "The Cingranelli and Rchards (CIRI) Human Rights Data Project," *Human Rights Quarterly* vol. 32(2010): 401–24; and Reed M. Wood and Mark Gibney, "The Political Terror Scale (PTS): A Re-Introduction and a Comparison to CIRI," *Human Rights Quarterly* vol. 32 (2010): 367–400.

49. Further discussion below: Ann Marie Clark and Kathryn Sikkink, "Information Effects and Human Rights Data: Is the good news about increased human rights information bad news for human rights measures?" *Human Rights Quarterly* vol. 35 (2013): 539–68. See also Christopher J. Fariss, "Respect for Human Rights has Improved Over Time: Modeling the changing standard of accountability," *American Political Science Review* vol. 108 (May 2014): 297–318; and Courtenay R. Conrad, Jillienne Haglund, and Will H. Moore, "Torture Allegations as Events Data: Introducing the Ill-Treatment and Torture (ITT) Specific Allegation Data," *Journal of Peace Research* vol. 51 (2014): 429–38.

50. PTS scores are usually inverted to allow comparison with CIRI, and I have followed that convention.

51. "If a report contains new information about earlier years that was not included in earlier reports, the relevant country-year scores will be revised if necessary." CIRI Coding Manual, p. 4, https://docs.google.com/file/d/0BxDpF6GQ-6fbWkpx TDZCQ01jYnc/edit (accessed 27 August 2014).

52. See Mohammed Raiss, *De Skhirat à Tazmamart: retour du bout de l'enfer* (Casablanca: Afrique Orient, 2011).

53. *Instance Equité et Réconciliation*, "Synthèse du rapport final," book 1, section 4, Royaume du Maroc, http://www.ier.ma/article.php3?id_article=1496 (accessed 27 August 2014).

54. CIRI authors report high levels of inter-rater reliability for 2004, available at http://www.humanrightsdata.com/p/data-documentation.html (accessed 17 June 2016). The reported correlation coefficients imply confidence in the scoring but are likely to disguise issues related to information effect (especially as regards information available after the reporting year) and what Fariss identifies as changing standards of accountability. Such changes may affect the recorded incidence of

disappearance in Morocco, for example. During the 1970s and 1980s, enforced disappearance was a prevalent form of human rights abuse, facilitated by laws that imposed no limit on indefinite and incommunicado detention. Hundreds of prisoners disappeared during this period, and while many of them eventually reappeared decades later, others did not. In the early 1990s Morocco's law on pre-trial detention was changed, and what had been a common practice of enforced disappearance fell into disuse. State Department reports nevertheless continued to report as "disappearances" the cases of political prisoners whose whereabouts were unknown for a brief time, though after a relatively short period of time they were brought to trial. (For example, see US State Department, Country Reports on Human Rights Practices: Morocco, 2010 (http://www.state.gov/j/drl/rls/hrrpt/2010/nea/154468.htm) and 2011 (http://www.state.gov/j/drl/rls/hrrpt/2011humanrightsreport/index.htm#wrapper); and Western Sahara, 2010 (http://www.state.gov/documents/organization/160080.pdf) and 2011 (http://www.state.gov/j/drl/rls/hrrpt/2011humanrightsreport/index.htm#wrapper), (accessed 27 August 2014).

55. Ann Marie Clark and Kathryn Sikkink, "Information Effects and Human Rights Data: Is the good news about increased human rights information bad news for human rights measures?" *Human Rights Quarterly* vol. 35 (2013): 539–68.

56. Ibid., 540.

57. Richard Carver cites this as the reason why a research project commissioned by the Association for the Prevention of Torture has decided not to use either the PTS scale or the CIRI index, but will instead begin with an alternative 5-point measure of torture (the Hathaway index), which will in turn be scrutinized and corrected before use in statistical tests (on a limited number of countries). See Richard Carver, "Does Torture Prevention Work?" http://www.apt.ch/content/files/apt%20institutional/Carver%20research%20project%20stage%201_report.pdf (accessed 21 August 2014). Further, authors of the CIRI index have recently decided not to continue their data collection efforts (author correspondence with David Richards, March 2014).

58. Clark and Sikkink, "Information Effects," p. 541.

59. Ibid., p. 563. Compare with Fariss, "Respect for Human Rights has Improved Over Time," *supra* n.40.

60. See Anita Godhes and Megan Price, "First Things First: Assessing Data Quality Before Model Quality," *Journal of Conflict Resolution* vol. 57 (2013): 1090–1108.

61. Hayner, *Unspeakable Truths*, p. 26.

62. Oskar N. T. Thoms, James Ron, and Roland Paris, "State-Level Effects of Transitional Justice: What Do We Know?" *International Journal of Transitional Justice* (2010); Olsen, Payne and Reiter, *Transitional Justice in Balance*; Wiebelhaus-Brahm, *Truth Commissions and Transitional Societies*; Hayner, *Unspeakable Truths*.

4. FOR THE SAKE OF PEACE OR JUSTICE? TRUTH, ACCOUNTABILITY, AND AMNESTY IN THE MIDDLE EAST

1. Johan Galtung, *Theories of Peace: A synthetic approach to peace thinking* (Oslo: International Peace Research Institute, 1967), p. 12.
2. Tricia D. Olsen, Leigh A. Payne, and Andrew G Reiter, *Transitional Justice in Balance* (Washington, DC: US Institute of Peace Press, 2010), p. 39.
3. Charles P. Trumbull IV, "Giving Amnesties a Second Chance," *Berkeley Journal of International Law* vol. 25 (2007): 314.
4. Andrew G. Reiter, "Examining the Use of Amnesties and Pardons as a Response to Internal Armed Conflict," *Israel Law Review* vol. 47, no. 1 (2014): 147.
5. Jack Snyder and Leslie Vinjamuri, "Trials and Errors: Principle and Pragmatism in Strategies of International Justice," *International Security* vol. 28, no. 3 (Winter 2003/4): 5–44.
6. Trumbull, "Giving Amnesties a Second Chance," p. 313.
7. Diane F. Orentlicher, "Settling Accounts: The duty to prosecute human rights violations of a prior regime," *Yale Law Journal* vol. 100, no. 8 (1991): 2537–615.
8. Mark Freeman and Max Pensky, "The Amnesty Controversy in International Law," in Francesca Lessa and Leigh A. Payne, eds, *Amnesty in the Age of Human Rights Accountability: Comparative and international perspectives* (New York: Cambridge University Press, 2012), p. 64.
9. See Mark Freeman, *Necessary Evils: Amnesties and the search for justice* (New York: Cambridge University Press, 2009).
10. Laura M. Olson, "Provoking the Dragon on the Patio. Matters of Transitional Justice: Penal Repression Vs. Amnesties," *International Review of the Red Cross* vol. 88, no. 862 (2006): 283; Trumbull, "Giving Amnesties a Second Chance," 306, 319.
11. Olsen, Payne, and Reiter, *Transitional Justice in Balance*, p. 39.
12. Juan E. Mendez, "Accountability for Past Abuses," *Human Rights Quarterly* vol. 19, no. 2 (1997): 256, 261.
13. Trumbull, "Giving Amnesties a Second Chance," 307.
14. Orentlicher, "Settling Accounts," 2542–3.
15. Mendez, "Accountability for Past Abuses.
16. Ibid., 275. Also see Trumbull, "Giving Amnesties a Second Chance," 308–12; Mark Freeman, *Necessary Evils*, pp. 20–21; Louise Mallinder and Kieran McEvoy, "Amnesties, Punishment, and the Calibration of Mercy in Transition," *Journal of Law and Society* vol. 39, no. 3 (2012): 426.
17. Amstutz, "Restorative Justice, Political Forgiveness," 166.
18. Rachel Kerr and Eirin Mobekk, *Peace and Justice: Seeking accountability after war* (Cambridge: Polity, 2007), p. 8.
19. Michael P. Scharf, "Swapping Amnesty for Peace: Was there a duty to prosecute

international crimes in Haiti?" *Texas International Law Journal* vol. 31, no. 1 (1996): 9–10.

20. Kerr and Mobekk, *Peace and Justice*, p. 9.

21. Mendez, "Accountability for Past Abuses," 256.

22. David Mendeloff, "Truth-Seeking, Truth-Telling, and Postconflict Peacebuilding: Curb the enthusiasm?" *International Studies Review* vol. 6, no. 3 (2004): 358.

23. Priscilla B. Hayner, *Unspeakable Truths: Transitional justice and the challenge of truth commissions*, 2nd edn (London: Routledge, 2010), p. 91.

24. Mendeloff, "Truth-Seeking, Truth-Telling, and Postconflict Peacebuilding"; Eric Brahm, "Uncovering the Truth: Examining truth commission success and impact," *International Studies Perspective* vol. 8 (2007): 16–35.

25. Klaus Bachmann, "Do Truth Commissions Make a Difference? When and how truth commissions contribute to reconciliation," *Review of International Affairs* vol. 60, no. 1138–9 (2010): 71–100.

26. Olsen, Payne, and Reiter, "The Justice Balance."

27. George Joffé, "National Reconciliation and General Amnesty in Algeria," *Mediterranean Politics* vol. 13, no. 2 (2008): 216.

28. Ibid.

29. Valerie Arnould, "Amnesty, Peace and Reconciliation in Algeria: Analysis," *Conflict, Security & Development* vol. 7, no. 2 (2007): 228.

30. Ibid.; Human Rights Watch (HRW), "Impunity in the Name of Reconciliation: Algerian president's peace plan faces national vote September 29" (New York: HRW, 2005), pp. 4–6.

31. Amnesty International, "Algeria: Truth and Justice Obscured by the Shadow of Impunity," Amnesty International, 2000, 8.

32. Arnould, "Amnesty, Peace and Reconciliation," 228.

33. Ibid., 229.

34. William Wallis, "Algeria claims overwhelming Yes vote in referendum," *Financial Times*, 1 October 2005, http://www.ft.com/intl/cms/s/0/19590300-3218-11da-9c7f-00000e2511c8.html?siteedition=intl#axzz3KXkkmiOS (accessed 17 June 2016).

35. Amnesty International, "A Legacy of Impunity: A Threat to Algeria's Future" (London: Amnesty International Publications, 2009), p. 13; Arnould, "Amnesty, Peace and Reconciliation," 247.

36. Arnould, "Amnesty, Peace and Reconciliation," 240–41; Joffé, "National Reconciliation," 222.

37. Arnould, "Amnesty, Peace and Reconciliation," 243–4.

38. Souad Mekhennet et al., "A ragtag insurgency gains a Qaeda lifeline," *New York Times*, 1 July 2008, http://www.nytimes.com/2008/07/01/world/africa/01algeria.html?pagewanted=all&_r=3&; David Gauthier-Villars, "Long insurgency gave rise to al Qaeda-linked group," *Wall Street Journal*, 16 January 2013, http://www.wsj.com/articles/SB10001424127887323968304578246302154535158

39. Arnould, "Amnesty, Peace and Reconciliation," 247.
40. Eric Stover, Hanny Megally, and Hania Mufti, "Bremer's 'Gordian Knot': Transitional justice and the US occupation of Iraq," *Human Rights Quarterly* vol. 27, no. 3 (2005): 834.
41. Erin Daly, "Transitional Justice in Iraq: Learning the hard way," *Israel Law Review* vol. 47, no. 1 (2014): 69.
42. Ibid., 840.
43. Stover, Megally, and Mufti, "Bremer's 'Gordian Knot,'" 841–3.
44. Daly, "Transitional Justice in Iraq," 69; Ewen MacAskill and Michael Howard, "How Saddam died on the gallows," *Guardian*, 1 January 2007, http://www.theguardian.com/world/2007/jan/01/iraq.iraqtimeline
45. Miranda Sissons and Abdulrazzaq Al-Saiedi, "A Bitter Legacy: Lessons of de-Baathification in Iraq," International Center for Transitional Justice, March 2013, p. 11.
46. Stover, Megally, and Mufti, "Bremer's 'Gordian Knot,'" 847.
47. Ibid., 848.
48. Daly, "Transitional Justice in Iraq," 72.
49. Terrence McCoy, "Camp Bucca: The US prison that became the birthplace of Isis," *The Independent*, 4 November 2014, http://www.independent.co.uk/news/world/middle-east/camp-bucca-the-us-prison-that-became-the-birthplace-of-isis-9838905.html
50. Pierre Hazan, *Morocco: Betting on a Truth and Reconciliation Commission*, Special Report 165 (Washington, DC: United States Institute of Peace, 2006), p. 2.
51. Laetitia Grotti and Eric Goldstein, *Morocco's Truth Commission: Honoring past victims during an uncertain present* (New York: HRW, 2005), p. 2; Hayner, *Unspeakable Truths*, pp. 43, 172; Luke Wilcox, "Reshaping Civil Society through a Truth Commission: Human rights in Morocco's process of political reform," *International Journal of Transitional Justice* vol. 3, no. 1 (2009): 55.
52. Amnesty International, *Broken Promises: The Equity and Reconciliation Commission and its follow-up* (London: Amnesty International Publications, 2010), p. 13; Grotti and Goldstein, *Morocco's Truth Commission*, p. 2; Hayner, *Unspeakable Truths*, p. 172.
53. Equity and Reconciliation Commission (ERC), *Summary of the Final Report of the Equity and Reconciliation Commission (IER)* (Rabat: National Human Rights Council, 2006), p. 9.
54. ERC, *Summary of the Final Report*, p. 29.
55. Amnesty, *Broken Promises*, p. 15.
56. Hayner, *Unspeakable Truths*, p. 44; ICTJ, "Truth and Reconciliation."
57. Agence France-Press, "Morocco repression of peaceful protests growing," Naharnet Newsdesk, 18 June 2014, http://www.naharnet.com/stories/en/135488-morocco-repression-of-peaceful-protests-growing (accessed 17 June 2016).

58. Hayner, *Unspeakable Truths*, pp. 43–4.
59. Controversially, the victims who testified at the public hearings were only permitted to do so after pledging not to name names. Grotti and Goldstein, *Morocco's Truth Commission*, p. 35.
60. Pierre Hazan, "The Nature of Sanctions: The case of Morocco's Equity and Reconciliation Commission," *International Review of the Red Cross* vol. 90, no. 870 (2008): 407.
61. Hayner, *Unspeakable Truths*, p. 44.
62. "Yemen's Saleh agrees to transfer power," Al Jazeera English, 24 November 2014, http://www.aljazeera.com/news/middleeast/2011/11/2011112355040101606.html (accessed 17 June 2016).
63. Snyder and Vinjamuri, "Trials and Errors," p. 39.
64. Author's interview with a waiter, Sanaa, Yemen, May 2012.
65. "Yemen: Three years on no justice for Sana'a protest killings," Amnesty International, 18 March 2014, http://www.amnesty.org/en/news/yemen-three-years-no-justice-sana-protest-killings-2014–03–18
66. Letta Tayler, *Unpunished Massacre: Yemen's failed response to the "Friday of Dignity" killings* (New York: HRW, 2013), http://www.hrw.org/sites/default/files/reports/yemen0213webwcover_0.pdf
67. Elham Manea, "Yemen's contentious transitional justice and fragile peace," Middle East Institute, 24 February 2014, http://www.mei.edu/content/yemen%E2%80%99s-contentious-transitional-justice-and-fragile-peace
68. Author's interview with Yaser al-Awadi, Sanaa, Yemen, May 2012.
69. Author's interview with Abudlhakim Helal, Sanaa, Yemen, May 2012.
70. Author's interview with Mahmoud Nasher, Sanaa, Yemen, May 2012.
71. Manea, "Yemen's contentious transitional justice and fragile peace."
72. Agence France-Press, "ICC refers Libya to Security Council over Gadhafi son," Naharnet, 11 December 2014, http://www.naharnet.com/stories/en/158676 (accessed 17 June 2016).
73. "Libya: Detainees tortured and denied medical care," Médecins Sans Frontières, 26 January 2012, http://www.doctorswithoutborders.org/news-stories/press-release/libya-detainees-tortured-and-denied-medical-care (accessed 17 June 2016).
74. Associated Press, "Al-Baghdadi Al-Mahmoudi, ex-Libya PM, extradited by Tunisia," *World Post*, 24 June 2012, http://www.huffingtonpost.com/2012/06/24/al-baghdadi-al-mahmoudi-extradited-libya-tunisia_n_1622294.html
75. Author's interview with former Libyan Islamist Fighting Group leader Sami al-Saa'di, Tripoli, Libya, December 2012.
76. Haizam Amirah-Fernández, "Libya and the problematic Political Isolation Law," Real Instituto Elcano, 20 June 2013, http://www.realinstitutoelcano.org/wps/portal/rielcano_eng/Content?WCM_GLOBAL_CONTEXT=/elcano/elcano_in/zonas_in/ari20–2013-amirah-fernandez-libia-ley-aislamiento-politico;

"Legislation No. 13 of 2013 of the Political and Administrative Isolation," *Libya Herald*, 14 May 2013, http://www.libyaherald.com/2013/05/14/political-isolation-law-the-full-text/#axzz2hJk0c7Z9 (accessed 17 June 2016).

77. Author's interview with revolutionaries picketing parliament, Tripoli, Libya, December 2012. For more about the motives behind the PIL, see Ibrahim Sharqieh, "An ill-advised purge in Libya," *New York Times*, 18 February 2013, http://www.nytimes.com/2013/02/19/opinion/an-ill-advised-purge-in-libya.html?_r=0

78. Author's interview with Muhammad Toumi, Tripoli, Libya, January 2013.

79. Author's interview with al-Hadi Bu Hamra, Tripoli, Libya, January 2013.

80. Michelle Nichols, "UN says Libya Political Exclusion Law likely violates rights," Reuters, 18 June 2013, http://www.reuters.com/article/2013/06/18/us-libya-un-idUSBRE95H15Y20130618 (accessed 17 June 2016).

81. "Libya: Amend new Special Procedures Law," HRW, 11 May 2012, http://www.hrw.org/news/2012/05/11/libya-amend-new-special-procedures-law

82. Author's interview with a tribal figure, Tripoli, Libya, January 2013.

83. Anas El Gomati, "Khalifa Haftar: Fighting terrorism or pursuing political power?" Al Jazeera English, 10 June 2014, http://www.aljazeera.com/indepth/opinion/2014/06/khalifa-hifter-operation-dignity-20146108259233889.html (accessed 17 June 2016).

84. Ryan Rifai, "Timeline: Tunisia's uprising," Al Jazeera English, 23 January 2011, http://www.aljazeera.com/indepth/spotlight/tunisia/2011/01/201114142223827361.html; "Tunisia says will track down Ben Ali family abroad," Reuters, 21 January 2011, http://af.reuters.com/article/tunisiaNews/idAFLDE70K23K20110121 (accessed 17 June 2016).

85. Author's interview with Salim Ben Humaidan, Minister of State Property and Land Affairs, Tunis, May 2013; Agence France-Presse, "Tunisia President wants graft suspects travel ban lifted," 11 May 2013, http://www.naharnet.com/stories/en/82699

86. Author's interview with Khaled Kashier, a history professor, Tunis, May 2013.

87. "ICTJ welcomes Tunisia's historic Transitional Justice Law," ICTJ, 16 December 2013, http://www.ictj.org/news/ictj-welcomes-tunisia%E2%80%99s-historic-transitional-justice-law (accessed 17 June 2016).

88. "ICTJ welcomes launch of Tunisia's Truth and Dignity Commission," ICTJ, 6 June 2014, https://www.ictj.org/news/ictj-welcomes-launch-tunisia%E2%80%99s-truth-and-dignity-commission (accessed 17 June 2016).

89. Author's interview with Mohamed Ben Aisa, Tunis, May 2013.

90. Author's interview with Souad Abdel Rahim, Tunis, May 2013.

91. Khaled Fattah, "The repercussions of the GCC tension in Yemen," *Sada* (blog), 8 April 2014, http://carnegieendowment.org/sada/index.cfm?fa=show&article=55276&solr_hilite=

92. See Ibrahim Sharqieh, "Yemen can't do it alone," *New York Times*, 1 June 2012,

http://www.nytimes.com/2012/06/02/opinion/yemen-cant-do-it-alone.html?_
r=0 (accessed 17 June 2016); and idem, "The price of abandoning Yemen," *New
York Times*, 22 September 2014, http://www.nytimes.com/2014/09/23/opin-
ion/the-price-of-abandoning-yemen.html (accessed 17 June 2016).

5. THE SCOPE AND BOUNDARIES OF TRANSITIONAL JUSTICE IN THE ARAB SPRING

1. See for example the edited volume by Kirsten J. Fisher and Robert Stewart,
   Transitional Justice and the Arab Spring (Abingdon: Routledge, 2014).
2. This is despite the fact there have been a number of initiatives aimed at dealing with
   the legacy of past abuses initiated in the Arab Middle East prior to the Tunisian
   revolution in 2011. These include the Algerian truth commissions, Iraq's purges,
   and trial processes that followed the US-led invasion of Iraq in 2003, and Morocco's
   truth commission, which had a limited temporal mandate.
3. While this literature is too broad to review here, a few indicative examples include
   Guillermo O'Donnell, Philippe C. Schmitter, and Laurence Whitehead, *Transitions
   from Authoritarian Rule in Latin America* (Baltimore, MD: Johns Hopkins
   University Press, 1986); Neil Kritz, ed., *Transitional Justice*, vols I-III (Washington,
   DC: United States Institute for Peace, 1995); Lavinia Stan, ed., *Transitional Justice
   in Eastern Europe and the former Soviet Union: Reckoning with the Communist Past*
   (Abingdon: Routledge, 2009); Olivera Simić and Zala Volčič, eds, *Transitional
   Justice and Civil Society in the Balkans* (London: Springer, 2013). In contrast, the
   Arab Middle East was often approached from the perspective of explaining author-
   itarian resilience. Jonathan Brownlee, *Authoritarianism in an Age of Democratization*
   (Cambridge: Cambridge University Press, 2007).
4. John L. Esposito, *Islam and Politics*, 4th edn (Syracuse, NY: Syracuse University
   Press, 1998). See also Reem Abou El Fadl, "Beyond Conventional Transitional
   Justice: Egypt's 2011 Revolution and the absence of political will," *International
   Journal of Transitional Justice* vol. 6, no. 2 (2012): 318–30.
5. Samuel P. Huntington, *The Third Wave: Democratization in the Late 20th Century*
   (Norman, OK: University of Oklahoma Press, 1991). Thomas Risse, Stephen
   C. Ropp, and Kathryn Sikkink, eds, *The Power of Human Rights: International
   norms and domestic change* (Cambridge: Cambridge University Press, 1999).
6. In 2012 our field research was funded by the American Institute for Maghrib Studies
   through a short-term travel grant that facilitated research at the Center for Maghrib
   Studies in Tunis; and for fieldwork carried out in 2013, I would like to thank the
   Center for Maghrib Studies in Tunis and the Middle East Partnership Initiative
   Tunisia and Algeria alumni branches.
7. Of course, in some respects Tunisia can also be argued to be an outlier in the Arab
   world in respect to its relative demographic homogeneity; however, at the same

time, given how far Tunisia's transitional justice process has progressed over the last three years, it provides a glimpse into political contestations over justice.

8. This observation is made in comparison to other states such as Egypt and Libya, which have witnessed a breakdown or reversal of transitional justice measures taken in the immediate aftermath of the 2011 uprisings. Within Tunisia, Islamists have argued that despite the establishment of the Truth and Dignity Commission in 2014, one of their major regrets is not having insisted upon the passage of a transitional justice law earlier in the transition. Fieldwork interview with Meherzia Labidi, Ennahdha's Deputy Speaker of the National Constituent Assembly, Tunis, 26 September 2014.

9. Tunisia's much heralded Ministry for Human Rights and Transitional Justice was established on 19 January 2012 and was incorporated into the Ministry of Justice following Ennahdha's voluntary withdrawal from government on 29 January 2014.

10. Confidential interview, Tunis, 8 March 2014. In the end, the establishment of the Truth and Dignity Commission in June 2014 can also be interpreted as a perpetuation of the Ministry, given the Commission's broad mandate.

11. The term "usable past" was used by Anna M. Grzymala-Busse, *Redeeming the Communist Past: The regeneration of Communist parties in East Central Europe* (Cambridge, Cambridge University Press, 2002).

12. For example, Fawzi Souid, the party secretary for communications from the Patriotic Democrats, noted that his Popular Front coalition feared that Ennahdha sought to use transitional justice to discredit Destourianism and the political opposition, rather than as an impartial tool to deal with past abuses. Fawzi Saouid, Party Secretary for Communications, Patriotic Democrats—Popular Front Coalition, 9 March 2014.

13. For example, a party official from Moubadara, a political party which is led by Ben Ali's former foreign minister, pointed out that unlike other parties which sought to claim the mantle of Destourianism, Moubadara proposed no alternative draft transitional justice law to that proposed by the Troika governing coalition, because the party did not feel that there was any need for extraordinary justice measures after 14 January 2011. Fieldwork interview with a Moubadara party official, 7 March 2014.

14. Grzymala-Busse, *Redeeming the Communist Past*, p. 5.

15. Ben Ali deposed Bourguiba in a bloodless coup in which Bourguiba was declared unfit for office due to health problems. Rachid Chelly, *Le Syndrome de Carthage: des Presidents Habib Bourguiba et Zine El Abinde Ben Ali* (Tunis: Impimerie Graphique du Centre—Tunisie, 2012), pp. 42–3.

16. Noura Borsali points out that at the time of independence, 1955–6, Tunisia's political scene was very close to reflecting what would be described today as a multiparty system with dissident voices among Saleh Ben Youssef's Youssefist movement, Marxists and Zeitounists, and *Swat et-taleb* or the Student Voice. Noura Borsali,

Bourguiba à l'épreuve de la démocratie (1956–1963) (Tunis: Imprimerie Carthage, 2012), pp. 9–11.

17. "*Dégager*" means "to go away" or "leave" in French.

18. Béji Caïd Essebsi argued that a key element of Bourguiba's modernization program was his promotion of women's emancipation: *Habib Bourguiba, le bon grain et l'ivraie* (Tunis: Sud Editions, 2009), pp. 62–3. For more on Bourguiba's promotion of education, see Dirk Vandewalle, "Bourguiba, Charismatic Leadership and the Tunisian One-Party System," *Middle East Journal* vol. 42, no, 4 (1980): 149–59.

19. Two senior Ben Ali era ministers contested the 23 November 2014 presidential elections. These included Ben Ali's former foreign minister, Kemal Morjane, and a former transport minister, Abdelrahim Zouari. This is in addition to the candidacy of Beji Caid Essebsi, who was a former minister of interior under Bourguiba. These campaigns lay the blame for Salafi violence that has plagued Tunisia's transition with the Islamist Ennahdha movement and present a nostalgic image of past stability and security.

20. Susan Waltz, "Islamist Appeal in Tunisia," *Middle East Journal* vol. 40, no. 4 (1986): 660. Vandewalle, "Bourguiba, Charismatic Leadership," pp. 149–59; Dirk Vandewalle, "From the New State to the New Era: Toward a Second Republic in Tunisia," *Middle East Journal* vol. 42, no. 4 (1988): 603–4.

21. Larbi Sadiki, "Political Liberalization of Bin Ali's Tunisia: Facade Democracy," *Democratization* vol. 9, no. 4 (2002): 122–41.

22. Christopher Alexander, "Back from the Democratic Brink: Authoritarianism and civil society in Tunisia," *Middle East Report* no. 205 (1997): 35; Sadiki, "Political Liberalization", pp. 132–3.

23. For members of Tunisia's Islamist opposition, the period of repression ushered in by Ben Ali constituted the bleakest period of Tunisia's recent past. In fact, Beya Jouadi, an Ennahdha deputy in the National Constituent Assembly and member of the Assembly's Commission on Martyrs and Injured, noted that in the 1990s "torture was most widespread, regime opponents were forced into exile, and women—in particular students—were violated." Fieldwork interview with Beya Jouadi, an Ennahdha deputy in the National Constituent Assembly, Tunis, 26 September 2014.

24. Alexander, "Back from the Democratic Brink," p. 37. In addition, Bourguiba turned against internal challengers within the nationalist movement, such as Saleh Ben Youssef.

25. Fieldwork interview, Ennahdha party official, Tunis, 7 March 2014.

26. The first two phases of Tunisia's transition were also presented in an early work that reflected upon transitional justice in Tunisia at a previous stage in the transition process. See Christopher K. Lamont and Hela Boujneh, "Transitional Justice in Tunisia: Negotiating justice during transition," *Politicka Misao: Croatian Political Science Review* vol. 49, no. 5 (2012): 32–49.

27. Jasmine Jawad, "A Gendered Perspective on the Arab Spring: Between internal and external conflict," in Christopher K. Lamont, Jan van der Harst, and Frank Gaenssmantel, eds, *Non-Western Encounters with Democratization* (Abingdon: Routledge, 2015).

28. Larbi Sadiki foreshadowed some of the underlying causes of the Tunisian revolution, such as inequality and political mobilization of marginalized groups, in *Rethinking Arab Democratization: Elections without democracy* (Oxford: Oxford University Press, 2009).

29. A participant in Tunisia's national consultation on transitional justice noted a strong demand for socio-economic justice. Fieldwork interview, National Dialogue participant, Tunis, October 2012.

30. Mohamed Ghannouchi was a long-time senior official, and held numerous ministerial positions in Ben Ali governments since 1989. Mohamed Ghannouchi shares no relation with Rashid Ghannouchi, the head of Tunisia's Islamist Ennahdha movement.

31. While *Kasbah 2* is used to describe protests leading to Ghannouchi's resignation, which began on 25 February, *Kasbah 1* occurred on 23–28 January 2011. During these demonstrations, protesters demanded the withdrawal of former RCD party members from the transitional government.

32. "La commission d'investigation présente son rapport final," *La Presse*, 5 May 2012, available at http://www.lapresse.tn/05052012/49324/la-commission-dinvestigation-presente-son-rapport-final.html (accessed 17 June 2016).

33. Bouazizi's act of self-immolation is a reference to an event that occurred on 17 December 2010, when Mohamed Bouazizi, a Tunisian fruit vendor, set himself on fire after having his stand confiscated. His death set off a wave of nationwide protests that eventually resulted in Ben Ali's ousting on 14 January 2011.

34. Wahid Ferchichi, "A Chronicle of Legislative Developments in the Aftermath of the Tunisian Revolution: A revolution seeks the means to succeed!" *Perspectives* 2 (2012): 248–57.

35. Ben Ali initially promised to create investigative commissions on 10 January and repeated this promise on 13 January 2011.

36. David Kirkpatrick, "Ex-Tunisian President Found Guilty, in Absentia," *New York Times*, 20 June 2011, available at http://www.nytimes.com/2011/06/21/world/middleeast/21tunisia.html

37. Fieldwork interview with a member of the Al Joumouhri executive board, 22 October 2012.

38. Human Rights Watch, "Tunisia: Injured of the uprising urgently need care," 28 May 2012, available at http://www.hrw.org/news/2012/05/28/tunisia-injured-uprising-urgently-need-care (accessed 2 December 2012).

39. The Carter Center identified a number of procedural problems with Article 15 that could result in the unjust exclusion of individuals from political participa-

tion. First, the High Commission on Political Reform, which was tasked with implementing political exclusion, failed to notify excluded persons; and second, the Commission failed to establish a process that would allow individuals to challenge their exclusion, meaning that effectively there was no due process remedy for those who felt they had been unjustifiably banned. Carter Center, *The National Constituent Assembly Elections in Tunisia October 12, 2011: Final Report*, p. 18.

40. Note that "time frame" in the table is used to refer to the period of time examined by a specific measure, and not the period of time when a particular measure was put in place. The effect of this was that earlier abuses, committed under Bourguiba, were left relatively untouched during a transitional period in which Tunisia was led by Bourguiba's former minister of interior, Beji Caid Essebsi.

41. Fawzi Saouid, Party Secretary for Communications, Patriotic Democrats—Popular Front Coalition, 9 March 2014.

42. Ennahdha Party Program, Tunis, 2011.

43. Fieldwork interview with Beya Jouadi, an Ennahdha deputy in the NCA and member of the Assembly Commission on Martyrs and Injured, Tunis, 26 September 2014.

44. Fieldwork interview with Jawahara Ettiss, an Ennahdha deputy in the NCA, Tunis, 26 September 2014.

45. Samir Dilou is a human rights lawyer who was initially detained for his participation in the 1984 bread riots and later spent a decade in prison under the Ben Ali regime. "Samir Dilou," Tunisia Live, 15 August 2011, available at http://www.tunisia-live.net/2011/08/15/samir-dilou/

46. Asma Ghribi, Debating Transitional Justice in Tunisia, Tunisia Live, 8 March 2012, available at http://www.tunisia-live.net/2012/03/08/debating-transitional-justice-in-tunisia/ (accessed 4 December 2012).

47. See http://www.tunisienumerique.com/samir-diloupas-questions-de-laisser-les-rcdistes-revenir-a-la-vie-politique/148587 (accessed 17 June 2016). It should be noted that Tunisia's electoral law, which authorized elections to parliament and the presidency in 2014, did not include a political exclusion provision. This is because Ennahdha later rejected political exclusions on the grounds that Ennahdha as a party had suffered from exclusion under the Ben Ali regime and it did not wish to bar individuals and parties from standing in elections. Fieldwork interview with Baya Jouadi, an Ennahdha deputy within the NCA. Jouadi also noted that in her view exclusion was inconsistent with Ennahdha's core values as an Islamist party, which emphasize coexistence and acceptance. However, while political exclusion was rejected, the vetting of state institutions will be the task of the newly established Commission on Truth and Dignity. Baya Jouadi, an Ennahdha deputy in the National Constituent Assembly, 26 September 2014.

48. Despite the establishment of the Technical Commission, strong criticisms were voiced that the Ministry of Human Rights and Transitional Justice effectively set

the parameters for transitional justice policy-making during this phase. Fieldwork interview, member of the executive board, Al Joumhouri, Tunis, 22 October 2012.

49. Each regional commission was responsible for four governorates.

50. Although the ICTJ hailed this law as being passed almost unanimously, the ICTJ fails to take note of the fact that opposition parties were boycotting the NCA at the time of the law's passage. This presents a distorted picture of consensus on transitional justice. See ICTJ Program Report, Tunisia, 3 June 2014, available at http://www.ictj.org/news/ictj-program-report-tunisia (accessed 17 June 2016).

51. Organic Law on Establishing and Organizing Transitional Justice, 13 December 2014. The Truth and Dignity Commission was launched on 9 June 2014.

52. Fieldwork interview, Baya Jouadi, an Ennnadha deputy in the National Constituent Assembly, 26 September 2014.

53. Fieldwork interview, member of Al Joumhouri executive committee, 22 October 2012.

54. Organic Law on Establishing and Organizing Transitional Justice, ratified 13 December 2013.

55. See interview with Bochra Belhadj Hamida, Nida Tounes parliamentary candidate. "Demonized, Insulted and Threatened," Development and Cooperation, 2 October 2014, available at http://www.dandc.eu/en/article/i-hope-tunisia-will-choose-well-time (accessed 17 June 2016).

56. Fieldwork interview with Nida Tounes party member, Sousse, Tunisia, 8 August 2014.

57. Fieldwork interview with Meherzia Labidi, Deputy Speaker of the National Constituent Assembly, 26 September 2014.

6. REFRAMING GENDER NARRATIVES THROUGH TRANSITIONAL JUSTICE IN THE MAGHREB

1. *Al-Qur'an*, A contemporary translation by Ahmed Ali (Princeton, NJ: Princeton University Press, 1988), p. 143.

2. Mark Freeman, *Truth Commissions and Procedural Fairness* (Cambridge: Cambridge University Press, 2006), p. 4.

3. See Laurel E. Fletcher and Harvey M. Weinstein, "Violence and Social Repair: Rethinking the contribution of justice to reconciliation," *Human Rights Quarterly* vol. 24 (2002): 573, available at http://scholarship.law.berkeley.edu/facpubs/545; and Elin Skaar, "Reconciliation in a Transitional Justice Perspective," *Transitional Justice Review* vol. 1 (2012): 54–103.

4. Vasuki Nesiah, *Truth Commissions and Gender: Principles, policies, and procedures* (International Center for Transitional Justice, Gender Justice Series, 2006), p. 2.

5. The run-off in the presidential elections in December 2014 occurred before the time of this writing.

6. For analysis and deconstruction of the "secular" myth created by the two previous Tunisian regimes, see Rory McCarthy, "Re-thinking Secularism in Post-
independence Tunisia," *Journal of North African Studies* vol. 19, no. 5 (2014):
733–50.

7. Personal interview by Doris Gray, Tunis, May 2014, based on previous interviews
2011–13.

8. Susanne Buckley-Zistel and Ruth Stanley, *Gender in Transitional Justice* (New
York: Palgrave Macmillan, 2011), p. 13.

9. Personal interview by Doris Gray, Tunis, June 2014, based on previous interviews
2011–13.

10. Personal interview by Doris Gray, Tunis, June 2014, based on previous interviews
2011–13.

11. Personal interview by Doris Gray, Tunis, June 2014.

12. The case of Sihem Bensedrine, one of the most prominent secular political opponents, is well known in Tunisia. Bensedrine now serves as president to the Truth
and Dignity Commission.

13. "Middle East: Women's rights under attack," www.amnesty.org/library/1995; and
"Tunisia: Rhetoric versus Reality; The failure of a human rights bureaucracy," www.
amnesty.org/library/1994

14. Corinne Mullin and Ian Patel, "Resisting Transitional Justice and Liberal
Governance in Revolutionary Tunisia," *Conflict and Society*, http://eprints.soas.
ac.uk/19376/

15. Béatrice Hibou, *The Force of Obedience: The political economy of repression in Tunisia*
(London: Polity Press, 2011), 287–8.

16. Ibid.

17. Personal interview by Doris Gray, Tunis, June 2014.

18. Priscilla Hayner, *Unspeakable Truths: Facing the challenge of truth commissions*
(London: Routledge, 2002), p. 77.

19. Chandra Lekha Sriram, "International law, International Relations theory and
post-atrocity justice: towards a genuine dialogue," *International Affairs* vol. 82
(2006): 467–78.

20. Hayner, *Unspeakable Truths*, p. 82.

21. Ibid.

22. Mullin and Patel, "Resisting Transitional Justice in Revolutionary Tunisia."

23. Catherine O'Rourke, "International Law and Domestic Gender Justice: Why case
studies matter," *Transitional Justice Institute Research Paper* no. 11–04 (Ulster,
7 April 2011): 10.

24. Teresa Godwin Phelps, *Shattered Voices—Language, violence, and the work of truth
commissions* (Philadelphia: University of Pennsylvania Press, 2004), p. 118.

25. Cardinal Paolo Arns was a key figure in the clandestine research project that in
1985 exposed the atrocities of the Brazilian military in *Brasil: Nunca Más* (Never

Again); Cardinal Juan Gerardi led efforts by the Catholic church in Guatemala that resulted in the 1998 publication of *Guatemala: Nunca Más*; and Bishop Sergio Valech of Chile headed the national commission that published a 2004 report chronicling systematic torture committed by the Pinochet regime.

26. As procedures for Members of the Truth Commission at the time of the interviews had not been decided, members preferred not to be named.

27. Personal interview by Doris Gray, Tunis, June 2014.

28. Ibid.

29. Virginia Guzman, Ute Seibert, Silke Staab, "Democracy in the Country but not in the Home? Religion, politics and women's rights in Chile," *Third World Quarterly* vol. 31, no. 6 (September 2010): 971–88.

30. Catherine O'Rourke, *Gender Politics in Transitional Justice* (London: Routledge, 2013), p. 212.

31. Bettina Dennerlein, "Remembering Violence, Negotiating Change: The Moroccan Equity and Reconciliation Commission and the politics of gender," *Journal of Middle East Women's Studies* vol. 8, no. 1 (2012): 10–36. The 2004 Moroccan Truth and Equity Commission did not follow a regime change and only addresses a particular set of human rights violations during King Hassan's II rule.

32. Ibid.

33. Personal interview by Doris Gray, Tunis, June 2014.

34. Nesiah, *Truth Commissions and Gender*, p. 8.

35. Tristan Ann Borer, "Gendered War and Gendered Peace: Truth commissions and post-conflict gender violence: Lessons from South Africa," *Violence Against Women* vol. 15, no. 10 (2012): 1177.

36. Olivera Simić, "But I Want to Speak Out: Making art from women's testimonies," *Australian Feminist Law Journal* vol. 40 (2014): 52.

37. Fionnuala Ni Aolain and Catherine Turner, "Gender, Truth and Transition," *UCLA Women's Law Journal* vol. 16, no. 2 (2007): 262.

38. Borer, "Gendered War and Gendered Peace," p. 1177; Simić, "But I Want to Speak Out," p. 52.

39. Nesiah, *Truth Commissions and Gender*, p. 19.

40. Freeman, *Truth Commissions and Procedural Fairness*, p. 261; Borer, "Gendered War and Gendered Peace," p. 1177.

41. O'Rourke, *Gender Politics in Transitional Justice*, p. 37.

42. Nesiah, *Truth Commissions and Gender*, p. 23.

43. Colleen Duggan and Adila Abusharaf, "Reparations of Sexual Violence in Democratic Transitions: The search for gender justice," in Pablo de Greiff, ed., *The Handbook of Reparations* (Oxford: Oxford University Press, 2006), p. 623.

44. O'Rourke, *Gender Politics in Transitional Justice*, p. 38.

45. Rita Schäfer, *Transitional Justice—Geschlechterpolitische Perspektiven für*

Übergangsgesellschaften (Gender-political perspectives in transitional societies) *Henrich Böll Stiftung*, vol. 10 (2013): p. 13.
46. Personal interview by Doris Gray, Tunis, June 2014.
47. Personal interview by Doris Gray, Bizerte, Tunisia, May 2014.
48. Personal interview by Doris Gray, Bizerte, Tunisia, June 2014.
49. Personal interview by Doris Gray, Bizerte, Tunisia, June 2014.
50. Personal interview by Doris Gray, Bizerte, Tunisia, June 2014.

7. MARTYRDOM IN NORTH AFRICA FOLLOWING THE ARAB SPRING AND THE PROCESS OF TRANSITIONAL JUSTICE

1. Although this paper deals exclusively with the Maghrebi countries of Algeria, Morocco, and Tunisia, it is important to note that the study of martyrdom in the MENA region is broad and deep. Outside the case of the Arab–Israeli conflict, recent works have begun to probe the post-conflict significance of martyrdom emerging out of the Iran–Iraq war (1980–88). Farideh Farhi's contribution ("The Antinomies of Iran's War Generation") to Lawrence Potter's edited volume entitled *Iran, Iraq and the Legacies of War* (Palgrave Macmillan, 2004) is especially useful in this regard. The term "friend of God" has been used by Muslim writers since the early medieval period to denote mystical, holy men whose unique attributes are viewed as signs of God's favor and grace.
2. At times, the word "victim" is employed in official reports or the media. In addition, it sometimes occurs that the status of the deceased will be contested between the state on the one hand and the relatives on the other, with the latter preferring the more politically charged term of "martyr" to describe the death of their loved ones. The phenomenon of "disappeared" persons in North Africa often constitutes a type of martyrdom in popular consciousness. One of the most famous cases of a "disappeared" martyr is that of Moroccan political leader Mehdi Ben Barka, who was probably killed by the security forces of King Hassan II in the 1960s.
3. Mohammed Bouazizi set himself on fire on 17 December 2010 in protest over police harassment. He expired in hospital on 4 January 2011. The following day he was buried with the participation of thousands of mourners in Sidi Bou Zid.
4. This marked one of the first documented occurrences of "mass self-communication" in North Africa. The term, coined by Manuel Castells in his work *Communication Power* (Oxford: Oxford University Press, 2009), refers to the ability of non-state actors (excluding major media outlets) to create content primarily via the use of mobile technology.
5. Both Chokri and Brahmi were charismatic political leaders who were affiliated with the leftist consortium of parties known as the "Popular Front." Although it would be wrong to describe both men as "secular" in the Western sense of the word, both Chokri and Brahmi spoke out against social policies promoted by the Ennadha party and other political Islamic organizations.

6. Didier Fassin, "The Humanitarian Politics of Testimony: Subjectification through trauma in the Israeli-Palestinian conflict," *Cultural Anthropology* vol. 23 (2008): 531–58.

7. Ibid., 555.

8. Fassin uses the Latin terms *testis* and *superstes* throughout his article to refer to the first-hand witness and third-party individuals respectively.

9. Ibid., 540.

10. Ruti G. Teitel. *Transitional Justice* (Oxford: Oxford University Press, 2000) [Kindle edn], p. 71.

11. David Cook, *Martyrdom in Islam* (Cambridge: Cambridge University Press, Themes in Islamic History, 2007), pp. 1–2.

12. The Arabic terms often associated with holiness in individuals range from *walī* to *qiddīs* to *sālih* and *sādiq*. In a general sense, such holy individuals approximate Christian saints in their importance to believers. See John Renard, *Friends of God: Islamic images of piety, commitment, and servanthood* (Berkeley, CA: University of California Press, 2008), p. 7.

13. The example of Che Guevara, a Cuban revolutionary leader who perished in Bolivia in 1967, is often cited as a Marxist "martyr." Similarly, the French *communards* who fell in Montmartre in 1871 are likewise venerated as nationalist "martyrs."

14. The case of Morocco is more complex than either Algeria or Tunisia. The northern half of modern-day Morocco has historically fallen under the Spanish sphere of influence (along with the Western Sahara). As a result, many Berber tribes of the Rif mountains considered the Spanish as the primary European antagonist, rather than the French. These conflicts came to a head during the "Rif War" of the 1920s, in which the forces of Abd al-Krim al-Khattabi fought the Spanish armies of Primo de Rivera.

15. Later King Mohammed V of Morocco.

16. Susan Gilson Miller, *A History of Modern Morocco* (Cambridge: Cambridge University Press, 2013), cited in ch. 5: "Framing the Nation (1930–1961)."

17. Renard, *Friends of God*, pp. 231–2.

18. Laleh Khalili, *The Politics of National Commemoration* (Cambridge: Cambridge University Press, 2007) [Kindle edn], p. 126.

19. Other works which make reference to martyrdom in an Arab context include Ted Swedenburg, *Memories of Revolt: The 1936–1939 rebellion and the Palestinian national past* (Fayetteville: University of Arkansas Press, 2003); Lisa Wedeen, *Ambiguities of Domination: Politics, rhetoric, and symbols in contemporary Syria* (Chicago: University of Chicago Press, 1999).

20. Luis Martinez and John Entelis. *The Algerian Civil War (1990–1998)* (New York: Columbia University Press, 2000); Abderrahmane Moussaoui, *De la culture de la violence en Algérie: les lois du chaos* (On the Culture of Violence in Algeria: The

laws of chaos) (Paris: Actes Sud, 2006); Hugh Roberts, *The Battlefield: Algeria, 1988–2002, studies in a broken polity* (London: Verso, 2003).

21. In the case of Algeria, the works of John Entelis, Mahfoud Bennoune, Isabelle Werenfels, and Miriam Lowi provide detailed analyses of the rise of Algeria's political economy based on a distributory state model after independence in 1962. John Entelis, *Algeria: The revolution institutionalized* (Boulder, CO: Westview Press, 1987); Mahfoud Bennoune, *The Making of Contemporary Algeria, 1830–1987* (Cambridge: Cambridge University Press, 1988); Isabelle Werenfels, *Managing Instability in Algeria: Elites and political change since 1995* (New York: Routledge, 2007); Miriam R. Lowi, *Oil Wealth and the Poverty of Politics: Algeria compared* (Cambridge: Cambridge University Press, 2009).

22. The term "maquis" often refers to a loosely organized paramilitary group in opposition to an established state.

23. Martinez and Entelis, *The Algerian Civil War (1990–1998)*, pp. 14–15.

24. This penchant for "memorializing" former combatants and martyrs of the Algerian War of Liberation extends to state and regional actors. As I argue elsewhere, the physical landscape of Algeria following the "dark decade" has seen a resurgence of physical memorials (museums, murals, sculpture) to the revolutionary generation. The hyper-visibility of such monuments is a testament to the fixation of the FLN (and other regional groups) upon the martyr/revolutionary as an enduring historical guide for Algerian society. See Thomas DeGeorges, "The shifting sands of revolutionary legitimacy: the role of former mujahidin in the shaping of Algeria's collective memory," *Journal of North African Studies* vol. 14 (2009): 273–88.

25. Ibid., 286.

26. Abdelaziz Bouteflika has a long history of government service in Algeria dating back to the war of liberation. Bouteflika was personally close to the military commander (and later President) Haouri Boumedienne and assumed ministerial portfolios immediately following Algeria's independence in 1962. His most important post prior to the death of Boumedienne in 1978 was that of foreign minister. He appears to have lost the competition to succeed Boumedienne as president and assumes a low-key political posture until the end of the 1990s, when he is selected as a candidate for president on a platform of restoring peace and security in the aftermath of the "dark decade." United States Institute of Peace, "Commission of Inquiry: Algeria," http://www.usip.org/publications/commission-of-inquiry-algeria (accessed 14 July 2014).

27. John Waterbury, *The Commander of the Faithful: The Moroccan political elite* (New York: Columbia University Press, 1970). Although Waterbury's thesis has remained important over time, recent works by historians tend to emphasize the broader cultural and local forces acting on the Moroccan political system in the nineteenth and twentieth centuries, rather than focusing on state institutions like the monarchy and the army. A good example of such revisionism is latest work of Susan

Gilson Miller, *A History of Modern Morocco* (Cambridge: Cambridge University Press, 2013).

28. United States Institute of Peace, "Truth Commission-Morocco," http://www.usip. org/publications/truth-commission-morocco (accessed 14 July 2014). Note the similarities to the Algerian truth and reconciliation commission which also lacked the ability to refer individual suspects for criminal prosecution.

29. Susan Slyomovics, *The Performance of Human Rights in Morocco* (Philadelphia: University of Pennsylvania Press, Pennsylvania Studies in Human Rights, 2005).

30. Slyomovics. *The Performance of Human Rights in Morocco*, p. 12.

31. Jonathan Smolin, *Moroccan Noir: Police, crime, and politics in popular culture* (Bloomington: Indiana University Press, 2013).

32. Ibid., ch. 6: "From Morocco's 9/11 to Community Policing: State advertisement and the new citizen."

33. See Mahmoud Ben Ramdhane, *Tunisie: Etat, Economie et Société: Resources politiques, légitimation, régulations sociales* (Tunisia: State, Economy and Society: Political resources, legitimation, social regulations) (Tunis: Sud Editions, 2011), pp. 175–8 and 234–40; Hakim Ben Hammouda, *Tunisie: Economie politique d'une révolution* (Tunisia: Political economy of a revolution) (Brussels: Groupe De Boeck, 2012) pp. 112–15; Hamadi Tizaoui, *Le Décrochage industriel des régions intérieures en Tunisie* (The industrial stagnation of the interior regions of Tunisia) (Tunis: Arabesques, 2013), ch. 4: "La consécration du déséquilibre régional Littoral Est Intérieur du pays et l'émergence de grandes régions industrialisées: le Nord Est et le Sahel Littoral."

34. The term "underemployment" is used here to reflect the fact that many Tunisians work at part-time, low-skilled, and precarious jobs that do not adequately reflect the wage expectations or job security desired by their holders.

35. Eva Bellin, *Stalled Democracy: Capital, labor, and the paradox of state-sponsored development* (Ithaca, NY: Cornell University Press, 2002); Christopher Alexander, *Tunisia: Stability and reform in the modern Maghreb* (New York: Routledge, 2010); Stephen J. King, *Liberalization against Democracy: The local politics of economic reform in Tunisia* (Bloomington: Indiana University Press, 2003).

36. Samples of such imagery from the first Casbah protests can be found in Viviane Bettaïeb, ed., *Dégage: La révolution tunisienne (17 décembre 2010 à 14 janvier 2011)* (Get Out: The Tunisian revolution) (Paris: Editions du Layeur, 2011), especially pp. 80–85.

37. The name of the former ruling party under President Zine el-Abidine Ben Ali.

38. DeGeorges, "The social construction of the Tunisian revolutionary martyr," p. 490.

39. The commission's final report is divided into five main parts: a chronology and documentation of the events and human rights violations before, during, and shortly after the Tunisian revolution; Noteworthy Items and Events (Prison Conditions, Snipers, Tribal Violence, Violations against Women, Violations

against Children); Responsibility for the Violations Documented; Recommendations; Lists and Explanatory Figures.

40. Taoufik Bouderbala, et al., *Taqrīr al-lujna al-wataniyya li-istiqsā' al-haqa'iq hawl al-tajāwuzāt wa al-intihākāt* (Report of the National Commission to establish the facts surrounding the illegal acts and infractions recorded over the period from 17 December 2010 to the end of the commission's mandate) (Al-lujna al-wataniyya li-istiqsa' al-haqa'iq hawl al-tajawuzat wa al-intihakat al-musajjila khilal al-fitra al-mumtadda min 17 december 2010 ila hin zawal mawjibiha) Tunis, April 2012, p. 25.

41. Taoufik Bouderbala, et al., *Report of the National Commission*, p. 35.

42. Taoufik Bouderbala, et al., *Report of the National Commission*, pp. 35–6.

43. Given the earlier complaint raised by the commission about the reluctance of the security forces and institutions to cooperate with its work, perhaps this finding is not as surprising as it first appears.

44. Taoufik Bouderbala, et al., *Report of the National Commission*, p. 13.

45. This may be due to the vital presence on the commission of notable advocates for women and children, including the lawyer Bushra Belhaj Hamida (former president of the Association of Democratic Women), as well as medical doctors such as Sarah Beltaji of the esteemed Charles Nicolle Hospital in Tunis.

46. Taoufik Bouderbala, et al., *Report of the National Commission*, pp. 507–13.

47. The formerly dominant post of president has been weakened so that, while the holder is still the commander-in-chief of the armed forces, no cabinet-level changes may be effected without the approval of the prime minister.

48. Teitel, *Transitional Justice*, p. 191.

49. Teitel, *Transitional Justice*, ch. 3.

50. *Dustūr al-jumhūriyya al-tūnisiyya* (The Constitution of the Tunisian Republic) (Tunis: Imprimerie Officielle de la République Tunisienne, 2014).

51. Teitel, *Transitional Justice*, p. 71.

8. POLITICAL EXCLUSION AND TRANSITIONAL JUSTICE: A CASE STUDY OF LIBYA

1. The authors wish to thank Razzaq Al-Saedi and Alexander Mayer-Rieckh, whose work on political isolation helped inform this chapter. An earlier and briefer version of this chapter appeared as Marieke Wierda and Mieczysław P. Boduszyński, "Accounting for the Past or Avenging in the Present? Transitional justice and Libya's Political Isolation Law," *Georgetown Journal of International Affairs* (Winter/Spring 2014).

2. Hisham Matar, "The Consequences of Dreams," *New Yorker*, 31 July 2014.

3. Alexander Mayer-Rieckh and Pablo de Greiff, eds, *Justice as Prevention: Vetting public employees in transitional societies* (New York: Social Science Research Council, 2007).

4. Ibid.

5. Ibid.

6. Roman David and Huma Mzioudet, "Personnel Change or Personal Change? Rethinking Libya's Political Isolation Law," *Brookings Doha-Stanford Paper*, March 2014.

7. Roger Duthie, "Introduction," in Mayer-Rieckh and Pablo de Greiff, eds, *Justice as Prevention*, pp. 15–34.

8. Herman Schwartz, "Lustration in Eastern Europe," in Neil J. Kritz, ed., *Transitional Justice Vol. I: General Considerations* (Washington, DC: United States Institute of Peace Press 1995), p. 16.

9. United Nations, "Updated Principles to Combat Impunity," Principle 36(a).

10. Mieczysław P. Boduszyński and Duncan Pickard, "Libya Starts from Scratch," *Journal of Democracy* vol. 24, no. 4 (October 2013).

11. Schwartz, *Transitional Justice*, p. 465.

12. Schwartz, *Transitional Justice*, p. 464.

13. Brian Grodsky, *The Costs of Justice: How new leaders respond to previous rights abuses* (South Bend, IN: University of Notre Dame Press, 2010).

14. Adam Przeworski, *Democracy and the Market: Political and economic reforms in Eastern Europe and Latin America* (New York: Cambridge University Press, 1991).

15. Samuel P. Huntington, *The Third Wave: Democratization in the late twentieth century* (Norman, OK: University of Oklahoma Press, 1991).

16. Monika Nalepa, *Skeletons in the Closet: Transitional justice in post-communist Europe* (Cambridge: Cambridge University Press, 2010).

17. Grodsky, *The Costs of Justice*.

18. ICTJ, "Vetting Lessons for the 2009–10 Elections in Afghanistan" (New York: International Center for Transitional Justice, 2009).

19. Even before the vetting law was passed, the National Transitional Council (NTC), Libya's interim government, passed a more comprehensive transitional justice law. This law went through several amendments and its implementation gradually stalled. The crux of the law was a Fact-Finding and Reconciliation Commission that never became functional.

20. David and Mzioudet, *Brookings Doha-Stanford Paper*.

21. Human Rights Watch, "Libya: June 1996 killings at Abu Salim prison," 27 June 1996, http://www.hrw.org/en/news/2006/06/27/libya-june-1996-killings-abu-salim-prison (accessed 17 June 2016).

22. Ian Black, "Libyan revolution casualties lower than expected, says new government," *Guardian*, 8 January 2013.

23. IRIN, "Libya's sidelined IDPs," 10 December 2014, http://www.irinnews.org/report/100931/libya-s-sidelined-idps (accessed 17 June 2016).

24. The current existence of tribal conflicts is based in part on Gaddafi's divide-and-rule tactics. Gaddafi co-opted or spread patronage among dueling ethnic groups

in order to extend his control over Libya's vast borderlands. He paid off certain tribal groups to keep order despite quarrels over claims to land and citizenship, tolerating some cross-border smuggling in the process. In other areas, he practiced the politics of divide-and-rule by encouraging rifts within tribes large enough to challenge the state.

25. UNMSIL, "Overview of violations of international human rights and humanitarian law during the ongoing violence in Libya," 4 September 2014.

26. Boduszyński and Pickard, *Journal of Democracy*.

27. Interviews with European officials in Brussels, June 2014.

28. Briefing of the Special Representative of the Secretary General and Head of UNSMIL to the Security Council, 18 June 2013: "In a number of detention centers, we have observed cases of torture. There is also evidence of deaths in detention due to torture."

29. Marie-Louise Gumuchian, "Libya's turmoil revealed in feud over custody of Gaddafi's son," Reuters Insight, 4 August 2013.

30. Just recently, the General National Congress created a committee to investigate and take measures in respect of the Abu Salim massacre. GNC Decision no. 59, 28 June 2013.

31. Anonymous interview with leading Libyan politician, October 2013.

32. In April 2012 the NTC passed laws immunizing revolutionaries who may have committed war crimes or human rights violations. They were given amnesty for acts "made necessary" by the February 17 revolution. See Paul Salem and Amanda Kadlec, "Libya's Troubled Transition" (Washington, DC: Carnegie Middle East Center, 2012).

33. In September 2012 the GNC mandated Libya Shield forces to make an armed incursion into Bani Walid, which was long considered a Gaddafi stronghold, to impose a new Local Council. The attack resulted in indiscriminate shelling, the deaths of dozens of civilians, and the unlawful detentions of hundreds.

34. Wolfram Lacher, "Fault Lines of the Revolution: Political actors, camps and conflicts in the new Libya," *Stiftung Wissenschaft und Politik Research Paper* (2013).

35. Mathieu Galtier, "Inside the Commission of Integrity and Patriotism," *Libya Herald*, 11 April 2013.

36. Interview with Mahmud Jibril, Al-Sharq al-Awsat Online, 7 June 2013.

37. Interview with Belhaj, Al Sharq Al-Awsat Online, 6 March 2013; and interview with Suwwan in Al-Hayat Online, 25 January 2013.

38. Anonymous interview with Islamist politician, May 2013.

39. Sami Zaptia, "GNC members held hostage by armed demonstrators—one member hit on the head," *Libya Herald*, 6 March 2013.

40. Tom Wescott and Seraj Essul, "Coffin march from Suq al Juma to Congress backs Political Isolation law," *Libya Herald*, 30 April 2013.

41. Frederic Wehrey, "Ending Libya's Civil War: Reconciling politics, rebuilding security," Carnegie Endowment for International Peace (September 2014).

42. Personal communication between authors and Libyans in exile, summer 2014.

43. Wehrey, "Ending Libya's Civil War."

9. TRUTH AND FACT-FINDING IN THE ARAB MONARCHIES

1. Rob Prince, "Tunisia: Siliana and the heritage of Farhat Hached sixty years after his assassination," *Open Democracy*, 5 December 2012, https://www.opendemocracy.net/rob-prince/tunisia-siliana-and-heritage-of-farhat-hached-sixty-years-after-his-assassination

2. Library of Congress Federal Research Division, "Country Profile: Morocco," Library of Congress, May 2006, http://lcweb2.loc.gov/frd/cs/profiles/Morocco.pdf (accessed 17 June 2016).

3. James Sater, *Morocco: Challenges to tradition and modernity*, 1st edn (London: Routledge, 2010), p. 23.

4. Tom Porteous, "Obituary: King Hassan II of Morocco," *Independent*, 26 July 1999, http://www.independent.co.uk/arts-entertainment/obituary-king-hassan-ii-of-morocco-1108768.html (accessed 17 June 2016).

5. BBC News, "On This Day 1971: Death for Moroccan rebel leaders," BBC News, 13 July 1971, http://news.bbc.co.uk/onthisday/hi/dates/stories/july/13/newsid_2503000/2503093.stm (last accessed 17 February 2016).

6. Encyclopedia Britannica, "Western Sahara," 4 February 2014, http://www.britannica.com/EBchecked/topic/640800/Western-Sahara/287330/History (accessed 17 June 2016).

7. International Court of Justice, "Western Sahara, Summary of the Advisory Opinion of 16 October 1975," http://www.icj-cij.org/docket/index.php?sum=323&p1=3&p2=4&case=61&p3=5 (accessed 17 June 2016).

8. Sidi Omar, "Mapping of the Conflict in Western Sahara," *Grupo de Estudios Estrategicos, http://www.*gees.org/articulos/mapping_of_the_conflict_in_western_sahara_6705 (last accessed 17 February 2016).

9. The Madrid accords provided that Morocco and Mauritania would exercise administrative control over the territory, but not sovereignty. See United Nations Treaty Series, "Declaration of Principles on Western Sahara by Spain, Morocco, and Mauritania 1975," http://peacemaker.un.org/sites/peacemaker.un.org/files/MA-MR-ES_751114_DeclarationPrinciplesOnWesternSahara_0.pdf (accessed 10 June 2014).

10. United States Department of State, *Western Sahara*, Bureau of Democracy, Rights, and Labour, 2007, http://www.state.gov/j/drl/rls/hrrpt/2007/102555.htm (last accessed 17 February 2016).

11. Joanna Quinn, ed., *Reconciliation(s): Transitional justice in post-conflict societies* (Montreal: McGill University Press, 2009), p. 59.

12. Human Rights Watch, "Morocco's Truth Commission: Honoring past victims during an uncertain present," vol. 17, no. 11, http://www.hrw.org/reports/2005/morocco1105/morocco1105.pdf (accessed 10 June 2014).

13. Ibid.

14. Quinn, *Reconciliation(s)*, p. 59.

15. ConstitutionNet, "Constitutional History of Morocco," International Institute for Democracy and Electoral Assistance, http://www.constitutionnet.org/country/constitutional-history-morocco (accessed 10 June 2014).

16. Catherine Sweet, "Democratization without Democracy: Political openings and closures in modern Morocco," *Middle East Report* vol. 218 (2001): 22–5.

17. United States Department of State, "Western Sahara," Bureau of Democracy, Rights, and Labour, 2005, available at http://www.refworld.org/docid/441821a63e.html%20also%20http://www.state.gov/j/drl/rls/hrrpt/2007/102555.htm

18. Frédéric Vairel and Joel Beinin, eds, *Social Movement, Mobilization, and Contestation in the Middle East and North Africa*, 2nd edn (Palo Alto, CA: Stanford University Press, 2011), p. 83.

19. Quinn, *Reconciliation(s)*, p. 63. In October 2003, the CCDH officially recommended that the King establish a new form to investigate past human rights violations. See Amnesty International, "Broken Promises: The Equity and Reconciliation Commission and its follow-up," Amnesty International, 2010, http://www.amnesty.org/en/library/asset/MDE29/001/2010/en/63d99172–428d-4717–8c25–866c879c80e9/mde290012010en.pdf (accessed 10 June 2014).

20. Ibid.

21. Human Rights Watch, "Morocco's Truth Commission," vol. 17, no. 11, p. 22.

22. National Commission for Truth, Justice and Reconciliation, "Summary of the Final Report," http://www.ccdh.org.ma/sites/default/files/documents/rapport_final_mar_eng-3.pdf, p. 5 (accessed 14 June 2014).

23. Website of Moroccan Equity and Reconciliation Commission, http://www.ier.ma/_fr_article.php?id_article=221 (accessed 12 January 2010).

24. Ibid.

25. Amnesty International, "Broken Promises," 2010, http://www.amnesty.org/en/library/asset/MDE29/001/2010/en/63d99172–428d-4717–8c25–866c879c80e9/mde290012010en.pdf (accessed 10 June 2014).

26. Ibid.

27. National Commission for Truth, Justice and Reconciliation, "Summary of the Final Report," http://www.ccdh.org.ma/sites/default/files/documents/rapport_final_mar_eng-3.pdf, p. 5 (accessed 14 June 2014).

28. Barbara Rose Johnston and Susan Slyomovics, eds, *Waging War, Making Peace: Reparations and human rights* (Walnut Creek, CA: Left Coast Press, 2009), p. 107.

29. Amnesty International, "Broken Promises."

30. Human Rights Watch, "Morocco's Truth Commission," vol. 17, no. 11, p. 24.
31. Amnesty International, "Broken Promises," p. 29.
32. Human Rights Watch, "Morocco's Truth Commission," vol. 17, no. 11, p. 24.
33. United States Department of State, "Country Report: Morocco," 2011, http://www.state.gov/documents/organization/186650.pdf (accessed 19 May 2014).
34. Report of the Follow-Up Committee to the CCDH, available online at http://www.arso.org/Report_on_Human_Rights_violations_in_Morocco.pdf
35. Moroccan American Center, "Morocco is Committed to Protecting Human Rights," http://moroccoonthemove.com/wp-content/uploads/2013/08/FS_MoroccoProtectingHumanRights10January2012.pdf (accessed 17 June 2016).
36. BBC News, http://www.bbc.com/news/world-africa-14121440 (accessed 17 June 2016).
37. Newsring, "Le Sahara Occidental, a-t-il le droit à l'indépendence?" 2 October 2013, http://www.mesdebats.com/monde/1246-le-sahara-occidental-a-t-il-le-droit-a-lindependance/17554-rapport-sur-les-tortures-et-traitements-cruels-et-inhumain-menes-par-le-maroc-au-sahara-occidental
38. See United States Department of State, "Western Sahara 2012 Human Rights Report," http://www.state.gov/documents/organization/204600.pdf (accessed 17 June 2016).
39. Activists representing the *Association Sahraouie des Victimes des Violations Graves des Droits Humains* state that although they notified authorities of the presence of a mass grave in February 2013, no investigation was carried out. As a result, the association brought together a team of 16 specialists to exhume and examine remains found in the area, revealing the identities of 14 individuals in the mass graves. These include 8 persons shot to death at close range in 1967, including Salama Ahmed, an 86-year-old identified as having died in military clashes in the town of Amgala by the CCDH report. According to the Sahrawi Association, this is evidence of inaccuracies within the commission's own reporting in Western Sahara. The association also states that it sent a letter to the CDDH and NHRC in March 2013 stating that they had evidence of remains near Layounne of another disappeared Sahrawi, but nothing was done to follow up.
40. The Emir appointed 20 members directly to the assembly, and held national elections for an additional 22 members. See Edward Burke, "Bahrain, Reaching a Threshold," Foundation for International Relations and Dialogue, June 2008, http://www.fride.org/descarga/FRIDEWP61INGLES_FINAL.pdf
41. Ibid.
42. The constitution also granted the Emir the authority to dissolve the assembly at his discretion, provided he make public the grounds for so doing; and provided that new elections take place within two months. Failing such conditions, any dissolution of the assembly would be invalidated and the dismissed members rein-

stated. See Library of Congress Country Studies Program, "A Country Study: Bahrain," Library of Congress, 27 July 2010, available at http://lcweb2.loc.gov/frd/cs/bhtoc.html (accessed 17 June 2016).

43. BBC News, "Bahrain Profile," 19 September 2013, http://www.bbc.com/news/world-middle-east-14541322 (accessed 17 June 2016).

44. Elham Fakhro, "The European Union and Islam: Democracy-Promotion in Bahrain and the Arab World," International Institute for Democracy and Electoral Assistance, Stockholm, 2010.

45. "February 14 Youths Media," downloaded 17 February 2011, https://ar-ar.facebook.com/14FebruaryYouthsMedia

46. Ibid.

47. Bahrain Independent Commission of Inquiry, *Report of the Bahrain Independent Commission of Inquiry* (Manama: BICI, final revision dated 10 December 2011), p. 71, available from www.bici.org.bh

48. Ibid., p. 75.

49. Ibid., p. 80.

50. Bahrain News Agency, "HM King Hamad's Decree Lifting the State of National Security on June 1 Hailed," 8 May 2011, http://www.bna.bh/portal/en/news/455777 (accessed 17 June 2016).

51. Cherif Bassiouni was renowned for leading a United Nations investigation into war crimes in Bosnia. The King also appointed four other legal experts as commissioners responsible for leading the inquiry, including Sir Nigel Rodley, a British lawyer who served as the United Nations Special Rapporteur on Torture for the years 1993–2001; Philippe Kirsch QC, a Canadian lawyer who served as a judge of the International Criminal Court; Dr Mahnhoush Arsanjani, an Iranian–American lawyer and the Vice President of the American Society of International Law; and Dr Badriya Al-Awadhi, a Kuwaiti Professor of International Law at Kuwait University.

52. Ibid.

53. Bahrain Independent Commission of Inquiry, *Report of the Bahrain Independent Commission of Inquiry*, p. 31.

54. Ibid., p. 266.

55. Ibid., p. 280.

56. Ibid.

57. Ibid., p. 299.

58. Ibid., p. 399.

59. Ibid., p. 383.

60. Bahrain Information Affairs Authority, "Press Release by the Special Investigations Unit at the Public Prosecution," 7 February 2013, http://www.iaa.bh/pressReleasedetails.aspx?id=416 (accessed 17 June 2016).

61. Trade Arabia, "Bahrain's Ombudsman's Office Probes 242 Claims," 29 May 2014, http://www.tradearabia.com/news/LAW_259058.html (accessed 17 June 2016).

62. Project on Middle East Democracy, "One Year Later: Assessing Bahrain's Implementation of the BICI Report," November 2012, http://pomed.org/wp-content/uploads/2013/12/One-Year-Later-Assessing-Bahrains-Implementation-of-the-BICI-Report.pdf (accessed 17 June 2016).

63. Trade Arabia, "Unrest Compensation Fund Draws 6.400 Claims," 22 March 2012, http://www.tradearabia.com/news/LAW_214607.html (accessed 17 June 2016).

64. Reuters, "Bahrain King toughens penalties for insulting King", 5 February 2014, http://www.reuters.com/article/2014/02/05/us-bahrain-law-idUSBREA140KX 20140205 (accessed 12 May 2014).

65. Human Rights Watch, "Bahrain's new Associations Law spells repression," 20 June 2013, http://www.hrw.org/news/2013/06/20/bahrain-new-associations-law-spells-repression (accessed 14 May 2013).

66. Ibid.

67. Ibid.

68. Elham Fakhro, "Bahrain's National Dialogue Faces a Stalemate," Al Jazeera Center for Studies, 10 November 2013, http://studies.aljazeera.net/en/reports/2013/10/2013101091036321935.htm (last accessed 17 February 2016).

69. Ibid.

70. Antoun Issa, "Bassiouni: Bahrain's progress limited by 'piecemeal' approach to reforms", *Al-Monitor*, http://www.al-monitor.com/pulse/originals/2014/06/cherif-bassiouni-bici-bahrain-uprising-violations.html?utm_source=dlvr.it&utm_medium=twitter# (accessed 13 June 2014).

10. "THE WALLS WILL NOT BE SILENT": A CAUTIONARY TALE ABOUT TRANSITIONAL JUSTICE AND COLLECTIVE MEMORY IN EGYPT

1. The quoted phrase refers to a painted wall image on Mohammad Mahmud Street in Cairo attributed to Mohamed Omar. See "Art and Culture: A year in review (Part 2)," *Daily News Egypt*, 13 December 2012, http://www.dailynewsegypt.com/2012/12/31/art-culture-a-year-in-review-part-2/ (accessed 21 December 2013).

2. This chapter employs the term "uprising," not revolution, to refer to the protests that led to Mubarak's removal. In places, however, it acknowledges popular Egyptian use of the term "25 January revolution." For discussion about terminology, see Robert F. Worth, "The Pillars of Arab Despotism," *New York Review of Books*, 9 October 2014, p. 24.

3. For a fascinating history of the intellectual origins of transitional justice, see Paige Arthur, "How Transitions Reshaped Human Rights: A conceptual history of transitional justice," *Human Rights Quarterly* vol. 31 (2009): 321–67.

4. Arthur, "How Transitions Reshaped Human Rights," 331, noted the descriptive title of an early collection of writings on the new field of transitional justice: Neil

Kritz, ed., *Transitional Justice: How emerging democracies reckon with former regimes* (Washington, DC: United States Institute of Peace, 1995).

5. Ibid., 337. She references W. W. Rostow's book, *The Stages of Economic Growth: A non-Communist Manifesto* (Cambridge: Cambridge University Press, 1960).

6. See their *Transitions from Authoritarian Rule: Tentative conclusions about uncertain democracies* (Baltimore and London: Johns Hopkins University Press, 1986). Other contending theories included dependency theory and world systems theory.

7. See, for example, Gene Sharp, *From Dictatorship to Democracy: A conceptual framework for liberation* (Boston, MA: Albert Einstein Institution, 2010, 4th edn); and Adrian Karatnycky and Peter Ackerman, "How Freedom is Won: From civic resistance to durable democracy" (Washington, DC: Freedom House, 2005), http://agnt.org/snv/resources/HowFreedomisWon.pdf (accessed 12 December 2013). They argue that "the force of civic resistance was a key factor in driving 50 of 67 transitions, or over 70 percent of countries where transitions began as dictatorial systems...", p. 6.

8. According to the International Center for Transitional Justice, transitional justice includes a range of goals and practices: 1) *criminal accountability* (trials of key perpetrators suspected of significant human rights violations or abuse of power); 2) *truth-telling* (truth commissions and other investigative bodies that expose and accumulate evidence illuminating systematic, underlying processes and structures that fostered impunity and the gross violation of human rights); 3) *institutional reforms* (reorganizing security forces to bring them under civilian control, disarming and decommissioning combatants, drafting new constitutions, reforming the judicial institutions, and implementing vetting or lustration policies that remove perpetrators from public institutions and create transparent rules and processes regulating who may run for elective office or serve in important public positions); 4) *material and symbolic reparations* (including financial compensation, restoration of confiscated property, facilitated access to health services for survivors of torture or violence, and public apologies by perpetrators to acknowledge guilt); and, 5) *memorialization and public memory projects* (including museums and memorials and reform of history and/or civics curriculum and pedagogy to promote critical thinking and understanding by future generations of the past). See http://www.ictj.org/about/transitional-justice (accessed 12 December 2014).

9. For a fuller discussion of the meaning of the term "reconciliation," see Judy Barsalou, "Reflecting the Fractured Past: Memorialisation, transitional justice and the role of outsiders," pp. 55–6, in Susanne Buckley-Zistel and Stefanie Schafer, eds, *Memorials in Times of Transition* (Cambridge: Intersentia, 2014).

10. For contending views on the goals and effectiveness of transitional justice interventions, see Chandra Lekha Sriram, "Transitional Justice in Comparative Perspective: Lessons for the Middle East," Ch. 2 in this volume; Tricia D. Olsen,

Leigh A. Payne, and Andrew G. Reiter, "The Justice Balance: When transitional justice improves human rights and democracy", *Human Rights Quarterly* vol. 32 (2010): 980–1007; "Peacebuilding Commission—Working Group on Lessons Learned," Justice in Times of Transition and the United Nations Peacebuilding Support Office, 29 February 2008, http://www.un.org/en/peacebuilding/pdf/doc_wgll/justice_times_transition/26_02_2008_chair_summary.pdf, accessed 27 September 2014); Eric Stover and Harvey M. Weinstein, *My Neighbor, My Enemy: Justice and community in the aftermath of mass atrocity* (Cambridge: Cambridge University Press, 2004); James L. Gibson, *Overcoming Apartheid: Can truth reconcile a divided nation?* (New York: Russell Sage Foundation, 2004); Hugo van der Merwe, Victoria Baxter, and Audrey R. Chapman, eds, *Assessing the Impact of Transitional Justice: Challenges for empirical research* (Washington, DC: United States Institute of Peace, 2009); and Jamie O'Connell, "Gambling with the Psyche: Does prosecuting human rights violators console their victims?" *Harvard International Law Journal* vol. 46 (2005): 295–345.

11. Researchers are now working to fix exactly when memorialization was first linked to transitional justice. Personal communication with Harvey Weinstein, University of California, Berkeley, December 2013.

12. Memorialization takes three basic forms: 1) *constructed sites* (monuments, museums, commemorative libraries, virtual memorials on the World Wide Web); 2) *found sites* (mass killing sites, graveyards, prisons and torture centers); and 3) *activities* (vigils, demonstrations, anniversaries of historical events, walking tours and parades, public place re-naming and apologies, and temporary exhibits). Different types of violence evoke different forms of memorialization, and in practice it can be both spontaneous and informal (e.g. laying flowers or pictures at the place where a death occurred) as well as highly organized (e.g. the creation of an historical site museum). Those who engage in memorialization range from individual survivors of violent conflict and the communities of which they are a part to government entities, civil society organizations, and corporations. See Judy Barsalou in Buckley-Zistel and Schafer, *Memorials in Times of Transition*.

13. Jeffry K. Olick and Joyce Robbins, "Social Memory Studies: From 'collective memory' to the historical sociology of mnemonic practices," *Annual Review of Sociology* vol. 24 (1998): 106.

14. Maurice Halbwachs, *On Collective Memory*, edited, translated and with an introduction by Lewis A. Coser (Chicago: University of Chicago Press, 1992).

15. David Berliner, "The Abuses of Memory: Reflections on the memory boom in anthropology," *Anthropological Quarterly* vol. 78 (2005): 197. As of the early 1970s, the study of collective memory was not a focus of political science research.

16. Buckley-Zistel and Schafer, *Memorials in Times of Transition*, p. 5.

17. Judy Barsalou, "Trauma and Transitional Justice in Divided Societies," Special Report 135 (Washington, DC: United State Institute of Peace, April 2005),

http://www.usip.org/publications/trauma-and-transitional-justice-in-divided-societies (accessed 10 December 2013).

18. See, for example, Vamik D. Volkan, "Traumatized Societies and Psychological Care: Expanding the concept of preventative medicine," *Mind and Human Interaction* vol. 11 (1991): 177–94. Preliminary findings from animal studies suggest that trauma and stress in early life may even affect DNA at the molecular level. Victoria Gill, "Early Life Stress 'Changes' Genes," BBC News, 8 November 2009, http://news.bbc.co.uk/2/hi/sci/tech/8346715.stm (accessed 10 December 2013).

19. Judy Barsalou, "Trauma and Transitional Justice in Divided Societies," 4.

20. International Center for Transitional Justice, "What is Transitional Justice?" http://www.ictj.org/about/transitional-justice (accessed 27 September 2014).

21. Olsen, Payne, and Reiter, "The Justice Balance," 997.

22. Sriram, Chapter 2 of this volume.

23. For analysis of political conditions during these phases, see R. Kent Weaver and Judy Barsalou, "Barriers to Democratization: A behavioral perspective," in Michele Micheletti, ed., *Democratization and Citizenship Discourses in the MENA Region* (Istanbul: Swedish Research Institute in Istanbul, 2013), p. 84.

24. "Popular Protest in North Africa and the Middle East (1): Egypt Victorious?" Middle East/North Africa Report, International Crisis Group 101 (2011), p. 19.

25. Egyptians love to joke about *Hizb al Kanabi* (the Sofa party) in describing those who stayed on the political sidelines.

26. Joel Beinin, "Was there a January 25 Revolution?" *Jadaliyya*, 25 January 2013, http://www.jadaliyya.com/pages/index/9766/was-there-a-january-25-revolution (accessed 18 January 2014). See also Hugh Roberts, "The Revolution that Wasn't," *London Review of Books* no. 35 (2013): 3–9, http://www.lrb.co.uk/v35/n17/hugh-roberts/the-revolution-that-wasn't (accessed 18 January 2014).

27. Roberts, "The Revolution that Wasn't" reviews three books that analyze Egyptians' complex and shifting orientation toward the military.

28. Rana Muhammad Taha, "Transitional Justice is Missing: NGOs," *Daily News Egypt*, 20 November 2013, http://www.dailynewsegypt.com/2013/11/20/transitional-justice-is-missing-ngos/ (accessed 13 January 2014).

29. Patrick Kingsley and Leyla Doss, "Egyptian Police 'Killed Almost 900 Protestors in 2011 in Cairo,'" *Guardian*, 14 March 2013, http://www.theguardian.com/world/2013/mar/14/egypt-leaked-report-blames-police-900-deaths-2011?view=mobile (accessed 13 December 2013). Yet, it is still early days: 11 Egyptian NGOs, along with Human Rights Watch and Amnesty International, jointly called for the investigation and release of findings regarding 13 major incidents occurring between January 2011 and October 2013 and resulting in the death of 2,329 persons. They also demanded that Egypt's then Minister of Transitional Justice, Amin Al-Mahdy, issue the complete reports from two earlier fact-finding committees. See Fady Ashraf, "Mass Protester Killings Going Unanswered: HRW, Amnesty

International and 11 NGOs," *Daily News Egypt*, 10 December 2013, http://www.
dailynewsegypt.com/2013/12/10/no-acknowledgment-or-justice-for-mass-pro-
tester-killings-hrw-amnesty-international-and-11-ngos/ (accessed 13 December
2013).

30. Sarah Raslan, "Newly Issued Lustration Law Slammed as Ineffective," *Ahram
Online*, 21 November 2011, http://english.ahram.org.eg/NewsContent/33/
100/27197/Elections-/News/Newly-issued-lustration-law-slammed-as-ineffective.
aspx (accessed 18 November 2014).

31. To put the Arab uprisings into comparative perspective, see Stephen R. Grand,
*Understanding Tahrir Square: What transitions elsewhere can teach us about the
prospects for Arab democracy* (Washington, DC: Brookings Institution, 2014).

32. The author conducted the fieldwork in Egypt between November 2011 and March
2012. Full findings are available in an unpublished paper (names withheld):
"Delayed or Denied: Egyptian expectations about justice in post-Mubarak Egypt,"
January 2013. Quotations included in this paper without references are from interviews conducted by the author during the fieldwork.

33. The term "statistically significant" means that the results reported would occur by
chance in 1 in 20 occasions, or less frequently. Statistical significance is measured
by "probability values" ("p" for short), so that the value where p is "1 in 20" is written as "$p = 0.05$." In the case above, where $p < 0.0001$, the probability is less than
one in 10,000 that the result would occur by chance, and is therefore statistically
highly significant.

34. A journalist, Alexander Marquardt, claimed that it was available in three versions.
See "Mubarak Becomes a Ringtone," ABC News, 4 August 2011, http://abcnews.
go.com/Blotter/mubarak-ringtone/story?id=14232084 (accessed 19 December
2013).

35. He was right. Mubarak's trial was postponed numerous times. In 2012 he was
found guilty of overseeing the killing of Egyptians by security forces during the
January–February 2011 uprising, but an appeals court overturned that decision.
David D. Kirkpatrick, "Mubarak tells court he gave all for Egypt," *New York Times*,
13 August 2014, http://www.nytimes.com/2014/08/14/world/middleeast/
egypt-hosni-mubarak-trial.html?_r=0 (accessed 18 August 2014). Citing a tech-
nicality, an appeals court overturned Mubarak's conviction on murder and corruption charges in November 2014. http://www.npr.org/blogs/thetwo-way/2014/
11/29/367363664/egyptian-court-overturns-mubaraks-murder-conviction
(accessed 12 December 2014).

36. A number of workshops and conferences were held in Cairo, including a conference organized by the International Center for Transitional Justice and the Cairo
Institute for Human Rights Studies in Cairo, 30–31 October 2011, entitled
"Transitional Justice and the MENA Region: Challenges and Possibilities"; and
an "Expert Conference" organized by the Center for International Peace Operations

and the Cairo Regional Center on Conflict Resolution and Peacekeeping in Africa in Cairo, 19–21 June 2012, entitled "Criminal Justice and Accountability in Arab Transition Processes."

37. For elaboration of these elements, see Barsalou, "Trauma and Transitional Justice in Divided Societies," 3–4.

38. For some idea of the range and scale of these activities, see Judy Barsalou, "Recalling the Past: The battle over history, collective memory and memorialization in Egypt," *Jadaliyya*, 22 June 2012, http://www.jadaliyya.com/pages/index/6007/recalling-the-past_the-battle-over-history-collect (accessed 21 December 2013).

39. To view some of these images, see http://suzeeinthecity.wordpress.com (accessed 21 December 2013).

40. Ahmed Nadi, activist/cartoonist, "Egypt Street Art Vents Anger at President after Whitewashing," Reuters, 20 September 2012, http://www.reuters.com/article/2012/09/20/us-egypt-tahrir-idUSBRE88J0VF20120920 (accessed 21 December 2013). See also Rana Muhammad Taha and Hend Kortam, "The Remains of Mohamad Mahmoud," *Daily News Egypt*, 19 November 2013, http://www.dailynewsegypt.com/2013/11/19/the-remains-of-mohamed-mahmoud/ (accessed 29 December 2013).

41. These festivals were banned by the el-Sisi government. Khaled Mahmoud, "Fighting Censorship, Al-Fan Midan Organisers Pledge to Continue Performing," Daily News Egypt, 24 September 2014, http://www.dailynewsegypt.com/2014/09/24/fighting-censorship-al-fan-midan-organisers-pledge-continue-performing/ (accessed 26 September 2014).

42. An example was a running skirmish relating to the "Mubarak" metro stop under Tahrir Square, subsequently renamed "Martyrs" by the SCAF government, but with pro-Mubarak supporters using graffiti to switch the name back.

43. The Egyptian government's removal of informal memorials constructed by demonstrators in Tahrir Square compares to measures undertaken by the South African government to preserve and reinterpret pre-existing memorials constructed by past regimes, notably the Voortrekker Monument and Freedom Park in Pretoria, where diverse perspectives about the past are narrated in an effort to reconstruct South Africa as an inclusive "rainbow" nation.

44. https://www.youtube.com/watch?v=gvop9dL36lI (accessed 21 December 2013).

45. Pew Research Center, "One Year Later... Egyptians remain optimistic, embrace democracy and religion in public life," Global Attitudes Project, 8 May 2012, p. 2, http://www.pewglobal.org/files/2012/05/Pew-Global-Attitudes-Project-Egypt-Report-FINAL-May–8–2012–2PM-ET.pdf (accessed 21 December 2013).

46. "Chapters Praising Mubarak's Regime Removed from Egyptian Textbooks," *Al Arabiya News*, 21 April 2011, http://english.alarabiya.net/articles/2011/04/21/146224.html (accessed 21 December 2013).

47. Merrit Kennedy, "Teaching Recent History in Egypt," National Public Radio,

5 October 2013, http://www.npr.org/templates/story/story.php?storyId= 229472257 (accessed 21 December 2013). Kennedy notes that NPR was not able to confirm the minister's remark.

48. Interview with Nora Soliman, a spokesperson of the Al-Adl party, 1 February 2012.

49. https://www.facebook.com/3askar.Kazeboon (accessed 27 September 2014).

50. See http://suzeeinthecity.wordpress.com/2012/02/06/war-on-graffiti-scaf-van-dalists-versus-graffiti-artists/ (accessed 21 December 2013).

51. Hiren Mistry, "Transitional Justice and the Arab Spring," Meeting Summary: International Law and Middle East Programme, Chatham House, 1 February 2012, p. 14, http://www.chathamhouse.org/sites/files/chathamhouse/public/Research/International%20Law/010212summary.pdf (accessed 26 September 2014).

52. Mistry, "Transitional Justice and the Arab Spring," p. 15.

53. Personal communication with the author, October 2012.

54. See Diana Sankey, "Towards Recognition of Substantive Harms: Reassessing approaches to socioeconomic forms of violence in transitional justice," *International Journal of Transitional Justice* vol. 8 (2014): 121–40; Evelyne Schmid and Aoife Nolan, "'Do No Harm'? Exploring the scope of economic and social rights in transitional justice," *International Journal of Transitional Justice* vol. 8 (2014): 362–82; Makau Mutua, "A Critique of Transitional Justice: The African experience," in Gaby Ore Aguilar and Felipe Gomez Isa, *Rethinking Transitions: Equality and social justice in societies emerging from conflict* (Cambridge: Intersentia, 2011), pp. 31–45; Lars Waldorf, "Anticipating the Past: Transitional justice and socioeconomic wrongs," *Social and Legal Studies* vol. 21 (2012): 171–86.

55. Partly, this knowledge gap reflects the challenge of conducting social science research in Egypt. The Central Agency for Public Mobilization and Statistics (CAPMAS), led since its establishment in 1964 by an army major general, asserts the right to review prospective research projects and forbid or modify those deemed politically or socially sensitive.

56. However, smartphone penetration is low (about 6 percent). "Smartphone Usage Soars Across the Middle East and Africa", *eMarketer*, 9 May 2014, http://www.emarketer.com/Article/Smartphone-Usage-Soars-Across-Middle-East-Africa/1010820 (accessed 9 December 2014).

57. Sara Aggour, "Social Networking Websites have over Two Billion Registered: Y2D," *Daily News Egypt*, 15 January 2014, http://www.dailynewsegypt.com/2014/01/15/social-networking-websites-have-over-2-billion-registered-users-y2d/ (accessed 19 January 2014). According to a report produced by the company Y2D, users based in Egypt generate 2.7 billion "likes" per day.

58. For example, amendments to Article 78 of the Egyptian Penal Code relating to the operation of organizations receiving foreign funding have raised the stakes of

opposition, including potential life sentences and even the death penalty." Foreign Funding Law Raises Concerns over Future of Human Rights Organizations, *Daily News Egypt*, 24 September 2014, http://www.dailynewsegypt.com/2014/09/24/foreign-funding-law-raises-concern-future-human-rights-organisations/ (accessed 26 September 2014).

59. A snowball sampling technique was used to build the sample. Patrick Biernacki and Dan Waldorf, "Snowball Sampling: Problems and techniques of chain referral sampling," *Sociological Methods and Research* vol. 10 (1981): 141–63. Some anonymous respondents did not provide identifying information.

60. We constructed this category on the basis of the last degree earned and employment. "Working class" respondents included persons who had not completed a high school degree, as well as those with higher levels of education but performing low-skill and low-income jobs. All others were coded in a single combined group (middle class and upper middle class).

61. We did not ask people their religion but inferred it from their names. If an inference could not be drawn or the respondent chose anonymity, we coded respondents' religion as "not applicable."

11. THEATER OR TRANSITIONAL JUSTICE: REFORMING THE JUDICIARY IN EGYPT

1. Professor Aziz thanks the Center for International Relations at Georgetown University in Qatar, Professor Mehran Kamrava, and Professor Zahra Babar for providing the opportunity to workshop earlier drafts of the paper. She also thanks Professors Adrien Wing, Chandra Sriram, and Nathan Brown for their insightful comments to earlier drafts. Special thanks to Deborah Bankhead, Brian Bailey, and Travis Gasper for their excellent research assistance. All errors are mine.

2. Human Rights Watch, "Egypt: Fresh Assault on Justice," 29 April 2014, http://www.hrw.org/news/2014/04/29/egypt-fresh-assault-justice (accessed 7 February 2015).

3. Nathan J. Brown, "Why do Egyptian courts say the darndest things?" *Washington Post*, 25 March 2014, http://www.washingtonpost.com/blogs/monkey-cage/wp/2014/03/25/why-do-egyptian-courts-say-the-darndest-things/ (accessed 7 February 2015); Tamir Moustafa, "Law Versus the State: The judicialization of politics in Egypt," *Journal of Law and Social Inquiry* vol. 3 (2003): 885 (discussing the effect of an independent judiciary free of governmental manipulation); Mahmoud Hamad, "When the gavel speaks: Judicial politics in modern Egypt" (PhD diss., University of Utah, 2008), pp. 19, 161–2 (noting "the connection between the existence of an independent judiciary, capable of upholding property rights and enforcing business contracts and attracting investment to achieve economic development," discussing the political significance of judicial independence).

4. Yussef Auf, "Prospects for Judicial Reform in Egypt," Atlantic Council, 21 October 2014, http://www.atlanticcouncil.org/blogs/egyptsource/prospects-for-judicial-reform-in-egypt (accessed 7 February 2015) (noting the judiciary is conservative by nature); Tom Ginsberg, "Courts and New Democracies: Recent works," *Law and Social Inquiry* vol. 37 (2012): 735 (noting the Chilean judiciary's similar conservative inclinations as an impediment to transition to democracy); Asli U. Bali, "The Perils of Judicial Independence: Constitutional transition and the Turkish example," *Virginia Journal of International Law* vol. 52 (2012): 235 (arguing that the Turkish judiciary's composition of secular elites caused it to constrain political liberalization rather than secure democratic space in Turkey).

5. Samer Soliman, *Autumn of Dictatorship* (Stanford, CA: Stanford University Press, 2011), p. 152; Thomas Carothers, ed., *Promoting the Rule of Law Abroad* (Washington, DC: Carnegie Endowment for International Peace, 2006), p. 3; Tom Ginsberg, "Courts and New Democracies, pp. 720, 736.

6. Sahar Aziz, "Bringing Down an Uprising: Egypt's stillborn revolution," in Bessma Momani et al., eds, *Tahrir Square and Beyond: Critical Perspectives on Politics, Law, and Security* (under review by Indiana University Press, 2015).

7. Soliman, *Autumn of Dictatorship*, p. 70; Roger Owen, *The Rise and Fall of Arab Presidents for Life* (Boston, MA: Harvard University Press, 2012), p. 189.

8. Nathan Brown, "Egypt's Judges in a Revolutionary Age," Carnegie Endowment for International Peace, 22 February 2012, http://carnegieendowment. org/2012/02/22/egypt-s-judges-in-revolutionary-age/9sri (accessed 7 February 2015); Hamad, "When the gavel speaks."

9. Steven A. Cook, *Ruling But Not Governing* (Washington, DC: Johns Hopkins University Press, 2007), p. 131; Tamir Moustafa, "Law in the Egyptian Revolt," *Middle East Law and Governance* vol. 3 (2011): 181–5.

10. Carothers, *Promoting the Rule of Law Abroad*, pp. 253–4.

11. Cook, *Ruling But Not Governing*, p. 148.

12. Marek M. Kaminski, Monika Nalepa, and Barry O'Neill, "Normative and Strategic Aspects of Transitional Justice," *Journal of Conflict Resolution* vol. 50 (2006): 296.

13. Reem Abou-El-Fadl, "Beyond Conventional Transitional Justice: Egypt's 2011 revolution and the absence of political will," *International Journal of Transitional Justice* vol. 6 (2012): 318, 319; Ivan Ivekovic, "Egypt's Uncertain Transition," in Dan Tschirgi, Walid Kazziha, and Sean McMahon, eds, *Egypt's Tahrir Revolution* (Boulder, CO: Lynne Rienner, 2013), p. 183 (noting the military's role as the most prominent player in the transition process).

14. Fadl, "Beyond Conventional Transitional Justice," p. 327.

15. "English Text of SCAF amended Egypt Constitutional Declaration," *Ahramonline*, 10 June 2012, http://english.ahram.org.eg/News/45350.aspx (accessed 7 February 2015).

16. David D. Kirkpatrick and Merna Thomas, "Egyptian judges drop all charges against Mubarak," *New York Times*, 29 November 2014.

17. Aziz, "Bringing Down an Uprising"; Nathan J. Brown, "Egypt's Failed Transition, Tracking the 'Arab Spring'," *Journal of Democracy* vol. 24 (2013): 4, 45, 50.

18. Soliman, *Autumn of Dictatorship*, p. 70; Nathalie Bernard-Maugiron, ed., *Judges and Political Reform in Egypt* (New York: American University in Cairo Press, 2008), p. 9.

19. Sean F. McMahon, "Egypt's Social Forces, the State, and the Middle East Order," in Tschirgi, Kazziha, and McMahon, eds, *Egypt's Tahrir Revolution*, pp. 157–8.

20. Brian Tamanaha, *On the Rule of Law: History, politics, theory* (Cambridge: Cambridge University Press, 2004), p. 113; Abou-El-Fadl, "Beyond Conventional Transitional Justice," 320.

21. Abou-El-Fadl, "Beyond Conventional Transitional Justice," p. 323.

22. Aziz, "Bringing Down an Uprising."

23. Moustafa, "Law Versus the State," pp. 893–4.

24. Ibid., p. 907.

25. Mark Wassouf et al., *Separating Law and Politics: Challenges to the independence of judges and prosecutors in Egypt* (London: International Bar Association Human Rights Institute, 2014), p. 12, http://www.ibanet.org/Article/Detail.aspx?ArticleUid=B30A63AE-8066–4B49–8758-C1684BE5E9B9 (accessed 7 February 2015).

26. Carothers, *Promoting the Rule of Law Abroad*, p. 67.

27. Ginsberg, *Courts and New Democracies*, p. 738.

28. Intisar Rabb, "The Least Religious Branch? Judicial Review and the New Islamic Constitutionalism," *UCLA Journal of International and Foreign Affairs* vol. 17 (2013): 124–6.

29. Brown, "Egypt's Failed Transition," pp. 4, 45, 53.

30. Moataz El Fegiery, "Truth and Reconciliation? Transitional justice in Egypt, Libya and Tunisia," RIDE Policy Brief no. 177, pp. 3–4 (March 2014), http://fride.org/descarga/PB_177_Truth_and_reconciliation.pdf; Luc Huyse, *Transitional Justice after War and Dictatorship* (Brussels: Centre for Historical Research and Documentation on War and Contemporary Society, 2013), pp. 22–3, http://www.cegesoma.be/docs/media/Recherche/TransJustFinalReport.pdf (accessed 11 November 2014).

31. Owen, *Rise and Fall*, p. 174; Abou-El-Fadl, "Beyond Conventional Transitional Justice," p. 323.

32. Abou-El-Fadl, "Beyond Conventional Transitional Justice," p. 323; Moustafa, "Egyptian Revolt," p. 185.

33. Abdul-Fatah Madi, "Where are the Youth of the Egyptian Revolution?" Al Jazeera, 19 November 2013, https://www.middleeastmonitor.com/articles/africa/8467-

where-are-the-youth-of-the-egyptian-revolution (accessed 7 February 2015); Tamanaha, *On the Rule of Law*, p. 112; Moustafa, "Egyptian Revolt," p. 190.

34. *Recommendations on the Conference "Transitional Justice and Institutional Reform"* (Cairo: Arab Center for the Independence of the Judiciary and the Legal Profession, 2013) (copy on file with author).

35. Brown, "Egypt's Judges," p. 7. Moustafa, "Egyptian Revolt," pp. 181–2.

36. Mohammed Al Shafey, "A talk with the Muslim Brotherhood's Ibrahim Munir," Ikhwanweb, 12 January 2011, http://ikhwanweb.com/article.php?id=27804&ref=search.php (accessed 7 February 2015) (discussing how the "existing laws must be applied to everyone"); "Muslim Brotherhood Praises Pro-Democracy Brussels Declaration," Ikhwanweb, 13 May 2014, http://ikhwanweb.com/article.php?id=31653&ref=search.php (accessed 7 February 2015) (discussing the MB's wish to reinstate Morsi and build upon the existing laws in furtherance of the democratic transformation).

37. Carothers, *Promoting the Rule of Law Abroad*, p. 21.

38. Tamanaha, *On the Rule of Law*, p. 43.

39. The Constitution of the Arab Republic of Egypt, available in English translation at http://www.sis.gov.eg/Newvr/Dustor-en001.pdf; Rabb, "The Least Religious Branch," p. 90.

40. Kora Andrieu, "Political Liberalism after Mass Violence: John Rawls and a Theory of Traditional Justice," in Susanne Buckley-Zistel et al., eds, *Transitional Justice Theories* (New York: Routledge, 2014), pp. 6, 85.

41. Wendy Lambourne, "Transformative Justice, Reconciliation and Peacebuilding," in Buckley-Zistel et al., eds, *Transitional Justice Theories*, pp. 19, 24.

42. Susanne Buckley-Zistel et al., introduction to *Transitional Justice Theories*, pp. 1, 6.

43. Brown, "Egypt's Failed Transition," pp. 4, 45, 56.

44. Andrieu, "Political Liberalism," p. 6.

45. Buckley-Zistel, *Transitional Justice Theories*, pp. 14–15.

46. Ibid., pp. 4, 19.

47. Randall Peerenboom, ed., *Asian Discourses of Rule of Law* (London: RoutledgeCurzon, 2004), p. 4; Tamanaha, *On the Rule of Law*, 96.

48. Peerenboom, *Asian Discourses*, pp. 35–6; Tamanaha, *On the Rule of Law*, pp. 42–3; Abou-El-Fadl, "Beyond Conventional Transitional Justice," p. 320.

49. Buckley-Zistel, *Transitional Justice Theories*, p. 9; Owen, *Rise and Fall*, p. 3.

50. Ruti Teitel, "Transitional Jurisprudence: The role of law in political transformation," *Yale Law Journal* vol. 106 (1997): 2020–21.

51. Buckley-Zistel, *Transitional Justice Theories*, p. 14.

52. Ibid., p. 4.

53. Wassouf, *Separating Law and Politics*, pp. 48–9; Emily C. Perish, Jenay Shook, and Eric Wiebelhaus-Brahm, "Transitional Justice in the Wake of the Arab Spring,"

9 June 2012, available at http://papers.ssrn.com/sol3/papers.cfm?abstract_id= 2087696

54. Abou-El-Fadl, "Beyond Conventional Transitional Justice," p. 326.

55. Kristen Stilt, "The End of 'One Hand': The Egyptian constitutional declaration and the rift between the 'people' and the Supreme Council of the Armed Forces," *Yearbook of the Islamic and Middle Eastern Law* (2012), pp. 16–19.

56. Jason Brownlee, *Democracy Prevention: The politics of the US–Egyptian alliance* (New York: Cambridge University Press, 2012), pp. xi-xii; Javed Maswood and Usha Natarajan, "Democratization and Constitutional Reform in Egypt and Indonesia: Evaluating the role of the military," in Bahgat Korany and Rabab El-Mahdi, eds, *Arab Spring in Egypt: Revolution and beyond* (Cairo: American University in Cairo Press, 2012), p. 244; "English Text of SCAF."

57. Al Masry Al Youm, "Jama'a al-Islamiya: SCAF is rigging election for Shafiq," *Egypt Independent*, 5 May 2012, http://www.egyptindependent.com/news/jamaa-al-islamiya-scaf-rigging-election-shafiq (accessed 7 February 2015) (discussing the SCAF's use of "unconventional methods that had not been used in the past").

58. Nathan J. Brown, "The Egyptian Political System in Disarray," Carnegie Endowment, 19 June 2012, http://carnegieendowment.org/2012/06/19/egyptian-political-system-in-disarray (accessed 7 February 2015) (discussing the SCAF's issuance of constitutional decrees and loophole-enforced laws to retain authority).

59. Brown, "Egypt's Failed Transition," pp. 4, 45, 50.

60. "Constitutional Timeline of Egypt," Constitutionnet, 8 August 2014, http://www.constitutionnet.org/country/constitutional-history-modern-egypt (accessed 7 February 2015).

61. Wassouf, *Separating Law and Politics*, pp. 14, 15.

62. Carothers, *Promoting the Rule of Law Abroad*, p. 20; Brown, "Egypt's Judges," p. 1.

63. Tom Ginsberg and Tamir Moustafa, eds, *Rule By Law: The politics of courts in authoritarian regimes* (New York: Cambridge University Press, 2008), p. 132; Moustafa, "Law Versus the State," p. 885; Hamad, "When the gavel speaks," p. 19.

64. Bjorn Bentlage, "Strife for Independence in an Autocratic Regime: The Egyptian Judges' Club 2000–2007," *Die Welt des Islams* vol. 50 (2010): 247.

65. Ginsberg and Moustafa, *Rule by Law*, p. 4; Jothie Rajah, "Punishing Bodies, Securing the Nation: How rule of law can legitimate the urbane authoritarian state," *Law and Social Inquiry* vol. 36 (2011): 4, 945, 948.

66. Ginsberg and Moustafa, *Rule by Law*, pp. 141–2.

67. Soliman, *Autumn of Dictatorship*, p. 137.

68. Tamir Moustafa, "The Political Role of the Supreme Constitutional Court: Between principles and practice," in Bernard-Maugiron, ed., *Judges and Political Reform in Egypt*, pp. 92–3.

69. Ibid.

70. Ibid., p. 93.

71. Ibid., p. 94.

72. Soliman, *Autumn of Dictatorship*, p. 142.

73. Ginsberg, *Courts and New Democracies*, p. 721; Auf, "Prospects for Judicial Reform."

74. The Constitution of the Arab Republic of Egypt, available in English translation at http://www.sis.gov.eg/Newvr/Dustor-en001.pdf.

75. Joshua Stacher, *Adaptable Autocrats: Regime power in Egypt and Syria* (Stanford, CA: Stanford University Press, 2012), p. 173.

76. Ibid., p. 38.

77. Ibid., p. 83.

78. Samer Shehata, ed., *Islamist Politics in the Middle East: Movements and change* (New York: Routledge, 2012), p. 124; Mona El-Ghobashy, "The Praxis of the Egyptian Revolution," in Jeannie Sowers and Chris Toensing, eds, *The Journey to Tahrir: Revolution, Protest, and Social Change in Egypt* (London: Verso, 2012), p. 21.

79. Stacher, *Adaptable Autocrats*, p. 35.

80. Ibid., pp. 38, 173.

81. Ibid., pp. 81–2.

82. Ibid., p. 173.

83. Ibid., p. 39.

84. Wassouf, *Separating Law and Politics*, p. 43.

85. The Constitution of the Arab Republic of Egypt, available in English translation at http://www.sis.gov.eg/Newvr/Dustor-en001.pdf

86. Wassouf, *Separating Law and Politics*, p. 22; Clark B. Lombardi, "Egypt's Supreme Constitutional Court: Managing Constitutional Conflict in an Authoritarian Aspirationally 'Islamic' State," *Journal of Comparative Law* vol. 3 (2008): 234, 235.

87. Wassouf, *Separating Law and Politics*, p. 43.

88. Ibid., p. 45.

89. Ibid., p. 43.

90. Ibid.

91. Ibid.

92. Ibid., p. 45.

93. Ibid.,p. 43; Bernard-Maugiron, *Judges and Political Reform in Egypt*, p. 21.

94. Abou-El-Fadl, "Beyond Conventional Transitional Justice," p. 327.

95. Wassouf, *Separating Law and Politics*, p. 44.

96. Ibid., p. 19.

97. Ibid., p. 7.

98. Ibid., p. 33.

99. Moustafa, "Law Versus the State," pp. 904–5.

100. The Military Court of Justice of Egypt, Article 6; Wassouf, *Separating Law and Politics*, p. 33.

101. Holger Albrecht, "Authoritarian Transformation or Transition from Authoritarianism? Insights on regime change in Egypt," in Bahgat Korany and Rabab El-Mahdi, eds, *Arab Spring in Egypt* (Cairo: American University in Cairo Press, 2012), p. 267; Abou-El-Fadl, *Beyond Conventional Transitional Justice*, p. 327.

102. Albrecht, *Authoritarian Transformation*, p. 267; Human Rights Watch, "Egypt: Q&A on the Trial of Hosni Mubarak" (28 May 2012), http://www.hrw.org/news/2012/05/28/egypt-qa-trial-hosni-mubarak (accessed 17 June 2016).

103. Ursula Lindsey, "Egypt's Judges Strike Back," *New Yorker*, 26 March 2014, http://www.newyorker.com/news/news-desk (last accessed 17 February 2016); Omar Mekky, "Evolution of the Rafaiest in Egyptian Politics," *Kuwait Times*, 17 September 2012, http://news.kuwaittimes.net/evolution-of-the-refaiest-in-egyptian-politics/ (last accessed 17 February 2016); Wassouf, *Separating Law and Politics*, p. 35.

104. Wassouf, *Separating Law and Politics*, p. 24.

105. Brown, *Egypt's Failed Transition*, pp. 4, 45.

106. Wassouf, *Separating Law and Politics*, p. 29.

107. Ibid., p. 7.

108. Leila Fadel, "Mubarak Trial a 'Decisive Moment' for Egypt," *Washington Post* (3 August 2011), http://www.washingtonpost.com/world/middle-east/mubarak-trial-a-decisive-moment-for-egypt/2011/08/01/gIQAfYCNpI_story.html (last accessed 17 February 2016); Jamie Dettmer, "Mubarak's Acquittal Signals Complete Triumph of Military Over Arab Spring," *Daily Beast* (29 November 2014), http://www.thedailybeast.com/articles/2014/11/29/mubarak-s-acquittal-signals-complete-triumph-of-military-over-arab-spring.html (last accessed 17 February 2016).

109. Jeannie Sowers, "Egypt in Transformation", in Jeannie Sowers and Chris Toensing, eds, *The Journey to Tahrir: Revolution, protest, and social change in Egypt* (London: Verso, 2012), p. 13.

110. Wassouf, *Separating Law and Politics*, pp. 46, 48.

111. "Key Events in Rule, Trial of Egypt's Hosni Mubarak," Associated Press, 22 August 2013, http://bigstory.ap.org/article/key-events-rule-trial-egypts-hosni-mubarak-0; Joe Stork, "Mubarak Convicted, but Abuses Continue in Egypt", Human Rights Watch, 20 June 2012, http://www.hrw.org/news/2012/06/10/mubarak-convicted-abuses-continue-egypt (accessed 17 June 2016).

112. Conal Urquhart, "Hosni Mubarak Sentenced to Life in Prison," *Guardian* (2 June 2012), http://www.theguardian.com/world/2012/jun/02/hosni-mubarak-sentenced-life-prison

113. Wassouf, *Separating Law and Politics*, p. 48.

114. Ibid.

115. Bahgat Korany, "Egypt and Beyond: The Arab Spring, the new Pan-Arabism, and the challenges of transition," in Bahgat Korany & Rabab El-Mahdi, eds, *Arab*

Spring in Egypt: Revolution and Beyond (Cairo: American University in Cairo Press, 2012), pp. 290, 291; Aziz, "Bringing Down an Uprising."

116. Ginsberg and Moustafa, *Rule by Law*, p. 14.
117. Ibid., p. 18.
118. Ibid., p. 14.
119. Wassouf, *Separating Law and Politics*, p. 22.
120. Ibid., p. 34.
121. Lombardi, "Egypt's Supreme Constitutional Court," p. 241.
122. Wassouf, *Separating Law and Politics*, p. 24.
123. Ibid., p. 23.
124. "Egypt refers 60 'pro-Brotherhood' judges to Disciplinary Board," *Al-Ahram Online*, 20 October 2014, http://english.ahram.org.eg/NewsContent/1/64/113517/Egypt/Politics-/Egypt-refers—proBrotherhood-judges-to-disciplinar.aspx (accessed 7 February 2015).
125. El-Ghobashy, "Praxis," p. 139.
126. Ibid.; Moustafa, "Law Versus the State," p. 889.
127. Ginsberg and Moustafa, *Rule by Law*, p. 134.
128. Judicial Authority Law of Egypt, Article 77.
129. El-Ghobashy, "Praxis," p. 139.
130. Wassouf, *Separating Law and Politics*, p. 28.
131. Mahmud al-Khudayari, "The Law on Judicial Authority and Judicial Independence," in Bernard-Maugiron, ed., *Judges and Political Reform in Egypt*, pp. 45, 47.
132. See Mohamed Sayed Said, "A Political Analysis of the Egyptian Judges' Revolt," in Bernard-Maugiron, ed., *Judges and Political Reform in Egypt*, pp. 19, 21–2; Sherif Younes, "Judges and Elections: The Politicization of the Judge's Discourse," in Bernard-Maugiron, ed., *Judges and Political Reform in Egypt*, p. 164.
133. Hamad, "When the gavel speaks," p. 33.
134. Judicial Authority Law of Egypt, Article 9.
135. Bernard-Maugiron, *Judges and Political Reform in Egypt*, p. 8.
136. El-Ghobashy, "Praxis," p. 139; Brown, "Egypt's Judges," p. 10; Bernard-Maugiron, *Judges and Political Reform in Egypt*, p. 10.
137. Wassouf, *Separating Law and Politics*, p. 26.
138. Wassouf, *Separating Law and Politics*, p. 26; Judicial Authority Law of Egypt, Articles 30–31, 36.
139. Wassouf, *Separating Law and Politics*, p. 7; Bernard-Maugiron, *Judges and Political Reform in Egypt*, p. 10.
140. "7 judges sent to retirement for MB affiliation," *Mada Masr*, 27 January 2014, http://www.madamasr.com/content/7-judges-sent-retirement-mb-affiliation (accessed 7 February 2015); Ginsberg and Moustafa, *Rule by Law*, pp. 138–9.
141. Wassouf, *Separating Law and Politics*, p. 41.

142. Samer Shehata and Joshua Stacher, "The Muslim Brothers in Mubarak's Last Decade," in Sowers and Toensing, *The Journey to Tahrir*, p. 167.
143. Ibid., p. 168.
144. Ibid., p. 167.
145. "Egypt refers 60."
146. Ibid.
147. Ibid.; "7 Judges"; "Judges investigated for Brotherhood ties," *Mada Masr*, 21 October 2014, http://www.madamasr.com/tags/judges-egypt (accessed 7 February 2015).
148. Nathan J. Brown, "Why do Egyptian courts say the darndest things?"
149. Wassouf, *Separating Law and Politics*, p. 26.
150. Ibid., p. 27.
151. Carothers, *Promoting the Rule of Law Abroad*, p. 120; Abou-El-Fadl, "Beyond Conventional Transitional Justice," pp. 322–3.
152. Wassouf, *Separating Law and Politics*, p. 25; Bernard-Maugiron, *Judges and Political Reform*, p. 8.
153. Wassouf, *Separating Law and Politics*, p. 25; Auf, "Prospects for Judicial Reform."
154. Carothers, *Promoting the Rule of Law Abroad*, p. 120.
155. Bernard-Maugiron, *Judges and Political Reform*, p. 13; Omar Mekky, "Evolution of the Rafaiest in Egyptian Politics," *Kuwait Times*, 17 September 2012, http://news.kuwaittimes.net/evolution-of-the-refaiest-in-egyptian-politics/ (accessed 7 February 2015).
156. Brown, "Egypt's Judges," p. 9. Mekky, "Evolution of the Rafaiest."
157. Brown, "Egypt's Judges," pp. 8, 10.
158. Ginsberg and Moustafa, *Rule by Law*, p. 2.
159. Alaa Al Aswany, *On the State of Egypt: What made the revolution inevitable*, trans. Jonathan Wright (New York: Vintage Books, 2011), p. 104; Bernard-Maugiron, *Judges and Political Reform*, pp. 13–14; Moustafa, "Law Versus the State," p. 897; Mekky, "Evolution of the Rafaiest."
160. Moustafa, "Law Versus the State," p. 897.
161. Tamir Moustafa, "Mobilising the Law in an Authoritarian State: The legal complex in contemporary Egypt," in Terence C. Halliday, Lucien Karpik, and Malcolm M. Feely, eds, *Fighting for Political Freedom: Comparative studies of the legal complex and political liberalism* (Portland: Hart Publishing, 2007), pp. 193–4.
162. Ginsberg and Moustafa, *Rule by Law*, pp. 14–15.
163. Said, "A Political Analysis," pp. 20–21; Mekky, "Evolution of the Rafaiest."
164. Bentlage, "Strife for Independence," p. 255.
165. Ibid.
166. Ibid.
167. Ibid., pp. 255–6.

168. Ibid.

169. Ginsberg and Moustafa, *Rule by Law*, pp. 12–13; Albrecht, "Authoritarian Transformation," p. 33; Moustafa, "Law Versus the State," p. 884; Lombardi, "Egypt's Supreme Constitutional Court," p. 244.

170. Ginsberg and Moustafa, *Rule by Law*, p. 16; Moustafa, "Law Versus the State," p. 903.

171. Ginsberg and Moustafa, *Rule by Law*, p. 151.

172. Nathalie Bernard-Maugiron, "Legal Reforms, the Rule of Law, and Consolidation of State Authoritarianism under Mubarak," in Said Amir Arjomand and Nathan J. Brown, eds, *The Rule of Law, Islam, and Constitutional Politics in Egypt and Iran* (Albany, NY: SUNY Press, 2013), p. 187.

173. Bentlage, "Strife for Independence," p. 264.

174. Bernard-Maugiron, *Judges and Political Reform*, p. 2; Bentlage, "Strife for Independence," p. 265.

175. Carothers, *Promoting the Rule of Law Abroad*, p. 120; Bentlage, "Strife for Independence," p. 249.

176. Mekky, "Evolution of the Rafaiest."

177. Moustafa, "Egyptian Revolt," pp. 181, 184.

178. Bernard-Maugiron, *Judges and Political Reform*, p. 3.

179. Mekky, "Evolution of the Rafaiest"; Bentlage, "Strife for Independence," p. 266.

180. Mekky, "Evolution of the Rafaiest."

181. Bernard-Maugiron, *Judges and Political Reform*, p. 3; Mekky, "Evolution of the Rafaiest."

182. Bentlage, "Strife for Independence," p. 266.

183. Bernard-Maugiron, *Judges and Political Reform*, p. 5.

184. Ibid., p. 4.

185. Ibid.

186. Mekky, "Evolution of the Rafaiest."

187. Tom Perry, "Egypt's Mursi faces judicial revolt over decree," Reuters, 24 November 2012, http://www.reuters.com/article/2012/11/24/us-egypt-president-idUS-BRE8AM0DO20121124 (accessed 7 February 2015); "Egypt judges call for national strike over Mursi decree," BBC News, 24 November 2012, http://www.bbc.com/news/world-middle-east-20476693 (accessed 7 February 2015).

188. Mara Revkin, "Egypt's injudicious judges," Middle East Channel, 11 June 2012, http://mideastafrica.foreignpolicy.com/posts/2012/06/11/egypts_injudicious_judges (accessed 7 February 2015); "Egypt: Behind Mursi's Decisions, II," *Daily Kos*, 29 November 2012, http://www.dailykos.com/story/2012/11/29/1165273/-Egypt-Behind-Mursi-s-Decisions-II# (accessed 7 February 2015).

189. Ginsberg and Moustafa, *Rule by Law*, pp. 17, 332.

190. Ibid., p. 18.

191. Bentlage, "Strife for Independence," p. 256.

192. Ibid.

193. Albrecht, "Authoritarian Transformation," p. 5.

194. Ginsberg and Moustafa, *Rule by Law*, p. 134.

195. Ginsberg, *Courts and New Democracies*, p. 725.

196. Moustafa, "Law Versus the State," p. 896.

197. Ibid., p. 913.

198. Ibid., p. 914.

199. Ibid., p. 917.

200. Ibid., p. 924; Bentlage, "Strife for Independence," p. 248.

201. Lombardi, "Egypt's Supreme Constitutional Court," p. 251.

202. Ibid.; Maswood, "Democratization and Constitutional Reform," p. 231.

203. Nathan Brown, "Judicial Turbulence Ahead in Egypt, Fasten Your Seat Belts," Carnegie Endowment for International Peace, 6 June 2012, http://carnegieendowment.org/2012/06/06/judicial-turbulence-ahead-in-egypt-fasten-your-seat-belts/b689 (accessed 7 February 2015).

204. Lombardi, "Egypt's Supreme Constitutional Court," p. 239.

205. "Egypt Justice Minister Mekky quits 'over cleansing call'," BBC News, 21 April 2013, http://www.bbc.com/news/world-middle-east-22240538 (accessed 7 February 2015).

206. Ginsberg, *Courts and New Democracies*, p. 727.

207. Brown, "Egypt's Failed Transition," pp. 4, 45, 53.

208. Rabb, "The Least Religious Branch," p. 116.

209. Sahar Aziz, "Egypt's War of Attrition," Al Jazeera English, 7 April 2013, http://www.aljazeera.com/indepth/opinion/2013/04/20134710923332904.html (accessed 7 February 2015).

210. Sahar Aziz, "Egypt's Protracted Revolution," *Human Rights Brief* vol. 19 no. 3 (2012): 9–10.

211. Rabb, "The Least Religious Branch," p. 121.

212. Ibid., pp. 81–2.

213. Wassouf, *Separating Law and Politics*, Annex B.

214. Ibid., p. 36.

215. Judicial Authority Law of Egypt, Article 41.

216. Wassouf, *Separating Law and Politics*, p. 23.

217. Ibid., Annex B.

218. Ibid.

219. Ibid.

220. Ibid.

221. Ibid., p. 30.

222. Ibid.

223. The Constitution of the Arab Republic of Egypt, available in English translation at http://www.sis.gov.eg/Newvr/Dustor-en001.pdf

224. Ibid., Article V.

225. Wassouf, *Separating Law and Politics*, p. 11.

226. Samer Al-Atrush, "Egypt judges back prosecutor against Morsi," *Morocco World News*, 12 October 2012, http://www.moroccoworldnews.com/tag/egypt-judges-back-prosecutor-against-morsi/?print=pdf-page (accessed 7 February 2015).

227. Wassouf, *Separating Law and Politics*, p. 6.

228. David Kirkpatrick and Kareem Fahim, "In Cairo, Effort to Broaden Support for Charter," *New York Times*, 11 December 2012, http://www.nytimes.com/2012/12/12/world/middleeast/egypt-morsi-referendum-International-Monetary-Fund-.html(accessed 7 February 2015).

229. Hamad, "When the gavel speaks"; "7 judges"; "Egypt Refers 60."

230. Mustapha Kamel al-Sayyed, "The Judicial Authority and Civil Society," in Bernard-Maugiron, ed., *Judges and Political Reform in Egypt*, pp. 227–31 (discussing the need for judicial independence); Younes, "Judges and Elections," pp. 155–6; Atef Shahat Said, "The Role of the Judges' Club in Enhancing the Independence of the Judiciary and Spurring Political Reform," in Bernard-Maugiron, ed., *Judges and Political Reform in Egypt*, pp. 129–30.

231. Carothers, *Promoting the Rule of Law Abroad*, pp. 23, 264; Ginsberg, *Courts and New Democracies*, p. 722.

232. Carothers, *Promoting the Rule of Law Abroad*, p. 90; Bentlage, "Strife for Independence," p. 257.

233. Carothers, *Promoting the Rule of Law Abroad*, p. 90.

234. Wassouf, *Separating Law and Politics*, pp. 36–7.

235. Hamad, "When the gavel speaks," p. 294; Ginsberg, *Courts and New Democracies*, pp. 735–6; Ginsberg and Moustafa, *Rule by Law*, p. 5.

12. SECURITY SECTOR REFORM AND TRANSITIONAL JUSTICE AFTER THE ARAB-MAJORITY UPRISINGS: THE CASE OF EGYPT

1. Omar Ashour argues that this term is more accurate than the "Arab Spring" or "Arab revolutions" given the participation of non-Arabs in the uprisings, the different transition trajectories, and the controversy around casting some of the 2010–11 events as "revolutions."

2. Omar Ashour, "History's Lessons: Dismantling Egypt's Security Agency," BBC Online, 9 March 2011, http://www.bbc.co.uk/news/world-middle-east-12679632

3. Then initial confrontations in late January and early February were mainly against other security and paramilitary forces, like the Central Security Forces and the Public (General) Security Sector who ran most of the local police stations.

4. Shaimaa Abdel Hady, "Tens of documents of State Security's leaks on Facebook," *al-Ahram*, last modified 6 March 2011, http://gate.ahram.org.eg/News/46337.aspx (last accessed 17 February 2016).

5. Dr Omar Ashour.

6. The former head of the Egyptian Police Academy.

7. Omar Ashour, "Egypt: Back to Generals' Republic?" BBC Online, 21 August 2013, http://www.bbc.co.uk/news/world-middle-east-23780839 (last accessed 17 February 2016). Please see the reasons below in the section entitled "The post-coup authorities." Yezid Sayigh, "Arab Police Reform: Returning to Square One," Carnegie Middle East Center, 9 January 2014, http://carnegie-mec.org/2014/01/09/arab-police-reform-returning-to-square-one/h3bh (last accessed 17 February 2016).

8. "Rasd: al-Sisi: al-Dabit Elly..." [The officer who...], https://www.youtube.com/watch?v=rF8Yz8J3MHI (accessed 14 January 2015).

9. The International Center for Transitional Justice, "What is Transitional Justice?" http://ictj.org/ar/about/transitional-justice (accessed 20 September 2014).

10. Islam Al-Raghy, "Chemical and Nuclear weapons in Rabaa Sit-in!" *Al-Akhbar Newspaper*, last modified 6 August 2013, www.al-akhbar.com (last accessed 17 February 2016).

11. More elaboration on TJ initiatives and their consequences are discussed in the following section, entitled "Transitional justice in Egypt."

12. Organization of Economic Co-operation and Development (OECD), *OECD-DAC Handbook on Security Sector Reform: Justice and Security* (Paris: OECD Publications, 2007), p. 20; Department for International Development (DFID), *Understanding and Supporting Security Sector Reform* (London, 2003), http://www.securitycouncilreport.org/atf/cf/%7B65BFCF9B-6D27–4E9C-8CD3-CF6E4FF96FF9%7D/supportingsecurity[1].pdf (last accessed 17 February 2016).

13. For more on the general objectives of SSR processes, see the UN Security Council Reports, for example "Security Sector Reform," report no. 1, 14 February 2007; the Organization for Economic Co-operation and Development (OECD) Handbook; or the UK Government's Global Conflict Prevention Pool (GCPP) reports.

14. OECD, *OECD-DAC Handbook on Security* Sector, p. 21

15. See for example OECD, *OECD-DAC Handbook on Security* Sector, pp. 112–18.

16. With some exceptions outlined below.

17. Wiki Thawra, "Statistical Database of the Egyptian Revolution," http://wikithawra.wordpress.com/ (accessed 20 September 2014).

18. In each of these cases, there were other protesters who did not fit the general description.

19. For some of the detailed violations, see Amnesty International's report entitled "Agents of Repression," http://www.amnesty.org/en/library/info/MDE12/029/2012/en (last accessed 17 February 2016).

20. Including 30 teenage girls and boys, 17 women, 8 journalists, 103 university stu-

dents. See Wiki Thawra, http://wikithawra.wordpress.com/2013/09/03/rabia-disperal14aug/ (last accessed 17 February 2016).

21. Human Rights Watch, "Libya: Abu Salim massacre remembered," 27 June 2012, http://www.hrw.org/news/2012/06/27/libya-abu-salim-prison-massacre-remembered (last accessed 17 February 2016).

22. Patrick Kingsley, "How did 37 prisoners come to die at Cairo prison Abu Zaabal?" *Guardian*, last modified 22 February 2014, http://www.theguardian.com/world/2014/feb/22/cairo-prison-abu-zabaal-deaths-37-prisoners (last accessed 17 February 2016).

23. Al-Masry Al-Youm, AFP, "Court overturns sentences given to officers over Abu Zaabal prisoner deaths," last modified 7 June 2014, http://www.egyptindependent.com/news/court-overturns-sentences-given-officers-over-abu-zaabal-prisoner-deaths (last accessed 17 February 2016).

24. Hisham Mubarak, *Diaries under Military Rule* (Cairo: Hisham Mubarak Law Centre, 2011), p. 6.

25. Joe Stork, Deputy Director for Middle East and North Africa, Human Rights Watch, "Egypt: Military Trials Usurp Justice System," last modified 29 April 2011, http://www.hrw.org/news/2011/04/29/egypt-military-trials-usurp-justice-system (last accessed 17 February 2016).

26. See for example Sherif Mohyeldeen et al., "Deep Justice: Dealing with the crimes of the past during the democratic transition", *Mishkat* no. 2 (August 2012), p. 4.

27. The statement was made by one of the military commanders in a meeting attended by several journalists, academics, and activists, including Sherif Mohyeldeen, in July 2011.

28. *Al-Jarida al-Rasmiyya* no. 27 (continued), 5 July 2012, Article 1, p. 2.

29. Human Rights Watch, "Egypt Report: The Background," January 2014, p. 2.

30. Ibid., p. 4.

31. *Warakum bi al-Taqrir*, http://nchrl.org/ar/taxonomy/term/11 (accessed 25 September 2014).

32. See for example http://eipr.org/pressrelease/2014/06/12/2105 (last accessed 17 February 2016).

33. See for example Rabi' al-Muhandis, "Abu Si'da: Dispersal of Raba'a and al-Nahda was done according to international human rights standards," *Masr al-Arabiya*, 11 August 2014, www.masralarabia.com. Ahmed Kamel, "Saad Eddine Ibrahim demands the transfer of schools and mosques to 'temporary' prisons," *Al-Watan*, 24 January 2014, http://www.elwatannews.com/news/details/403381 (last accessed 17 February 2016). "Saad Eddine Ibrahim demands the transforming of mosques into detention centres for the Brothers," *Al-Maseryoon*, 24 January 2014, http://goo.gl/7wUdeS (last accessed 17 February 2016).

34. Ibid.

35. This included pro-coup "human rights" activists mainly from the Nasserist and

Nationalist-Socialist camp, such as Nasser Amin, Ragia Omran, George Saad, and others.

36. Kareem Fahim, "Memory of mass killings becomes another casualty of Egypt protests," *New York Times*, 13 November 2013, http://www.nytimes.com/2013/11/14/world/middleeast/memory-egypt-mass-killing.html?pagewanted=all&_r=0 (last accessed 17 February 2016).

37. Human Rights Watch, "Egypt: Rab'a killings likely crimes against humanity," 12 August 2014, http://www.hrw.org/news/2014/08/12/egypt-rab-killings-likely-crimes-against-humanity (last accessed 17 February 2016).

38. See for example Amr al-Shalakany, *Tarikh al-Nukhba al-Qanunya fi Misr* (The History of the Judicial Elite in Egypt) (Cairo: al-Shuruq, 2012).

39. Amnesty International, "Egypt, roadmap to repression: No end in sight to human rights violations" (London: Amnesty International, 2014), p. 33.

40. Ibid.

41. Wafaa' Farrag, "Transitional justice in Egypt, a death before birth," *Al-Ahram*, 2 November 2013, http://digital.ahram.org.eg/articles.aspx?Serial=1453823&eid=894 (last accessed 17 February 2016).

42. Amr Sherif, *Masr al Arabia*, "Minister of Transitional Justice: No time for transitional justice," last modified 3 January 2014, www.masralarabia.com (last accessed 17 February 2016).

43. Ragab Galal, "Beblawi defines the functions of the Ministry of the Transitional Justice 6 months after his appointment," *Al Masry Al Youm*, last modified 23 January 2014, http://www.almasryalyoum.com/news/details/380005# (last accessed 17 February 2016).

44. Nourhan Hassan, "Minister of Transitional Justice: Egypt is really in need of this type of Ministries," *Youm 7*, 6 June 2014, www.youm7.com (last accessed 17 February 2016).

45. Former MP, interview by Omar Ashour, Cairo, April 2012.

46. Mohammed Selim Al-Awa, interview by Omar Ashour, Cairo, 19 September 2011. Dr Al-Awa was referring to the Egyptian armed forces after the humiliating defeat by the Israeli defence in June 1967.

47. Mansour Issawi, interview by Youssef Ahmad, *Al-Sharq al-Awsat*, 14 July 2011, p. 5.

48. Mohammed Salah, interview by Ahmad Mukhtar, *al-Ahram al-Masa'i*, 16 May 2012, p. 8.

49. Halim al-Deeb, GCPO member, interview by Omar Ashour, Cairo, 2 April 2012.

50. For more on the Post Said tragedy, see Sherif Mohyeldeen, "Egypt: a common sense of injustice forces the people to publicly disobey and collect arms," *Al-Akhbar*, last modified 18 February 2013, http://www.al-akhbar.com/node/177763 (last accessed 17 February 2016). Interview by Omar Ashour, Cairo, March 2012.

51. Omar Ashour was one of the experts consulted in five different sessions in the National Security and Foreign Affairs Committee.

52. Omar Ashour was one of the experts who outlined the document.

53. Interview by Omar Ashour, Cairo, 27 February 2012.

54. This tentative conclusion is based on Omar Ashour's observations, interactions, and meetings with police officers involved in SSR initiatives (both official and unofficial) between May 2011 and April 2013.

55. Ibid.

56. Jumhurriyyat Misr al-Arabiyya [Arab Republic of Egypt], *Al-Bayan al-Mali 'an Mashru' al-Muwazana al-'amma lil dawla 2013–2014* [Financial Statement for the General Budget Project of the State for the year 2013–2014] (Cairo, 2013), p. 1.

57. Al-Jumhurriyya al-Tunisiya—Wizarat al-Maliyya [Tunisian Republic—Finance Ministry], *Taqrir Hawl Mashru' Mizaniyat al-Dawla li Sanat 2013* [Report on the Draft Budget for the year 2013] (Tunis, 2012), p. 97.

58. Jumhurriyyat Misr al-Arabiyya, *Al-Bayan*, p. 21.

59. Abdulrhman Aboughait, "Sisi calls for austerity, and the government increase the interior's budget," *Al Jazeera*, last modified 11 March 2014, www.aljazeera.net

60. This conclusion is based on Omar Ashour's observations, interactions, and meetings with MPs involved in SSR initiatives (from both the upper and lower chambers) between February 2012 and April 2013.

61. Ali Larayedh (former Interior Minister of Tunisia), conversation with Omar Ashour, Geneva. 22 November 2012.

62. Wiki Thawra, http://wikithawra.wordpress.com/2013/09/03/rabiadisperal 14aug/ (last accessed 17 February 2016).

63. "Cabinet requests amending protest law to include tougher penalties," *Al-Masry Al-Youm*, last modified 2 September 2014, http://www.egyptindependent.com/news/
cabinet-requests-amending-protest-law-include-tougher-penalties?mc_cid=9bcc3ccaa5&mc_eid=3eeeb932dd (last accessed 17 February 2016).

64. "Egypt sentences a further 183 people to death in new purge of political opposition," Amnesty International press release, 21 June 2014, http://www.amnesty.org/en/for-media/press-releases/egypt-sentences-further-183-people-death-new-purge-political-opposition-201 (last accessed 17 February 2016).

65. "Egypt: Dozens of disappeared civilians face ongoing torture at military prison," Amnesty International press release, 22 May 2014, http://www.amnesty.org/en/for-media/press-releases/egypt-dozens-disappeared-civilians-face-ongoing-torture-military-prison-201 (last accessed 17 February 2016).

66. Conversation with one of the activists involved, by Omar Ashour, London, August 2013.

INDEX

INDEX